Rabban Gamaliel II

BROWN UNIVERSITY
BROWN JUDAIC STUDIES

Number 8

Rabban Gamaliel II
The Legal Traditions

by Shamai Kanter

Rabban Gamaliel II
The Legal Traditions

by
Shamai Kanter

Scholars Press

Distributed by
SCHOLARS PRESS
101 Salem Street
Chico, CA 95926

Rabban Gamaliel II
The Legal Traditions

by
Shamai Kanter

Library of Congress Cataloging in Publication Data

Kanter, Shamai.
Rabban Gamaliel II, the legal traditions.

(Brown Judaic studies ; no. 8 ISSN 0147-927X)
Bibliography: p.
Includes index.
1. Gamaliel II, fl. 80–110. 2. Talmud—Criticism, Form. I. Title. II. Series.
BM502.3.G35K36 296.1'2 80-12229
ISBN 0-89130-403-7
ISBN 0-89130-404-5 (pbk.)

Printed in the United States of America
1 2 3 4 5
McNaughton & Gunn
Ann Arbor, Michigan 48106

LZKR ʾMY

Śʾśʾ BT YʿQB HYRŠ

Ṫ Ṅ Ṩ Ḃ Ḣ

RABBAN GAMALIEL II

THE LEGAL TRADITIONS

TABLE OF CONTENTS

Introduction

Rabban Gamaliel II succeeded Yoḥanan b. Zakkai as head of the academy at Yavneh. As the head of the Jewish community of Palestine bearing the title of Patriarch (Nasi), he founded a dynasty of leadership which was to endure through the first quarter of the 5th century, C. E. In addition to his administration of internal affairs of the Jews on behalf of the Roman government, Gamaliel is commonly credited with the promulgation of the 18 blessings of the ʿAmidah prayer in its official text, and with prescribing the liturgical core of the Passover Seder. The adoption of Hillelite norms as the official halakah, and the fixing of the biblical canon, are assumed to have taken place during his administration.

This study of Gamaliel's legal traditions builds upon methods which have been developed by Jacob Neusner in The Rabbinic Traditions about the Pharisees before 70 and Eliezer Ben Hyrcanus. These works subject all available rabbinic traditions to literary-critical and form-critical analysis, to the end of determining their value for historical purposes. The development of traditions is charted through the legal and non-legal traditions, according to the documents in which they appear, and through the named authorities who attest to the various pericopae through their comments about them. The value of Neusner's method is demonstrated by the results described in the works named. Our following of a similar method here supplies one additional value: the possibility of comparison of the characteristics of Gamaliel's traditions with those of the pre-70 Pharisees and Eliezer b. Hyrcanus, in some objective fashion. In this way, some conclusions concerning the development of rabbinic Judaism -- through Yavneh and beyond -- may be perceived.

In Part One: The Traditions, the corpus of legal traditions of Gamaliel, using the topical divisions of the Mishnah, is subject to analysis and comment as follows:

a) Traditions appearing in the Mishnah

b) Traditions appearing in the Tosefta

c) Related later materials from other rabbinic collections -- the Tannaitic midrashim, Palestinian Talmud and Babylonian Talmud

d) Pericopae found in the later collections, but unrelated to anything appearing first in the M.-Tos. stratum.

Such treatment has the advantage of preserving the centrality of the M.-Tos. stratum, and the light which parallel pericopae from the later collections can cast upon it. The disadvantage of this organization of the materials is clear: traditions appearing in the later documents, e.g., the Babylonian Talmud, may be scattered, some serving as "commentary" to a M.-Tos. pericope, some appearing later. But since the M.-Tos. pericopae overshadow those of other strata, in both bulk and reliability, this inconvenience is minor.

The non-legal materials which comprise the rest of the Gamaliel traditions (historical, exegetical, moral, theological, biographical and legendary) still await study. Nevertheless, even at this point some observations and generalizations may be made.

One problem of the materials lies in determining, in many passages, *which* "Gamaliel" is meant. The rabbinic literature mentions no less than five authorities with the name of Gamaliel: Gamaliel I (the Elder), Gamaliel II, Gamaliel III (son of Rabbi Judah the Patriarch), Gamaliel IV (great-grandson of Rabbi Judah), Gamaliel V, and Gamaliel VI (d. 425 C. E.) the last patriarch of Palestine.

The nature of the documents Mishnah and Tosefta rules out the presence of references to Gamaliels III-VI. As a practical matter, the question is to distinguish between Gamaliel I and Gamaliel II. But the problem is complicated by the fact that, through haplography, the name of Simeon b. Gamaliel frequently becomes Gamaliel. For evaluations of the ms. problems, Epstein (*Mišnah*) and Lieberman (*T.K.*) provided authoritative solutions. In analyzing passages, the following criteria were observed:

1. The presence or absence of the term "the Elder" usually helpful, was not always determinative. That term is absent from early traditions, having probably been added *after* the currency of traditions about Gamaliel II.

2. Citation in the same pericope of views of Gamaliel II's Yavnean contemporaries, Eliezer, Joshua, ʿAqiva, Ilai, or Onqelos (described in b. Meg. 3a as student of Joshua and Eliezer) would indicate our Gamaliel. Conversely, pre-70 authorities such as Admon indicate Gamaliel I.

3. Quotation of Gamaliel's words by a contemporary (such as ʿAqiva) or an Ushan in direct line of transmission of Gamaliel's views (such as Judah b. Ilai or Eleazar b. Ṣadoq) would indicate our Gamaliel.

4. Consistency with other views of Gamaliel II, or conversely, conflict with known views of Gamaliel I, would indicate our Gamaliel.

5. Historical context: a Gamaliel described on the undestroyed Temple mount would be Gamaliel the Elder. (Yet there is sufficient evidence that the Passover sacrifice and the Nazirite vow continued after the destruction of the Temple. So we may not identify a pericope with Gamaliel the Elder on the grounds of a mention of those practices alone.)

The largest number of pericopae pose no problem in identification of Gamaliel II. However, in those which do, no single one of these criteria is taken as sufficient; usually a number of them operate in concert.

The translation of the pericopae has been freshly made, though Danby's classic translation of the Mishnah, and the Soncino translation of the Talmud, have been consulted. For translation of the Tosefta passages, the extended commentary of Saul Lieberman, Tosefta ki-Fshuṭah, on Zeraʿim, Moʿed and Našim, was indispensable. The translation has attempted as literal as possible a rendering of the Hebrew and Aramaic, within the limits of intelligibility in English. The same English terms have been used for the same words throughout. Where meaning is the same, if the Hebrew uses two different words, alternate words have been used. The purpose of this has been to make possible, where literary analysis is significant for the understanding of a passage, the demonstration of a literary-critical point through the translation itself. Where deemed helpful, Hebrew words have been supplied in transliteration. Rather than using English circumlocutions when the text is oblique, connecting words or phrases have been supplied within brackets. The passage read without bracketed material should give a fair idea of the text itself, even though every translation is of course an interpretation.

The comments on the pericopae assembled in Part One, though not rigidly structured, include all or almost all of the following elements:

1. Exegesis: The meaning of the pericope, its legal issue in relation to other legal pericopae is exposited. Relevant traditional and modern commentaries have been consulted for the meaning of the passage, and Gamaliel's ruling within it.

2. Literary-critical analysis: The unitary or composite nature of the pericope, and the relationships of its parts, is discussed. The ms. variations of the Kaufmann, Parma, Naples, and Cambridge manuscripts of the Mishnah, the variants assembled by Rabbinovicz in Sefer Diqduqé Soferim for the Talmud, and variants noted in the Zuckermandel and Lieberman editions of the Tosefta, were regularly used for any light they could cast. For passages in the order Našim of the Talmud, the literary-critical work of Weiss-Halivni, Meqorot uMesorot, was consulted.

3. Form-criticism: Formal attributes of the pericope (as dispute, debate, narrative, etc.) are noted and discussed.

4. Attestations: Indications that the pericope was known at one of the following stages of the tradition -- Yavneh, Ushah, the circle of Rabbi Judah the Patriarch, or Mishnah-Tosefta are registered, for later note.

5. Redactional issues: Redactional history, the way in which the pericope developed, and the point (or points) of view standing behind the pericope, are hypothesized.

6. Historical issues: The value of the above for determining any historical assertions to be made, about the Gamaliel-tradition and Gamaliel himself, is determined.

Part Two: The Forms of the Legal Tradition attempts to draw together some of the characteristics which have been observed through the analysis of individual pericopae. The forms are listed and described, and the significance of the disputes and narratives for Gamaliel's tradition is discussed.

In Part Three: The Content of the Early Legal Tradition, a summary of Gamaliel's rulings is given, and his legal agenda compared with the interests of the pre-70 Pharisees. The attitude toward Gamaliel in the narratives is surveyed, and differing attitudes toward him noted.

Between the time this investigation was begun, as a doctoral thesis, and the present writing, progress in rabbinic studies has raised serious questions about the use of rabbinic traditions for biographical purposes. Such questions arise not from simple skepticism about the events those traditions allege to have occurred. Rather, they come from the investigation of the nature of the documents in which the traditions appear, as well as the nature of the forms of the traditions.

William Green's survey of the problematic of rabbinic biography, as it pertains to the masters of Yavneh (roughly, 70-135 C.E.) asserts the following:

1. Analysis of the documents of Mishnah and Tosefta reveals thier own inner structure and forms, imposed upon the materials they contain.

2. The nature of the forms employed for conveying the tradition works to conceal or suppress individuality of expression. Thus (1) and (2) call into question any supposition that we may have the exact words of the rabbis mentioned within the documents.

3. In rabbinic disputes, the language of the individual is secondary to the frame, which defines the problem. Stereotypical answers (forbidden/permitted, we accept his words/we do not) conceal or suppress individuality, and provide an illusion of consistency.

4. In Mishnah and Tosefta, the forms in which we encounter traditions are unconnected to specific masters or generations: they appear to be characteristic of the specific M.-Tos. chapters in which they appear.

5. Further, both Neusner and Towner are forced to assume the unreliability of the attribution of traditions to specific masters, except as indicative of generational strata. From this perspective, the real heroes of the traditions are the penultimate (or in some cases ultimate) redactors who actually give form to its materials, rather than the authorities who appear to teach and adjudicate and decree.

Green concludes that since rabbinic materials are structured not to reveal much about individuals, they contain insufficient material for Tannaitic biography, whether personal or intellectual. He finds that the value of name-studies lies in the fact that named traditions provide the previously-mentioned element of generational development. They serve as a sample, cutting across the various documents, which can indicate how a tradition develops historically.

The study of Gamaliel's legal traditions certainly reveals this. We can see its core of Mishnah-Tosefta materials and their elaboration in later documents. Our problem is: can we also reach back further than this description of a legal tradition, toward the figure of the individual about whom the tradition purports to speak? In some few respects we may answer affirmatively.

First, since Gamaliel was a figure of some controversy, within his own time and thereafter, we may discern differing attitudes toward him reflected in the traditions. The collections of M. and Tos. give evidence of this: the editor of M., Rabbi Judah the Patriarch, often tends to select materials more favorable to his grandfather than does the editor of Tos. Further, within those documents themselves, pericopae reveal views both critical and supportive of Gamaliel. Thus we may perceive some of the currents beneath the surfaces of M. and Tos. as well as differences between them. And on those points of description where positive and negative views of Gamaliel coincide, we may assume firm grounds for associating the issue that prompted both attack and defense with Gamaliel the individual.

Second, the more that current studies point to the autonomy of the individual chapter of M. or Tos., in terms of viewpoint and conform, the stronger becomes the value of evidence of internal consistency within the named traditions. Assumptions about the individual's role as teacher or decisor, or a concern for certain legal issues or theoretical problems behind the pericopae, become more valuable the more other evidence enlarges the role played by the redactor of the individual chapter or tractate. Strongest of all would be formal characteristics, not fully assimilated into the style of the chapter, which are shared with other pericopae of a named master in other chapters or tractates. The imposition of such consistency would have to precede the penultimate redaction. This would lead us back to the point where traditions were part of a collection assembled by the circle of tradents of a master. It means that we are two stages earlier than the M.-Tos. redaction, and fairly close to Yavnean times. We may imagine the stages of development of the traditions roughly as follows:

M.-Tos.	200-225 C.E.
Penultimate basic chapter redaction	150-175
Ushan collections of traditions	140-150
Pre-bar Kokhba named-master collections	100-125
Activity of Gamaliel	80-115

We note that the last two items on the list overlap in time. To speak of a collection of named traditions at the very beginning of the second century is to locate a time so close to the circle of the master as to warrant correspondingly greater reliance upon the accuracy of tradents.

Third, while other named legal traditions are clearly subject to Green's strictures, it is possible for a certain portion of the Gamaliel tradition to elude them. Here I refer to the legal narratives which, as we shall see, comprise such a high proportion of the legal traditions. Green's argument applies, in most part, to named rulings (required/not required, permitted/forbidden) which clearly originated in more lengthy statements: Rabbi X says ± problem ± ruling. Within the dispute-form, now only the attribution ± ruling remain. The statement of context or problem has been recast into the dispute framework. Further, examples abound in which the attributions of the rulings are reversed: later authorities exchange the positions of the disputants.

But the legal narrative is less amenable to such manipulation. Rabban Gamaliel did such, or Situation ± Rabban Gamaliel ruled such, carries its own context or problem within itself. Even when it is incorporated into a dispute-form, it is less dependent upon the framework of the dispute for its definition. It has not been recast completely, in order to fit smoothly into the structure of the dispute. Thus it stands one step closer to the hypothesized named master collection, and to greater reliability. (This is not to claim that legal narratives as a group are free of contradiction or fabrication -- only that their form indicates greater closeness to original formulation, as compared to other elements of a dispute.)

The study of the Gamaliel tradition is thus valuable for a number of reasons. Since its materials are primarily from the M.-Tos. stratum, it depends on the most reliable of our collections. Through it we may perceive differences within M.-Tos., as well as the development of the tradition in later documents. And lastly, though our materials about Gamaliel are admittedly sparse, the nature of the traditions themselves may be more reliable. Thus the Gamaliel tradition may serve as a valuable control for, and comparison with, other studies of other masters of Yavneh and beyond. This study of the legal tradition of Gamaliel is, then, as its title declares, primarily the description of the way a tradition unfolds. Yet laying no claim to personal or intellectual biography, it points in numerous details beyond the tradition, to the rootedness of that tradition in the deeds and concerns of the person it describes.

It is fitting to acknowledge personal debts connected with this work which are immeasurable. Professor Jacob Neusner, teacher for a decade and friend for more than two, provided careful guidance, unflagging urgency and a model of scholarly integrity and creativity. Professors Ernest Froerichs and David Blumenthal carefully read the first version of this work as a doctoral thesis, at Brown University, and provided detailed, helpful comments. Professor William Green's conversations on mutual problems were invaluable, far more than the quotations appearing on these pages would indicate. The inadequacies of the work which follows should not be ascribed to them, though they certainly may claim credit for its value.

Mrs. Marilyn Kogos prepared the original manuscript through many metamorphoses, a work of friendship, devotion, and patient skill. Mrs. Pearl Ostroff typed this new version of the manuscript for photocopying, one of many valuable deeds of assistance to me.

Public acknowledgement is also due to my parents, David and Doris Kanter, who encouraged a rabbinic career combined with the published word; to my children, Raphael, Elana and Ethan, whose growing years were defined by the progress of this work; and to my wife, Jeannette Elizabeth Kanter, for whom ʿAqiva's praise (b. Ket. 63a) would have to be invented, did it not exist.

The index was prepared by Mr. Arthur Woodman, for whose skill and patience my thanks are due.

The effort reflected in the following pages would never have seen completion in this volume, were it not for the support of the following persons: Malcolm and Linda Glazer, Harold and Helen Hecker, Morris and Jennie Levinson, Theodore and Tillie Levinson, William and Sheila Konar, Neil and Sharon Norry, and Norman and Glenna Spindelman. As individuals and as members of Congregation Beth El, Rochester, New York, they share a proud tradition of identification with serious Jewish scholarship which spans, in immediate congregational perspective, several generations, and in greater perspective, several millenia. I am honored to count them as friends.

Within a few days the Fast Day of destruction of Jerusalem will be observed, its 1,907th anniversary. That such observance would be held both in the Diaspora and in a rebuilt Jerusalem, using in part a liturgy for which he bore responsibility, would surely not have surprised Rabban Gamaliel too much.

July 23, 1979
28 Tammaz, 5739

Rochester, New York

NOTES

[1]William S. Green, "What's in a Name?--the Problematic of Rabbinic Biography," *Approaches to Ancient Judaism*, W.S. Green, ed., pp. 77-96.

Abbreviations

Albeck, = H. Albeck
Commentary to the Mishnah
Jerusalem-Tel Aviv, 1953)

Allon, *Toledot* = G. Allon,
A History of the Jews in Palestine During the Period of the Mishnah and the Talmud (Toledot HaYehudim B'Ereṣ Yisrael, Bitequfat HaMišnah VeHatalmud [Tel Aviv, 1970]

ʿA.Z. = ʿAvodah Zarah

B.B. = Bava Batra

b. = Bavil, Babylonian Talmud

b. = ben

B.Q. = Bava Qamma

Ber. = Berakhot

Beṣ. = Beṣah

Bik. = Bikkurim

B.M. = Bava Meṣiaʿ

Camb. = H. Loew, *The Mishnah of the Palestinian Talmud (HaMišnah al pi Ketav-Yad Cambridge* [Jerusalem, 1967]

Danby = H. Danby, translator, *The Mishnah* (London, 1933)

Dem. = Demai

ʿEd. = Eduyyot

Eliezer = J. Neusner, *Eliezer ben Hyrcanus* (Leiden, 1974)

Epstein, *Mišnah* = J. N. Epstein, *Introduction to the Text of the Mishnah (Mavo LeNusaḥ HaMišnah* Jerusalem, 1964)

ʿEruv. = ʿEruvin

Frankel, Mišnah = Z. Frankel, Darké HaMišnah, ha-tosefta, mekhilta, safra ve-sifré (Tel Aviv, 1959)

Freedman, Shabbat = H. Freedman, translator, Shabbath (London, 1938)

Giṭ. = Giṭṭin

GRA = Abraham ben Elijah, of Vilna, Commentary on the Mishnah (Jerusalem, 1948)

Green, Joshua = W. S. Green, Joshua ben Ḥananiah (unpublished PhD. thesis, Brown University, 1974)

Ḥag. = Ḥagigah

Ḥal. = Ḥallah

Halivni, Meqorot - David Weiss Halivni, Meqorot uMesorot (Tel Aviv, 1948)

HD = David Pardo, Sefer Hasdé David (Jerusalem, 1970-71)

Ḥul. = Ḥullin

Hyman, Toledot = A. Hyman, Biographies of the Tannaim and Amoraim (Toledot Tannaim VeAmoraim Jerusalem, 1964)

Hyman, T.K.M. = A. Hyman, Biblical References in Rabbinic Literature (Torah haKetuvah v'ha-Mesorah Tel Aviv, 1936)

Jastrow = M. Jastrow, A Dictionary of the Targumim, the Talmud Babli and Yerushalmi, and the Midrashic Literature (New York, 1943)

K = Faksimile-Ausgabe des Mischnacodex Kaufmann A50, mit Genehmigung der Ungarischen Akademie der Wissenschaften in Budapest, besorgt von Georg Beer (HaMishnah al pi Ketav Yad Kaufmann, [Jerusalem, 1967])

Kel. = Kelim

Kil. = Kilaʾim

Life = J. Neusner, A Life of Yohanan ben Zakkai (2nd ed., Leiden, 1970)

Lightstone, "Ṣadoq" = J. Lightstone, "Ṣadoq the Yavnean," Persons and Institutions in Early Rabbinic Judaism, W. S. Green, ed., (Missoula, 1977, pp. 49-147)

M. = Mishnah

Maimonides = M. Maimonides, Commentary to the Mishnah (Jerusalem, 1948)

Ma. = Maʿaserot

Meg. = Megillah

Mek. = Mekhilta

Men. = Menaḥot

Mevoʾot = J. N. Epstein, Introductions to Tannaitic Literature (Mevoʾot leSifrut HaTannaʾim [Jerusalem, 1957])

Miq. = Miqvaʾot

M.Q. = Moʿed Qaṭan

M.S. = Mʿaser Šeni

N = Naples ed. of Mishnah (Mishna im perush ha-Ram'Bam, defus rishon, Napoli, 252 [1492], divré mavo meʿet A. M. Habermann. [Jerusalem, 1970])

Naz. = Nazir

Ned. = Nedarim

Neg. = Negaʿim

Neusner, Development = J. Neusner Development of a Legend (Leiden, 1970)

Neusner, History = J. Neusner, A History of the Jews in Babylonia, vols. i - v, (Leiden, 1965-1970)

Neusner, Kelim = J. Neusner, A History of the Mishnaic Law of Purities (Leiden, 1974)

Nez. = Nezirot

Nid. = Niddah

Oh. = Ohalot

P = Parma ms. of Mishnah (Shisha Sidré Mishnah, Ketav Yad Parma ... [Jerusalem, 1970])

Par. = Parah

Pes. = Pesaḥim

Pharisees = J. Neusner, The Rabbinic Traditions about the Pharisees before 70, vols. i-iii (Leiden, 1971)

Politics = J. Neusner, From Politics to Piety (Englewood Cliffs, 1973)

Qid. = Qiddušin

R. = Rabbi

Rabbi = Rabbi Judah the Patriarch

Rabbinovicz, D.S. = R. N. Rabinowitz, Variae lectiones in Mischnam et in Talmud Babylonicum (Sefer Diqduqê Soferim [New York, 1960])

R.H. = Rosh Hashanah

R'Š = Asher ben Yeḥiel, Commentary on the Talmud (Jerusalem, 1948)

San. = Sanhedrin

Sens = Samson of Sens Commentary on M. Kelim (Jerusalem, 1948)

Shab. = Shabbat

Shav. = Shavu'ot

Sheq. = Sheqalim

Shev. = Shevi'it

Slotki, Kelim - I. Slotki, Translator, Kelim (London, 1948)

Slotki, Yev. = J. Slotki, Translator, Yebamoth (London, 1936)

Soṭ. = Soṭah

Suk. = Sukkah

Ta. = Ta'anit

Ter. - Terumot

T.K. = S. Lieberman, A Comprehensive Commentary on the Tosefta (Tosefta ki-Fshuṭah [New York, 1955-1967])

Ṭoh. = Ṭoharot

Tos. = Tosefta

T.R. = S. Lieberman, Commentary on the Tosefta (Tosefet Rišonim)

y. = Yerušalmi, Palestinian Talmud

Y.Ṭ. = Yom Ṭov

Yad. = Yadayim

Yev. = Yevamot

Zer. = Zera'im

Zev. = Zevaḥim

Transliterations

א	=	ʾ	מ,ם	=	M
ב	=	B	נ,ן	=	N
ג	=	G	ס	=	Ś
ד	=	D	ע	=	ʿ
ה	=	H	פ,ף	=	P
ו	=	W	צ,ץ	=	Ṣ
ז	=	Z	ק	=	Q
ח	=	Ḥ	ר	=	R
ט	=	Ṭ	שׁ	=	Š
י	=	Y	שׂ	=	S
כ,ך	=	K	ת	=	T
ל	=	L			

PART ONE: THE TRADITIONS

i. Berakhot

A. From what time do they recite the Shemaʿ in the evening? From the hour that the priests enter [the Temple] to eat their Heave-offering.

B. "Until the end of the first watch," the words of Rabbi Eliezer.

C. And sages say, "Until midnight."

D. Rabban Gamaliel says, "Until the dawn comes up."

E. (MʿSH Š) His sons came from a [wedding] feast. They said to him, "We have not recited the Shemaʿ ." He said to them, "If the dawn has not come up, you are required (ḤYYBYN) [K, P: MWTRYN, permitted] to recite it."

F. And not just [in] this [case], but in every case concerning which sages said, "Until midnight," the obligation (MṢWTN) lasts until the dawn comes up: [for instance, for] burning the fat pieces and limbs [of the sacrifices], the obligation lasts until the dawn comes up; [and for] all [offerings] that must be eaten on the same day, the obligation lasts until the dawn comes up.

G. If so, why did sages say, "Until midnight"? In order to keep a man far from transgression.

M. Ber. 1.1

Comment: The obligation to recite the Shemaʿ , evening and morning, is taken for granted here. There is no dispute here over the start of the time for the evening Shemaʿ : only the conclusion of the time period is at issue. B, C and D present three answers, in chronological order, all beginning with the same word "until," ʿD. After the illustration of Gamaliel's view (E), F-G harmonizes the view of the sages with Gamaliel. They really agree with him that the time for Shemaʿ is until dawn. In fact, everywhere they state a midnight deadline, the act is valid until dawn. The earlier time is a "fence," to prevent violation of the law.

Neusner (Eliezer, i, p. 19) suggests A as an original Temple rule, since the hour of nightfall is described in terms of the Temple ritual. B-E are Yavnean glosses, and F-G are a later harmonization of the sages' position with Gamaliel's; thus far Neusner.

The language of Gamaliel's statement, D, is fairly close to that used in the story, E. Considering the uniformity of style imposed upon B-D, the word "until" + time-designation, it could not be closer. The Kaufmann and Parma manuscript variants in E provide a suggestion for determining whether one of the two units, D and E, is derived from the other.

It is easy to see how, in the context of the dispute over the final time for reciting the Shemaʿ, "permitted" could become "required". But it is hard to understand how the reverse could have taken place. If "permitted" is indeed the correct reading, what we have is a story about Gamaliel's enthusiasm for reciting the Shemaʿ. The man about whom it was told that he recited the Shemaʿ on his wedding night (M. Ber. 2.5) would certainly seek to extend the time permissible to "assume the yoke of the kingship of Heaven". The story about what Gamaliel felt was permissible to the individual has been converted to a statement of what is a requirement for all. This points to D being derived from the story, rather than the reverse. Gamaliel's part of the dispute is post-Yavnean, created to join the story to the dispute of Eliezer and the sages.

The same hand responsible for adding D-E to the pericope supplied F-G. From A-E nothing in the pericope suggests that the sages would agree with Gamaliel. The joining-language of F implies it ("and not just in this case") but does not state it, using D-E as an introduction to the general rule: wherever the sages state "until midnight" the requirement lasts until dawn. Neither of the two cases cited in F states this; the generalization is imposed upon them. The passage on burning the limbs and fat pieces (and reaping the ʿOmer, found in M. Meg. 2.6) does not mention midnight. It states a different principle that something required to be done at night is valid "all the night". Likewise, the listing of offerings eaten on the same day (M. Zev. 5.3, 5,6) says "until midnight", with no hint of validity until dawn.

The reason for adding Gamaliel to the dispute A-C may well be found here: it helps provide a basis for, and a third example of, the principle stated in F: anywhere the sages said "midnight" really means "until dawn". That principle is created here.

In the eyes of the party responsible for D-F, the story about Gamaliel is a valid source for derivation of a law. Further, the law is presented in a way that harmonizes the view of the sages with Gamaliel, rather than the reverse. Eliezer's rule might also have been interpreted to agree with Gamaliel, but there is no effort to do so.

Said Rabban Gamaliel, "There are times when a man recites the Shemaʿ twice in one night: once before the dawn comes up and once after the dawn comes up; and with that, he fulfills his obligation both for the day and for the night."

ARNA 2.8

Comment: The statement follows from Gamaliel's view in M. Ber. 1.1: it assumes that the current practice is according to his view, as does the conclusion to that pericope. Further, the statement here exactly fits the situation of the MʿSH in that pericope: the sons coming home from their feast, close to dawn, are in a position to fulfill both requirements within the same brief time. Thus this pericope may be a simple observation on the consequence of Gamaliel's ruling, any time after that ruling had become normative.

A. A bridegroom is exempt from reciting the Shemaʿ on the first night [of his marriage. He is exempt] through the end of the Sabbath, if he has not performed an act [of intercourse].

B. (MʿSH B) Rabban Gamaliel recited [the Shemaʿ] on the first night he was married.

C. His students said to him, "Master, didn't you teach us that a bridegroom is exempt from reciting the Shemaʿ?"

D. He said to them, "I will not listen to you to free myself from the kingship of Heaven, even for an hour."

E. He bathed himself the first night after his wife died.

F. His students said to him, "Master, didn't you teach us that a mourner is forbidden to bathe?"

G. He said to them, "I am not like other men: I am infirm."

H. And when Ṭabi his slave died, he accepted condolences for him.

I. His students said to him, "Master, didn't you teach us that condolences are not accepted for slaves?"

J. He said to them, "My slave Ṭabi was not like other slaves: he was fit (KŠR)."

M. Ber. 2.5-7 (E-G = Sem. 6.1; H-J = Sem. 1.4)

Comment: These three pericopae, A-D, E-G and H-J, follow consecutively in the Mishnah, and must be considered together as well as individually.

A states the anonymous law. It exempts the bridegroom from reciting the Shemaʿ, since his mind would be preoccupied with the consummation of his marriage. The law is illustrated by the story B-D. According to C, Gamaliel taught his students the anonymous law. Personally, however, he rejected its leniency. According to M. Ber. 2.8, the sages permit a groom to recite the Shemaʿ, if he wishes; but R. Simeon b. Gamaliel considers it a mark of special piety, reserved for only a few outstanding individuals. We cannot be sure which Simeon this is, whether the father or the son of our Gamaliel.

The story seems unlikely to be historically-based. It describes Gamaliel as a mature teacher with his own disciples, at the time of his marriage. The son of a wealthy family would marry at a much younger age, since no economic hindrances would have delayed this religious obligation. Since we have no traditions of any remarriage, we must assume that this story was told about Gamaliel in his maturity, or after his lifetime, to show his special dedication to the "kingship of Heaven".

E-F depends upon the preceding pericope. Gamaliel is not identified by name. There is no statement of the law the story presumably illustrates, either anonymously or in Gamaliel's name. Indeed, the only source for the law seems to be a short statement on b.M.Q. 15b:

> A mourner is forbidden to bathe, as it is written, And anoint not yourself with oil (II Sam. 14:2); for bathing is implied in "anointing".

Bathing the body is considered one of the physical comforts denied to a mourner during the first week of mourning. The custom is certainly very old, and Gamaliel cannot be considered its innovator. F states that he taught it as accepted law. Therefore, for him to extend such a leniency toward himself would be noteworthy. Though Gamaliel explains his behavior satisfactorily, the story is implicitly critical of him. It may have been formulated as an answer to such criticism.

In H-J there is again no statement of the law the story refers to. But b. Ber. 16b does supply an anonymous baraita:

> Our Rabbis taught: For male and female slaves no row [of comforters] is formed, nor is the blessing of mourners said, nor is condolence offered.

This is followed by a well-developed narrative about Eliezer. Eliezer repeatedly avoids his students, who wish to offer him condolences for the death of a servant. There Eliezer states that he taught them the established law. There is no mention of Gamaliel.

I M. Ber. 2.5	II M. Ber. 2.6	III M. Ber. 2.7
B. MʿSH B	--	--
When R. Gamaliel married	--	H. And when Ṭabi his slave died
he recited the <u>Shema</u>	E. He bathed	he accepted condolences
C. His students said Master, didn't you teach us that	"	I. "
bridegroom exempt	mourner forbidden	condolences not accepted
D. He said, to them	G. "	J. "
I will not listen to free myself	I am not like other men	Ṭabi was not like other slaves

These three pericopae entered the Mishnah as a unit. Gamaliel is identified by name only in the first; II and III, which depend upon it, deal with mourning, rather than either bridegrooms or the <u>Shemaʿ</u>; although II refers to the first night of mourning for Gamaliel's wife, paralleling the reference in I to the first night of their marriage.

In structure they are the same: Gamaliel acts contrary to the alleged accepted practice; the students question him about this deviation from his own teaching; and he explains why he constitutes an exception to the rule.

Behind this trio of stories seems to stand an editor who arranged material both positive and negative toward Gamaliel into a structure which would stress it as positive. The redactor was not forced to use I at all, since the sages give a groom permission to recite the <u>Shemaʿ</u> in M. Ber. 2.8.

A. Rabban Gamaliel says, "Every day a man prays [the] Eighteen [Blessings]."

B. R. Joshua says, "[A prayer] like the Eighteen."

C. R. ʿAqiva says, "If his prayer is fluent in his mouth he will pray the Eighteen, but if not, [a prayer] like the Eighteen."

D. R. Eliezer says, "He who makes his prayer routine (QBʿ), his prayer is not supplications."

M. Ber. 4.3, 4A

Comment: Gamaliel requires the Eighteen Blessings of the daily prayer, in the order established under his leadership at Yavneh (b. Ber. 28b, below). Joshua requires only that the themes of the blessings be expressed. ʿAqiva suggests a compromise: the person familiar with the official text should use it; otherwise he need only pray the substance of the Eighteen. But his compromise is really a support for Joshua's position, since it implies that one is not obliged to learn the official text.

Eliezer's lemma has been added from M. Ber. 4.4, on the basis of the insight of S. Lieberman (T.K., Seder Zeraim, I, pp. 31-32) that Eliezer's contrast of routine prayer with "supplications" completes the pericope. The scribes were misled by the fact that Eliezer is usually quoted first, and placed his lemma at the start of the next pericope. According to Lieberman, Eliezer objects to ʿAqiva's statement about prayer which is "fluent in his mouth"; but Lieberman also quotes L. Ginzberg (p. 32, n. 13) who reads Eliezer as disputing all three colleagues, by objecting to a fixed text of the prayers, *per se*. (For more complete discussion of Eliezer's position, cf. J. Neusner, *Eliezer*, pp. 23-24.)

The pericope is in modified dispute form. Gamaliel's assertion, A, and the topic sentence are identical. A and B seem to have been shaped for memorization, but C and D do not. The latter may be part of the original dispute, or they may be later, independent comments upon it, ʿAqiva providing a compromise, Eliezer either disputing with ʿAqiva's emphasis on fluency, or rejecting the terms of the discussion entirely.

From this pericope it is not possible to assess the force of Joshua's lemma. The custom of pre-Pharisaic, and pre-70 Pharisaic, prayer is well-attested. Does Joshua refer to an established custom outlining the themes of the daily prayer, saying that therefore the specific wording of the Blessings need not be recited? Or is his remark dependent upon some newly-published text, saying that one need only abstract its themes? We cannot determine from his remark the exact nature of the liturgical project of the Yavneh synod under Gamaliel.

The roles played by all of the men are similar to other pericopae. Gamaliel and Joshua are in conflict (M.R.H. 2.9, b.Ber.

28b). Eliezer is apart from his colleagues (b. B.M. 59b). ʿAqiva is intermediary and conciliator (b. Ber. 28b, b. B.M. 59b). ʿAqiva's support for Joshua nevertheless shows deference to Gamaliel.

A. Our Rabbis taught (TNW RBNN): Simeon HaPaquli arranged [the] Eighteen Blessings in the [official] order, before Rabban Gamaliel in Yavneh.

B. Rabban Gamaliel said to the sages, "Can anyone among you frame (LTQN) a blessing relating to the Minim?" Samuel the Little arose and composed it (WTQNH).

C. The next year (LŠNH ʾḤRT) he forgot it. So he tried to remember it [lit., he looked for it: WHŠQYP BH] [for] two and three hours. And they did not remove him [from his place as leader].

b. Ber. 28b-29a

A. It was taught (DTNYʾ): Simeon HaPaquli arranged [the] Eighteen Blessings in the [official] order, before Rabban Gamaliel in Yavneh.

B. R. Yoḥanan said -- and some say it was taught in a matnita -- "One hundred and twenty elders, among them a number of prophets composed [the] Eighteen Blessings in the [official] order."

b. Meg. 17b

Comment: We cannot determine what exactly was done under Gamaliel's authority in Yavneh, by Simeon HaPaquli. HŚDYR ʿL HŚDR, "arranged in the order" does not imply composition; yet something beyond editorial work must have been involved.

B-C refers to the composition of the blessing against the Jewish-Christians. Epstein (Mišnah, p. 66) and Frankel (Mišnah, p. 70) place Samuel the Little as the contemporary of our Gamaliel. Hyman, however, brackets Samuel's life between Hillel and Eliezer b. Hyrcanus, on the basis of y. Sot. 9.13 and Sem. 8.7; he assigns the mid-point of Samuel's life to the time of Gamaliel the Elder (Toledot, iii, p. 1148). It is more probable that the y. story connecting Samuel to Hillel is unreliable, and that Gamaliel II is the subject here, as Epstein and Frankel assume. The version of the story in Tos. Śoṭ. 13.3 has the key references to Hillel and Samuel in two separate stories, joined by ŠWB PʿM ʾḤT. Further, were Gamaliel the Elder the one responsible for the blessing against the Jewish-Christians, it would be strange for him to receive such favorable mention in Acts 5:34-39.

A and B-C were joined by the editor of b. As we see, in b. Meg. 17b, A occurs alone. The statement of R. Yohanan, a Palestinian Amora, testifies to his sense of the antiquity of the Eighteen Blessings, but I do not think it can be relied upon for more than that.

The relation of Gamaliel to Samuel the Little will be discussed below, regarding the pericopae Tos. Pes. 1.2 and b. San. 11a. Here let us note that in B Samuel is possibly presumptuous in composing the blessing without further invitation. This may account for his forgetting it later (C) since forgetfulness is usually taken as a sign of punishment for arrogance (e.g. Hillel in b. Pes. 66a-b). So the story has possible unfavorable implications for Samuel the Little.

Gamaliel is represented in charge of the liturgical work of Yavneh, which is evidently considered one of its important achievements. The term LPNY in "before Rabban Gamaliel in Yavneh" refers to a formal session, over which he presided. Other elements of the ʿAmidah must have been current and accepted; for, the blessing directed against the Minim cannot have been the sole liturgical composition of the Pharisaic movement prior to Yavneh.

A. [If a man] ate figs, grapes or pomegranates,

B. "He says Three Blessings after them," the words of Rabban Gamaliel.

C. And sages say, "One blessing, like the Three [K, P omit: like the Three]."

D. Rabbi ʿAqiva says, "If he only ate steamed vegetables, but that is his meal, he blesses Three Blessings after it."

M. Ber. 6.8

Comment: The three fruits listed in A are meant to be representative of the "Seven Species" of the Land of Israel mentioned in Deut. 8:8 and M. Bik. 1.3. This is clear from parallel passages in Tos., y. and b., below; but there is no indication why these three are chosen from the seven (which also include: wheat, barley, olives and date honey).

Gamaliel requires the full text of the Grace after meals (blessings for divine sustenance, the goodness of the Land, and the rebuilding of Jerusalem). The sages require only a single blessing, expressing these themes. ʿAqiva extends the scope of Gamaliel's rule, making any food subject to the Three Blessings.

A-C is in standard dispute form, with the topic incorporated into Gamaliel's ruling, followed by the sages' dissent. The end of C, "like the Three", does not occur in the Tosefta; it is probably a post-Yavnean addition, and the original dispute was three blessings vs. one. ʿAqiva's lemma, D, really does not deal with the proper form of the Grace. He takes Gamaliel's view for granted, and is concerned with the type of food to which Grace is applicable, i.e., anything which constitutes a meal. D, also has little in common with the concise answers of B and C, which are capable of easy memorization. ʿAqiva's answers, here and in M. Ber. 4.3C, may be ʿAqivan supplements to disputes of Gamaliel with the sages and Joshua, respectively.

No pericope directly identifies Gamaliel as the author of the Grace, or as the authority who commissioned its composition. The third of the Three Blessings provides a terminus ante quem with its theme of the rebuilding of Jerusalem, and Gamaliel is the first to mention the obligation to say the Three Blessings. The formulation of the blessings is generally assumed to be part of the liturgical work of the Yavneh synod, under Gamaliel's direction, as is the case with the Eighteen Blessings of the daily prayer.

A. This is the general rule:

B. [After eating] anything of the kind of Seven (MMYN ŠBʿ) [Species of foods] or of grain,

C. Rabban Gamaliel says, "He blesses three blessings afterwards."

D. And sages say, "One blessing."

E. (MʿSH B) Rabban Gamaliel and Elders were reclining in Jericho. They brought dates before them and they ate.

F. R. ʿAqiva quickly said one blessing afterwards.

G. Rabban Gamaliel said to him, "ʿAqiva, why do you poke your head into a dispute?"

H. He said to him, "You taught us to follow the majority (Ex. 23:2). Even though you say [one thing], and your colleagues say [another], the halakah is according to the words of the majority."

I. R. Judah says in his name, "[After eating] anything of the Seven Species which is not of a kind of grain, or of grain which has not been made into bread,

J. "Rabban Gamaliel says, 'He blesses three blessings afterwards,'

K. "And sages say, 'One blessing.'

L. "[After eating] anything which is neither of the Seven Species nor of a kind of grain,

M. "Rabban Gamaliel says, 'He blesses one blessing afterwards,'

N. "And sages say, 'Nothing at all.'"

Tos. Ber. 4.15 (Lieberman ed. p. 21, line 52 -- p. 22, line 61)

Comment: Tos. supplies two versions of Gamaliel's dispute with the sages over the grace. Both are in standard dispute form -- topic sentence followed by brief answers. The first version, A-D, is parallel to the Mishnah; however, it specifies the "Seven Species" and grain as the subject of the dispute, rather than "figs, grapes or pomegranates". And it makes clear that the issue is three blessings vs. one blessing. R. Judah gives different language for essentially the same dispute in I-K, presumably in Gamaliel's name. He adds a further refinement in L-N: for a food neither of the Seven Species nor of grain, Gamaliel requires one blessing and the sages none at all.

ʿAqiva's lemma, M. Ber. 6.8D, applying Gamaliel's ruling to any kind of food, is missing from the dispute A-D here, strengthening the inference that it was not a part of the original dispute. Rather, it was a later gloss on this dispute of Gamaliel and the sages. The same ʿAqivan principle would also supercede both Gamaliel and the sages in L-N, since ʿAqiva would require the full Three Blessings there too.

The story separating the two versions of the dispute, E-H, shows ʿAqiva siding with the sages against Gamaliel on this issue. Further, he has the last word in the debate. Gamaliel's question to ʿAqiva (G), with ʿAqiva's reply, "You have taught us: follow the majority," occurs in a story about straightening a candelabrum on a holiday (Tos. Y.Ṭ. 2.21), as well as here. Significantly, the redactor of the Mishnah chooses to include a tradition in which ʿAqiva implicitly supports Gamaliel, rather than the negative tradition expressed here.

A. For we have learned (DTNY): This is the general rule -- for R. Judah used to say, in the name of Rabban Gamaliel,

B. "[After eating] anything of the kind of Seven [Species of foods] which is not of a kind of grain or of a kind of grain which has not been baked into bread --

C. "Rabban Gamaliel says, 'He blesses three blessings after it.'

D. "And sages say, 'One blessing.'

E. "[Concerning] anything neither of the Seven Species nor of a kind of grain --

F. "Rabban Gamaliel says, 'He blesses before and after it.'

G. "And sages say, 'He blesses before it but not after it.'"

y. Ber. 6.1

<u>Comment</u>: Not only are there two versions of the dispute between Gamaliel and the sages over the grace in Tos. (the anonymous rule's and R. Judah's). We also have a second version of R. Judah's pericope extending the dispute to food neither of the Seven Species nor of grain. A, here, clarifies what was possibly ambiguous in Tos. Ber. 4.15 I: even though Rabban Gamaliel is mentioned in the third person in the pericope, R. Judah's statement is in Gamaliel's name, not ʿAqiva's.

Of the body of the pericope here, only F-G differs from Tos. Ber. 4.15M-N. It is otherwise identical to Tos. The added detail about a blessing before eating the food is a simple elaboration. Though a new issue here, it is treated elsewhere; so it is probably taken for granted in the parallel pericopae. F implies the same ruling by Gamaliel as in Tos. The blessing after eating would be like the blessing before, i.e., one blessing.

A. (DTNYʾ) As it has been taught: This is the general rule:

B. [After eating] anything that is of the Seven Species (MŠBʿT HMYNYM) --

C. Rabban Gamaliel says, "Three blessings."

D. And sages say, "One blessing that is like three."

E. (WMʿSH B) When Rabban Gamaliel and the elders were reclining in an upper chamber in Jericho, they brought dates before them and they ate.

F. Then Rabban Gamaliel gave permission to R. ʿAqiva to say grace.

G. R. ʿAqiva quickly said (QPṢ WBRK) one blessing that is like three.

H. Rabban Gamaliel said to him, "ʿAqiva, how long will you poke your head into a dispute?"

I. He said to him, "Master, although you say [one thing] and your colleagues say [another], you have taught us, master, [when an] individual and the majority [dispute], the <u>halakah</u> is like [the opinion of] the majority."

J. R. Judah says in his name, "[After eating] anything of the Seven Species which is not of a kind of grain, or of grain which has not been made into bread --

K. "Rabban Gamaliel says, 'Three blessings,'

L. "And sages say, 'One blessing.'

M. "[After eating] anything which is neither of the Seven Species nor of a kind of grain, like bread or rice or millet --

N. "Rabban Gamaliel says, 'One blessing that is like three.'

O. "And sages say, 'And nothing at all.'"

b. Ber. 37a

Comment: A comparison of b. with Tos. reveals that b. has taken the Tos., and added to it some details from the Mishnah, together with some narrative improvements.

Tos. Ber. 4.15	b. Ber. 37a
1. This is the general rule:	1. DTNY': This is the general rule:
2. Anything that is of the kind of seven or of grain	2. " " " Seven Species,
3. Rabban Gamaliel Says,	3. " " "
"He blesses	- - -
three blessings	" " "
afterwards."	" " "
4. But sages say, "One blessing - - - ."	4. " " " that is like three."
5. (M'SH B:) When Rabban	5. (WM'SH B) " "
Gamaliel and Elders were	and the elders "
reclining in Jericho, they	in an upper chamber "
brought dates, before them	" " "
and they ate.	" " "
6. - - -	6. Then Rabban Gamaliel gave permission to R. 'Aqiva to say grace.
7. R. 'Aqiva quickly said one blessing afterwards.	7. R. 'Aqiva quickly said one blessing that is like three.
8. Said Rabban Gamaliel to	8. " " "
him, "'Aqiva, why do you	"'Aqiva, how long will
poke your head into a	you poke " "
dispute?"	
9. He said to him,	9. " " "

10. "You taught us <u>to follow the majority</u>.	10. "Master, although you say one thing and your colleagues say another
11. Even though you say [one thing] and your colleagues say [another] the <u>halakah</u> is according to the words of the majority."	11. You have taught us, master, [when an] individual and the majority [dispute], the <u>halakah</u> is like [the opinion of] the majority."
12. R. Judah says in his name, "After eating anything of the Seven Species which is not of a kind of grain, or of grain which has not been made into bread -- Rabban Gamaliel says, 'Three Blessings.' And the sages say, 'One Blessing.' After anything which is neither of the Seven Species nor of a kind of grain --	12. " " " / " " " / " " " / " " " / " " " / " " " / " " " / " " " / " " " / " " " / " " " / " " "
13. - - -	13. "like bread of rice or millet --
14. "Rabban Gamaliel says, 'He blesses one blessing afterwards.' "And sages say, 'Nothing at all.'"	14. " " " 'One blessing that is like three.' "And sages say, 'And nothing at all.'"

b. makes use of the Seven Species (2) as a well-established technical term (MŠBʿT HMYNYM) as opposed to the Tosefta's (and y.'s) less polished "kind of Seven (MMYN ŠBʿ)".

b. also adds the detail, "One blessing that is like Three," to the sages' reply in 4, from the Mishnah, and even to ʿAqiva's action in 7. It adds the same phrase to Gamaliel's answer in 14, probably to bring the two sides into balance: three <u>vs</u>. one-like-three, then one-like-three <u>vs</u>. nothing. It adds the detail of the upper chamber to 5, and a few terms of respect to soften the force of ʿAqiva's reply in 11. The only really significant addition is in 13, an explanatory gloss about what constitutes food neither of the Seven Species nor of a kind of grain.

In sum, b. synthesizes and polishes the traditions it has received, but here supplies nothing of importance. It knows nothing of the version of R. Judah contained in y. Ber. 6.1.

A. Scribes for Torah-scrolls, tefillin and mezuzot stop [work] to recite the Shemaʿ, but do not stop for the Tefillah.

B. Rabbi says, "Just as they do not stop for the Tefillah they do not stop to recite the Shemaʿ."

C. R. Hananya b. Aqavya says, "Just as they stop to recite the Shemaʿ they also stop for the Tefillah."

D. R. Eleazar b. R. Ṣadoq said, "When Rabban Gamaliel and his court were in Yavneh, and were occupied with the needs of the community, they did not stop, in order not to distract their minds [from the needs of the community]."

Tos. Ber. 2.6 (Lieberman ed. p. 7, lines 12-17)

Comment: According to M. Shab. 1.2, a worker interrupts his work to recite the Shemaʿ, but does not do so to recite the Tefillah. Our pericope (A) applies this rule to scribes.

Since Hananya b. ʿAqavya was a contemporary of Rabbi's (Rabbi Judah the Patriarch's] father, A + B + C is an artificial dispute. It was created by interpolating Rabbi's comment B into A + C.

We consider B below. In C, Ḥananya disputes the anonymous rule. He treats the scribes more strictly than other workers: they must stop work to recite the Tefillah. The issue of the dispute appears to be kavvanah (attention in prayer). A shows the concern that the worker interrupting his work would not be able to give sufficient attention to the prayer. But Ḥananya assumes that the scribe will not be bothered by the need to return to his work, which is also a sacred task, and will be able to pray with proper kavvanah. C depends upon A.

Rabbi's view (B) is the most extreme. He frees the scribe from all responsibility for prayer while he is at work. Lieberman (T.K., Ber. -- Ter., p. 16, line 13) follows Jacob Tam in interpreting Rabbi's reason in connection with D: the scribe is engaged in the "needs of the community". His activity, of the highest priority, is not to be interrupted. The leniency afforded other workers, in connection with the Tefillah, is extended for him to include the Shemaʿ. B depends upon A for its substance, and upon C for its form. We would expect B to follow C, but Rabbi's view has been given priority.

Eleazar's report (D) has no explicit connection with the substance of the pericope. It says that Gamaliel's court "did not stop" because they were engaged in the "needs of the community".

However, we are not told what their "not stopping" excluded: the Tefillah, or both Tefillah and Shemaʿ, or indeed whether the statement refers to prayer at all. Lieberman's explanation provides us with a plausible understanding of the redaction of the pericope. The editor understands D to mean that the court did not stop for prayer. D has been added to support Rabbi's position, with evidence about the practice of the Yavnean court under Gamaliel.

The reference to Gamaliel and his court appears more an indication of Yavnean consensus than a tradition specific to Gamaliel. This may be seen from the tradition cited on b. Shab. 11a, attested no earlier than 4th c. Babylonia (cf. Friedman, Shabbat, p. 41, n. 2): "For R. Adda b. Ahava and the Elders of Hagrunya recited likewise: R. Eleazar b. Ṣadoq said, 'When we were engaged in intercalating the year in Yavneh, we did not stop, neither to recite the Shemaʿ nor for the Tefillah.'" This latterly-attested lemma specifies "the needs of the community" as the fixing of the calendar, and refers to the two prayers. Though it is most probably an elaboration of the Toseftan pericope, the reference to Gamaliel and his court has not been retained.

A. It was taught [TNYʾ] there: What is the law about the evening prayer?

Rabban Gamaliel says, "Compulsory."

R. Joshua says, "Optional."

B. R. Hiyya said, "This dispute is like the previous dispute: the one who says 'Obligatory' holds that the neʿilah prayer does not absolve one from reciting the evening prayer; and the one who says 'Optional' holds that the neʿilah prayer frees one from reciting the evening prayer."

y. Ber. 4.1

Comment: This pericope renders in dispute-form the difference of views contained in the narrative of Gamaliel's deposition immediately following. The comment of R. Ḥiyya, the student-colleague of R. Judah the Patriarch, indicates an early-3rd century terminus ante quem for this form of the material. Though arguments from silence are inconclusive, the absence of this pericope from M. does suggest its unavailability to Rabbi, except in association with the story notoriously unfavorable to his ancestor. This may account for its omission from M.

A. (WMʿSH B) A certain student came and asked R. Joshua, What is the law about the evening prayer?" He said to him, "Optional."

[The student] came and asked Rabban Gamaliel, "What is the law about the evening prayer?" He said to him, "Compulsory."

[The student] said to him, "But (WHʾ) R. Joshua said 'Optional'!" [Rabban Gamaliel] said to him, "Tomorrow, when I come into the meeting-house (BYT HVʿD) get up and ask about this law."

The next day that same student got up and asked Rabban Gamaliel, "What is the law about the evening prayer?" He said to him, "Compulsory." He said, "But R. Joshua said 'Optional'."

Rabban Gamaliel said to R. Joshua, "Is it you who says 'Optional'?" He said, "No."

[Rabban Gamaliel] said to him, "Stand on your feet, and let them bear witness against you." And Rabban Gamaliel sat and expounded, and R. Joshua remained standing, until all the people shouted and said to R. Ḥuṣpit the Meturgeman, "Dismiss the assembly!"

B. They said to R. Zenun the Ḥazzan, "Say..." He began to speak. All the people began to get up and say to him [Gamaliel], "'For upon whom has not come your unceasing evil (Nah. 3:19)'?"

C. 1. They went and appointed (MYNW) R. Eleazar b. ʿAzariah into the Academy (BYŠYBH).

C. 2. (He was sixteen years old, and all his hair turned gray.)

D. 1. R. ʿAqiva was sitting sorrowfully and saying, "not that he is more learned (BN TWRH) than I, but he is of more illustrious parentage (BN GDWLYM) than I. Happy the man whose fathers have gained him merit! Happy the man who has a peg upon whom to hang!"

D. 2. (And what was R. Eleazar b. ʿAzariah's peg? He was the tenth generation in descent from Ezra.)

E. (And how many benches were there? R. Jacob b. Sisi said, "There were eighty benches there, of students, besides those standing behind the fence." R. Yosé b. R. ʾAbun said, "There were 300, besides those standing behind the fence.")

H. [This is the reference of] <u>what we learn elsewhere</u>: "On the day they seated (HWŠYBW) R. Eleazar b. ʿAzariah in the Academy" (M. Zev. 1.3; M. Yad. 3.5; 4.2).

I. (<u>We learn elsewhere</u>: "This is a <u>midrash</u> which R. Eleazar b. ʿAzariah expounded before the Sages at the Vineyard in

Yavneh" [M. Ket. 4.6]. But was there a vineyard there? Rather, these are the students who were arranged in rows, as in a vineyard.)

J. 1. Rabban Gamaliel immediately went to the home of each person to appease him.

J. 2. He went to R. Joshua; he found him sitting making needles. He said to him, "Are these how you make your living?" He said, "And are you just now trying to find out? Woe to the generation of which you are the steward (PRNŚ)."

K. Rabban Gamaliel said to him, "I submit to you."

L. 1. And they sent a certain laundry-worker (QṢR) to R. Eleazar b. ʿAzariah

L. 2. (but some say it was R. ʿAqiva).

[Sections M-N in b. only.]

O. [The messenger] said to him, "The sprinkler, son of a sprinkler, should sprinkle; shall he that is neither a sprinkler nor the son a sprinkler say to the sprinkler, son of a sprinkler, 'Your water comes from a cave, and your ashes from roasting'?"

P. [R. Eleazar b. ʿAzariah] said to them, "Are you satisfied? You and I shall wait at R. Gamaliel's door."

Q. Nonetheless, they did not depose [R. Eleazar b. ʿAzariah] from his high dignity, but rather appointed him ʾAv Bet Din.

y. Ber. 4.1 (y. Taʿan. 4.1)

(Aramaic in italics. Variant readings of Taʿan. in footnotes to Appendix, ad. loc.)

Comment: The narrative of Gamaliel's deposition from leadership of the Academy at Yavneh, and its parallels in y. Taʿan., b. Ber. and b. Bek., have been subjected to careful analysis and evaluation by R. Goldenberg (JJS, vol. XXIII, No. 2, 1972, pp. 167-190). Because of its direct pertinence, that analysis has been reproduced as an Appendix to this study. The comments which follow sum up those aspects of Goldenberg's work on this pericope directly applicable to us, and supplement them where necessary:

1. Goldenberg demonstrates the priority of y., and the ways in which b. expands its narrative. Even the detail of the appointment of Eleazar to the presidency, explicit only in b. (see below), is clearly implied by y. (Q). The alterations in the story from y. to b. indicate a shift from the political to the personal, though such a process was already underway prior to the version of the story we have in y.

2. Clearly, Gamaliel-circles took over a story unfavorable to Gamaliel (b. Bek. 36a indicates that the part of the whole story critical of Gamaliel circulated independently) and chose to present its least damaging version.

3. Unique to y. is the group nature of the protest against Gamaliel. The humiliation of Joshua is the trigger: many political upheavals turn upon a seemingly-minor incident. But y. emphasizes the mass nature of the reaction. We note the two quotations associated with the event, one scriptural (B=Nah. 3:19) and one a popular saying (J.2="Woe to the generation of which you are the steward"). For the latter, each Talmud supplies an explanatory setting; but the saying itself reveals more widespread discontent than the context of Joshua's dialogue with Gamaliel, in which it is placed. Further, Gamaliel goes to apologize to all the sages, not just to Joshua (J.1); his restoration is linked to this fence-mending.

4. Though deposition would have proved embarrassing to Gamaliel, he still would have retained the authority flowing from his appointment as Patriarch by the Romans, together with the eminence of personal wealth, learning and descent. Only the last of these, however, forms the basis of the appeal he makes in the message to Eleazar (O). The sprinkler-metaphor states: just as a priest (as was Eleazar) has his lineal prerogatives, so does a descendant of Hillel and Gamaliel the Elder. This is elaborated twice over by b., using the metaphor of "one accustomed to wear the garment [of authority]" and in the explicit statement, to Joshua, "Do it out of respect for my father." (See b., below).

5. This narrative contains the sole reference in the Gamaliel traditions to an ʾAv Bet Din. It is probably a later solution to the problem of how the rabbis avoided embarrassing Eleazar, similar to the explanation of why ʿAqiva was not chosen president. The baraita in b. (R) which refers to Eleazar's "week" need not refer to a sharing of power.

6. As we shall see (M.R.H. 2.7) the Gamaliel tradition contains a number of humiliation- and confrontation-stories, of which the opening part of this narrative would be one. We will reserve comment on the genre until the discussion of y. Sanh. 1.2. However, let us re-emphasize that here the quotations attached to Gamaliel, with differing contexts supplied by the different versions, rebuke Gamaliel for arrogance not only toward individuals but towards the sages as a group. That is unique to this narrative.

[Concerning] the evening prayer -
Rabban Gamaliel says, "Compulsory."
R. Joshua says, "Optional."

b. Ber. 27b

Comment: The b. quotation of the baraita is by R. Judah, in the name of Samuel. The narrative follows immediately.

A. Our Rabbis taught (TNW RBNN: M'SH B): A certain student came before R. Joshua. He said to him, "Is the evening Tefillah optional or obligatory?" He said to him, "Optional."

He came before Rabban Gamaliel. He said to him, "Is the evening Tefillah optional or obligatory?" He said to him, "Obligatory."

He said to him, "But did not R. Joshua say, 'Optional'?" [Rabban Gamaliel] said to him, "Wait until the Shield-bearers enter the house of study."

When the Shield-bearers entered, the questioner stood and asked, "Is the evening Tefillah optional or obligatory?" Rabban Gamaliel said to him, "Obligatory."

Rabban Gamaliel said to the Sages, "Is there anyone who disagrees in this matter?" R. Joshua said to him, "No."

He said to him, "But did they not tell me 'Optional' in your name?" He said to him, "Joshua, stand on your feet, and let them bear witness against you."

R. Joshua rose to his feet and said, "If I were alive and he [the witness] were dead, the living can contradict the dead. But now that I am alive and he is alive, how can the living contradict the living?"

And Rabban Gamaliel sat and expounded, and R. Joshua remained standing, until the whole assembly shouted and said to Ḥuṣpit the Turegeman, "Stop!" So he stopped.

[Section B lacking in b.]

C. 1. They said, "How long will he go on insulting him? Last year he insulted him [on Rosh Hashanah], he insulted him in the incident of R. Ṣadoq [in Bekhorot], and now he has insulted him again. Let us remove him! Whom shall we appoint (NWQYM)? Shall we appoint R. Joshua? He is a party to the dispute. Shall we appoint R. 'Aqiva? He might be punished, since he has not ancestral merit. Let us rather appoint R. Eleazar b. 'Azariah, since he is wise, and he is rich, and he is tenth in descent from Ezra."

C. 1. (He is wise, [that is] if questioned, he can answer; he is rich, [that is] if [Rabban Gamaliel] has to go to pay honor to Caesar, he too can go pay honor; he is tenth in descent from Ezra, [that is] he has ancestral merit, and he cannot be punished.)

C. 3. They came and said to him, "Would the Master consent to become head of the Academy?"

C. 4. He said to them, "Let me go consult my household." He went and consulted his wife.

She said to him, "They may remove you." He said to her, "Let a man use a valuable cup one day, and let it be broken the next."

She said to him, "You have no white hair." That day he was eighteen years old. A miracle occurred to him and eighteen rows of his hair turned white.

C. 5. (That is [why] R. Eleazar b. ʿAzariah said, "Behold, I resemble one [lit., am like] seventy years old," and not, "am seventy years old".)

[Section D lacking in b.]

E. 1. It was taught (TNʾ): That day (ʾWTW HYWM) they removed the doorkeeper, and the students were given permission to enter. For Rabban Gamaliel used to proclaim and say, "Any student whose outside is not like his inside shall not enter the house of study."

E. 2. (On that day (HHWʾ YWMʾ) a number of benches was added. R. Yohanan said, "The matter is disputed by ʾAbba Joseph b. Dostai and the rabbis: one holds four hundred benches were added, and the other, seven hundred.")

E. 3. Rabban Gamaliel was greatly disturbed, and said, "Perhaps, God forbid, I have withheld Torah from Israel!" In a dream, he was shown white casks filled with ashes [to indicate that he had acted correctly]. But that was not [the case]. He was shown that just to calm his mind.

F. 1. It was taught (TNʾ): ʿEduyot was reviewed on that day (BW BYWM)

F. 2. (and wherever it says "on that day" the reference is to that day)

F. 3. and there was no law which had been left pending in the house of study which was not decided.

G. And even Rabban Gamaliel did not absent himself from the study house for as much as one hour, as we learn: On that day (BW BYWM) Judah, an Ammonite proselyte, came before them in the house of study. He said to them, "Am I permitted to enter the congregation?" Said to him Rabban Gamaliel, "You are forbidden to enter the congregation." Said to him R. Joshua, "You are permitted to enter the congregation."

Said to him Rabban Gamaliel, "But has it not already been said, 'An Ammonite or a Moabite shall not enter the congregation of the Lord' (Deut. 25:4)?"

Said to him R. Joshua, "Then do Ammon and Moab dwell in their own places? Sennacherib, King of Assyria, has already come up and mixed together all the nations, as it is said, 'And I have removed the boundaries of the peoples, and have plundered their treasures; like a bull I have brought down those who sat on thrones' (Is. 10:13) - and anything which comes out [of a composite mass is assumed to have] come from its largest element."

Said to him Rabban Gamaliel, "But has it not already been said, 'And afterwards I shall restore the former condition of the children of Ammon, says the Lord' (Jer. 49:6) - so they have returned!"

Said to him R. Joshua, "But has it not already been said, 'And I shall restore the former condition of my people Israel (Amos 9:14)'? And they have not yet returned!"

They immediately permitted him to enter the congregation.

J. 1. Said Rabban Gamaliel, "Such being the case, I shall go and appease R. Joshua."

J. 2. When he got to his house, he saw that its walls were black. He said to him, "From the walls of your house, I see that you are a charcoal-maker." He said to him, "Woe to the generation whose steward (PRNŚ) you are! You do not know of the troubles of the scholars and how they support and sustain themselves."

K. [Rabban Gamaliel] said to him, "I submit to you; forgive me." He paid him no attention.

"Do it out of respect for my father." [R. Joshua] was appeased.

L. They said, "Who will go and inform the rabbis?" A certain laundry-worker (KWBŚ) said to them, "I shall go."

M. So R. Joshua sent [a message] to the house of study, "Let him who wears the garment wear the garment; should he who does not wear the garment say to him who wears it, 'Take off your garment and let me wear it'?"

N. Said R. ʿAqiva to the rabbis, "Shut the doors, so that Rabban Gamaliel's servants do not come and disturb the rabbis."

Said R. Joshua, "I had better go to them myself."

O. He came and knocked on the door and said to them, "The sprinkler, son of a sprinkler, should sprinkle; should he who is neither a sprinkler nor the son of a sprinkler, say to the sprinkler, son of a sprinkler, 'Your water comes from a cave, and your ashes from roasting'?"

P. Said R. ʿAqiva to him, "R. Joshua, have you been appeased? We have done nothing except for your honor. Tomorrow, you and I shall wait at [Rabban Gamaliel's] door."

Q. <u>They said, "How shall we act? Shall we remove</u> Eleazar b. ʿAzariah? <u>Tradition holds that</u> one may increase the holiness of an object, but not diminish it. <u>Should each Master expound one Sabbath</u> [alternately]? <u>That will lead to jealousy. Rather let Rabban Gamaliel expound three Sabbaths and R. Eleazar b. ʿAzariah one Sabbath."</u>

R. (<u>That is what the Master meant when he said</u>, "Whose Sabbath was it? R. Eleazar b. ʿAzariah's."

S. (And that student who started the whole episode was R. Simeon b. Yoḥai.)

b. Ber. 27b-28a

<u>Comment</u>: Cf., Appendix, for extended literary analysis.

A. Our rabbis taught (TWN RBNN): [If] oil and myrtle are brought before him -

B. The House of Shammai say, "He says a blessing over the oil and afterwards says a blessing over the myrtle."

C. And the House of Hillel say, "He says a blessing over the myrtle and afterwards says a blessing over the oil."

D. Said Rabban Gamaliel, "I will tip the balance [in favor of the House of Shammai].

E. "Oil - we enjoy its fragrance and we enjoy anointing with it. Myrtle - its fragrance we enjoy but anointing with it we do not enjoy."

b. Ber. 43b

<u>Comment</u>: The oil, brought at the end of a meal, cleanses the hands; the myrtle is for scent. The Houses indicate the relative importance of the two substances, by determining which is blessed first. Gamaliel decides in favor of the Shammaites (D) and supplies his reason (E). E appears to be a gloss, yet Gamaliel's words would be meaningless without it. The pericope is in standard Houses-dispute form. The answers are perfectly balanced: oil-myrtle <u>vs</u>. myrtle-oil. Gamaliel's answer, however, is not part of that balanced dispute: it is a comment upon it.

Gamaliel comments directly upon Houses-disputes in only three other pericopae: M. Beṣ. 1.8, M. Ket. 8.1 and M. Ṭoh. 9.1. In Beṣ. and Ṭoh., he adopts a position more lenient than the Hillelite view. The tradition reporting his view in M. Ket. is not completely clear, but it cannot be grouped with the House of Shammai in any case. One must wonder why this pericope is not to be found in the M.-Tos. stratum of Gamaliel traditions; perhaps it may be because of this espousal of the Shammaite view.

ii. Pe'ah, Demai, Kila'im, Shevi'it

A. As for carob trees, all [that are] within sight of each other [require a single Pe'ah].

B. Said Rabban Gamaliel, "In my father's house, they used to give a single Pe'ah

C. "for the olive trees that belonged to them in each quarter [of the city],

D. "and for carob trees [a single Pe'ah for] all [that were] within sight of each other."

E. R. Eliezer b. R. Ṣadoq says in his name, "[A single Pe'ah was given,] even for the carob trees that belonged to them throughout the whole city."

M. Pe. 2.4 (Sifra, Qed. 2.4)

Comment: Carob and olive trees are listed among those trees which, like vegetables, require a portion to be set aside as Pe'ah, the "corner" of the field reserved for the poor (M. Pe'ah 1.5). While vegetables in separated fields usually may not be donated as Pe'ah for each other, the fruits of trees constitute one of the exceptions to the rule. According to A, carob from a tree in one field may be given as Pe'ah for trees in another field, within sight of the first. Gamaliel testifies to the practice of his father's house in accordance with the anonymous law. But R. Eleazar b. R. Ṣadoq revises the statement in Gamaliel's name, extending the area of carob trees, which can be used as Pe'ah for each other, to the whole city.

Gamaliel's comment is in the form of a testimony to the practice in his father's house. Since he refers to both olive and carob trees, B-D was not originally intended as an illustration of the anonymous law, though it has been redacted here to serve as such. Eleazar's revision converts the testimony from an illustration to a dispute: Simeon b. Gamaliel applied the agricultural law much more leniently than does A. If we examine the two parts of Gamaliel's statement, C-D, we note that the language of the first part, C, referring to olive trees, is similar to the language of Eleazar's revision, E; while the wording of the second part, D, is identical with the anonymous law of the Mishnah, A. It is possible that Eleazar presented his revision in a style to match the first part of the statement.

Eleazar's Ushan statement here attests to the contents of A-D. E certainly derives from a patriarchal redactional circle; and A-D probably does also.

A. [The poor make] three searches [for Pe'ah, Gleanings, etc.] during the day: in the morning, at noon, and at sunset (WBMNḤH).

B. Rabban Gamaliel says, "They said this so that they [the poor] should not decrease [their searches]."

C. R. ʿAqiva says, "They said this so that they [the poor] should not increase [their searches]."

D. [The men] of Bet Namer used to reap their crops by the [measuring] rope, and leave Pe'ah from every furrow.

M. Pe. 4.5

Comment: Gamaliel views the number of times the poor may come to the field, to collect their due, as a minimum. More times are permitted for the convenience of the poor. ʿAqiva views the law as a maximum, to assure that produce will be available when they come. The harvest custom of Bet Namer, cited in D, makes frequent visits to the field worthwhile, because some crops will be available to the poor at any hour. D thus seems to agree with Gamaliel, yet in a way that takes account of the reason we have attributed to ʿAqiva. The dispute has been edited in accord with Gamaliel's view.

A. If the sheaf contains two se'ahs, and he forgets it, it is not [subject to the law of] a Forgotten Sheaf.

B. If there are two sheaves with two se'ahs between them, Rabban Gamaliel says "[They belong] to the owner."

And sages say, "To the poor."

C. Rabban Gamaliel said, "Is the owner's claim strengthened or weakened, according to the greater number of sheaves?"

They said, "It is strengthened."

D. He said to them, "Then if one sheaf containing two se'ahs, when forgotten, is not [called] a Forgotten Sheaf, does it not follow that two sheaves, containing two se'ahs, will not be [called] a Forgotten Sheaf?"

E. They said to him, "No. Would you say about one sheaf, which is as [big as] a stack, what you would say of two sheaves which are as [small as] bundles?"

M. Pe. 6.6 (Sifré, Ki Teṣé 283)

Comment: The traditions available to the rabbis at Yavneh use two standards for determining the quantity of grain defined as the "Forgotten Sheaf" to be left for the poor. One is number (one or two sheaves together, no more); the other is volume (a sheaf up to two se'ahs in volume, no more).

The quantity disputed here would be assigned to the poor if defined in terms of the number of its sheaves. But it is retained by the owner of the field if it is considered according to its volume. For Gamaliel, volume is determinative. The sages reject his argument on the grounds that a sheaf of under two se'ahs is considered like any other small bundle, and that number is determinative. They decide this borderline case in favor of the poor, rather than the owner.

Behind this dispute lies a more comprehensive Yavnean issue: whether individual items or acts are to be considered as a unit, to fall into a particular legal category. Here Gamaliel holds that the two sheaves are added together, and thus excluded from the Forgotten Sheaf law. The sages hold that they are considered separately. We shall see that Gamaliel's position is consistent (see below, M. Shab. 12.6).

In this pericope, A is the undisputed antecedent law. B is in dispute-form, with Gamaliel preceding the sages, and the answers balanced, one word each. C-E sets out a debate between Gamaliel and the sages. As with the Houses-debates (cf. Neusner, Pharisees, iii, pp. 16-23) Gamaliel's opening question is phrased in terms of a premise the other side would share. The sages' response distinguishes between the two kinds of sheaves. However, rather than exploring the reasoning behind the positions of the opposing parties, the debate-form here only restates their views in a different way.

Gamaliel speaks first, but the sages have the last word and defend their point of view. Whatever prominence Gamaliel may have in A-B is cancelled in C-E, which implicitly supports the sages.

A. [MʿSH B] R. Yeshovav once arose and distributed all his possessions to the poor.

B. Rabban Gamaliel sent him [a message]: "Have they not said, 'A fifth of your possessions toward the _miṣvot_'?'

C. But wasn't Rabban Gamaliel before Usha?

D. R. Yosé b. R. Bun [said] in the name of R. Levi, "That was the _halakah_ in their hands, but they forgot it; and the second [group of scholars in their action] agreed with the view of the first ones."

y. Pe. 1.

Comment: The anonymous questioning of the attribution of B to Gamaliel (in C) leads Epstein to postulate a time of Ushan residence for the Sanhedrin during Gamaliel's days (_Misnah_, p. 141). Hyman objects to this (_Toledot_, ii, p. 816). It is indeed anachronous to have Yeshovav and Gamaliel illustrate an Ushan decree.

A. They feed _Demai_-produce to the poor, and [K, P, Camb.: they feed] _Demai_ to transient guests.

B. Rabban Gamaliel used to feed _Demai_ to his workers.

M. Dem. 3.1

Comment: In contrast to produce which definitely has not been tithed (WDʾY) and which is subject to all the laws of tithing before it may be used, _Demai_ is produce which may possibly have been tithed. Since its status is doubtful, some tithes (the priest's portion of the First Tithe; Second Tithe) must be set aside from it, but not all (the Levite's portion of the First Tithe; the Poorman's Tithe). Only then may the produce be used; so Danby (_Mishnah_, p. 20, n. 9).

Our pericope deals with another situation involving _Demai_. Here the owner is not to use it himself; he is giving it to someone else. In this case it becomes the recipient's responsibility to tithe the food before consuming it. In the statement about Gamaliel, B, Gamaliel's workers, rather than the employer, in effect, bear the cost of tithing. This is consistent with his position in M. Pe. 6.6, which also favors the farm-owner.

B was not created to illustrate A. It deals with workers, rather than transients or the poor. B was added to supply another category of recipients for _Demai_, by a redactor who felt that Gamaliel's practice was significant for legal precendent. A tradition about him is used, rather than a statement in his name.

A. If one buys [produce] from a merchant who says, "This has been tithed, and this has not," he is not believed, even about [what he claims has been] tithed.

One whose practice is to sell Demai is believed.

B. If a ḥaver usually sells wholesale, and [only] tithed [produce], and is assigned something which is Demai, he must announce [that fact].

C. Rabban Gamaliel used to feed Demai to his workers, and announce (WMWDYʿ) [it].

D. If it is known that the owner does [not] have that kind [of produce] he is not required to announce [that it is Demai].

Tos. Dem. 3.15 (Lieberman ed. p. 77, lines 56-61)

Comment: The reference to Gamaliel here does not seem appropriate to the context. Gamaliel is, in C, a farmer; the context deals with a wholesale merchant and his customers.

The presence of a single word, WMWDYʿ, "announce", makes it fitting to the issue. Yet the version in the Mishnah (M. Demai 3.1) is actually no more appropriate to its setting, which likewise does not speak of employer-worker relations. The connection there is the theme of giving Demai to others for food.

Thus while at first glance the reports might seem to be simply illustrations of the theme, their unfittingness in both cases would point to an independent tradition, used in each place to illustrate something slightly different. The original form of the tradition must be here in Tos. Had the version in M. been primary, we would have to posit a redactor seeing its possible relevance to the Toseftan case of a produce merchant by adding the word WMWDYʿ. It is more likely that the tradition was added to the Toseftan pericope because of the common theme of the responsibility to announce the character of the Demai. It was redacted into M. because of the common reference to feeding Demai to others, where the additional detail of WMWDYʿ was dropped.

We cannot determine whether the tradition was originally favorable to Gamaliel, only that the redactor considers his behavior as legal precedent.

A. R. Simeon says, "There are three decrees concerning Demai-produce."

B. (MʿSH Š) Our rabbis entered the Samaritan villages which are beside the road [between Judea and the Galilee]. They brought vegetables before them. R. ʿAqiva quickly rose and tithed them as untithed food (WDʾY).

C. Rabban Gamaliel said to him, 1. "How did your heart prompt you to transgress the words of your colleagues" -- 2. "or, who gave you permission to tithe?"

D. He said, "Did I establish the halakah in Israel [by doing this]? Didn't I only [WHLW : so Lieberman's emendation. Zuck.: ʾMR LW, He said to him] tithe my own vegetables?"

E. He said to him, "Know that you did establish a halakah in Israel by tithing your own vegetables."

F. And when Rabban Gamaliel went among them [i.e., the Samaritan villages] he declared their produce and beans Demai, and [declared] all the rest of their fruits certainly untithed (WDʾY).

G. And when Rabban Gamaliel [so Lieberman's emendation. Zuck.: Rabban Simeon b. Gamaliel] returned through them, he saw that [their observance] had deteriorated; and he declared all their fruits untithed.

Tos. Dem. 5.24 (Lieberman ed. p. 93, lines 100-106)

Comment: This entire pericope may have been intended as a continuation of Simeon's lemma (A), since it is possible to find "three decrees" within it. But it is more likely that the rest of the pericope was appended to A, to explain it.

Lieberman explains B as follows (T.K. Zer., I, p. 262): The vegetables brought to the rabbis came from the homes of the Samaritans. According to Tos. Dem. 5.23, Samaritans are like Israelites, as far as the food they use, or send to an Israelite, is concerned. It is considered Demai. ʿAqiva's act is unfriendly toward the Samaritans, since he classes them with gentiles by declaring their produce as untithed.

Gamaliel's question to ʿAqiva (C) may contain an elaboration (C.2). Until this point, B-E has resembled other stories (Tos. Ber. 4.15, Tos. Beṣ. 2.12) about Gamaliel dining with a group of elders which includes ʿAqiva. In those, too, ʿAqiva "quickly" does something contrary to Gamaliel's opinion (QPṢ RBY ʿQBʾ W). But ʿAqiva justifies his actions on the grounds that a majority of the sages has ruled that way, and that Gamaliel himself taught the principle of majority rule. Here, however, it is ʿAqiva who violates the consensus of the sages by his actions.

ʿAqiva's defence is that his action was individual, and not meant as a legal precedent (D) but Gamaliel replies that he has, nevertheless, established a precedent.

F-G now shows ʿAqiva's action to be predictive of decrees that Gamaliel will make. On Gamaliel's first inspection of the Samaritan villages, he compromises between the position of ʿAqiva and the sages: he rules the Samaritan produce and beans to be Demai and the rest of their fruit untithed. (These would be the first two "decrees" mentioned in A.) Lieberman explains that the produce and beans are either grown by the Samaritans for their own consumption, or imported for sale from Jewish farms. But the rest of the fruits from the Samaritans' fields are untithed, because the Samaritans do not tithe food they do not intend to consume.

By the time F-G has appeared, the question of the sages' consensus is no longer a factor in the story. Gamaliel is in a position of authority. As Patriarch he himself rules on the status of the Samaritan foods. G describes Gamaliel's return trip, at some later time, through the same area. The Samaritan observance of the laws of tithing has declined. Gamaliel now rules all Samaritan food to be considered untithed. (This would be the third "decree".) The passage of time has vindicated ʿAqiva's personal ruling.

Thus we have two short stories, B and F-G, connected by a dialogue, C-E. The first story (B) is one of the stories of ʿAqiva's quick action, as occurs elsewhere in Tos. The latter story describes how Gamaliel at first ruled on the Demai question in compromise between ʿAqiva and the sages, but later reversed himself to follow ʿAqivan precedent. The connecting dialogue, probably the last addition to the pericope, explains how Gamaliel realized that ʿAqiva's action, though contrary to the sages' consensus, would eventually become the halakah.

B is, of course, an ʿAqivan story. C-E has the secondary purpose of justifying an act by ʿAqiva contrary to majority rule. F-G is a Gamaliel-story, about the Patriarch's travels and decrees, which has been incorporated into the ʿAqivan tradition; its point is not to show ʿAqiva besting Gamaliel (as in Tos. Ber. 4.15 and Tos. Beṣ. 2.12) but rather to describe how circumstances themselves required Gamaliel to accept his views.

Rabban Gamaliel and his court decreed (HTQYNW) that a distance of four cubits was to be made from the root of the grapevines to the fence [of the vineyard].

Tos. Kil. 4.1 (Lieberman ed. p. 217, lines 1-3)

Comment: This would permit seeds to be sown on the other side of the fence, without violating the prohibition against mixed seeds.

A. [if a man] pickles three [kinds of] vegetables in a single jar,

B. R. Eliezer says, "They eat according to the first."

C. R. Joshua says, "Even (ʾP) according to the last."

D. Rabban Gamaliel says, "Each (KL) [vegetable] whose type has ceased from the field -- let him remove its type from the jar."

E. And the halakah is according to his words [P omits].

M. Shev. 9.5
(y. Shev. 9:4, b. Pes. 52a)

Comment: Vegetables gathered during the Sabbatical year may be eaten while there are vegetables of the same type still growing in the fields (M. Shev. 9.4). When those crops begin to wither, picked vegetables also must be removed from the household.

Both Eliezer and Joshua make a distinction between vegetables pickled together, and those lying separate in the house. Eliezer permits the mixture only until the first-ripened vegetable disappears. Joshua permits the mixture until the last-ripened vegetable is gone. Gamaliel does not make such a distinction. His position is intermediate: each vegetable is removed from the jar as its type disappears from the field.

In this dispute, B and C both respond to the topic sentence, A; but further, C depends upon B. Gamaliel's lemma depends upon A for its definition, but its phrasing is independent of B-C. A separate Gamaliel-tradition may here be used to comment upon an Eliezer-Joshua dispute. The redaction of the pericope, as well as the decision, E, supports Gamaliel's intermediate position on the issue.

A. From the field you shall eat the crops (Lev. 25:12) -- all the time you eat from the field, you eat within the house. When [the food has] ceased from the field, it ceases from the house.

B. Based on this, they said: If a man pickles three [kinds of] vegetables in a single jar --

C. R. Eliezer says, "Since one type has ceased from the field, the whole jar is to be removed."

D. R. Joshua says, "He continues and eats until the last one in it [has ceased from the field]."

E. Rabban Gamaliel says, "A type (MYN) [of vegetable] whose type has ceased from the field -- let him remove its type from the jar."

F. And the halakah is according to his words.

Sifra, Behar 3.4-5

Comment: Sifra supplies an exegesis for the time-table of removing crops from the household during the Sabbatical year. Then the editor quotes the topic sentence of M. Shev. 9.5, with a pericope different in wording but identical in substance. The statements attributed to Eliezer and Joshua, C-D, may be explanations of their terse formulations in the Mishnah. Only Gamaliel's words, E, are identical in both pericopae, with the exception of the first word, KL vs. MYN, which may be an error by the Sifra. The redactional process here treats Gamaliel much more carefully than his colleagues, in the preservation of words in his name: and the exegesis conforms to his opinion.

iii. Terumot, Maʿaserot, Maʿaser Sheni

A. A jar of Heave-offering, concerning which there was born the suspicion of uncleanness (SPQ Ṭ\M'H) --

B. R. Eliezer says, "If it was lying in an exposed place (MQWM HTRPH), he should put it in a hidden place; and if it was uncovered, he should cover it."

C. And R. Joshua says, "If it was lying in a hidden place, he should place it in an exposed place; and if it was covered, he should uncover it."

D. Rabban Gamaliel says, "Let him not do anything new with it."

M. Ter. 8.8 (y. Ter. 6.4;
b. Bek. 33b)

Comment: The jar of Heave-offering may not be used, since we suspect it to be unclean. Eliezer's concern is that the Heave-offering should be protected from definite defilement, since we now are not sure whether it is clean. Joshua recommends its defilement, so that it can be disposed of. Gamaliel rejects

Eliezer's requirement for protection and Joshua's for defilement: nothing should be done to it.

B and C, Eliezer's and Joshua's parts in the dispute, contain the identical words, in reverse order. Gamaliel's lemma is placed as if it were a compromise position, but it is not. Again, he appears to comment upon an Eliezer-Joshua dispute.

A. [Concerning a] ship which comes from outside the Land [of Israel] to the Land, with fruit in it: from the boundary-line eastward if it touches bottom it is liable [to give tithes] according to the [prescribed] reckoning.

B. One that goes outside the Land is not liable, according to the [prescribed] reckoning [of tithes].

C. R. Leazar says, "Dust [of the Land of Israel, carrying fruit, bound for] outside the Land is liable for the reckoning [of tithes]."

D. But ʿorlah and kilaʿim of the vineyard are the same for a gentile in the Land of Israel [and] in Syria, [and for an Israelite] outside the Land;

E. except that R. Judah [alt.: Yudan] says, "The law of the Fourth Year for a vineyard does not [apply] to a gentile in Syria."

F. And sages say, "It does." [Vienna omits.]

G. R. Judah said, "(MʿSH B) Segavyon [alt: SʿBYWN] chief of the synagogue of Akziv, brought a fourth [-year] vineyard in Syria from a gentile, and paid him for it. He came to ask Rabban Gamaliel, who was traveling from place to place.

H. "He [Gamaliel] said to him, 'Wait until we are [concerned] with halakah.'

I. "He said to him[self], 'There is proof from that [: since he did not declare it forbidden, it is permitted].'

J. "But (ʾP) he sent him [a message] by a mute messenger [i.e., secretly]. 'What you have done you have done, but do not teach [that it is permissible] to do so.'"

Tos. Ter. 2.13 (Lieberman ed.
p. 115, lines 50-58)

Comment: A-C discuss the application of the laws of tithing to territory within, and outside of, the Land of Israel, and do not directly concern us.

D-I discuss the difference in location as it affects the laws of ʿorlah. Lev. 19:23-25 states that fruit borne by a tree during its first three years may not be used. It is considered ʿorlah, lit. "uncircumcised". Fruit of the fourth year may be used only for a pilgrimage to Jerusalem.

D declares that gentile-owned land within the Land of Israel, and in Syria, is subject to these laws. E-F registers a dispute on one aspect of the law, the restriction on use of the fourth-year fruit to a pilgrimage. Judah rules (E) that this aspect of the law does not apply to gentile-owned Syrian land. A Jew may use that fruit. The sages (F) insist that all of the law applies to Syria. (E-F = M. Ter. 3.9.)

G now supplies a precedent, in Judah's name, in the form of a story about Gamaliel, agreeing with Judah's view. Segavyon bought a gentile's vineyard: Gamaliel does not directly forbid his use of the fourth-year fruit (H), and Segavyon concludes that it is permitted (I).

J appears to be an addition, explaining why there is no well-known tradition, in Gamaliel's name, supporting Judah. HD understands Gamaliel's message to mean that while use of a gentile's Syrian-raised fruit is biblically permissible, it is subject to a rabbinical prohibition. Since Segavyon had already purchased the field, Gamaliel permitted him to use the fruit, lifting the prohibition for him because of the economic loss involved. However, we do have one example (Tos. M.Q. 2.14) of a ruling held by Gamaliel, more lenient than popular practice, which he did not teach publicly. This may be another.

The way Gamaliel is represented here must be compared to M. Ḥal. 4.7 and Tos. Ḥal. 2.5. In M. there, Gamaliel relinquishes any claim to Syria as Jewish territory, and the redactor of M. claims popular acceptance of his view. Tos. there, on the other hand, presents a revision of Gamaliel, by Eleazar b. Ṣadoq, portraying him closer to the nationalist position attributed to Eliezer b. Hyrcanus. The story in our pericope, as presented by Judah, would accord with the evidence from both M. and Tos. Ḥal. Our pericope shows Gamaliel ruling that Syrian land is not subject to the law of fourth-year fruit when owned by a gentile. Syria is considered foreign territory in this respect (as in M. Ḥal.). But Gamaliel's ruling, according to J, is not one which he or anyone else should teach publicly.

A. Rabban Gamaliel says, "The stalks of fenugreek (TLTN), of mustard and of white beans are all subject to tithes."

B. R. Eliezer says, "Caperbush is tithed as to stalks, caperberries and caperflowers."

C. R. ʿAqiva says, "Only the caperberries are tithed, because they are the fruit."

M. Ma. 4.6 (y. Ma. 1.1)

Comment: All four plants mentioned in the pericope have stalks and flowers as well as their seeds (mustard, fenugreek), beans or berries (caperbush). In A, Gamaliel asserts that the stalks of the plants he lists -- as well as the seeds or beans -- are to be considered food. Hence they too are to be tithed.

Gamaliel's lemma (A) is independent of the Eliezer-ʿAqiva dispute. It was added to B-C because it mentions other examples of plants whose stalks are tithed. His view has been given priority in the newly-created dispute.

A. What kind of garlic is Baalbek [garlic] [BʿL BKY; or garlic that causes tears]? One which has only one capsule [of seeds] (DWR; alt.: ZWR, DYR) surrounding the stem.

B. What kind of onion is the Rikpa [onion]? One in which the stalk is not squeezed inside.

C. Rabban Simeon b. Gamaliel says, "One which has only one husk."

D. These are the Sicilian beans: ones which are large and square.

E. Rabban Gamaliel [so Erfurt, Geniza fragments; Vienna: Simeon b. Gamaliel] says, "There has been nothing [created perfectly] square since the six days of Creation."

F. These are Egyptian lentils: ones with sharp seeds.

G. Rabban Gamaliel [so Erfurt, Geniza fragments; Vienna: Simeon b. Gamaliel] says, "One which has no 'stone'."

H. R. Meir says, "Even the colocasia, [so Danby] for its stalks are small, yet (W) its pods are many."

Tos. Ma. 3.15 (Lieberman ed.
p. 241, line 51-p. 242, line 55)

Comment: Because the following plants grow wild, M. Ma. 5.8 lists them as exempt from tithes: Baalbek garlic, Rikpa onions, Sicilian beans and Egyptian lentils. Meir adds colocasia (QLQŚ, QRQŚ, a plant which Lieberman is unable to define, T.K. II, p. 709, line 56) to the list. Our pericope supplies a commentary to M., defining its terms.

C, E and G depend upon, and comment upon, B, D and F respectively. Meir's addition to the list provides a reason for his words in M., but does not attest to what precedes him.

The definition of liability for tithes is certainly a Yavnean preoccupation, so that it is not impossible to assign these comments to Gamaliel. But ms. differences preclude certainty about which name really belongs in E and G, Gamaliel or Simeon. Since Simeon is quoted in C, according to all the mss., this pericope may consist of a series of his comments on the anonymous definitions. The Vienna reading in E is supported by y. Ma. 5.3F and its parallels, below. But upon comparison with y., the terms and definitions are so confused as to suggest only that this is a collection of patriarchal comments upon M.

A. What kind of garlic is Baalbek [garlic] [Bʿ L BKY; or: garlic that causes tears]? One which has only one capsule [of seeds] (HWR) surrounding the stem.

B. Said to R. Simeon b. Gamaliel, "One which has only one husk."

C. What kind of onion is the Rikpa [onion]? One in which the stalk is squeezed inside.

D. Rabban Gamaliel says, "One which has no penetrating moisture (ʾYRŚ)."

E. These are the Sicilian beans: ones which are square.

F. It was taught (TNY): Rabban Simeon b. Gamaliel says, "There is nothing [perfectly] square from the six days of Creation."

y. Ma. 5.3 (F = y. Ned. 3.2,
y. Shav. 3.1)

Comment: Simeon's definition of Baalbek garlic (B) appears in Tos. Ma. 3.15C as a definition of the Rikpa onion. The anonymous definition of the Rikpa onion (C) is the reverse of the one in Tos., since the negative Lʾ does not appear. The definition of the Rikpa onion here attributed to Gamaliel (D) does not occur in Tos. at all. As we noted above, F here supports the Vienna ms. reading of Tos. Ma. 3.15E.

A. Samuel said, "A cucumber which was perforated while growing - the whole stalk is forbidden."

B. It is even so with the stems of palm-branches:

C. R. Yosé said, "Jonathan b. Ḥarsha of Genossar asked Rabban Gamaliel and the sages at Yavneh, 'What is the law regarding moist perforations of palm-leaves still growing on the stem?' They said to him, "That whole palm is forbidden.'"

y. Ma. 1.2

Comment: The plant which has been pierced is forbidden, for fear that it has been poisoned by snake-bite. Jonathan b. Ḥarsha appears only in this pericope (Hyman, Toledot, ii, p. 702). The reply to his question indicates a general consensus of the Yavneans, reported by R. Yosé, rather than a ruling by Gamaliel.

A. The House of Shammai say, "A man may not change his śelas [of Second Tithe money] for gold dinars."

But the House of Hillel permit it.

B. R. ʿAqiva said, "I changed silver for gold dinars, for Rabban Gamaliel and R. Joshua."

M. M. S. 2.7

Comment: Whatever the intention of the Shammaite rule in A, its effect is to decrease the demand for gold coins, and hence their price. The Hillelite rule (B) disregards any inflationary effects for the convenience of transporting the more valuable gold coins, and the encouragement of pilgrimage to Jerusalem. Neusner (Pharisees, ii, pp. 96-98) argues that A-B was created well after the destruction of the Temple. No one knew the views of the Houses on this point, and ʿAqiva's statement supplied evidence for Hillelite practice.

Gamaliel's reported behavior again is considered as a source for law, indeed for the source of a Houses-dispute created after his time. But this tradition (C) is at odds with a number of other themes in other pericopae: those which represent Gamaliel as following Shammaite rulings, and those which represent him in opposition to Joshua.

B also stands in contrast to many of the materials involving Yoḥanan b. Zakkai, which assume that Jerusalem was no longer a focus for pilgrimages, or other religious observances, after the destruction in 70 C. E.

A. One whose fruit is far away from him must designate [its tithes] (LQRʾ BHM ŠM).

B. (MʿSH B) When Rabban Gamaliel and the elders were going by ship, said Rabban Gamaliel, "The tithe which I am going to measure [as First Tithe] is given to Joshua, and the land it grows on is rented to him; the other Tithe which I am going to measure [as Poorman's Tithe] is given to ʿAqiva b. Joseph, that he may possess it on behalf of the poor, and the land it grows on is rented to him."

C. Said R. Joshua, "The tithe which I am going to measure [as Heave-offering of Tithe] is given to Eleazar b. ʿAzariah, and the land it grows on is rented to him."

D. And they each received rent from the other.

M.M.S. 5.9 (b. Qid. 26b-27a; b. B.M. 11a-b)

Comment: M.M.S. 5.6 states that tithes of the fourth and seventh years are "removed" from the possession of their owner on the eve of the last day of Passover. Here A states a law concerning the removal of those tithes. If the owner is far away from his field, he must "designate" fruit from the field for tithes (QRʾ BHM Š̌M). According to M. Ter. 3.5 and M.M.S. 4.7, "designation" involves naming the exact location, and possibly even the amount of produce to be removed.

The story B-D does not illustrate that act of designation. Rather it shows how, at a distance, tithes are assigned to a specific recipient. Renting the land on which the tithes grow is a way of accomplishing this transfer of possession. The summing-up sentence (D) indicates that as the point of the story, B-D is independent of A, not created for it. It was added either in error or as a reinterpretation of the phrase LQRʾ BHM Š̌M, understanding it as "specifically naming their recipient".

Two of the other narratives about Gamaliel and the elders (in a number of versions) during their voyage to Rome connect their trip with the Sukkot festival instead of Passover. A voyage between Palestine and Rome spanning the two seasons is conceivable. But so is the possibility that the famous quartet was used freely to illustrate a number of situations, here the procedure of tithing at a distance, and transferring ownership. Since Gamaliel and the sages consist of the Patriarch plus a Kohen, Levi and Israelite, their group invited such use.

The structure of this story somewhat resembles one of those Sukkot holiday stories. It concerns multiple use of a lulav; each of the sages takes possession of the lulav from the other (Sifra Emor 16.2, b. Sukk. 41b). The opening phrases are identical, "When Gamaliel and the elders were going by ship," they describe a chain of reciprocal actions among the sages, and they conclude with a short summation. The summation here, D, "And they each received rent from the other," does not exactly describe the action (rather, Gamaliel receives rent from Joshua and ʿAqiva; and Joshua receives rent from Eleazar). So this pericope may be modeled after the Sukkot story there.

iv. Ḥallah, Bikkurim

A. [As to] Israel[ites] who are tenant-farmers of gentiles in Syria, Rabbi Eliezer makes their produce subject (MḤYYB) to the laws of Tithes and the Sabbatical year.

But Rabban Gamaliel exempts (PWṬR) [them].

B. Rabban Gamaliel says, "Two Dough-offerings [are given] in Syria."

Rabbi Eliezer says, "One Dough-offering."

C. They adopted the leniency of Rabban Gamaliel and the leniency of Rabbi Eliezer. They reversed themselves and followed the words of Rabban Gamaliel in both ways.

M. Ḥal. 4.7 (y. Ma. 5.2)

Comment: Syria was not part of the land originally divided among the Israelite tribes by Joshua. It became part of the "Land of Israel" through the Davidic conquest. The dispute of Eliezer and Gamaliel, over how much biblical agricultural law applies to the area, reflects their respective views of Syria as Jewish territory.

Eliezer considers Syria legally identical to Palestine, and the tenant-farmer relationship similar to a partnership. Since the Jew is, in effect, part-owner of Israelite land, Eliezer declares the produce of such land subject to the laws of Tithes and the Sabbatical year. But Gamaliel holds Syria to be foreign land, in this respect. He requires the full ownership of such land by a Jew before it becomes subject to these laws. (Of course, land which is in no way to be considered "Land of Israel", when owned by a Jew, is not subject to biblical agricultural law at all.)

The same attitudes are carried over into B. Gamaliel holds Syria, as "foreign" land, and ritually unclean, to have its Dough-offering removed but burnt (similar to the unclean dough of Palestine) and a second portion of dough given to the priest as a pedagogic device, to maintain the custom. Eliezer requires only one offering, given to the priest, since the land is in the same category of ritual purity as Palestine itself.

Differences in both content and form clearly show the nature of the pericope. A reports the views of the men in the third person (MḤYYB, PWṬR) about tithes and Sabbatical year; B quotes them directly (ʾWMR) about the Dough-offering; and C comments from a later perspective.

The sequence within units A and B is the same: first the more demanding view, then the more lenient. Thus there is no way to determine whether there is special significance to Eliezer's precedence in A and Gamaliel's precedence in B.

The subject of C appears to be the Jewish population of Syria, who adopted the leniencies (lit. "grasped" ʾḤZW) and then reversed themselves and followed (lit. "they turned around and behaved," ḤZRW LNHWG) Gamaliel's ruling. We shall see immediately below that R. Eleazar b. R. Ṣadoq explains unit A and revises unit B, thus providing an Ushan terminus a quo for that part of the pericope. Let us only note here that the author of C did not have to bring A and B together. They had probably been collected together before he made his comment. We shall further argue that C could not have been added at Usha, nor could the change it describes have taken place until after the Ushan period.

The significance of Gamaliel's ruling, in political terms, is that it gives up any Jewish claims to Syria as Jewish territory (Neusner, Eliezer, i , pp. 80-81). For Gamaliel as Patriarch, this submission to Roman authority over Syria was an obviously necessary accomodation. The redaction of the pericope stresses that Gamaliel's view was adopted popularly, even though such a reversal meant the adding of a second Dough-offering. In other words, the Jews living in Syria are represented as coming to regard that area as non-Jewish land. The shift from following two lenient rulings, to following both of Gamaliel's rulings, has clear political implications, since the common element of Gamaliel's rulings is only this attitude toward Syria.

A. R. Leazar b. R. Ṣadoq said, "Even though Rabban Gamaliel would free tenant farmers in Syria [from the obligations of tithes and the Sabbatical year] he would forbid tenant-farming [ab initio].

B. "If he did tenant-farm [however] he is not liable [to tithes and Sabbatical year prohibitions] provided that he did not pick [fruit] and they [his gentile workers] bind it beside him, that he did not harvest [the grapes] and they trample them beside him, that he did not harvest [the olives] and they pack the vat beside him; rather, they pick [the fruit] and he binds it beside them, they harvest [the grapes] and he tramples them beside them, they harvest [the olives] and he packs the vat beside them."

C. R. Leazar b. R. Ṣadoq would also say, "For Syria, Rabban Gamaliel required only one single Dough-offering."

Tos. Ḥal. 2.5 (Lieberman ed. pp. 280-281, lines 20-25)

Comment: In A-B, R. Eleazar b. R. Ṣadoq makes specific reference to M. Ḥal. 4.7A, the dispute of Gamaliel and Eliezer. His remarks clearly depend upon it. Eleazar explains Gamaliel's exemption of the tenant farmer from the laws of tithing and Sabbatical year, in context of an outright prohibition of tenant-farming. Presumably, this is to help stem emigration from Palestine into Syria.

In B, he qualifies and narrows Gamaliel's position, bringing him much closer to Eliezer. The land would be subject to the agricultural laws if worked by a Jew. But since the tenant farmer does not own the land, and since he does not come into direct control over the crops while they are still attached to the soil, the laws do not apply. If the Jew did have direct contact with the crops, before they were harvested, they would be subject to tithes and the Sabbatical year, as Eliezer contends.

Within this pericope the same principle may underlie C. The making of the bread is done by the Jew; therefore it is subject to a Dough-offering. On the other hand, C may stand alone, dependent neither upon the Gamaliel-Eliezer dispute in M. Ḥal. 4.7B, nor upon A-B, above. It is in direct contradiction to the Mishnah, and agrees with the position of Eliezer. Eleazar b. R. Ṣadoq has revised the understanding of M. Ḥal. 4.7A, and revised the text of M. Ḥal. 4.7B. He knows nothing of the adoption of practice favored by Gamaliel, over that of Eliezer, as described in the Mishnah. Perhaps this claim was made after Eleazar's time. The development of these pericopae would then be as follows:

1. M. Ḥal. 4.7A-B are one version (probably the correct one) of the Yavnean disputes of Eliezer and Gamaliel. Eliezer lays claim to Syria as Jewish territory; Gamaliel relinquishes Syria as unclean.

2. Tos. Ḥal. 2.5 is Eleazar b. R. Ṣadoq's late-Yavnean or Ushan attestation to, and revision of, the traditions recorded in the Mishnah. He reinterprets Gamaliel's words in a way closer to Eliezer, in A-B; and he revises Gamaliel's words completely in C. Now Gamaliel is represented with Zealot sympathies, and in agreement with Eliezer that Syria is Jewish. His authority is claimed for both sides of the question.

3. M. Ḥal. 4.7C is the Ushan, or post-Ushan, comment on the traditions reported in M. The redactor declares popular acceptance of Gamaliel's relinquishing of any claim to Syria. The Mishnah, reflecting the Patriarchate and its relation to the Roman government, selects the traditions on Gamaliel which fit attitudes common to them both.

A. Rabban Gamaliel says, "Three lands [differ in applying the law] of the Dough-offering.

B. "In the Land of Israel as far as Keziv, one Dough-offering [is given].

C. "From Keziv to the River and to Amanah, two Dough-offerings, one for the fire and one for the priest.

D. "[The one] for the fire has [the prescribed] measure, and [the one] for the priest has no [prescribed] measure.

E. "From the River and from Amanah, beyond, two Dough-offerings, one for the fire and one for the priest."

F. "[The one] for the fire has no measure, and the one for the priest has the [prescribed] measure."

G. And one who had immersed [himself on the same] day [because of uncleanness] eats it.

H. R. Yosé says, "He does not need immersion. And it is forbidden to zavim and zavot, [or to] menstruants or women after childbirth. It is eaten with a non-priest at the same table, and is given to any priest."

M. Ḥal. 4.8

Comment: Albeck (Zeraʿim, pp. 154, 286) explains as follows. The "Land of Israel as far as Keziv [Ecdippa]" (B) is considered unquestionably Jewish territory, since it is biblical Israel, resettled by the returnees from Babylon, in the sixth pre-Christian century. To that territory applies the law of the Dough-offering, as a gift to the priests. The area of Syria "from Keziv to the River and to Amanah" (C) was part of biblical Palestine, but was not settled during the Return. Gamaliel considers it to be unclean foreign territory. The prescribed Dough-offering (1/24 of the dough) has to be removed (because it comes from Palestinian soil) but it must be burned, as unclean dough in the Land of Israel would be burned. Gamaliel then requires that an additional bit of dough be given to the priest, to maintain the custom of the gift, while demonstrating that the first Dough-offering was considered unclean.

The area of Syria between "the River and Amanah" (E) was always non-Israelite territory. Nevertheless, Gamaliel requires two offerings here too. First, a symbolic bit of dough is removed for the sake of the custom; it is burned because the land is unclean. This is done to demonstrate the status of the second Dough-offering. The latter is the regular, prescribed 1/24 of the dough, but it is added for the sake of supporting the priests living in the area, not to fulfill the biblical agricultural law.

Even though the area of Syria from Keziv to the River and to Amanah is declared as unclean, Gamaliel treats it differently from territory which was never biblical Israel. The fact that he requires the prescribed Dough-offering to be taken indicates that the biblical law of ḥallah applies to the area; the fact that it is burned implies that the area is unclean, but not inherently and permanently. It would seem that Gamaliel's relinquishment of the claim to Syria does not attempt to void its biblical status completely. The area between the River and Amanah is treated exactly the opposite; the contrast emphasizes the permanence of the status of the area.

Gamaliel's lemma consists of A + B + C + E; D and F are explanatory glosses. G is probably not a continuation of Gamaliel's pericope, which means that Yosé's Ushan revision of G attests only to G, and not to the foregoing parts of the pericope.

A. "[One] who buys from a professional baker in Syria must separate [a] Dough-offering [from dough about which we are] doubtful [whether a Dough-offering has been taken]," the words of Rabban Gamaliel.

B. And sages say, "It is not necessary to separate doubtful Dough-offerings."

C. From the southern river of Keziv and onwards [there is liability for] two doubtful Dough-offerings.

Tos. Ḥal. 2.6 (Lieberman ed.
p. 281, lines 26-28)

Comment: According to Gamaliel (A), someone buying dough from a commercial baker in Syria could not be sure whether the baker had removed the dough for the Dough-offering. Gamaliel requires the customer to remove the dough in order to make sure it has been done. The unnamed sages (B) do not assume a baker will be negligent, and do not require an offering removed solely for the purpose of relieving doubt.

As it stands, A-B may be understood to accord either with Gamaliel's ruling in M. Ḥal. 4.7B (two Dough-offerings) or with Eleazar b. Ṣadoq's revision in Tos. Ḥal. 2.5C (one Dough-offering). Lieberman's commentary, ad. loc., sees A-B as a continuation of the small collection of Gamaliel-materials transmitted by Eleazar b. Ṣadoq, in Tos. Ḥal. 2.5. This pericope would then agree with R. Eliezer's view that there is only one Dough-offering given in Syria, as in the Land of Israel.

But Lieberman's comment does not take C into account. C defines more precisely the northern boundary of Israel with Syria (the southern river of Keziv) and indicates the responsibility for two doubtful Dough-offerings beyond it. True, the words of C are not attributed to Gamaliel. But the editor must have added C to the dispute to indicate that the dispute applies to Gamaliel's view as stated in the Mishnah, and not to Eleazar b. Ṣadoq's revision.

Thus we cannot know for certain where the "sages" here stand on the dispute between Gamaliel and Eliezer in M. Ḥal. 4.7, or which version of Gamaliel is presupposed. Adding A-B to the other traditions transmitted by Eleazar b. Ṣadoq implies a continuity with his version of Gamaliel (assuming that A-C was not a unit when this happened). But adding C to A-B shows that that editor (assuming he is separate from the one who added this pericope to the other Gamaliel-materials) understood A-B as agreeing with the Mishnah version, rather than with Eleazar b. Ṣadoq.

A. "The etrog [tree] is like a tree in three ways (BŠLŠH DRKYM) and [like] a vegetable in one way.

B. "It is like a tree in applying the laws of ʿOrlah, the Fourth Year, and the Seventh Year. And it is like a vegetable in one way: that [the year of] its tithing [is determined] at the hour of its picking,"

C. the words of Rabban Gamaliel.

D. R. Eliezer says, "[It is] like a tree in all things (BKL DBR)."

M. Bik. 2.6 (b. R.H. 14b,
b. Suk. 39b-40a)

Comment: In addition to the yearly "First Tithe", given to the Levite, biblical agricultural law sets aside certain years within the seven-year cycles for specific offerings and tithes. Crops of the first, second, fourth and fifth years are tithed for pilgrimages to Jerusalem. Crops of the third and sixth years are tithed for the poor. Because vegetation grows during the spring and summer of one calendar year, but is harvested in the fall at the start of another calendar year, the law defines which kind of plant is assigned to which year, to be subject to its offerings.

For fruit-trees, the year the fruit appears on the branch determines when that fruit becomes subject to all agricultural laws. Besides tithing, this includes the law of ʿOrlah (fruit from the first three fruit-bearing years of a tree, which may not be used) or the Fourth Year fruit offering (i.e., of the first useable fruit of a tree); or whether it is considered fruit of a Sabbatical year, and hence forbidden. When the fruit appears upon the branch it is marked, and assigned to the year of its growth. The laws of that year apply to it, no matter when it is harvested.

On the other hand, vegetables are assigned to the year of their harvesting, though they may have first appeared during a previous year.

According to Gamaliel, the citron tree falls into the category of a fruit-tree, insofar as the three laws mentioned above apply to it. But when it comes to the laws of tithes, those laws apply to the year of its harvesting, as is the case with all vegetables. Eliezer, in contrast, makes the tithing laws apply to the etrog at the time of its emergence, as with all other fruit.

This pericope is part of a collection of examples of mixed legal categories, things to which certain laws apply only in certain cases. Gamaliel's statement may include a later elaboration, B, explaining it. If the original statement were only A+C, the entire pericope of A+C+D would look as if it had been shaped with memorization in mind. Numerical listing is, of course, a common mnemonic aid.

Eliezer's dissent does not mention the subject, so that D depends upon A-C. It is unusual for him to follow Gamaliel as he does here. This may point to the shaping of the pericope in Gamaliel's circle of redaction or transmission, though this is hardly decisive.

A. (MʿSH B) R. ʿAqiva picked an etrog on the first of Shevat, and did with it according to the words of the House of Shammai and according to the words of the House of Hillel.

B. R. Yosah b. R. Judah [said], "According to the words of Rabban Gamaliel and according to the words of R. Liezer."

Tos. Shev. 4.21 (Lieberman
ed. p. 185, lines 71-73;
y. Bik. 2.9; R.H. 1.2;

b. Eruv. 7a; R.H. 14a;
Yev. 15a; Suk. 40a)

Comment: The House of Shammai (M.R.H. 1.1) designate the "new year" for trees as the first of Shevat. Fruit picked on that day would be liable to the Poorman's Tithe of the third year. The House of Hillel date the new year on the fifteenth of Shevat. Therefore fruit picked on the first would be liable to the Second Tithe of the second year.

When ʿAqiva (as explained by Lieberman, T.K., Seder Zeraʿim II, pp. 545-546) picked the etrog on the first of Shevat of the third year, he separated the Second Tithe, then redeemed the fruit for money which he gave to the poor. In doing so he complied with the stringencies of both Houses. Since according to Gamaliel the etrog was liable to the Poorman's tithe (year it was picked) and according to Eliezer the etrog was liable to the Second Tithe (year of its emergence) he also complied with both of these authorities. Hence R. Yosah's revision of the story, in B, interprets the action equally well.

Yosah's comment provides an attestation for the pericope in M. Bik. 2.6, contemporary with R. Judah the Patriarch.

v. Shabbat

Rabban Simeon b. Gamaliel said, "[Those of] my father's house were accustomed to give white garments to the gentile laundryman three days before the Sabbath."

M. Shab. 1.9

Comment: Gamaliel's household is identified with Shammaite practice here. The injunction of Sabbath rest was extended to include even inanimate objects. The extended time provided by bringing the laundry in, so many days before the Sabbath, assured that work on them would not take place on the Sabbath.

R. Leazar b. Ṣadoq said, "Those of the house of Rabban Gamaliel would bring their white garment[s] to the gentile laundryman three days before the Sabbath, and colored [ones] on the eve of the Sabbath.

"According to our way, we learned that white ones are harder to make [clean] than colored ones."

Tos. Shab. 1.22 (Lieberman ed. p. 5, lines 52-54)

Comment: Neusner (Pharisees, ii, p. 130) points out that the Tos. superscription here is the original, that the story was reframed in the name of Simeon b. Gamaliel as a first-person recollection, and that Rabbi Judah the Patriarch preferred to use the version in his father's name for M. Shab. 1.9.

It was taught (TNY'): R. Ṣadoq said, "This was the custom of those of the house of Rabban Gamaliel: they used to give white garment[s] to the laundryman three days before the Sabbath, but colored [ones] even on the eve of the Sabbath."

b. Shab. 19a

Comment: The superscription of b. and Tos. demonstrate one of the channels of transmission for narrative traditions about Gamaliel: from Ṣadoq, Gamaliel's contemporary, to his son Eleazar, contemporary of Simeon b. Gamaliel.

[If a man] writes two letters, during two [acts of] forgetting, once in the morning and once towards evening,

Rabban Gamaliel [holds him] liable [MḤYB);

And sages exempt (PWṬRYN) [him].

M. Shab. 12.6

Comment: Writing two letters on the Sabbath violates the prohibition against Sabbath labor; its penalty is the bringing of a Sin-offering. This law is taken for granted by the pericope. But what if the two acts of writing are separated in time? Gamaliel considers the total of the number of physical acts performed, rather than the time-period. Since they both add up to a violation, the penalty is imposed. The sages consider the acts only within the context of the times in which they take place. Thus separated, neither one alone incurs a penalty.

The pericope is in standard dispute-form, with Gamaliel's opinion first.

This issue appears to be an offshoot of a problem extensively discussed at Yavneh: whether individual items or acts are to be considered separately or together in the application of a law. In M. Pe. 6.6 the problem is discussed in terms of individual sheaves combining to be excluded from the category of pe᾽ah. Elsewhere, the question is whether multiple violations committed during a single "act of forgetting" require a single Sin-offering or multiple Sin-offerings. The problem is discussed by the Yavneans in terms of sacrilege, illicit intercourse and Sabbath violation in M. Ker., chapters 2 and 3. Eliezer (M. Ker. 3.10) and Gamaliel and Joshua (M. Ker. 3.7) all rely on the same tradition (to the effect that intercourse with five menstruant wives requires five separate offerings) in declaring that multiple transgressions even within the same act of forgetting require multiple offerings (cf. Neusner, Eliezer b. Hyrcanus, pp. 256-258). The act, rather than the occasion, seems to be the primary consideration. Likewise here, Gamaliel holds that the act alone is the determining factor. A single violation, even though interrupted in time ("two acts of forgetting") requires an offering. For the sages in M. Ker., the single time-frame requires a single offering, even with multiple acts; while here the partial violation within a single period exempts the man entirely.

There is an underlying consistency in Gamaliel's rulings in M. Pe. and M. Shab. Partial acts or quantities do combine, in his view, to make up a single Sabbath-violation, on the one hand, and a quantity of produce too large to be considered pe᾽ah, on the other. While there may seem to be a conflict between these rulings and the reliance upon the tradition of M. Ker. (multiple acts requiring multiple offerings) the distinction between them can be made clear. In M. Ker. the individual culpable acts are separately liable, therefore not combined; in M. Pe. and M. Shab. the acts/quantities would not be separately considered, and so are combined.

A. It was taught (TNY᾽): R. Judah said in Rabban Gamaliel's name, "Even if he only writes two letters of the same kind, he is liable;

B. "for example, ŠŠ, TT, RR, GG, ḤḤ."

b. Shab. 103b

Comment: A of the baraita further explains Gamaliel's position in M. Shab. 12.6, adding that conditions mentioned in M. Shab. 12.3 apply to it: the two letters written on two separate occasions may be not only two different ones, but even the same letter twice.

B is an explanatory gloss, probably from Judah himself. All of its examples make up words: ŠŠ = silk, TT = give, RR = flow,

GG = roof, ḤḤ = hook. Judah often provides revisions of Gamaliel's lemmas, and this gloss may intend to qualify the restriction in A, by saying that only those doubled letters which make up a word, like the examples given, incur a penalty. The same letter, written at two different times, which did not make up a word, would not incur a penalty. Judah's gloss would move Gamaliel's position slightly closer to the position of the sages, who would exempt the man in any case.

The pericope provides an Ushan attestation for the substance of Shab. 12. 6, upon which it depends for its intelligibility.

Said R. Ḥisda, "Whence do I derive this? Since it was taught (DTNY'): If a man writes two letters during one [act of] forgetting, he is liable.

"In two [acts of] forgetting --

"Rabban Gamaliel [holds him] liable;

"and sages exempt [him].

"And Rabban Gamaliel admits that if he wrote one letter on this Sabbath and one letter on another Sabbath, he is exempt.

"But it was taught in another [baraita]: [If a man] writes two letters on two Sabbaths, one on one Sabbath and one on another Sabbath --

"Rabban Gamaliel [holds him] liable.

"And sages exempt [him]."

b. Ker. 16b

Comment: The two baraitot quoted by R. Hisda further refine distinctions concerning "two acts of forgetting". B is identical with part of M. Shab. 12.4, and C is identical with M. Shab. 12.6. The issue is: granted that Gamaliel disregards an interval of time, in totalling up partial acts in violation of the law, what is the limit of the period within which he will do this? A day, a week, or more? Here the question concerns two letters written on two successive Sabbaths. But the baraitot report contradictory views: the first having Gamaliel agree with the sages, the second having him retain his position even in this extreme case. Since neither baraita is a direct quotation, it is possible that both are assumptions, and that his views on this were not known. The authors of both baraitot evidently felt it valuable to frame a statement on this extreme case in Gamaliel's name. Their work may be simultaneous with Judah's elaboration at Ushah (b. Shab. 103b).

The Ushans were thus completing the exploration of this important problem of Yavnean legal theory. The presence of

Gamaliel, Eliezer, Joshua and ʿAqiva, in the pericopae dealing with this issue, attests to its importance on the Yavnean agenda.

A. [If] a gentile sets up a gangplank for disembarking, an Israelite disembarks after him;

B. but if it were done for the sake of the Israelite, it is forbidden [to use it].

C. (MʿSH B) Rabban Gamaliel and [the] elders were traveling on a ship, and a gentile set up a gangplank for disembarking.

D. And Rabban Gamaliel and the elders disembarked by it [Camb., P omit: And Rabban Gamaliel].

M. Shab. 16.8

<u>Comment</u>: A Jew may benefit incidentally from an act performed by a gentile on the Sabbath, provided that the act was done for the gentile's own sake, and not for the Jew. M. Shab. 16.8 consists of three illustrations of this principle. Our pericope is the third such case in the series.

C-D, the story of Gamaliel and the elders, does not mention the important detail that the gentile disembarked first. The omission of this demonstration that the gentile had set up the gangplank for his own use shows that the story is independent of A. C-D tells us only that a gangplank was set up and the elders (possibly Gamaliel, depending upon our text) made use of it.

C-D is another example of legal material, involving Gamaliel, which is formulated as narrative rather than as a legal statement in his name. The redactor of the Mishnah added it to A-B with the assumption that it did, in fact, illustrate the law, and that narratives about Gamaliel's behavior carry the force of a legal lemma.

A. At that time a gentile set up a gangplank and disembarked by it.

B. They said to Rabban Gamaliel, "May we use it to disembark?"

C. He said to them, "Since he did not set it up in our presence, we are permitted to disembark by it."

D. And the elders disembarked by it.

Tos. Shab. 13.11B
(Lieberman ed. p. 62,
lines 64-66)

<u>Comment</u>: This story is added to Tos. Shab. 13.11. First comes a law about disembarking from a ship, on Sabbath, only if it

had entered the Sabbath limit before the Sabbath began. The law is followed by an illustrative story about Gamaliel and the elders. Then our story follows, as an added narrative; no law is quoted.

Our story begins parallel to the law as stated in M. Shab. 16.8: the gentile sets up a gangplank and makes use of it. However, when the elders ask Gamaliel whether to disembark, his answer (C) is not as we might expect, "Yes, because he disembarked first." He says instead, "He did not set it up in our presence," a different way of expressing the idea that it was not done for their sake. The dialogue of our story, B-C, seems to differ from the introduction, A, which appears to be influenced by the law as stated in the Mishnah.

Having acknowledged a difference between A and B-D, we may attempt to account for the redactional development of the stories in M. and Tos. A Gamaliel-story consisting roughly of M. Shab. 16.8C + Tos. Shab. 13.11B-D is posited: A gentile sets up a gangplank. Gamaliel rules that since it has not been done in their presence, they may descend. (We note that in the Cambridge and Parma mss., D of the Mishnah = D of Tos.) This story enters the Tosefta with its introduction revised to conform with the law as stated in the Mishnah. Since it was added to a context of a sea voyage of Gamaliel and the elders, its introduction required a revision. On the other hand, the story enters the Mishnah minus its dialogue, revised in this way to conform to the law which it is supposed to illustrate.

A. [Concerning] one who says, "He heals! [i.e., _Gesundtheit_]" -- this is one of the "ways of the Amorites".

B. R. Leazar b. Ṣadoq says, "He does not say, 'He heals!' because of waste of [time to be spent studying] Torah."

C. [Those] of the house of Rabban Gamaliel did not say "He heals!" because of the "ways of the Amorites".

Tos. Shab. 7.5 (Lieberman
ed. p. 26, lines 7-9)

Comment: "Ways of the Amorites" are gentile customs or superstitions which, though not considered idolatry, are forbidden with reference to Lev. 18.3 (_nor shall you follow their customs_; cf. M. Shab. 6.10, Sifra 13.9). Lieberman finds textual difficulties in this pericope (_T.K._, III, pp. 93-95). He corrects A to read, "This is _not_ one of the ways of the Amorites." Blessing the one who sneezes is permitted.

Similarly, he points out that in C, the Ehrfurt and London mss. omit the phrase "ways of the Amorites" while London ms. omits "did not"! Because of this, he understands B-C as follows: Eleazar forbids taking time away from study in order to bless the one who sneezes (B). C reads "The house of Rabban Gamaliel did not say 'He heals!'," and possibly continues, "in the House of Study." Then the redactor, or possibly Eleazar himself, cites the custom of Gamaliel's house, as he often does, to support Eleazar's view.

It was also taught thus (TNY' NMY HKY): [Those] of the house of Rabban Gamaliel would not say, "He heals!" in the House of Study, because of waste [of time in] the House of Study.

b. Ber. 53a

Comment: This *baraita* is in accord with other textual evidence discussed by Lieberman, mentioned above, applying Gamaliel's family precedent to a category other than "ways of the Amorites".

The *baraita* may have been amplified to agree with Eleazar's saying about time-wasting; but its language is not the same, BṬWL TWRH *vs*. BṬWL BYT HMDRŠ.

A. [Concerning] one who binds a thread upon a red [...], Rabban Gamaliel says, "That is not one of the 'ways of the Amorites'."

B. R. Leazar b. Ṣadoq says, "Behold, this is one of the 'ways of the Amorites'."

Tos. Shab. 7.11 (Lieberman ed. p. 26, line 16-p. 27, line 17)

Comment: Lieberman indicates difficulties with the text and attribution (*T.K.* III, p. 96). The London ms. attributes B to R. Ṣadoq, as do related quotations from several medieval works.

A probably is connected with the custom of tying a red thread around a part of the body as a means of warding off disease (cf. Tos. Shab. 7.1 and *T.K. ad. loc*.). Lieberman explains meaning of the current text as: "He sews a thread upon a red garment or patch, so that it will appear as two." I am unable to visualize this.

B depends upon A, but it is remarkable for Eleazar (or Ṣadoq, for that matter) to dispute a lemma of Gamaliel's.

[Those of] the house of Rabban Gamaliel did not fold up their white garments [on Sabbath,] because they would change [into others].

Tos. Shab. 12.16 (Lieberman ed. p. 56, lines 75-76; b. Shab. 113a)

Comment: M. Shab. 15.3 states: "A man folds up his garments [that he wears on Sabbath] as many as four or five times." The anonymous description of the practice of Gamaliel's household indicates the practice of the affluent, who do not need to fold their garments (to preserve their appearance for wearing later on Sabbath).

Gamaliel's name here is probably synonymous with prominent wealth.

A. [If Scriptures] were written [in Aramaic] translation, or in any language, they save them [from fire] and they store them away.

B. Said R. Yosé [alt.: Yoseh], "(M'SH Š) R. Ḥalafta once went to Rabban Gamaliel in Tiberias, and found him sitting at the table of Yoḥanan b. Hanazuf [Vienna: Nazif] with a translation of the book of Job in his hand, reading it.

C. "R. Ḥalafta said to him, 'I used to remember that Rabban Gamaliel the Elder, your father's father, was sitting at the top of the stairs on the Temple Mount. They brought before him a book of Job in translation. He told a builder [Vienna: his sons], and they built it [Vienna: stored it away] under the brickwork.'"

Tos. Shab. 13.2 (Lieberman ed. p. 57, lines 4-9)

Comment: M. Shab. 16.1 states that (a) Scriptures in Hebrew, whether publicly read in the synagogue or not, are saved from fire, and (b) Scriptures in any language are stored away when unusable. Omitted is the question of whether Scriptures in translation are saved from fire. Tos. functions here as a commentary, adding (A) that the translations are indeed saved from fire.

B-C adds a disputing opinion from Yosé b. Ḥalafta, in the form of a story about his father and Gamaliel. The point of Ḥalafta's reminiscence (C) is that Gamaliel the Elder stored away the Job translation because it could not be saved, in event of fire. If he were to make use of it, eventually it might be destroyed.

The pericope cannot be complimentary to Gamaliel. In B he is following the practice of the anonymous law (A) while in C he must be reminded of the tradition of his own family, as shown by the behavior of his grandfather (cf. M. Yev. 16.7, which suggests that this may be an ʿAqivan pericope also).

(MʿSH B) Rabban Gamaliel was standing near the building on the Temple mount, and they brought him the book of Job written [in Aramaic] translation. He spoke to the builder and he stored it away, under the brickwork.

y. Shab. 16.1

Comment: Ḥalafta's story is here independent of the Tos. framework about Gamaliel II. It may have circulated separately from Yosé's narration.

A. (DTNYʾ) For it was taught: [If Scriptures] were written [in Aramaic] translation, or in any language, they save them from the fire.

B. R. Yosé says, "They do not save them from the fire."

C. Said R. Yosé, "(MʿSH B) My father, Ḥalafta, went to Rabban Gamaliel Beribbi (BRYBY) in Tiberias, and found him sitting at the table of Yoḥanan Hanazuf. In his hand was a book of Job [written in Aramaic] translation, and he was reading it.

D. "He said to him, 'I remember that Rabban Gamaliel, your father's father, was standing on the step on the Temple mount, and they brought before him a book of Job in translation. He said to a builder, 'Bury it under the brickwork.'

E. "He [Gamaliel II] too commanded it to be stored away."

F. R. Yosé b. R. Judah says, "They overturned a tub of mortar on it."

G. Said Rabbi, "There are two objections to this. One, where did mortar come from, on the Temple mount? And further, is it permitted to destroy them personally (BYD)? Rather, they put them in a neglected place, and they decay on their own."

b. Shab. 115a

Comment: Either b. has preserved the Toseftan dispute or the editor has restored it by supplying Yosé's dissent (B). Aside from the honorific title BRBY (in C) the story C-D is identical with Tos. E then adds that Gamaliel II followed the advice given him by Ḥalafta.

F-G which depend upon A-E, provide an attestation for the pericope which is rather late, from Beth Shearim. Since the entire pericope was edited within the circle of Rabbi Judah the Patriarch, this may explain the presence of the title BRBY, usually applied to Rabbi's descendants but here attached to the name of his ancestor.

A. (MʿSH B) R. Ḥalafta went before Rabban Gamaliel, and found him sitting at his table. In his hand was a translation of the book of Job, and he was reading it.

B. He said to him, "Master, will you permit me to say what my eyes have seen?"

C. He said to him, "Say [it]."

D. "I was watching Rabban Gamaliel the Elder, your father's father, who was sitting beside the building on the Temple mount. They brought a translation of Job before him, and he said to the builder, 'Remove a line [of stones] and bury this beneath it.'"

E. Rabbi says, "There are two objections to this. One, where did mortar come from on the Temple mount? And further, he is not permitted to destroy them personally; rather, he puts them not in a place of defilement but in a neglected place, and they decay by themselves."

Sof. 5.15

<u>Comment</u>: Except for the single elaboration of B, Sof. briefly retells the story A-D in language that recalls both the Tos. and y. versions. E seems to depend upon the <u>baraita</u> of b., though Sof. has omitted the lemma of Yosé b. Judah, about the "tub of mortar," (which E presupposes).

(MʿSH B) There were four sisters in Sepphoris, where the first, second and third circumcised [their sons] and they died. The incident came before Rabban Gamaliel, who said, "The fourth shall not be circumcised."

Tos. Shab. 15.8 (Lieberman
ed. p. 70, lines 27-29)

<u>Comment</u>: The Vienna ms. has the incident come before "the sages", while other texts, and b. Yeb. 64b, assign it to R. Simeon b. Gamaliel. Lieberman accepts the latter as correct (<u>T.K</u>. III, p. 250, line 28).

vi. ʿEruvin

A. [A man] whom gentiles or an evil spirit took out [beyond the Sabbath limit] has only four cubits [area to move in]. If they brought him back, it is as though he had never gone out.

B. [If] they brought him to another town, or put him in a cattle-pen or corral,

C. Rabban Gamaliel and R. Eleazar b. ʿAzariah say, "He walks around the whole [area]."

D. R. Joshua and R. ʿAqiva say, "He has only four cubits [area to move in]."

E. (MʿSH Š) They came from Brindisium (FRNDYSYN) and their ship was sailing on the sea. Rabban Gamaliel and R. Eleazar b. ʿAzariah walked around the whole [area of the ship].

F. R. Joshua and R. ʿAqiva did not move beyond four cubits,

G. since they wished to be more strict with themselves.

M. ʿEruv. 4.1

Comment: A presents an anonymous, undisputed law, based on Ex. 16:29. Once outside the Sabbath limit of the town which is his "place", a man may move only within a four-cubit area. B-D presents a dispute, raising the question of movement when one has been involuntarily transported to another enclosed area. According to Gamaliel and Eleazar b. ʿAzariah, a man brought outside his Sabbath residence to another enclosed area may use the latter as his "place". Joshua and ʿAqiva (D) consider that, once outside the Sabbath limit, he may only occupy the six-foot module which is his personal space. Gamaliel's view is stated first. He is paired with Eleazar b. ʿAzariah as co-author of the lemma C.

E-F, the incident which follows, is not an illustration of this dispute. Not only do the specific terms differ (cattle-pen vs. ship) but also the underlying issues of the two enclosed spaces. As Albeck's commentary, ad. loc., makes clear, one could not necessarily deduce the reported behavior of Joshua and ʿAqiva from the preceding law in their names. They could well decide that, since they had made the ship their residence before Sabbath, they have its entire area at their disposal. Or they could assume that the moving craft is bringing them into a new four-cubit area at each moment, so that they have full freedom to move within these successive areas, as the ship passes through them. Finally,

b. ʿEruv. 43a, which depends upon E-F, treats the dispute and the story as two separate issues.

G explains the self-restriction of Joshua and ʿAqiva as an act of added piety. As far as the law is concerned, they are really in agreement with Gamaliel. We shall suggest below (in the comment on b. ʿEruv. 43a) that G is an editorial addition, explaining Joshua's and ʿAqiva's behavior in a way that harmonizes it with Gamaliel and Eleazar; and that E-F is a separate dispute, coming to us in narrative form. At this point we can note that E-G is an independent story, related in theme to the preceding law. Gamaliel and Eleazar are related in the story, as they had been in the law, and their actions are described first. The story implies the agreement of Joshua and ʿAqiva with them; and the placement of the story following the dispute endorses their views in B-D, since Joshua and ʿAqiva are represented as taking their position merely as a self-restriction.

The form of the dispute B-D is unusual in several respects. It starts with a standard announced topic, a further refinement of the law stated in A, but the two sides of the dispute show no balance in language: MHLK ʾT KLH vs. ʾYN LW ʾLʾ ʾRBH ʾMWT. This suggests that independent lemmas have been placed into a dispute form. But the co-authorship of the lemmas in C and D is also a problem. How do two authorities come to join as the spokesmen for a single lemma, and how does it occur that it happens simultaneously on both sides of an issue, rather than, e.g., Gamaliel vs. Joshua-ʿAqiva? One possibility for an answer will be raised in connection with b. ʿEruv. 43a.

It was also taught (WHTNYʾ): Ḥanania (son of the brother of R. Joshua) [Munich ms. omits parenthetical material] says, "All that day they sat and discussed the question of the halakah, and in the evening my father's brother decided that the halakah was in agreement with Rabban Gamaliel in the case of a ship, and the halakah was in agreement with R. ʿAqiva in that of a cattle-pen and a corral."

b. ʿEruv. 43a (y. ʿEruv. 4.2)

Comment: This baraita depends upon the story told in M. ʿEruv. 4.1E-G, and claims the ultimate agreement of Joshua with Gamaliel, on the permissibility of roaming the entire area of a ship, rather than being restricted to a four-cubit area. However, some key details are different. At first, Joshua does not agree with Gamaliel on the law. The matter is discussed all day, and only after the Sabbath does Joshua agree. The implication of this, clearly, is that M. ʿEruv. 4.1E-F originally represents a dispute between Gamaliel-Eleazar and Joshua-ʿAqiva. The element bringing the latter two into harmony with Gamaliel, claiming they were in agreement all along, cannot be known by this story. Joshua would not be represented as discussing the halakah all day, if his decision reflected only an added act of piety. M. ʿEruv. 4.1G must be an editorial addition, bringing M. into line with the tradition about Joshua's decision.

The role of Joshua is markedly different in the two pericopae. In M. ʿEruv. 4.1, Joshua and ʿAqiva are co-disputants against Gamaliel-Eleazar in the law, and also (if our analysis is correct) in the story. Here the dispute lies between Gamaliel and ʿAqiva only. Eleazar does not appear at all. And Joshua plays a third-party role. He is objective and impartial, and able to decide between the conflicting arguments. He almost seems pre-eminent over both Gamaliel and ʿAqiva, here reflecting the perspective of his family or disciples. Nothing of this appears in M., where Gamaliel's primacy is taken for granted.

One suggestion may be advanced concerning the co-authorship of the lemma in M., based upon consideration of this baraita. M. ʿEruv. 4.1C-D was originally, like E-F, a Gamaliel-ʿAqiva dispute. Since Joshua is represented here as deciding in ʿAqiva's favor on the issue of the cattle-pen, he is included in M. as co-author with ʿAqiva. The presence of Eleazar in M., absent from the baraita may not be satisfactorily resolved. Its difficulty may point to authenticity within the dispute. Yet either Eleazar or ʿAqiva may have been added for balance, given the presence of the other.

Though the final forms of the pericopae in the Mishnah are not supported by the baraita here, the name of Ḥanania, nephew and disciple of Joshua, provides a Yavnean attestation for the substance of the disputes transmitted in both the lemmas and the story. And further, since M. ʿEruv. 4.1B-D and E-G depend upon the anonymous law of M. ʿEruv. 4.1A, our baraita attests to it as part of the Yavnean legal agenda as well.

Once they did not enter the harbor until it became dark [on the Sabbath].

They said to Rabban Gamaliel, "May we disembark?"

He said to them, "It is permitted, for I have already made

observation, and we were within the [Sabbath] limit before it became dark."

M. ʿEruv. 4.2

Comment: The preceding pericope (M. ʿEruv. 4.1) told of a sea voyage of Gamaliel, Eleazar, Joshua and ʿAqiva, with reference to the Sabbath limit. This pericope supplies another, without mentioning the names of the other rabbis.

Had the ship not entered the Sabbath limit, of 2,000 cubits beyond the port, before the onset of the Sabbath, the rabbis would not have been able to disembark. Since they were within the limit before the Sabbath, the town was their "place" and they could move about within it. The point of the story is not this law, which is taken for granted. It is Gamaliel's ability to measure the distance from shore correctly, and also his pre-eminence in authority over his companions.

The pericope is identical with M. ʿEruv. 4.1 in its setting (shipboard, Sabbath, MʿSH Š) and depends upon it for the names of the other rabbis. But the incident it recounts is separate in time ("Once" = PʿM ʾḤT) and was probably originally independent, since a new issue has been raised.

A. They do not land from a ship that has been at sea, unless (ʾLʾ ʾM KN) they were within the [Sabbath] limit before it became dark.

B. (MʿSH B) Rabban Gamaliel and elders were traveling on a ship, and the [Sabbath] day had descended upon them (WQDŠ ʿLYHN HYWM).

They said to Rabban Gamaliel, "May we disembark?"

He said to them, "I had been watching, and we were within the [Sabbath] limit before it became dark, but the ship was thrown back many times."

Tos. Shab. 13.11A
(Lieberman ed., pp. 61-62,
lines 61-64)

Comment: The story common to this pericope (B) and M. ʿEruv. 4.2 here serves to illustrate the legal principle stated in A. The Mishnah does not state the law at all. The story here is more elaborate than in M., in that it explains why the elders needed to ask Gamaliel whether they could disembark: they had been traveling an unusually long time since it had become dark. Gamaliel's answer implies that the elders know the law as well as he does. They were just unsure of their distance from shore at the time the Sabbath began.

It is unlikely that B was created for the purpose of serving as an example for A. Its point is not the law but Gamaliel's ability to measure the distance accurately. And also, the story occurs independently of the law in the Mishnah.

A single story lies behind the two stories of M. ʿEruv. 4.2 and Tos. Shab. 13.11A, though some of their details differ, for redactional reasons. The main dialogue of the stories is identical: "They said to Rabban Gamaliel, 'May we disembark?' He said to them, '[I had been watching/ It is permitted, for I had already made observation] and we were within the Sabbath limit before it became dark.'"

In both stories, the names of the elders are not mentioned. Only Gamaliel, as leader of the group, is named. The tradition is part of the extensive references to the voyage of Gamaliel and his colleagues to Rome, and Gamaliel is in a position of authority throughout them.

A. "[If a man] lives in the same courtyard with a gentile or with one who does not admit [the lawfulness of] an ʿEruv, this restricts him [from using the courtyard]," [N adds:] The words of Rabbi Meir. [K, P, Camb. omit.]

B. Rabbi Eliezer b. Jacob says, "He can never restrict him until there are two Israelites, who would restrict each other."

C. Said Rabban Gamaliel, "(MʿSH B) A Sadducee once lived with us in the same alley in Jerusalem, and my father said to us, 'Hurry, bring all the vessels out into (WHWṢYW ʾT KL HKLYM L) the alley, before he brings out [his] and restricts you.'"

D. Rabbi Judah says [it] in another version (BLŠWN ʾḤR): "Hurry, and do all you need to do in (WʿSW ʾT KL ṢRKYKM B) the alley, before he brings [something] out and restricts you."

M. ʿEruv. 6.1-2

Comment: The ʿEruv arrangement joins a number of private homes, sharing a common courtyard, into a single "household" for the Sabbath; objects may be carried freely throughout the area on Sabbath, as in a private dwelling. According to A, the presence of the household of a gentile, or of one not agreeing with the validity of the practice, prevents this arrangement from taking place. No one may carry within the common area. (The presence of such an alien differs from the presence in the courtyard of a conforming Jew who may have forgotten to take part in the ʿEruv.

With the latter, the ʿEruv will still take effect; cf. the rest of M. ʿEruv., ch. 6.)

Eliezer b. Jacob (B) revises the law: the alien's presence does not affect the ʿEruv, for only Israelites can restrict each other. Eliezer's revision (B) depends upon A for its context, providing an Ushan attestation for the mishnah.

The two versions of Gamaliel's words (C-D) are addressed to the case of a Sadducee, "one who does not admit an ʿEruv", and omit any reference to the gentile. Further, the story refers to an alley (MBWY) and not a courtyard (ḤṢR). Thus C-D was originally independent of A.

At issue between C and D is the legal status of the Sadducee. In C, the Sadducee is considered like any Jew, whose rights to the courtyard have not been claimed. R. Simeon b. Gamaliel instructs his family, on the Sabbath, to make use of the yard. Even if the non-participant were to lay claim to the yard by moving objects into it, his claim to the yard has already been pre-empted, so Simeon's family may continue to use it.

The redaction of C here, with its omission of any mention of a gentile and with its treatment of the Sadducee as any Jew, implicitly supports Eliezer b. Jacob's amendment of A.

D depends upon C. It is another example of Judah's frequent revisions of Gamaliel-materials. This version implies that the Sadducee is more like a gentile, as viewed by A. Simeon commands his family to finish their work before the Sabbath (or perhaps even rent the rights to the yard from the Sadducee) since his presence at any time can restrict them. Judah also provides, in D, another Ushan attestation within the pericope.

Once more the Gamaliel material appears not as a lemma but in the form of a story (this time in the first person); and the editor, considering it of legal significance as such, did not need to change its form.

A. Who mentioned the name of a Sadducee? [This indicates a clause is] missing, and this is the [correct] reading:

> A Sadducee has the same status as a gentile.
>
> Rabban Gamaliel says, "A Sadducee does not have the status of a gentile."
>
> And Rabban Gamaliel said, "A Sadducee once lived with us in the same alley in Jerusalem, and father said to us, 'Hurry, bring all the vessels out into the alley, before he brings out [his] and restricts you.'"

B. And so it was taught (WHTNYʾ): [If a man] lives [in the same alley] with a gentile, a Sadducee or a Boethusian, these restrict him. Rabban Gamaliel says, "A Sadducee and a Boethusian do not restrict."

C. (WMʿSH B) A Sadducee lived with Rabban Gamaliel in the same alley in Jerusalem, and Rabban Gamaliel said to his sons, "Hurry, my sons, and carry out what you desire to carry out, or take in what you desire to take in, before this abomination carries out his [things] and restricts you. For [right now] he has given up his rights in your favor." The words of R. Meir.

D. R. Judah says [it] in another version (BLŠWN ʾḤRT): "Hurry and do what you need in the alley before nightfall, when he would restrict you."

b. ʿEruv. 68b

Comment: The Amoraic reconstruction of the text of the Mishnah, A, seeks to provide a transition between the dispute of M. ʿEruv. 6.1A-B and Gamaliel's story which follows it. Thus b. adds a dispute on the status of the Sadducee. In doing so, it provides Gamaliel with a position which we have seen implicit in the story: Unlike the anonymous law, Gamaliel declares the Sadducee not similar to a gentile; the Sadducee restricts use of the yard as would any Jew.

The baraita quoted in B directly contradicts the story from M. ʿEruv. 6.1, above. Gamaliel amends B's anonymous lemma, to the effect that a Sadducee does not restrict. B is more specific than the Mishnah, using the names Sadducee and Boethusian, rather than the more general "one who does not admit an ʿEruv", probably an indication of later elaboration.

C tells the story of M. ʿEruv. 6.2C in more detail, and attributes it to R. Meir. There is one significant difference. Whereas M. tells the story of the Sadducee as a quotation directly from Gamaliel about his father, the baraita tells the story in the third person about Gamaliel and his sons. Provided that the attribution to Meir was not added by the baraita editor, to balance Judah's name below, we may assume that Meir's story about Gamaliel was changed to a first-person story about Gamaliel in the version which entered the Mishnah without Meir's name attached. But the expanded language of C also points to later elaboration by the baraita narrator.

The lack of uniformity of the traditions must be noted. In A, a story indicates that the Sadducee is like a Jew, and restricts. In B, a lemma states that the Sadducee is like a Jew, and does not restrict. In C, another version of the story occuring in A indicates that the Sadducee is like a Jew and restricts. While in D, the revision of the story indicates that the Sadducee is like a gentile, and restricts. So that while the Gamaliel-story is important to both Meir and Judah, there is no agreement about its actual content.

A. [If a man] finds _tefillin_ [in the open field, on Sabbath], he brings them in one pair at a time.

B. Rabban Gamaliel says, "Two pairs at a time."

C. To what do these words apply? Old ones, but with new ones he is free [of the obligation to bring them in].

D. If he found them in sets or bundles, he waits until nightfall and brings them in.

E. And in [time of] danger, he covers them up and goes on his way.

F. R. Simeon says, "He gives them to his fellow, and his fellow to his fellow, until it reaches the outer courtyard [of the town]. And also with his child [born in the field, on Sabbath]: he gives him to his fellow, and his fellow to his fellow, even a hundred."

G. R. Judah says, "A man gives a jar to his fellow, and his fellow to his fellow, even beyond the Sabbath limit."

They said to him, "It cannot go farther than the feet of its owner [may travel]."

M. ʿEruv. 10.1-2

Comment: According to Jer. 17:21-22 and M. Shab. 1-10, objects may not be carried into, or out of, the household on the Sabbath (M. Shab. 10.3 specifically mentions handcarrying). M. Shab. 6.2 prohibits going out of the house wearing _tefillin_ on Sabbath, though no Sin-offering is required. The anonymous law in A lifts this prohibition against wearing the _tefillin_ so that they may be saved. The leniency cannot extend to bundles of _tefillin_ (D) since they cannot be worn, and carrying them would involve the suspension of a biblical law.

(The phrase "brings them in", in A, cannot refer to carrying. Permission to carry the _tefillin_ runs counter to the entire law of M. Shab., and would leave some trace of a dispute, of which there is none; and there are no grounds for a distinction between one set and more, except on the basis that the former may be worn.)

However, in B Gamaliel allows a second set to be worn as well, in order to save the _tefillin_.

A and D stem from Yavneh or even earlier law: a single pair of tefillin may be brought from the field by wearing them; many pairs should be guarded until after the Sabbath and then brought in. B is Gamaliel's Yavnean dispute with the anonymous law, permitting two pairs to be worn. Thus the original pericope is A+B+D.

C and E are anonymous interpolations to the Mishnah. C restricts the application of A-B to old tefillin, on the grounds that they can assume to be kasher, while new ones might be invalid. E reflects conditions of the Hadrianic persecutions, with the "danger" of possessing tefillin in public.

The conclusion of the pericope, F-G, depends upon D-E, since F refers to the bundles or sets of tefillin. The names of R. Simeon (b. Yoḥai) and R. Judah (b. ʾIlai) there attest that pericope was shaped in Usha.

A. [If a man] finds tefillin [in the open field, on Sabbath] -- he brings them in one pair at a time.

B. Rabban Gamaliel [First printed ed., Vienna ms. and Geniza fragments: R. Judah] says, "Two pairs at a time."

C. It is the same whether [the finder be] a man or a woman, the same whether they be new ones or old.

D. R. Judah forbids [bringing them in] with new ones, and permits it with old ones.

Tos. ʿEruv. 11.14 (Lieberman ed. pp. 136-137, lines 53-54)

Comment: A-B here is identical with M. Part D identifies R. Judah as the author of the view stated anonymously in M. ʿEruv. 10.1C., to the effect that only old tefillin may be brought in from the open field on Sabbath. He is probably responsible for the transmission of Gamaliel's views in both M. and Tos., which would account for the fact that his name replaces Gamaliel's in part B, in some manuscripts of Tos.

A. [If a man] finds tefillin [in the open field, on Sabbath] -- he brings them in one pair at a time,

B. by means of wearing them: one on his head, one on his arm.

C. Rabban Gamaliel says, "Two pairs at a time:"

D. Two on his head, two on his arm.

y. ʿEruv. 10.1

Comment: A and C are identical with M. They have been glossed to explain the method of bringing in the tefillin (B, D).

A. [Concerning] a bolt with a knob on its end [which is not hung on, or fastened to, a door] and is to be used to shut the door on the Sabbath,

B. R. Eliezer [Camb., P, K, N, y.,: Leazar] forbids [using such a bolt to close a door on the Sabbath].

C. And R. Yosé permits.

D. Said R. Eliezer [Eleazar], "[There was] (M'SH B) a synagogue in Tiberias where they would deem it permitted, until Rabban Gamaliel and the elders [P omits: elders] came and prohibited it."

E. R. Yosé says, "They deemed it prohibited. Rabban Gamaliel and the elders [P omits: Rabban Gamaliel and the elders] came and permitted it for them."

M. ʿEruv. 10.10 (y. ʿEruv. 10.10; b. Eruv. 101b)

Comment: Eliezer considers the knob not integral to the bolt. Not an utensil in its own right, when it is placed in the door it constitutes a kind of "building" on the Sabbath. Yosé permits the bolt, since he considers the knob as an utensil, and its placement not a form of building. Eliezer [Eleazar] cites a story (D) to show that Gamaliel and the elders agreed with him. Yosé reverses the key terms of the story, to show it supports him.

A-C is in standard dispute form. Eliezer's story (D) depends upon the foregoing for its context, and Yosé's reversal of the story (E) in turn depends upon D. There is no way of determining which of several Eliezer/Eleazars and Yosés are involved here, and no way of determining whether Yosé corrects his opponent on the basis of logic or of his own received tradition of the incident. Both sides in the dispute claim Gamaliel's precedent as authority for their respective positions. They are most likely Ushans, for whom Gamaliel's authority was of great importance.

The story can only be seen as another example of the great number of traditions involving Gamaliel's travels with an entourage of elders, sometimes specified and sometimes, as here, unnamed. Since Tiberias was a major Jewish population center, the locale for the story is appropriate.

A. [Pertaining to] a channel outside the window: one lowers [a bucket] and fills [the bucket] from it on Sabbath, provided that there is not [a space of] four handbreadths between it and the wall for a man to walk [on].

B. This is the way it was with the channel of Tripolis [alt.: TRBLYŚ, PRṬLYŚ]. The matter came before Rabban Gamaliel [so Erfurt and London mss.; Vienna, first printed ed. and b. ʿEruv. 87a: Simeon b. Gamaliel], who said, "Since there aren't four handbreadths between it and the wall, so that a man could walk [there] in any case, (BYN KK WBYN KK) they fill [buckets] from it on Sabbath."

Tos. ʿEruv. 9.25 (Lieberman ed. p. 125, lines 81-85)

Comment: Despite the conflicting mss. readings, since B resembles other Gamaliel precedent-stories, the pericope probably should be assigned to our Gamaliel.

A describes a water-channel less than four handbreadths from the window. Since it is so close to the wall of the house, it is considered within the house's domain, rather than in the public domain. Therefore, on the Sabbath, a bucket may be lowered from the window to be filled from the channel. B cites a story of a ruling by Gamaliel. Its language is almost the same as A. The phrase, "in any case (BYN KK WBYN KK)" is problematic here. However, part of Tos. ʿEruv. 9.24, just above our pericope, reads:

> A. [Pertaining to] a well outside the window: one lowers [a bucket] and fills from it on Sabbath, provided that there is not [a space of] four handbreadths between it and the wall for a man to walk [on]. And if the mouth of the well is four by four handbreadths [in area], in any case (BYN KK WBYN KK) [i.e., whether or not it is less than four handbreadths from the wall] one lowers and fills [a bucket] from it on Sabbath.

Lieberman explains our pericope in accordance with the sense of 9.24B, "Whether or not [the area of the water channel] is four by four handbreadths," if it is less than four handbreadths away from the wall one may fill the bucket. But it may be simply that the phrase BYN KK WBYN KK has contaminated our pericope from 9.24B, since they are so similar.

It seems clear that B has been formulated as an illustration of A, on the basis of a tradition, similar to the "ovens of Kefar Signah" (M. Kel. 5.4B). If the latter is any indication, the tradition available was, "(MʿSH B) the channel of Tripolis. The matter came before Rabban Gamaliel, who said, 'They fill from it on Sabbath.'" The specific details were added by the tradent.

We may be dealing with fragments of a collection of precedent-stories, formulated on this model: problem + place + Gamaliel-decision.

vii. Pesaḥim

A. R. Meir says, "They eat [ḥameṣ] through the fifth [hour on the eve of Passover] and they burn it at the beginning of the sixth."

B. And R. Judah says, "They eat through the fourth hour, suspend it through the fifth, and burn it at the beginning of the sixth."

C. And further, said R. Judah, "Two loaves of the Thanks-offering which had become unfit were placed on the roof of the [Temple] portico. All the time they were placed there, all the people ate. [When] they took one away, they suspended: they did not eat and did not burn; [when] they took them both away, all the people began to burn [the ḥameṣ]."

D. Rabban Gamaliel says, "Common food (ḤWLYN) is eaten through the fourth and Heave-offering through the fifth; and they burn it at the beginning of the sixth."

M. Pes. 1.4-5 (b. Pes. 21a)

Comment: According to Ex. 12:18-19, no leavened food (ḥameṣ) is to be eaten, or even present in the house, during the Passover festival. In this pericope Meir and Judah agree that the ḥameṣ must be burned at the sixth hour of the fourteenth of Nisan. They dispute when, on that day, the last ḥameṣ may be eaten. Meir (A) says it is eaten through the fifth hour. Judah (B) says it is eaten only through the fourth hour, and that there is an hour of "suspension" during the fifth hour, when nothing is done to the ḥameṣ.

C is an addendum to the dispute on Judah's behalf, joined to the preceding by "and further (WʿWD)". Judah shows that his position corresponds to a description of the practices in Jerusalem in Temple times. The populace was given signals for the disposal of ḥameṣ. The signal-code included an hour of "suspension", which could only have been during the fifth hour.

A lemma of Gamaliel's is now added (D), introducing a new distinction between the treatment of common food (ḤWLYN) and of terumah, which A and B do not mention. Gamaliel makes an exception for Heave-offering (terumah), in order that this offering not be burned. Heave-offering may be consumed by the priests during the fifth hour. During this hour nothing at all is done with the common food: this is the "hour of suspension" to which Judah refers. D serves an added purpose in assimilating Meir's statement into Judah's position: the ḥameṣ Meir asserts is eaten during the fifth hour may be understood to be only Heave-offering. The redaction not only supports Judah but reinterprets Meir to agree with him.

So we have, in A-B, an Ushan dispute carrying on a problem of Yavnean law. An editorial disciple of Judah has added two things to the pericope to support Judah: the historical description from Temple times, and the lemma of Gamaliel's which we may assume was also transmitted by Judah's tradents.

R. Judah says, in the name of Rabban Gamaliel, "Two loaves of the Thanks-offering which had become unfit were placed on the roof of the [Temple] portico. All the time they were placed there, all the people ate common food (ḤWLYN). [When] one of them was taken away, all the people would eat Heave-offering; [when] both of them were taken away, they would burn both."

Tos. Pes. 1.4 (Lieberman
ed. p. 141, lines 15-17)

Comment: Tos. presents another version of Judah's description of Jerusalem practices in Temple times, with some details different from M. Pes. 1.4-5. The pericope here is given in Gamaliel's name with Judah as tradent, rather than in Judah's own name (as in M.). The references to terumah are also absent from the description in M., where they occur in Gamaliel's separate lemma.

Assuming the priority of the pericope in M., the added details may be explained simply through the incorporation of the distinction between common food and Heave-offering from M. Pes. 1.5D ("Rabban Gamaliel says, 'Common food is eaten through the fourth etc.'") into M. Pes. 1.4B ("And further, R. Judah says, 'Two loaves etc.'"). The incorporation of Gamaliel's name into the superscription here, with the resultant attribution of the entire pericope to him, is unusual, and cannot be satisfactorily explained. The alternative possibility, that Tos. is prior, and that in the Mishnah the name of the source, Gamaliel, dropped out, while the name of the tradent, Judah, was retained, would be even more unusual.

A. Rabban Gamaliel says, "Three women knead [dough] at the same [time]; and they bake in one oven, one after the other."

B. And sages say, "Three women work with the dough: one kneads, and one shapes and one bakes."

C. R. ʿAqiva says, "Not all women and not all [kinds of] woods and not all ovens are alike.

D. "This is the general rule: [if] it [the dough] rises, let her smooth it (TLṬS) with cold [water]."

M. Pes. 3.4 (y. Pes. 3.4)

Comment: Gamaliel permits women to prepare dough for the Passover maṣṣah simultaneously, even though they may have to wait to use the same oven successively. He is not apprehensive that the dough might rise during the interval of waiting, while two batches of maṣṣah are baked. The sages permit the women to work only in sequence, so that they do not have to wait for use of the oven (B)

In C, ʿAqiva observes that no two sets of circumstances are identical. The last woman in the series may have prepared her dough quickly, while the stove may bake slowly. It is impossible to give a fixed rule. Instead, ʿAqiva advances the "general rule" of D: possible rising of the dough may be prevented by wetting it with cold water.

A and B are independent lemmas, each setting its own time limit for the preparation of the dough. C-D supports the position of A, since it explains how to prevent the dough from rising while waiting for the oven. ʿAqivan material is thus being used to support Gamaliel's position, even though ʿAqiva's rule might have even broader application. The redaction of the pericope attests to a pro-Gamaliel editor here.

It was taught (TNYʾ): R. ʿAqiva said, "I discussed [this] before Rabban Gamaliel, 'Let our Master teach us, [does your statement refer] to energetic women or to women who are not energetic, to damp wood or to dry wood, to a hot oven or a cool oven?'

"He said to me, 'You have only what [the] sages learned: [If] it rises, let her smooth it with cold [water].'"

b. Pes. 48b

Comment: This baraita depends upon M. Pes. 3.4 for its intelligibility. A spells out in detail ʿAqiva's objection to any specific time-limit. It is phrased as a first-person report of a question respectfully presented to Gamaliel.

Gamaliel's answer is a quotation of ʿAqiva's general rule (B), presented as a generally-accepted early law. He uses the rule as the reason why the three women may work with the dough simultaneously; they can retard any possible rising through the application of cold water. A pro-Gamaliel redactor here seems to use ʿAqivan material to support Gamaliel's position. (This is true of some, but not all, other first-person ʿAqivan pericopae referring to Gamaliel, M.M.S. 2.7, M. Yev. 16.7, and M. Ker. 3.7.)

A. The Passover-offering is roasted neither on a [metal] spit nor on a grill.

B. R. Ṣadoq said, "(MʿSH B) Rabban Gamaliel said to his servant Ṭabi, 'Go out and roast the Passover-offering for us on the grill.'"

C. [If] it touched the earthenware of the oven, that part must be pared away.

D. [If] some of its juice dripped on to the earthenware and dripped again on part of the carcass, that part must be taken away.

E. [If] some of its juice dripped on to the flour, he must take a handful away from that place [and burn it].

M. Pes. 7.2

Comment: According to Ex. 12:8, the Passover-offering must be roasted by fire. The anonymous law in A declares that the indirect heat of the spit or grill cannot fulfill the biblical injunction because a direct flame is necessary. Gamaliel's behavior, recounted by Ṣadoq (B) is explained differently by y. and b. According to y. (Albeck, ad. loc.) Gamaliel views the heat of the metal as the equivalent of the direct heat of the flame. However, b. Pes. 75a assumes that the text of the Mishnah is defective. b. emends it by adding a statement about the validity of a perforated grill, which the statement of R. Sadoq then illustrates. It is understandable that b. wishes to harmonize the extreme position of Ṣadoq/Gamaliel with the anonymous law, which is more literally in accord with Ex. 12:8.

In any case, C and D follow the position of A. Nothing but direct fire may cook the offering. Parts of the meat which may have been cooked by the side of the oven, or the juice, must be removed. So A+C+D is really a composite, working out the same principle.

Though B might have been more simply stated, "And Rabban Gamaliel permits", as in numerous other cases a story about Gamaliel is used, rather than a lemma in his name. B is independent of A, since it mentions the grill but does not refer to a spit. It creates the dispute A-B by interrupting the composite A+C+D.

There is some question about the identities of the Gamaliel and Ṣadoq of the pericope. The reference to the Passover-offering might lead us to connect the story with Gamaliel I and the pre-destruction Jerusalem, and the Ṣadoq who was contemporary with Yoḥanan b. Zakkai. But Ṣadoq here is a tradent of Gamaliel; and Ṭabi is represented as the contemporary of Gamaliel II. G. Allon argues (Toledot, vol. i, p. 165) that our Gamaliel attempted to retain as much of the observance of the Passover-offering as could be carried out in the absence of the Temple. And he adduces evidence that the custom of roasting a kid for Passover was observed long after the destruction. This would satisfactorily explain a narrative connecting our Gamaliel with roasting the Passover kid.

A. Rabban Gamaliel used to say, "Whoever did not say these three things on Passover has not fulfilled his obligation. And they are these: the Passover-offering, maṣṣah and bitter herbs.

B. "The Passover-offering, because the Omnipresent passed over the houses of our fathers in Egypt; the maṣṣah because our fathers were redeemed from Egypt; [and] the bitter herbs, because the Egyptians embittered the lives of our fathers in Egypt."

M. Pes. 10.5

Comment: The duty about which Gamaliel speaks is the father's obligation to explain the Exodus to his son (Ex. 12:26-27). The Mishnah text in the printed versions of b. goes further, and supplies scriptural verses for the three explanations. The context is an extended description of the Passover evening observance. B may be a later expansion of Gamaliel's words. There is no reason to doubt the attribution of A to him. Likewise, there is no reason to assume that the origin of the Passover seder would be found here. Gamaliel seems to play the same liturgical role we have previously observed: he formalizes and regulates an accepted practice.

A. [Concerning one] who finds leavened [bread] (ḤMṢ) in the road, if the majority [of the travelers are gentiles] the bread (ḤMṢ) is permitted [as a source of benefit for a Jew] but if not, it is forbidden [to derive any benefit from it].

B. (M‘SH B) Rabban Gamaliel and R. Ilai were traveling from Akko to Keziv. He saw a glusqin [loaf of expensive white bread].

He said to Ṭabi, his slave, "Take up that glusqin."

C. He saw a gentile and said to him, "Mabgai, take this glusqin,"

D. R. Ilai ran after him and said to him, "What is special about you?"

He said to him, "I am from the [Vienna: those] towns of the station keepers (BWRGNYN)".

"And what is your name?"

He said to him, "My name is Mabgai."

He said to him, "Has Rabban Gamaliel ever known you?"

He said to him, "No."

E. From this we learned that Rabban Gamaliel divined by means of the Holy Spirit.

F. And from his words we learned three things: (a) 1, that leavened bread of a gentile [which has existed during Passover] is permitted [as a source of benefit] immediately after Passover; (b) 2, that one does not pass by foodstuffs [without picking them up]; and (c) 3, that we follow the majority of travelers [in determining whether the bread originally belonged to a gentile or Jew].

G. When he reached Keziv, a man came and asked him [to release him] from his vow.

H. He said to one who was with him, "Have we perhaps drunk a quarter [log] of Italian wine?"

He said to him: "Yes."

He said to him: "If so, let him walk after us until the effects of our wine have worn off."

I. He walked with him until they reached the ladder of Tyre.

J. He got off his donkey, wrapped himself [in his cloak], sat down and released him of his vow.

K. We learned many things on that day: we learned that a quarter [of a log] of wine intoxicates; that travel takes away [the effect of] wine; that they do not teach [law] having drunk wine; and that they do not release vows either walking, riding or standing, but wrapped [in a cloak] and sitting.

Tos. Pes. 1.27-28 (Lieberman
ed. pp. 146-148, lines 32-45;
Lev. R. 37.3; J = b. Ned. 77b)

Comment: A Jew may not use, after Passover, any leavened bread which has been baked, or owned, by a Jew during the Passover week. Leavened bread made or owned by a gentile before the end of Passover is permissible afterwards (M. Pes. 2.2). In A, the bread is of questionable status: since it is found in the road, we cannot be sure whether a Jew or a gentile baked it. A rules that we follow the majority of travelers on the road, in assigning status to the bread.

B-F has been added to illustrate the law. Of the three things learned from the story (in F) only the third illustrates A. The story is independent of A, not created for it. B-F appears to have its own inner history, since all three things learned in F are derived from Gamaliel's words in B. The exchange with Magbai, the gentile, (C-E) is irrelevant to B + F. Further, E functions as a conclusion to C-E, while F is the conclusion for B. If all this were unitary, the conclusion would simply read, "And from his words we learned four things: Holy Spirit + leavened bread + not pass by + majority of travelers." As it stands, the story has two endings: "From this we learned . . . And from his words we learned . . ." in succeeding sentences. Thus, C-E was interpolated into the story after B + F were a unit. The name of Ilai would have been added to B at the same time.

C-E is related to the theme of the story (B) only in a forced way. In B, we assume that Gamaliel orders Ṭabi to pick up the bread so that he can use it himself. But in C, the only "benefit" Gamaliel receives from the bread is that he makes it a gift to someone else. The point of C-E is Gamaliel's supercognition; he identifies the gentile by name without having seen him before. Ascription of access to the Holy Spirit by Gamaliel does not occur in any other early tradition, though it befits the supernatural powers of a second-century holy man. Allowing time for it to be added to the tradition before the two stories B + F and C-E were joined in Tos., but as much time as possible after Gamaliel's death for the idea to arise, would make the terminus ad quem of the story the early third century.

The second half of the pericope (G-K) is independent of the material which precedes it. It has its own, similar conclusion (K: "We learned many things on that day . . ."). Gamaliel's companion, identified in B as Ilai, is anonymous in H: "one who was with him". Further, the place-reference at the beginning of G, "When he reached Keziv . . ." creates difficulties for the rest of the story. Gamaliel arrives at his destination, and immediately sets out again. Yet in the meantime he has managed to drink about three ounces of wine, which the conclusion claims is sufficient to intoxicate. The reference to Keziv was probably added to join the stories together. However, G-K was added after A-F was complete. Had C-E been interpolated after B + F and G-K were a unit, any editor noticing that K contains four things learned, and that E-F also contains four things learned, could not have overlooked bringing the two halves of the pericope into explicit balance: Here we learned four things, there we learned four things.

G-K is tightly organized; all details in the story are accounted for in the conclusion. But the story could not have been created to account for such a set of observations. Rather, they are derived from an analysis of the story, as indeed the rules of F are derived from B. We have seen innumerable times that one basic form of Gamaliel traditions is law transmitted as a story about Gamaliel's behavior. In this pericope we may see how a story can be transmuted into example and law, through the careful analysis of the master's actions. We have no indication of the time when this takes place, though the name of Ilai suggests that the pericope may derive from Judah b. Ilai, and hence Usha. Needless to say, this is not the sole way Gamaliel's legal traditions come to us.

The ascription of access to the Holy Spirit by Gamaliel requires further consideration. In his discussion of Tos. Soṭ. 13.3, Neusner (Pharisees, i, pp. 237-240) notes the following: A divine echo tells the sages that Hillel is worthy of the Holy Spirit, but his generation is not sufficiently righteous for him to receive it; at another time, an echo proclaims the same about Samuel the Little, then called Hillel's disciple. Neusner writes that the point of the pericope is "to stress that the true disciple of Hillel is not Gamaliel his descendant, but [Samuel] the pious, modest sage." The allegation in our pericope of Gamaliel's divination by means of the Holy Spirit may, then, be an answer to the superiority claimed on Samuel's behalf by Samuel's circle. The involvement of Samuel with the humiliation-story form suggests him to be considered an antagonist of Gamaliel, similar to Joshua (see Appendix). The claim to the Holy Spirit would then be: granted that a divine echo called Samuel worthy of the Holy Spirit; still, he did not attain that gift. Yet Gamaliel did attain it! This detail of Tos. confirms a post-Ushan estimate for C-E. Through both Yavnean and Ushan times, the patriarchal group would, like the Shammaites, "deny that anyone could draw upon heavenly revelation in the formation of the law (Neusner)," in their affirmation of the authority of the patriarchal court.

1. R. Zeʿira in the name of R. Yosé, and R. Abba and R. Ḥiyya in the name of R. Yoḥanan, said, "You shall show them no mercy (Lʾ TḤNM) (Deut. 7:2) means do not ascribe grace to them (Lʾ TTN LHM ḤN). You shall show them no mercy means do not give them a free

gift (L' TTN LHM MTNT ḤNM). You shall show them no mercy means do not give them a resting-place in the Land (L' TTN LHM ḤNYH B'RṢ) . . .

A. "Do not give them a free gift": But have we not learned: (M'SH B) Rabban Gamaliel was traveling on the road and saw a glusqin lying in the road. He said to Ṭabi his slave, "Pick up that glusqin."

B. He saw a gentile, and when he came up to him he said, "Magbai, take this glusqin."

C. R. Ilai ran after him and said to him, "What is your name?"

He said to him: "Magbai."

"And where are you from?"

He said to him, "From the towns of the station keepers (BWRGNYN)."

"And has Rabban Gamaliel ever known you?"

He said to him: "No."

D. Rabban Gamaliel divined this by means of the Holy Spirit.

E. And we learned three things from him: we learned (a) 2, that one does not pass by foodstuffs; (b) 1, that the leavened bread of a gentile is permitted [as a source of benefit] immediately after Passover; and (c) 3, that we follow the majority of travelers.

F. Said R. Jacob b. Zivdi in the name of R. Abbahu, "This was said at first, but now we pass by foodstuffs [on the road] because of witchcraft."

G. When he was about to leave Keziv, a man came to him to ask him [to release him] from his vow.

H. He said to the one who was walking with him, "Say if we have drunk a quarter [log] of wine, of the Italian kind."

He said to him, "Yes."

He said to the questioner, "Walk with us until we remove [the effects of] our wine."

I. When he reached the Ladder of Tyre,

J. Rabban Gamaliel descended, wrapped himself [in his cloak], sat down and released him of his vow.

K. From his words we learned: (a) that a quarter [log] of wine intoxicates, (b) that travel takes away [the effect of] wine; (c) that one is not asked about vows nor teaches [law] having drunk wine; and (d) that one does not release vows while traveling, but wrapped [in a cloak] and seated.

y. 'A.Z. 1.9

Comment: The material in y. has undergone a different redactional process from that in Tos. Unit 1 shows the context of y.: the pericope has been quoted here because of the "gift" idea of in the interpolation B-D, important to the exegetical subject here but irrelevant to the Toseftan context.

In A Gamaliel is traveling alone, except for his servant. Though Ilai appears in the Magbai-story, he has not been incorporated into the introduction, A. The place-names "from ʿAkko to Keziv" are replaced here by "on the road". This may suggest that, in Tos., the place-names are an elaboration, based on the mention of Keziv in G. In B and C the gentile's name is Magbai, rather than Mabgai. In C, when Ilai questions Magbai, the dialogue proceeds in a more logical fashion than in Tos. First he asks his name, then where he is from, and finally whether Gamaliel has ever met him. This may point to y. as the more accurate version, though Tos. has a claim as the more difficult reading, with the reference to the cryptic "towns of the station-keepers" coming at the start of the dialogue there. D lacks the repetitive heading, "From this we learned", so C-D may show signs of retouching at this point. In E, the sequence of the three things learned from the story is different from Tos.; but as we shall see below, the order in the three parallel pericope is totally random. F is an Amoraic comment on the pericope. The question of magic does not concern the version in b., below.

The second half of the pericope (G-K) also shows differences from Tos. G does not have the logical difficulties of its counterpart in Tos. Gamaliel is "about to leave Keziv" here, so there is no problem of his having drunk wine, or of ending one trip only to begin another. In H, Gamaliel's companion is the one "walking with him" rather than "with him"; and Gamaliel speaks directly to his questioner, rather than to his companion. The language of y. here is close to, but never identical with, Tos. In J, the donkey is not mentioned, though Gamaliel "descends". In K, point (d) is simpler: "walking, riding or standing" is instead: "traveling". The order of the four points in y. is identical with that of Tos.

In brief, y. appears smoother than Tos. As far as Gamaliel is concerned, nothing has been added to the pericope. The Amoraic interpolation (F), and the exegetical framework (1) involve the names of Amoraim of the early fourth century. So the probable later redaction of y. may account for its smoother narration of the common source.

A. (WHTNY') Have we not learned: (M'SH B) Rabban Gamaliel was riding on a donkey, and was traveling from 'Akko to Keziv. R. Ilai was traveling after him.

B. He found a glusqin in the road. He said to him, "Ilai, take that glusqin from the road."

C. He found a gentile. He said to him, "Mabgai, take these glusqins from Ilai."

D. R. Ilai joined him. He said to him, "Where are you from?" He said to him, "From the towns of the station keepers."

"And what is your name?"

"My name is Mabgai."

"Rabban Gamaliel has never known you before [has he]?"

He said to him, "No."

E. At that time we learned that Rabban Gamaliel divined this by means of the Holy Spirit.

F. And we learned three things at that time. We learned: (a) 2, that one does not pass by foodstuffs; (b) 3, and we learned that we follow the majority of travelers; (c) 1, and we learned that the leavened bread of a gentile is permitted for use after Passover.

G. When he reached Keziv, a man came to ask him [to release him] from his vow.

H. He said to the one who was with him, "Have we, perhaps, drunk a quarter [log] of Italian wine?"

He said to him, "Yes."

"If so, let him walk after us until the effects of our wine have worn off."

I. And he walked after them three mil, until he reached the ladder of Tyre.

J. When he reached the ladder of Tyre, Rabban Gamaliel got off the donkey, wrapped himself [in his cloak], and sat down and released him of his vow.

K. We learned many things at that time: (a) we learned that a quarter [log] of Italian wine intoxicates; (b) and we learned that an intoxicated person shall not give decisions [of law]; (c) and we learned that travel takes away [the effects of] wine; and (d) we learned that they do not release vows either riding, or walking, or standing, but sitting.

b. 'Eruv. 64b

Comment: The context of b. involves the power of travel to dispel the effects of wine. The pericope is quoted for the sake of G-K, rather than either of the other two elements in it. It seems that the redactor of b. has reworked Tos., for there is only one possible detail common to b. and y. together.

A adds the donkey Gamaliel is riding, following Tos., incorporating the detail from J, which mentions his dismounting. Ilai is mentioned at the beginning, having displaced the servant, Ṭabi, entirely. C follows Tos. in giving the gentile's name as Mabgai, and gains a rhyme: Mabgai/Ilai. D retains the order of questioning from Tos., but revises the opening question in order to make sense out of it. "What is special about you?" becomes, "Where are you from?" In E we may note a stylistic unity to the pericope, imposed by the repetiion of the phrase "at that time" in C, D and H.

In F, we note that the three things listed occur in a different order in each document [numbering follows appearance in Tos.]:

Tos. F	y. D	b. F
1	2	2
2	1	3
3	3	1

They are completely random.

G and H follow Tos. I brings "walked with him" from Tos., into conformity with H: "walked after them," and specifies the distance traveled as three miles. J repeats the phrase "ladder of Tyre" from the previous sentence. This may reflect a conflate of Tos. (I) and y. (I): if so, it is the only indication of knowledge of the y. version. But it may just as well be a matter of narrative style, without any influence of y. K adds the adjective "Italian" from H. K retains the three terms "riding, walking or standing" from Tos., although in different order, and drops the detail "wrapped [in a cloak]".

In brief, b. has retold the story from Tos., changing it slightly to create greater internal harmony and stylistic unity. Other slight differences seem to be accidental.

And we do not provide an opening by [means of] the following, which, said Rabban b. bar Ḥannah, said R. Yoḥanan: "What opening did Rabban Gamaliel provide for that old man? [He quoted] <u>There is such that expresses himself like the piercings of a sword; but the tongue of the wise performs healing</u> (Prov. 12:13). [This means, he suggested,] anyone who expresses [a vow] is worthy to be pierced by the sword, <u>but the tongue of the wise performs healing</u> [by absolving vows]."

b. Ned. 22a

Comment: Gamaliel suggests, through quoting the biblical verse, that the man should arrange to have his vow absolved. This may possibly refer to the conclusion of Tos. Pes. 1.27; but there the man approaches Gamaliel to release him of his vow, and Gamaliel does not prompt him to do so.

A. "[As to] the fourteenth [of Nisan] which fell on the Sabbath, they burn everything [ḥameṣ] before Sabbath; and he bakes maṣṣah for himself on the eve of the Sabbath.

B. "[As to] Heave-offering, [both] clean and unclean, they burn them before the Sabbath," the words of R. Meir.

C. And sages say, "[Both kinds of ḥameṣ are burned] at their [proper] time: [even] clean and unclean Heave-offering, they burn them on Sabbath."

D. R. Eleazar b. Ṣadoq says, "Heave-offering [which is ḥameṣ is to be burned] before the Sabbath, since those who eat it are few, and common food (ḤWLYN) [is to be burned] on the Sabbath, since those who eat it are many."

E. Said R. Eleazar b. Ṣadoq, "Once the fourteenth [of Nisan] fell on Sabbath, and we were sitting before Rabban Gamaliel in the house of study in Lud. Zunin the official came and said, 'The time for burning [the] ḥameṣ has come.'

"My father and I went to the house of Rabban Gamaliel, and we burned [the] ḥameṣ."

Tos. Pes. 2.9-11 (Lieberman
ed. pp. 153-154, lines 32-39)

Comment: Tos. here explains the rulings set forth in M. Pes. 3.6. The problem concerns a conflict of Passover and Sabbath laws when the eve of Passover falls on a Sabbath. The obligation to burn ḥameṣ conflicts with the prohibition to burn anything on the Sabbath. In M., Meir rules that all ḥameṣ (meaning, both common food and Heave-offering) is to be burned before Sabbath; the sages rule that all ḥameṣ is burned at its proper time on the Sabbath; and Eleazar b. Ṣadoq holds the intermediate view, that Heave-offering is to be burned before Sabbath, and common food on the Sabbath.

Tos. adds some details (A, B, C) and supplies Eleazar with a reason for his position: burning the common food is delayed so that it can be used up by the many people who would otherwise have to destroy it. E adds a first-person account by Eleazar, about himself and his father burning the ḥameṣ with Rabban Gamaliel, on a Sabbath morning. There is no mention made in the story of any distinction between Heave-offering and common food. Nothing in story would rule out the view of the sages, that people would be burning Heave-offering then as well as common food. Indeed, to assume that Gamaliel would agree with Eleazar's distinction here would seem to contradict the priority Gamaliel gives to Heave-offering in M. Pes. 1.4-5D. There Gamaliel extends the time Heave-offering may be eaten, beyond that of common food, by one hour, in order that it not have to be burned. Here, Eleazar would have us believe that Gamaliel would agree to have it burned half a day earlier! While the pericope in M. comes from Judah b. Ilai, who often revises Gamaliel's traditions, it is simpler to assume that the redactor of Tos. supplied the Gamaliel-story (silent on this distinction) to illustrate Eleazar's view. Meir's affirmation of the priority of the Sabbath over Passover is certainly Ushan. Gamaliel would not have known of it, nor of Eleazar's attempt to save the older law in the majority of cases, though not in all.

It was taught (TNY'): R. Eleazar b. Ṣadoq says, "Once father [spent a] Sabbath in Yavneh, and the fourteenth [of Nisan] fell on the Sabbath. Zunin, Rabban Gamaliel's official, came and said, 'The time for burning the ḥameṣ has come.'

"I went after father and we burned the ḥameṣ."

b. Pes. 49a

Comment: The b. version of Eleazar's story has revised several of the puzzling details of Tos. Gamaliel is placed in Yavneh, where we would expect him, rather than in Lud (scene of a number of other pericopae related to Passover, Tos. Pes. 10.12, y. Pes. 2.4). Zunin, the official, has been made Gamaliel's official. Yet though Ṣadoq is a guest at Yavneh, where it would make sense for him to go to Gamaliel's house to burn the ḥameṣ, that detail is not present.

A. After the Passover [sacrificial meal] they do not conclude [with] afiqomon,

B. for example: nuts, dates or parched grain (QLYWT),

C. and a man is required to busy himself with [the study of] the laws of Passover,

D. even by himself alone, [or] together with his household, [or] together with his student.

E. (M'SH B) Rabban Gamliel and elders were reclining in the house of Boethus b. Zunin, in Lud, and were discussing the laws of Passover all that night, until the cock crowed.

F. They removed [the scraps from the table] before them, and swept [the floor] and went to the House of Study.

Tos. Pes. 10.11-12 (Lieberman ed. pp. 198-199, lines 30-35; A = M. Pes. 10.8)

Comment: A is a quotation from M. Pes. 10.8, in order to present an explanation of the term afiqomon as kind of snack (B) rather than in terms of its Greek etymology as after-dinner entertainment (see Danby, Mishnah, p. 151, n. 9). C-D is a separate issue, but also related to the theme of what one does after the Passover meal.

E cites a story to illustrate C: Gamaliel and his accompanying elders, in Lud, discussed the laws of Passover through the night. The story is similar to the more famous version incorporated into the Passover Haggadah (Haggadah, E. D. Goldschmidt ed., p. 118; see also p. 19). The latter story takes place in B'nei Beraq; though Eliezer, Joshua, Eleazar b. ʿAzariah, ʿAqiva and Tarfon are present, Gamaliel is not mentioned. Eleazar is central to the latter version, as he is to M. Ber. 1.5, which also speaks of "telling of the going out of Egypt". E is thus the counterpart, in Gamaliel's tradition of the ʿAqivan story.

F. recalls M. Beṣ. 2.7, illustrating Gamaliel's ruling that it is permissible to sweep the dining-area floor on a festival. Since it alters the focus of the story, it may be an addition together with the glosses B and D. In fact, since D serves to introduce the story, D and F might have been interpolated into an original pericope of C + E.

It is clear that both the ʿAqivan and patriarchal circles preserved stories of an all-night Passover meal. The point of the ʿAqivan story is the elaboration of the miracle of the Exodus. For the Gamaliel-story it is the study of Torah, in this case the laws of Passover.

Boethus b. Zunin appears in another pericope related to Passover laws (y. Pes. 2.4), while "Zunin the official" appears in the House of Study in Lud in another Passover pericope (Tos. Pes. 2.11). The latter may be connected with the "Zenun the Ḥazzan" who figures briefly in the story of Gamaliel's deposition (y. Ber. 4.1).

A. 1. We fulfill our obligations [to eat maṣṣah on Passover] with Syrian cakes, whether decorated with figures or not decorated with figures, even though they said,

2. "One may not make Syrian cakes decorated with figures for Passover."

B. We have learned (TNY): Said Rabbi Judah, Boethus b. Zunin asked Rabban Gamaliel and the sages in Yavneh, 'What is the law about making figured Syrian cakes for Passover?'

C. "They said to him, 'It is forbidden, because a woman delays while making them, and causes it to leaven.'

D. "He said to them, 'If so, they can make them with a mold.'

E. "They said to him, 'If so, they will say all Syrian cakes are forbidden but the Syrian cakes of Boethus b. Zunin are permitted!'"

y. Pes. 2.4

Comment: In order to avoid the possibility of leavening, the dough for maṣṣah should be baked immediately after kneading. A. 1 revises an earlier law, which forbids the making of decorated unleavened cakes for Passover, because the extra time required for them might give the dough a chance to leaven (A. 2). As with many reversals of previous law, the prohibition is allowed to stand, but the cakes may be used anyway, if they have already been baked.

B-E is a debate expressing the original prohibition and its reason. Boethus has a method for guarding against using up extra time, but the sages will not allow his special method an exemption from the rule. B-E is separate from A; its superscription indicates its redaction by the editor of y. (TNY). The debate B-E is attributed to the Ushan Judah b. Ilai; its content indicates A. 2 to be a Yavnean law. So the revision, A. 1, is probably Ushan. The nature of the Ushan discussion will be commented upon further, in the next pericope.

As in y. Ma. 1.2, the phrase "Rabban Gamaliel and the sages in Yavneh," (together with the plural verb, "They said") appears to express a Yavnean consensus rather than a ruling by Gamaliel himself.

A. 1. [TNW RBNN] they fulfill [their obligation to eat maṣṣah] on Passover, with fine [-flour] bread, and with coarse [bread], and with Syrian cakes [decorated] with figures, even though they said,

2. "They do not make Syrian cakes [decorated] with figures on Passover."

B. Said Rav Judah, "This thing asked Beothus b. Zunin of the sages: 'Why was it said that "They do not make Syrian cakes [decorated] with figures on Passover"?

C. "They said to him, 'Because a woman takes time over it, and it leavens.'

D. "He said to them, 'It is possible to make it in a mold, and form it immediately.'

E. "They said to him, 'Shall they say, "All Syrian cakes are forbidden, but the Syrian cakes of Boethus are permitted"?'"

F. Said R. Eleazar b. Ṣadoq, "Once I followed my father into the house of Rabban Gamaliel, and they brought before him Syrian cakes [decorated] with figures on Passover.

G. "I said, 'Father, did not the sages say thus: "They do not make Syrian cakes [decorated] with figures on Passover"?'

H. "He said to me, 'My son, they did not speak of [the cakes of] all people, but they referred to bakers'."

I. Others say, "He said thus to him, 'They did not of [the cakes of] bakers, but of all [other] men.'"

b. Pes. 37a (Aramaic italicized)

Comment: A-E expands on y. Pes. 2.4, in the following details: A. 1 adds the reference to fine and coarse flour as permissible for maṣṣah; D adds a reference to time, "and form it immediately;" otherwise the pericopae are essentially identical. However, B refers to Rav (not Rabbi) Judah, and omits the names of Gamaliel and Yavneh.

F-I quotes a story from the Ushan Eleazar b. Ṣadoq, another reminiscence of his father and Gamaliel. The earlier rule is quoted (G) and Ṣadoq reassures Eleazar that Gamaliel's behavior is correct. The reassurance is given in two versions. According to H, the prohibition applies only to commercial bakers, who make the cakes in large quantities, which may have time to leaven. But individuals make the cakes in small batches, with no chance of this, and are permitted. According to I, the prohibition applies only to the individual bakers, who must hand-make the cakes, taking a long time. Commercial bakers, however, use molds to shape the cakes quickly. So they are permitted to do so. By the time of redaction of the pericope F-I in b., it was not clear how the prohibition was to be restricted, whether before the fact (A. 1) or by applying it to a specific kind of decorated cake (H or I).

In any event, Eleazar's story uses a Gamaliel-precedent to support the Ushan revision of the Yavnean law. We have seen other examples of the employment of Gamaliel-stories against Judah b.

Ilai, assuming that y. is correct in its reference to Rabbi (rather than Rav) Judah.

Both sides at Usha were able to appeal to a Gamaliel-tradition for support. However, if Gamaliel's opinion is to be consistent with his opinion in M. Pes. 3.4, Eleazar's report is more acceptable. This would confirm our previous interpretation of the phrase "Rabban Gamaliel and the sages in Yavneh" as consensus rather than specific to Gamaliel.

Boethus b. Zunin appears in another pericope related to Passover. Tos. Pes. 10.12 relates that Gamaliel and the Elders celebrated the Passover at his house in Lud. A "Zunin the official" announces the time for burning the _ḥameṣ_ in Tos. Pes. 2.11; Eleazar b. Ṣadoq is the tradent there too.

A. Have we not learned (WHTNY'): They do not knead dough, on Passover, with wine, or oil or honey.

B. And if he kneaded [it] -
Rabban Gamaliel says, "It shall be burned immediately."
And sages say, "It is eaten."

C. And said R. ʿAqiva, "My stay [one Passover] was with R. Eliezer and R. Joshua, and I kneaded dough for them with wine, or oil or honey; and they did not say a word to me."

b. Pes. 36a

Comment: The dough for _maṣṣah_ is not to be mixed with wine, oil or honey, because these substances might speed up the fermentation process, and leaven the dough (A). This anonymous law is followed by a dispute over a _post facto_ situation (B). Gamaliel insists on destroying the dough immediately, so that it should not have a chance to leaven. The sages allow it to be baked and eaten. ʿAqiva (C) supplies a personal narrative in illustration of the sages' view: Eliezer and Joshua did not forbid him to use dough that had been kneaded with the prohibited substances.

Though there are instances of ʿAqivan comment upon Yavnean pericopae, this appears to be an illustration for the sages' position, rather than a participation by ʿAqiva in the dispute. First, the story uses the same general terms for the forbidden substances: "wine, or oil or honey (BYYN WŠMN WDBŠ)". A plausible independent narrative would not include all three terms. Second, ʿAqiva is not arguing on behalf of the sages' view, but only saying that they acted in accord with their view. Further, ʿAqiva's lemma is indefinite as to whether it refers to a situation before or after the fact. Had the dispute been "they do not knead _vs_. they knead",

ʿAqiva's story would support the latter (as, e.g., in M.M.S. 2.7). The alternative to seeing C as an illustration for B is to say that C really disputes A, and that the sequence of the pericope should be A+C+B. In that case, ʿAqiva would dispute the anonymous law; after the fact, however, Gamaliel still follows that law, while the sages compromise with ʿAqiva. However, we have not seen ʿAqiva play that central role in any Gamaliel pericopae.

viii. _Sukkah_

A. A man who sleeps under a bed in the _sukkah_ [F, P, Camb. omit: in the _sukkah_], has not fulfilled his obligation.

B. Said R. Judah, "It was our custom to sleep under the beds in the presence of the elders, and they said nothing to us [K, P, Camb. omit: and they said nothing to us]."

C. Said R. Simeon, "(MʿSH B) Ṭabi, the slave of Rabban Gamaliel, slept under the bed. And said Rabban Gamaliel to the elders, 'You have seen Ṭabi, my slave. He is a student of the wise (TLMYD ḤKM) and knows that slaves are exempt from [the law of] the _sukkah_; and accordingly (LPYKK) [K, P, Camb. omit: LPYKK] he sleeps under the bed.'

D. "So incidentally (LPY DRKYNW) we learn that [a man] who sleeps under a bed has not fulfilled his obligation."

M. Suk. 2.1

Comment: A bed ten handbreadths high would interpose a second "roof" between the person sleeping under it and the roof of the _sukkah_. The man would thus not fulfill the commandment to sleep under the _sukkah_-roof. Judah dissents from this anonymous law, on the basis of the permission actually granted by the elders. Simeon, however, supports the law with another report, a story of Gamaliel stating that only someone _not_ observing the law of the _sukkah_ would sleep under a bed there.

A states the anonymous law. B is Judah's dissent, reporting his experience with the elders. He does not mention the _sukkah_ directly, so B depends upon A for this. C is Simeon's illustration of the law in A. Though redacted as an answer to B, it does not depend upon it. B and C may be independent responses to the earlier anonymous law, here redacted by a disciple of Simeon to support A.

Simeon's story does not follow the pattern of the other "faithful servant" stories of Gamaliel and Ṭabi. With the others, the point usually is that Ṭabi (or the maidservant Ṭabita) is both knowledgeable and observant of Jewish law. Here the point is the opposite: Ṭabi's behavior teaches us what _not_ to do. Only someone free of the law may sleep under the bed in the _sukkah_. It is also strange to have a Gamaliel-story quoted against Judah, who is often a channel for traditions about Gamaliel -- especially by Simeon, who occurs only here as a tradent of Gamaliel. It would almost seem that a Ṭabi-story demonstrating that it is _permissible_ to sleep under the bed in the _sukkah_ is here revised by Simeon, by adding: "And knows that slaves are exempt from [the law of] the _sukkah_; and accordingly . . ." This makes it fit his own view: "So, incidentally, we learned . . . he has not fulfilled his obligation." The import of the story could be the opposite of what Simeon derived from it. Certainly Simeon does not quote Gamaliel directly as teaching the validity of the act; Gamaliel speaks mainly to praise his servant. Gamaliel may have implicitly agreed with the elders; but using his example could be Simeon's strongest possible argument against Judah.

Setting aside this speculation, we may note only that the story is unusual in its tradent, and in its use of the servant as example. The pericope was shaped at Usha by a disciple of R. Simeon b. Yoḥai. Not only is Gamaliel's own practice considered good evidence for accepted law, but as we have seen in other Ṭabi stories, even the servant of the Patriarch teaches the law through his own behavior. This favorable view of the Patriarch contrasts, for example, with some of the stories told of the servants of the Exilarch (cf. Neusner, _History_, vol. iii, pp. 83-87).

It was taught (TNY'): Said R. Simeon, "From the [casual] conversation of Rabban Gamaliel we learned two things: we learned that slaves are exempt from [the law of] the _sukkah_; and we learned that one who sleeps under a bed [in the _sukkah_] has not fulfilled his obligation."

b. Suk. 21b

Comment: Simeon's lemma is a re-phrasing of Gamaliel's remark in M. Suk. 2.1C, and of Simeon's own deduction in 2.1D. It is almost a programmatic statement of the way the law is learned from the behavior of Gamaliel.

A. The views of Rabban Gamaliel switched. For we have learned [DTNY]:

B. (1) Ṭabi, the slave of Rabban Gamaliel, used to put on [HYH NWTN] tefillin, (2) and the sages did not protest against it.

C. And yet here they protested against [Ṭabi's observing the laws of the sukkah].

-- [He only lay under the bed in the sukkah] so as not to discomfort the sages.

-- If it were not to discomfort the sages [because of crowding in the sukkah] he could have sat outside the sukkah.

-- Ṭabi, slave of Rabban Gamaliel, wanted to hear the words of the sages.

y. Suk. 5.3 (y. ʿEruv. 10.1)

Comment: B is the baraita quoted in this Amoraic discussion. Its key verb differs from its parallel (Mek. Pisḥa 17): HYN NWTN vs. HYH MNYḤ. The latter half of the sentence (B.2) may be an Amoraic gloss. C is not relevant to our purpose here, or to M. Suk. 2.1, since it is clearly the product of Amoraic supposition.

A. On this basis, sages said, "All are required to put on tefillin, except women and slaves."

B. Michal, the daughter of Kushi used to put on tefillin.

C. The wife of Jonah used to go up to Jerusalem for festivals.

D. Ṭabi, the slave of Rabban Gamaliel, used to put on tefillin.

Mek. Pisḥa, 17 (Lauterbach I,
p. 153, line 160-
p. 154, line 164)
(y. ʿEruv. 10.1)

Comment: The larger passage, of which this pericope is the conclusion, discusses the basis for exemption of women from certain commandments. This may explain the intrusion of C, which is not part of our pericope. B and D provide two exceptions to the rule that women and slaves do not don tefillin: Michal, daughter of King Saul, and Ṭabi, Gamaliel's slave. A number of traditions describe Ṭabi as knowledgeable and observant of Jewish law, so he is the natural example to cite.

A. (MʿSH W) They brought cooked food to Rabban Yoḥanan b. Zakkai to taste, and two dates and a pail of water to Rabban Gamaliel. And they said, "Bring them up to the sukkah."

B. And when they gave R. Ṣadoq less than an egg's bulk of food, he took it in a towel and ate it outside the sukkah, and did not say the blessing after it.

M. Suk. 2.5

Comment: J. Neusner (Development, p. 43) concludes that since Gamaliel is mentioned together with Yohanan b. Zakkai, this story derives from Rabban Gamaliel I, between ca. 35 and ca. 50, c.e. not our Gamaliel. Accordingly, its parallel and amplifying baraita (b. Yoma 79a) are also omitted from consideration here.

A. And where do they shake [the lulav]?

"At the beginning and the end of the psalm, O give thanks unto the Lord (Ps. 118) and at Save now, we beseech Thee O Lord (Ps. 118:25A)," [K, P, N, Camb.: like] the words of the House of Hillel [Munich: the words of the House of Shammai].

The House of Shammai [Munich: House of Hillel] say, "Also (ʾP) at O Lord, we beseech Thee, send now prosperity (Ps. 118:25B)."

B. R. ʿAqiva said, "I was watching Rabban Gamaliel and R. Joshua, and while all the people were shaking (MNʿNʿYN) [P, N, CAMB.: MṬRPYN] their lulavs, they shook them only at Save now, we beseech Thee, O Lord [K, P, N, Camb., Munich add: alone (BLBD)]."

M. Suk. 3.9 (y. Suk. 3,8,
b. Suk. 37b)

Comment: Neusner (Pharisees, ii, pp. 154-155) notes that the form of the dispute does not follow the usual form for the traditions of the Houses: Hillel precedes Shammai. On form-critical grounds he suggests a rearrangement, in which the House of Shammai are mentioned first (as in the Munich ms.) and shake only at a single verse, Ps. 118:25B. The placement of ʿAqiva's story then comes to reveal that Gamaliel and Joshua followed Shammaite practice. This is disguised by quoting Ps. 118:25A for them and Ps. 118:25B for the House of Shammai.

Since, however, the two halves of Ps. 118:25 are cited separately here, Neusner's more conservative suggestion seems stronger: Gamaliel and Joshua followed a third position from either of the two Houses. They waved the lulav only at Save us, we beseech thee, O Lord.

The analysis of W. S. Green (Joshua, p. 182) arrives at a similar conclusion: ". . . although ʿAqiva's lemma [in B] may seem to line up Joshua and Gamaliel with the Shammaite opinion in . . . the revised version, it does not necessarily presuppose the dispute . . . as a background. [B] is intelligible by itself, and it suggests that while the people shook their lulavs throughout the recitation of Ps. 118, Joshua and Gamaliel shook theirs only once, at Ps. 118:25A. The BLBD of the five manuscript editions tends to confirm this interpretation. The lemma thus appears attached to a Houses-dispute to which it does not refer and with which it does not agree."

As in M.M.S. 2.7, Gamaliel's co-exemplar is Joshua, and the tradent is ʿAqiva. While Gamaliel's behavior is significant for law, a difference may be noted between the ʿAqivan redaction and the Patriarchal editor. Here Gamaliel does not play a pre-eminent role; rather he is a major figure equal to Joshua.

A. "[On] the first day of the [Sukkot] festival, a man does not fulfill his obligation [to take up the lulav] with the lulav of his fellow,"

B. unless [the latter] gives it to him as a valid gift.

C. (WMʿSH B) Rabban Gamaliel and elders were traveling on a ship, and they had no lulav.

D. Rabban Gamaliel took up (NṬL) a lulav worth a gold dinar.

E. When he had fulfilled his obligation, he gave it as a valid gift to his fellows, so that they all could fulfill their obligation. Afterwards, they returned it to him.

Tos. Suk. 2.11
(Lieberman ed. p. 265,
lines 66-70)

Comment: M. Suk. 3.13 describes how, on the first day of Sukkot, each person provides his own lulav. It then quotes, "For sages said, 'A man does not fulfill his obligation [to take up the lulav] on the first day of the [Sukkot] festival with the lulav of his fellow'." A of Tos. rephrases M. slightly and then adds its comment (B) that a person may use another's lulav, provided that he receives it as an actual gift.

C-E now illustrates the comment of B, with a story of Gamaliel and the elders. Except for the detail of the cost of the lulav (D) the story echoes the situation and language of A-B exactly ("fulfill his obligation," "valid gift").

C-E appears to have been created for the purpose of illustrating A-B and shows no sign of being independent of it. The stories of Rabban Gamaliel's travels both at home and abroad were widespread. Gamaliel is portrayed as the leader of the group, indeed here the only member named. He is credited with the foresight of purchasing a lulav in advance, and with the willingness to spend a great sum to buy it. The others are dependent upon him. (This contrasts with b. Hor. 10a-b, for example, a Joshua-story in which Gamaliel is dependent upon Joshua's knowledge and foresight, for supplies on a sea voyage.)

A. And you shall take for yourselves (Lev. 23:40) -- each one individually. For yourselves -- and not a stolen one.

B. On the basis of this verse, they said, "A man does not fulfill his obligation [to take up the lulav] on the first day of the [Sukkot] festival with the lulav of his fellows."

C. But if he wishes, [the latter] gives it to him as a gift, and he [in turn may give it] to another, [in a series of] even a hundred [men].

D. (M'SH B) Rabban Gamaliel and the Elders were traveling on a ship; there was no lulav,

E. except [one] in the possession of Rabban Gamaliel alone.

F. Rabban Gamaliel gave it as a gift to Joshua, Joshua gave it to Eleazar b. 'Azariah, Eleazar b. 'Azariah gave it to R. 'Aqiva; and they all fulfilled their obligation.

Sifra, Emor. 16.2

Comment: As befits a midrash collection, the Sifra version begins with exegesis. The Scriptural verse states that the palm branch is to be taken for yourselves, i.e., your own.

B-F illustrates only the first of the two exegetical points raised in A. B quotes M. Suk. 3.13 exactly. The comment upon it (C) expands the concept of a gift into that of a serial gift, which is not really present in Tos. This is the real contribution of Sifra to the subject. The story which follows has no reference to the price paid for the lulav (D) and illustrates the serial-gift idea by naming the three other rabbis who figure in stories of Gamaliel's voyage to Rome (E). The order of the names reflects the official status of the sages during the patriarchate of Gamaliel: Gamaliel as Patriarch, Joshua as his Av Beth Din, Eleazar having served as Patriarch temporarily, and finally 'Aqiva.

The lulav-story is used, this time, to illustrate the serial-gift idea. Since the language and details of Tos. and Sifra are not similar, and since the mention of the gold dinar is not present, Sifra has probably adapted the tradition (Sukkot voyage and lulav) for its own purpose. But since the story illustrates only the first point of exegesis, and not the second (no stolen lulav),

Sifra probably made use of an extent tradition, instead of creating one to illustrate both points.

A. How do we know this? From what our rabbis taught (DTNW RBNN): <u>And you shall take</u> (Lev. 23:40) means that there shall be a "taking" by the hand of each individual. <u>For yourselves</u> -- of your own, excluding one either borrowed or stolen.

B. On the basis of this verse, sages said, "A man does not fulfill his obligation [to take up the <u>lulav</u>] on the first day of the [Sukkot] festival with the <u>lulav</u> of his fellow",

C. unless the latter gives it to him as a gift.

D. (WMʿSH B) Rabban Gamaliel, Joshua, R. Eleazar b. ʿAzariah and R. ʿAqiva were traveling on a ship,

E. and Rabban Gamaliel alone had a <u>lulav</u>, which he had obtained for a thousand <u>zuz</u>.

F. Rabban Gamaliel took it, fulfilled his obligation, and gave it as a gift to R. Joshua. R. Joshua took it, fulfilled his obligation, and gave it as a gift to R. Eleazar b. ʿAzariah. R. Eleazar b. ʿAzariah took it, fulfilled his obligation, and gave it as a gift to R. ʿAqiva. R. ʿAqiva took it, fulfilled his obligation, and returned it to Rabban Gamaliel.

b. Suk. 41b

<u>Comment</u>: The pericope in b. appears to depend upon both Tos. and Sifra. A expands the exegesis, adding the idea of a personal "taking", and including not only a positive statement of "your own" but a full negative statement as well (not borrowed or stolen). B retains the full M. quotation in the proper order from Sifra. C depends upon Tos., since this is the point at which Sifra introduces the concept of the serial gift (while b. only describes it later, in the story). D follows Sifra again, with the names of all four rabbis. E depends upon Tos., mentioning the high price of the <u>lulav</u>, but increasing it 400%! Finally, F. returns to Sifra, but spells out the serial gift in even greater detail, repeating the phrase "fulfilled his obligation" from M., and mentioning the eventual return of the <u>lulav</u> to Gamaliel. In sum, b. synthesizes and makes explicit what is in the earlier sources.

A. We have learned (TNY): Just as they clear out [the sukkah] because of rain, so [do they do it] because of heat or because of flies.

B. Rabban Gamaliel would enter and leave all night. R. Liezer would enter and leave all night.

y. Sukk. 2.10

Comment: The point of Gamaliel and Eliezer was to spend as much time as possible in the sukkah, conditions permitting; so they would return whenever the rain stopped.

Gamaliel and Eliezer appear together infrequently. Here their precedents are cited together, without being combined into a single sentence. In M. Ket. 1.6-9, on the other hand, their traditions were formulated as a co-statement. Here the citations in B may have been assembled by the redactor of y. and not subjected to the redactional process which produced the joint quotation of M. Ket. But as in M., Gamaliel is cited first.

A. According to whom is our Mishnah? According to R. ʿAqiva.

B. As it was taught (DTNYʾ): [As to one] who makes his sukkah [b. Suk. 7b adds: on top of a wagon or] on the deck of a ship -

C. Rabban Gamaliel [declares it] unfit.

D. And R. ʿAqiva [declares it] fit.

E. (MʿSH B) Rabban Gamaliel and R. ʿAqiva were travelling by ship. R. ʿAqiva arose and made a sukkah on the deck of the ship.

F. On the next day, the wind blew and tore it away.

G. Said to him Rabban Gamaliel, "ʿAqiva, *where is* your sukkah?"

b. Suk. 23a (B-D = b. Suk. 7b:
G: Aramaic italicized)

The anonymous law of M. Sukk. 2.3 states, "[Concerning one] who makes his sukkah on top of a wagon or on the deck of a ship- it is valid, and they go up to it on the festival." The baraita in b. presents this view as the ʿAqivan side of a Gamaliel-ʿAqiva dispute (B-D). The version of the baraita on b. Sukk. 7b conforms to the text of the anonymous law in M., while the version here conforms to the story which follows in E-G.

E-G presents a critique of the ʿAqivan position from Gamaliel's viewpoint: a sukkah erected upon a moving vehicle cannot last for the week of the festival, and is consequently invalid. The incident itself has shown the absurdity of ʿAqiva's ruling. Thus, both B-D and E-G reflect Gamaliel's viewpoint: his opinion is recorded first in the dispute, and is vindicated in the story.

There is reason to assume that, unlike other pericopae in which a MʿSH is the precedent for a law, this story is an illustration supplied for the dispute. Though we have a number of traditions about the famous voyage of Gamaliel, Joshua, Eleazar, and ʿAqiva to Rome, that tradition does not seem to be reflected in this story. Joshua and Eleazar are not present nor are the "elders" as a unit mentioned. Further, the story does not raise any question regarding M. Sukk. 2.4, "Those sent on a mission of religious importance are exempt from the [requirement to enter a] sukkah" (cf. also b. Sukk. 26a). Since the four sages in the Rome-stories were on such a communal mission - and exempt from the commandment - one would expect at least mention of ʿAqiva's sukkah as an act of special piety (similar to M. ʿEruv. 4.1). None of the later traditions raises this question. The story exists in an historical vacuum. It seems likely to have been created to show the absurdity of the ʿAqivan view, with the shipboard setting suggested by the many other traditions circulated about Gamaliel's travels.

The dispute attributes the opinion validating such a sukkah to Gamaliel. The story shows a defense of his view by circles favoring him. Perhaps the existence of this pericope may explain why the redactor of M. incorporated ʿAqiva's view anonymously, rather than in named preference to Gamaliel.

ix. Beṣah

A. [If a man] picks out pulse on a festival, The House of Shammai say, "He picks the food [edible parts] and eats."

B. And the House of Hillel say, "He picks according to his usual fashion (KDRKW),

C. "in his lap, or in a dish; but not on a board or in a sifter or a sieve."

D. Rabban Gamaliel says, "He even (ʾP) rinses and removes (MDYḤ WŠWLH)."

M. Beṣ. 1.8 (y. Beṣ. 1.10,
y. Shab. 7.2)

Comment: Pulse are legumes, a class of vegetables bearing edible seeds within an inedible pod (e.g., lentils, beans, peas, etc.). The pod is opened, and the seeds are thus shelled to be eaten raw or cooked.

On a festival one may prepare food only for consumption during the festival, not for consumption after the festival. The question of the pericope is: how much pulse may be podded at one time, to be considered as intended for use during the festival alone?

In A the Shammaites permit picking out only those seeds a man intends to eat immediately, presumably a handful at a time. The Hillelites permit doing it in the usual way: preparing a quantity in advance, and then eating (B). Neusner has pointed out (Pharisees, II, p. 165) that C is a restrictive gloss, narrowing some of the latitude of the Hillelite rule. But the gloss, in effect, provides us with a commentary on the meaning of the "usual way", since all the ways mentioned are methods of advance preparation of a quantity of food for serving at a meal. The issue between the houses is, then, picking-and-eating vs. preparation of a quantity.

Gamaliel's comment on the Houses-dispute is presented as an extension of the leniency of the Hillelite rule: "He even (ʾP) rinses and removes." Since rinsing does not help to remove the pods from beans or lentils, this seems to be a further step, beyond the "usual way". One common procedure for softening legumes after their removal from the pods is soaking (ŠWRH). Though none of the readings supports such a conjecture, the R and L are graphically so close that the possibility must be raised, at least, that Gamaliel's lemma should read ʾP MDYḤ WŠWRH, "He even rinses and soaks," rather than ʾP MDYḤ WŠWLH, "He even rinses and removes." Nevertheless, let us retain the latter, more difficult reading. Ambiguous as it may be, it can only refer to a further step in the preparation of already-shelled pulse, perhaps as Tos. understands it, the separation of dirt or stray pods from a quantity of the legumes.

Again Gamaliel is presented taking a position related to a Houses-dispute but independent of it, and more lenient than the Hillelite ruling.

Said R. Eleazar b. Ṣadoq, "[Those] of Rabban Gamaliel's house used to fill a pail with lentils, and let it overflow with water, and skim it. The pebbles would sink to the bottom and the food [would rise] to the top."

Tos. Beṣ. 1.22

Comment: Eleazar b. Ṣadoq explains Gamaliel's lemma, quoted in the Mishnah, by describing the practice in Gamaliel's household. We seem to have shelled lentils, among which there is sand. The water causes the lentils to rise to the top, the sand to sink to the bottom. It is clear that we are dealing with an extension of the Hillelite view, since a quantity of food is being prepared, and the added step is the washing.

We note that the term used in the illustration is lentil rather than pulse. The former is a specific vegetable, the latter a general term, but the principle of seed-bearing pods is the same. The difference in terms may help explain the ambiguity and brevity of Gamaliel's lemma in M. Gamaliel's saying may have originally referred to lentils, and his view may have been edited when it was added to the Houses-dispute in the Mishnah.

Personal experience of Gamaliel's household is elsewhere attributed to Eleazar (e.g., Tos. Y.Ṭ. 2.13) as well as to his father.

It was taught (TNY'): R. Eleazar b. R. Ṣadoq said, "This was the practice in the house of Rabban Gamaliel: They would bring a pail full of lentils, and pour water over them. The result was that the food [remained] below and the refuse [floated] to the top."

b. Beṣ. 14b

Comment: Except for the name of Eleazar, and the key words "pail" and "lentils", this *baraita* is different in language from the Tos. version, though it has obvious similarities. Pouring water could not separate the seeds from the pods of unshelled lentils. We have already-shelled lentils, but here they are mixed with stray pods and stems or leaves. When water is poured over the lentils, the refuse can be removed from the surface of the water in the pail. The *baraita* in b. has reversed the process described in Tos. Either the editor had an independent version, or he reconstructed the pericope from some vague report.

It was taught (TNY'): Rabban Gamaliel said, "To what do these words [of the House of Hillel] apply? [To a case] where the food is more than the refuse. But when the refuse is more than the food, all agree that he takes the food and leaves the refuse."

b. Beṣ. 14b

Comment: Here Gamaliel reinterprets the Hillelite position in the dispute of M. Beṣ. 1.8. He claims that the Hillelites too accept the Shammaite rule, when the pods are more prevalent than the seeds of the pulse. In such cases, the seeds are eaten piecemeal, and a quantity is not prepared for serving. Since, with unshelled pulse, the inedible pods always represent a greater bulk than the edible seeds, the Hillelite disagreement is shown to be nonexistent. Only the Shammaite rule remains. The Hillelites' dissent would apply only to a dish of shelled pulse, with a few unshelled pods -- a situation which fits Tos. Beṣ. 1.22, but which is not the situation disputed in M.

Neusner's observation on M. Beṣ. 1.8B pointed out the restrictions upon the "usual way" of preparing the pulse added by the gloss. In effect, it was a way of bringing the Hillelite view closer to the position of the House of Shammai, by restricting the types of permissible preparation. The same tendency seems to be at work in the baraita here. It presents a "Shammaite" Gamaliel, in contrast to the Mishnah, which shows Gamaliel as more lenient than the Hillelite view. However, it may be merely that a later desire to harmonize legal disputes presents Gamaliel in this way. His name is attached to the compromise position.

A. In three things Rabban Gamaliel [gives the more] stringent [ruling], according to the words of the House of Shammai,

B. "They do not cover up hot [food] on a festival day for the Sabbath; and they do not re-assemble a candelabrum on a festival; and they do not bake bread in large loaves but only as thin cakes."

C. Said Rabban Gamaliel, "Never did my father's household bake bread in large loaves, but only as thin cakes."

D. They said to him, "What shall we do with your father's household, who used to be strict with themselves, but lenient with all Israel, so that they [Israel] could bake large loaves and thick cakes!"

E. Moreover (ʾP) he said three things [which are more] lenient, "They sweep between the couches, and put spices on the fire, on a festival; and they prepare [lit., make] a kid roasted whole for Passover evening."

F. And sages prohibit.

M. Beṣ. 2.6-7 (M. ʿEd. 3.10-11; A-C = b. Shab. 39b; D = b. Pes. 36b-37a)

Comment: The rulings of A are explained as follows: Cooking is permitted on a festival day for the needs of that day, but not for preparation for another day. Covering up hot food, to retain its warmth for the Sabbath, is considered by Gamaliel to be tantamount to cooking for the Sabbath; so it is a form of unnecessary labor on the festival. The same principle is involved in the third ruling. Since it is possible that a large loaf of bread might not be entirely consumed on the festival, what is left over may be construed as having been prepared on the festival for the sake of the following day. The candelabrum mentioned is composed of sections which are put together in the evenings, when the lamps are lit, and dis-assembled in the morning for storage. Gamaliel considers the re-assembly of such a candelabrum to be building, and hence forbidden on the festival.

The lenient rulings of D are as follows: The couches mentioned are for dining, in Roman style, and the area between them, where the food would be brought, would collect scraps and crumbs in the course of a meal. The sages prohibit sweeping, to prevent inadvertent smoothing of the earthen floor; but Gamaliel is not concerned about such a possible violation of the festival prohibitions against labor. Similarly, the sages prohibit the burning of incense, an air-freshener, as unnecessary labor; but Gamaliel does not. Finally, the sages prohibit the roasting whole of a kid on Passover, because it resembles the biblical Passover-offering, which should be prepared only at the Temple (now destroyed). Gamaliel wishes to establish a continuity between the Yavnean Passover Seder and the predestruction Temple observance, and permits it. (See Allon, Toledot, I, pp. 164-166.)

Turning to the structure of the pericope, B presents the three Shammaitic rulings of Gamaliel. We assume Hillelite opposition, but where we would expect, "And the sages permit", it does not appear. C presents a saying by Gamaliel about the third of the three rulings; D turns it into a debate. Since C-D does not respond to the whole of B, but only to its third ruling, C-D is probably independent of A-B. This supposition is strengthened by the triumph of the anonymous sages over Gamaliel, silencing him, in C-D. It contrasts with B, which is not framed as a dispute. C-D has been supplied to represent the opposition to Gamaliel's views in B. Gamaliel points to the precedent of his father's house, but the sages reinterpret the situation in accord with their own view. Their reply is standard for dealing with Shammaitic opinion. "Shammaitic teachings . . . generally are made to apply to the authority himself, but the rule for the people is different (Neusner, Pharisees, ii, p. 380)."

Concerning the third ruling, we also note that (in contrast with the first two rulings) neither in the lemma (B) nor in the story (C) is there a mention of the festival. It is possible that C is the source for the law in B; but the third ruling was not connected with a festival until its redaction into B. The "thin cakes" may reflect the tradition of the delicacy of the Patriarch, as in M. Ber. 2.6. The development of this part of the pericope would then be: C, the first-person story, gives rise to the lemma-formulation, redacted into B; A + B + D are joined for a balanced pericope of 3 + 3 rulings. If the original pericope were A + B + D, the latter would be easily joined to B by ʾP, "moreover". Then C-D is added to supply opposition to B.

Our pericope is the only source identifying these three rulings as opinions of the House of Shammai. However, two baraitot on b. Beṣ. 22b identify the ruling on baking thick cakes as a Shammaite rule. One connects the rule with Passover; the other applies it to any festival. This ambiguity suggests that the Shammaite rule may have been formulated on the basis of the Gamaliel-pericope, which lacked such specificity. Could it be that the method of opposition used in the debate, C-D, led to the supposition that the strict rulings were an opinion of the House of Shammai, and that the words, "According to the words of the House of Shammai" in A are a gloss? Certainly the phrase is absent from E, where it might be expected on the grounds of balance; and we have lists of rulings where the Shammaites were more lenient than their opposition.

The collection of rulings in this pericope is also found in M. ʿEd., the anthology of laws according to the names of their authors. We note that two of the stringent rulings concern food-preparation on a holiday, in order to avoid the possibility of cooking something for the day following the holiday. This stands in contrast to M. Beṣ. 1.8; there the same issue is involved (the preparation of beans) and Gamaliel is more lenient than the Hillelites, permitting a larger amount to be prepared for a meal.

A. In Rabban Gamaliel's house they did not reassemble a candelabrum on festival nights.

B. 1. (WMʿSH B) Rabban Gamaliel and the elders were reclining [First printed edition, Vienna and London mss. add: in Rome] and the candelabrum fell [apart] on a festival night. 2. R. ʿAqiva rose and re-assembled it.

3. Said Rabban Gamaliel to him, "ʿAqiva, why do you poke your head into the dispute?"

4. He said to him, "You taught us to follow the majority (Ex. 23:2). Even though you forbid and they permit [it], the halakah is according to the words of the majority."

C. R. Judah says in the name of Rabban Gamaliel, "They carry the candelabrum on a festival, but they do not re-assemble it."

D. In Rabban Gamaliel's house they used to sweep between the couches on a festival.

E. Said R. Leazar b. R. Ṣadoq, "We ate at Rabban Gamaliel's house many times, and I never saw them sweep between the couches. Rather they used to spread sheets [on the ground] from the eve of the holiday. When the guests entered, they'd remove them."

They said to him, "If so, it is even permitted to do so on the Sabbath."

F. In Rabban Gamaliel's house they used to bring [burning] incense [into the dining room, on a holiday] in an airtight container.

G. Said R. Leazar b. R. Ṣadoq, "We ate at Rabban Gamaliel's house many times, and I never saw them bring incense in an airtight container. Rather: they used to [fill] casks [with the] smoke [of spices] from the eve of the holiday, and when the guests came they'd open them."

They said to him, "If so, it is even permitted to do so on the Sabbath."

Tos. Beṣ. 2.12-14 (Lieberman
ed. pp. 289-290, lines 43-56)

Comment: The Toseftan Gamaliel-materials transmit one of the strict rules of M. Beṣ./M. ʿEd. (candelabrum) and two of the leniencies (sweeping, spices). There is no mention of relation to a Houses-dispute, strengthening the supposition that this was a later ascription of Shammaite character to those Gamaliel-rulings.

A presents Gamaliel's prohibition of re-assembling a candelabrum on a festival as a report of the practice in his household. A short story follows (B. 1-2) in which ʿAqiva acts on the more lenient position of the sages, in Gamaliel's presence. This is followed by a dialogue (B. 3-4) in which ʿAqiva answers Gamaliel's objection by quoting Gamaliel's own principle of majority rule. (This dialogue is also used in different stories, in Tos. Ber. 4.15 and Tos. Dem. 5.24.) But as B stems from an anti-Gamaliel point of view, C once again adds material from Gamaliel's own tradition. Judah (C) quotes another version of the ruling, in Gamaliel's name, with the added detail that a candelabrum may be carried on the festival. This seems to be an elaboration of the story in A, and thus provides an Ushan attestation for the law, and for the priority of the story-form of the legal ruling.

D-E and F-G provide two revisions, by Eleazar b. Ṣadoq, of the leniencies of Gamaliel. In each case, the rule is reported as a practice in Gamaliel's house (they swept between the couches, they brought spices in a sealed container). Eleazar reports that the practice was not as narrated; rather it was done in a way which did not contradict the ruling of the Hillelites, thus emphasizing Gamaliel as a Hillelite. Sheets spread on the ground to catch the crumbs were removed before guests arrived. Thus there was no sweeping of the floor on the festival. The smoke of incense was caught in sealed casks before the festival, and later opened; so spices were not burned on the festival. After Eleazar's report, revising the tradition both here and, in a different form, in the Mishnah, Eleazar's anonymous contemporaries reply that there would be no disagreement between the sages and Gamaliel. The method he used was even acceptable on the Sabbath, and certainly on a festival. Eleazar's revision has removed the conflict between Gamaliel and the sages, by reinterpreting Gamaliel to agree with them. But if that were the case, why is a dispute recorded? Their answer implicitly challenges Eleazar's revision of Gamaliel's position.

Both Judah and Eleazar provide Ushan attestation for the substance of M. Beṣ. 2.6-7. Judah does so directly, in an independent statement. Eleazar does so indirectly, through his perplexity in squaring Gamaliel with the majority view. This would point to the tradition of M. Beṣ. 2.6-7 A + D as being fixed rather early in Usha.

A. In Rabban Gamaliel's house they used to sweep between the couches [on a festival].

B. R. Leazar b. R. Ṣadoq said, "Many times I dined at Rabban Gamaliel's; and they did not sweep between the couches. Rather they used to spread sheets on the ground. When the guests would leave, they'd fold them up."

C. They said to him, "If so, it is even permitted to do so on the Sabbath."

D. In Rabban Gamaliel's house they used to bring [burning] incense [into the dining room, on a holiday] in an air-tight container.

E. R. Eleazar b. R. Ṣadoq said, "Many times I dined at Rabban Gamaliel's; and they did not bring in the incense in an airtight container. Rather: they used to [fill] casks [with the] smoke [of spices] from the eve of the holiday, and when the guests came they'd open them."

F. They said to him, "If so, it is even permitted to do so on the Sabbath."

y. Beṣ. 2.7

Comment: Except for minor variations in language, y. is identical with Tos. Y.Ṭ., D-G.

A. An objection was raised: They do not sweep between the couches on a festival, but in the house of Rabban Gamaliel they sweep.

B. Said R. Eliezer b. Ṣadoq, "Many times I entered the house of Rabban Gamaliel after my father, and they did not sweep between the couches on a festival. Rather, they would sweep them [the areas] on the eve of the festival and cover them with sheets. On the next day, when guests would enter, they would remove the sheets and the house was found to be already swept."

C. They said to him, "If so, it is even permitted to do so on the Sabbath."

D. And they do not put incense [on the fire] on a festival, but in the house of Rabban Gamaliel they put [incense on the fire].

E. Said R. Eliezer b. Ṣadoq, "Many times I entered the house of Rabban Gamaliel after my father, and they would not put incense [on the fire] on a festival. Rather, they would bring in iron casks and [fill] them [with] smoke on the eve of the festival. On the next day, when guests would enter, they would open the holes, and the house was found to be already perfumed."

F. They said to him, "If so, it is even permitted to do so on the Sabbath."

b. Beṣ. 22b

Comment: b. supplies a few variations of language to what is a re-telling of the Toseftan pericope, with some added details (house was found to be swept, iron casks).

A. In Rabban Gamaliel's house they used to grind pepper in their mills [on the holidays].

B. Said R. Leazar b. R. Ṣadoq, "Once father was reclining [at dinner] before Rabban Gamaliel and they brought him elaiogaron and exagaron [sauce] with ground pepper on it. Father withdrew his hand from them.

"Said to him Rabban Gamaliel, 'Don't worry about them: they were ground before the eve of the festival.'"

Tos. Beṣ. 2.16 (Lieberman ed. p. 291, lines 62-66; y. Shab. 7.2)

Comment: This is the third pericope in the small collection of Gamaliel's leniencies in festival law. All share the same structure: In Gamaliel's house + leniency + Eleazar b. Ṣadoq's denial. Eleazar takes pains to show that Gamaliel really acted in accord with the sages in these cases; he is probably responsible for the collection (Tos. Beṣ. 2.13, 14, 16).

Here A represents Gamaliel as permitting the use of a pepper-mill on the festival; but in B Eleazar recounts an incident to show he did not. Lieberman explains the sauces as flavoring a muries, a fish appetizer which could have a wine-sauce (elaiogaron) or vinegar-sauce (exagaron). He notes that M. has accepted Eleazar's revision, since M. Beṣ. 2.8 assigns the view permitting grinding pepper to Eleazar b. ʿAzariah (T.K., IV, p. 960).

A. In Rabban Gamaliel's house they used to grind pepper in their mills [on the holidays].

B. Said R. Eleazar b. R. Ṣadoq, "Once father dined at Rabban Gamaliel's. They brought him elaiogaron [sauce] with ground peppers in it. When he had tasted them, he withdrew his hand from them.

"Said to him Rabban Gamaliel, 'Don't worry, they were ground on the eve of the holiday.'"

C. And would Rabbi Ṣadoq act as one unknowing, at Rabban Gamaliel's, and eat? Rather: [he refrained from eating so that people would] not [think that] Rabban Gamaliel permitted work [on a holiday].

y. Beṣ. 2.8

Comment: The y. version varies slightly, and adds an Amoraic comment (C).

A. [If] traps for animals, birds or fish were set before the eve of a festival (MʿRB YWM ṬWB), [a man] does not take anything out of them on the festival, unless he knows they were caught before the festival [began].

B. (WM‘SH B) A gentile brought fish to Rabban Gamaliel. He said, "They are permitted, but I have no wish to accept them from him."

M. Beṣ. 3.2

<u>Comment</u>: M. Shab. 1.6 states: "The House of Shammai say, 'They spread traps for animals or birds or fish only in order that they may be caught while it is still day (MB‘WD YWM).' And the House of Hillel permit."

The anonymous law in A of our pericope takes that Hillelite permission for granted, and applies its view to the situation of a festival. It is assumed that traps may be set prior to a festival, just as before the Sabbath. The question now concerns an animal which may have been trapped on the festival. Something not intended for use on a festival may not be handled on that day. If it is not known whether an animal was caught before the festival, it could not have been intended for use on the festival. Therefore it may not be handled.

The story in B is used to make the opposite point: the fish are permitted. But considered out of context, there is nothing in the story itself to tie it to a festival, or to a trap set before a festival, or to the removal of fish from a trap. B might equally concern some aspect of Sabbath law, or the permissibility of a species of fish, or of food prepared by a gentile. The redactor of the pericope, adding the story with a simple conjunction (W), has created a dispute which presents Gamaliel as stating a view more lenient than the Hillelite position, and independent of both the Houses. That he does not accept the fish could be a momentary preference, or a voluntary self-restriction, a mark of extra piety. We do have other pericopae in which Gamaliel declares certain things permitted, yet submits to a stricter law (Tos. Ter. 2.13, Tos. M.Q. 2.14).

Once again, a narrative has been used, when "And Rabban Gamaliel permits" could have served.

x. Rosh Hashanah

A. For two New Moons they profane the Sabbath: for Nisan and Tishré;

B. for on them messengers would go out to Syria, and by them they would set the festivals;

C. and when the Temple still stood they would profane [the Sabbath] for all of them, in order to set the [time of the New Moon] offering.

D. Whether it is clearly seen or whether it is not clearly seen, they profane the Sabbath for it.

E. R. Yosé says, "If it is clearly seen, they do not profane the Sabbath for it."

F. (M‘SH Š) More than forty pairs [of witnesses] came forward, but Rabbi ‘Aqiva stopped them in Lud. Rabban Gamaliel sent [a message] to him, "If you stop the multitude from coming, you will find yourself causing them to stumble in the future."

M. R.H. 1.4-6 (y. R.H. 1.5;
D = y. M.Q. 3.1)

Comment: The court, on its authority, proclaims the New Moon as a legal fact. Since this fixing of the calendar is necessary for determining the dates of the New Year and Passover, witnesses coming to testify that they had seen the New Moon are allowed to travel to the seat of the Sanhedrin, even on the Sabbath.

A states the law; B and C explain it, in terms of post-70 and pre-70 practice. D-E depend upon A: D elaborating upon A with Yosé's lemma disputing the anonymous statement. Yosé's dispute provides an Ushan attestation for A if not A-C.

F is the proper continuation of A; since it makes no reference either to the New Moon or to the violation of the Sabbath, it depends upon A. Gamaliel is concerned that witnesses may assume that others would be making the journey to testify to the appearance of the moon, and that the court would be deprived of valid witnesses. His exception to the prohibition against Sabbath travel appears to be an extension of the policies of Gamaliel I, who eased the restrictions on movement within Jerusalem for witnesses to the New Moon (M.R.H. 2.5).

The story (which could be reformulated as a Gamaliel-‘Aqiva dispute) reflects Gamaliel's emphasis on the importance of the

Patriarchal court as successor to the Temple's prerogatives. We assume that the location of the court would be Yavneh; but the phrase "in Lud" (BLWD) could stand at the end of one sentence, or at the beginning of the other. It might also refer to Gamaliel's temporary residence. Some other pericopae do place Gamaliel at Lud (Tos. Pes. 2.11, Tos. Pes. 10.12).

F may have been part of the pericope prior to Yosé's comment (E); or it may equally-well have been added by the redactor of the Mishnah, with his penchant for Patriarchal illustrative material.

A. (M'SH Š) More than forty pairs of witnesses came forward, but R. 'Aqiva stopped them in Lud.

B. (Because there were forty pairs; but if there had been one pair, he would not have stopped them.)

C. Rabban Gamaliel sent [a message] to him, "If you stop the multitude from coming, you will find yourself causing them to stumble in the future."

D. Do not be found stopping the multitude from performing a _miṣvah_, for anyone who stops the multitude from performing a _miṣvah_ must be placed under a ban.

E. R. Judah said, "Shall we conclude [there]?" Heaven forbid! Rabbi 'Aqiva was not placed under the ban: rather, it was the officer of Geder [who stopped the witnesses] and Rabban Gamaliel sent [word] and removed him from his post.

y. R. H. 1.5

Comment: Once again Judah presents a revision of a tradition about Gamaliel, in this case M.R.H. 1.6. A + D are the story from M.; B is an anonymous comment in 'Aqiva's defense, and D states a legal penalty which can apply to A. Judah's remark depends upon all of the foregoing. It refers to the ban, as well as to the story. Judah understands 'Aqiva's role in the narrative as uncomplimentary to 'Aqiva, probably since Gamaliel criticizes his actions. Judah substitutes a nameless local official, who is fired for his error. Without Judah's defense of 'Aqiva, we would not have considered the incident as so serious in nature. It indicates again the importance of fixing the calendar, and of the court which has that power. This in turn helps explain the desire of the Patriarch to guard the prerogatives of his office, in making such decisions.

It was taught (TNY'): R. Judah said, "Heaven forbid [that we think] that R. 'Aqiva prevented them! It was Shazpar, head of

Geder who prevented them; and Rabban Gamaliel sent [a message] and they deposed him from his greatness [of office]."

b. R. H. 22a

Comment: The b. version of Judah's comment is briefer than y., and makes no reference to the ban. But b. does supply a name for the official, and the name of the town is the same, so perhaps b. may depend upon y.

A. Rabban Gamaliel had pictures of the shapes of the moon on a tablet and on the wall of his upper room, which he used to show to the untrained people (HDYWṬWT) and say, "Did you see it in this way or in that?"

B. 1. (M‘SH Š) Two came and said, "We saw it in the east in the morning and in the west in the evening."

2. R. Yohanan b. Nuri said, "They are false witnesses."

3. When they came to Yavneh, Rabban Gamaliel accepted [their evidence].

C. 1. Again, two came and said, "We saw it at its expected time, yet in the night of the added day it did not appear."

2. And Rabban Gamaliel accepted [their evidence].

3. R. Dosa b. Harkinas said, "They are false witnesses: how can they testify about a woman that she has given birth if the next day her belly is between her teeth?"

4. R. Joshua said to him, "I approve your words."

D. Rabban Gamaliel sent him [a message], "I charge you to come to me, with your staff and your money, on the Day of Atonement as it falls according to your reckoning."

E. R. ‘Aqiva went [to R. Joshua] and found him troubled. He said to him, "I am able to learn that whatever Rabban Gamaliel has done is done, for it is written, *These are the set feasts of the Holy Lord, holy convocations, which you shall proclaim* (Lev. 23:4). Whether in their time or whether not in their time, I have no other *set feasts* but these."

F. [R. Joshua] went (B’ LW) to R. Dosa b. Harkinas. He said to him, "If we come to judge [the decisions of] the court of Rabban Gamaliel, we shall have to judge [the decisions of] every court which has arisen from the days of Moses until now.

G. "For it is written, *Then went up Moses and Aaron, Nadav and Avihu, and seventy of the elders of Israel* (Ex. 24:9). And why are the names of the elders not spelled out (NTPRŠW)? Rather, it is to teach that any three [judges] who arise as a court over Israel are like the court of Moses."

H. He took his staff and his money in his hand, and went to Yavneh to Rabban Gamaliel on the day which fell as the Day of Atonement according to his reckoning. Rabban Gamaliel stood up and kissed him on his head. He said to him, "Come in peace, my master and my disciple: my master in wisdom, and my disciple, in that you have accepted [K, P, Camb.: upon yourself; N.: upon himself] my words."

M. R.H. 2.8-9
(A = b. A.Z. 43a; b. R.H. 25a)

Comment: This pericope is unusual in its length and sustained, careful development. One must go to the most highly reworked pericopae in b. for a comparably polished narration. This testifies to the importance of the traditions dealt with here, in the eyes of the Patriarchal tradents whose authority the pericope supports. I rely in great part upon the insights of W. Green (Joshua, ad. loc. and have indicated this by [WG] where I have not quoted him directly.

A serves to link the pericope with the subject of M.R.H. 2.6: the detailed examination of the witnesses to the alleged appearance of the New Moon (see Epstein, Mevo'ot, p. 366). Its function within the narrative is to soften the effects of B-C. The latter units will show Gamaliel in error, accepting improper testimony. A asserts Gamaliel's careful examination of the witnesses available to him.

The body of the pericope depicts the two phases of the action: in B-C Gamaliel accepts incorrect reports about the new moon; in D-H Gamaliel orders Joshua to appear at Yavneh, and Joshua complies.

There is a doubling of material in each of these phases. B and C each report an objection to Gamaliel's acceptance of false testimony. E and F-G both supply counsel to Joshua, justifying Gamaliel's power to achieve a fait accompli in his fixing of the calendar. In each case, one of the units appears intrusive.

B is an addition to the pericope, unrelated to the main line of the narrative, and not sympathetic to Gamaliel. It says: Even Yoḥanan b. Nuri, elsewhere represented as a partisan of Gamaliel and one of his officials, once publicly stated that the Patriarch accepted false testimony about the new moon. The editor did not intend to connect Yoḥanan b. Nuri directly with the events of the Joshua story, as indicated by the joining language of C. 1: "And more, two came" (W'WD B'W ŠNYM). But he did wish to incorporate stories circulated by others, uncomplimentary to Gamaliel, within a structure that would at least neutralize their effect.

B does help, however, to cast light upon the original form of C [WG], since it follows the pattern of a number of M'SH stories about Gamaliel: (1) M'SH + action (2) + question or contrary opinion (3) + Gamaliel's answer or ruling. Gamaliel's answer would come last, since he is the focus of the M'SH. C has reversed elements (2) and (3), in order to add Joshua's agreement with Dosa. Without it, C would follow the pattern of B by the sequence C.1 + 3 + 2.

E is also an addition: it has ʿAqiva, who is previously unmentioned, visit Joshua, and give him an interpretation of Lev. 23:4. Indications of the relative autonomy of this unit in the pericope are: (a) ʿAqiva's intrusion; (b) [WG] ʿAqiva's support of the Patriarch, contrary to M.R.H. 1.6, where he attempts to prevent witnesses from testifying before Gamaliel; and (c) the sole use of an adjective descriptive of emotions (MṢR) whereas elsewhere we have only descriptions of behavior.

G also, which affirms the equality of all courts with that of Moses, is probably another elaboration, providing F with an exegetical base.

With B and E, and possibly G, as another exegesis -- removed from our narrative, we are left with C+D+F+G, a non-repetitive story with three characters, Gamaliel, Joshua and Dosa b. Harkinas -- all of whom appear in both parts of the action. It is important to observe [WG] that, in contrast to Dosa, Joshua is named only once (C. 4) within the narrative, when he agrees with Dosa. In F, where Dosa seems curiously to reverse himself, the words make more sense if said to Dosa than by him [WG]. In other words, as Green suggests, C+D+F+H carefully examined reads as a story about a disagreement between Dosa and Gamaliel, which has been converted into a Joshua-Gamaliel story by the addition of C. 4.

Dosa appears often, Green points out, as a representative of priestly interests. Since, in the Temple, the priesthood was in charge of the calendar, this was a prerogative they were reluctant to surrender. Neusner has suggested (Life, 214-215) that Gamaliel had need of priestly co-operation after he succeeded Yoḥanan b. Zakkai. The narrative, representing a conflict between Gamaliel and Dosa, may be seen as (1) Gamaliel's assertion of Patriarchal authority over the priestly circle, (2) his concurrent attempt to mollify them by explaining that the decisions of any court (not just Gamaliel's) must stand, and (3) his compliment to their statesmanship in accepting his authority for the good of society ("my master in wisdom").

As Green concludes, "When priestly opposition died out, but rabbinical-Patriarchal conflict persisted, the insertion of C. 4 would have been a convenient way to allow the pericope to serve other purposes." From then on, the narrative would make the same point for the Patriarchate against the rabbis, through Joshua, who would be seen as representative, and also assert Gamaliel's magnanimity in victory.

The point at issue, the determination of the New Year, must be seen in the light of Yavnean claims to the Temple's religious authority. The Temple expressed sacred reality not only in space but also in time. Just as the sacrificial rites, by conformity with laws of the Torah, gave the priesthood a measure of participation in and control over aspects of the sacred, so too did the priests' role in proclaiming the sacred times of the year provide them with the power to define reality, both sacred and profane. We know from the example of Qumran that the proper calendar was an issue of sectarian division: to deviate from the proper time of the sacred calendar would be to violate the divine will. After the fall of the Temple, when Yoḥanan ben Zakkai established the precedent of sounding the *shofar* at Yavneh, he preempted from the priests that single aspect of sacred reality which survived the destruction, the temporal. Gamaliel here followed Yoḥanan's example in clearly establishing his prerogative for this act of religious definition. Indeed, the remarkable claim of this pericope, contrary to Dosa and Joshua's assumption that the correct time of the New Moon is a natural fact to be *discovered*, is that Gamaliel's action shows astronomical facts to be secondary to the power of the court to *decree* the sacred time, in effect to create it. Insofar as the sacred seasons reflect the divine will for celebration, the assertion that the court does not merely find out what is in God's mind, but actually decides what God's will is to be, is a dazzling declaration.

Our narrative goes only so far as to claim that Gamaliel was able to impose this view upon the rabbis. Whether the patriarchal authority to declare the calendar extended beyond Yavneh and the rabbinic group cannot be determined. But implicitly, this subject was one on which the rabbinic practice could reach out to affect the world of the ordinary Palestinian Jew, who may not have adopted the rabbinic definition of proper behavior regarding tithes, blessings or the intricacies of purity laws. Rather than keeping his own calendar, the ordinary person would be likely to accept an official proclamation about *when* the New Year and Day of Atonement would take place, whatever the details of his holy day behavior.

And accepting a Yavnean decree in one matter potentially could lead to accepting Yavnean authority in other matters too. Further, this was an area of authority which held the potential for reaching out to Diaspora Jewry as well, and reforging the link which had existed between the Temple authorities and the communities of Jews within the Roman world and beyond it. The implications of Diaspora wealth and influence were never lost to any leader. Thus the issue of the narrative is at once economic and political, as well as theological.

It was taught (TNY'): Rabban Gamaliel said to the sages, "Thus was it received by me [in tradition] from the house of my father's father: There are times when it comes by a long [way] and there are times when it comes by a short [way]."

b. R.H. 25a

Comment: This is understood by the redactor of b. to refer to the decision criticized by Yoḥanan b. Nuri in M.R.H. 2.8-9B. Gamaliel appeals to a family tradition that it is possible for the moon to be seen in the eastern sky in the morning and in the west in the evening of the same day. Gamaliel would have reasons behind his acceptance of the witnesses' testimony, and this baraita provides one, in a form characteristic of Gamaliel pericopae. M. was not interested in Gamaliel's reasoning, even though Dosa's critique is given there. M. is interested rather in Gamaliel's authority.

Our rabbis taught (TNW RBNN): Once the heavens were covered with clouds, and the shape of the moon was seen on the twenty-ninth of the month. Since the people thought a new moon should be declared, and the bet din sought to sanctify it [the new moon], Rabban Gamaliel said to them, "Thus was it received by me [in tradition] from the house of my father's father, that the renewal of the moon does not take place until after twenty-nine and a half days, and two-thirds of an hour, plus 73 ḥalaqin [= 73/1080 hrs.]."

B. On that same day the mother of Ben Zaza died. And Rabban Gamaliel gave an extensive eulogy on her behalf; not because she was worthy of it, but in order that the people should know that the court had not sanctified the month.

b. R.H. 25a

Comment: Just as in the previous baraita Gamaliel accepted visual evidence, on the basis of a tradition indicating it was reliable (though the sighting seemed remarkably early) in A he rejects visual evidence, on the same grounds of family tradition. Together, the two baraitot establish a theoretical defense for Gamaliel's actions in M.R.H. 2.6-8.

The day of the New Moon was a minor holiday, and eulogies were prohibited, since they added to the grief of the community. Once more, in b. Gamaliel's action is pointed to, instead of quoting his words.

A. Just as the agent of the congregation (ŠLYḤ ṢYBWR) is required [to say the blessings of the Rosh Hashanah prayer], so is each individual person required [to do so].

B. Rabban Gamaliel says, "The agent of the congregation fulfils that requirement for the many [K omits: for the many]."

M.R.H. 4.9

Comment: Our explanation of this dispute follows the discussion in Tos. R.H. 2.18, below. The anonymous law (A) makes the ʿAmidah prayer by the leader, on behalf of the congregation, a vicariously effective act only for those persons who do not know the prayer. Those who know it must recite it themselves; his action is not effective on their behalf.

Gamaliel (B) insists that the leader's recitation of the Rosh Hashanah ʿAmidah is effective in fulfilling the obligation of all of the congregation. This appears to be inconsistent with Gamaliel's view in M. Ber. 4.3. There he requires every individual to recite the daily Eighteen blessings of the ʿAmidah. Bertinoro assumes that, since the Rosh Hashanah prayer is more complex, Gamaliel does not require its memorization. This would be consistent with Gamaliel's requirement of an official text of the prayer. If the anonymous view (A), like Joshua in M., required only something "like" the Rosh Hashanah prayer, an epitome, each individual could also be required to recite it on his own. In other words, Gamaliel's stringency in M. Ber. 4.3 accounts for his leniency here; and the case is reversed for the anonymous law in A.

Maimonides assumes a more complete harmony between the dispute of M. Ber. 4.3 and the one here: Gamaliel requires the official text of all blessings of the ʿAmidah, daily as well as Rosh Hashanah. Therefore, the leader's role becomes crucial at all times; and he is able to discharge the obligation of the entire congregation.

Though in B Gamaliel appears to be commenting on an earlier law, Tos. R.H. 2.18 shows this not to be the case. His argument is with the "sages", his contemporaries. So the question of the function of the prayer leader may be assigned to the liturgical agenda of Yavneh under Gamaliel's reign. The role of the leader, in Gamaliel's ruling, appears quite "priestly" on behalf of the congregation. This may be another indication of the desire to transfer as many overtones of the Temple as possible to the post-70 institutions of synagogue and court.

A. Rabban Gamaliel says, "The agent of the congregation fulfills the requirement [of reciting the Rosh Hashanah Prayer] for the many."

B. And sages say, "Each individual fulfills his own [obligation]."

C. He said to them, "If so, why do they bring him down before the Ark?"

D. They said to him, "In order to fulfill [the obligation of] one who does not know [how to pray]."

E. He said to them, "Just as he fulfills [the obligation of] one who doesn't know, he fulfills [the obligation of] one who does know."

F. They said to him, "If so, why does each individual pray by himself?"

G. They said, "In order that the leader should [have time to] prepare himself."

Tos. R.H. 2.18 (Lieberman
ed. p. 321, lines 96-104)

Comment: The pericope has some textual difficulties. In the Lieberman text, C-D is repeated twice within the pericope: Its units are as follows, A-B-C-D-F-G-C-D-E. Besides this difference in order, the Lieberman text of F begins, "He said to them", rather than the reverse.

There is one further logical problem involving the speakers in F-G. F is a question asked by the sages, who hold the obligation of the individual to pray. G is logically Gamaliel's reply, since he must justify the congregation's individual prayer, holding as he does that the leader's prayer will fulfill the obligation of the many. Despite the agreement of other mss. to the contrary, G should read, "He said", as in the London ms. and the first printed Tos.

A-B presents the dispute, with Gamaliel's ruling equivalent to the topic sentence, followed by the sages' dissent. C-G presents a debate, with two exchanges. Gamaliel challenges the sages in C-E, and disposes of their reply. They ask a further question of him (F), but he answers their objection (G). It is clear that Gamaliel predominates in the dispute; in contrast to M., his view comes first. In the same way, he predominates in the debate. It is unusual for M. to have selected material less favorable to Gamaliel than that in Tos.

A. It was taught (TNY'): They said to Rabban Gamaliel "[According] to your words, why does the congregation pray?"

B. He said to them, "In order for the agent of the congregation to arrange his prayer."

C. Rabban Gamaliel said to them, "[According] to your words, why does the agent of the congregation go down before the Ark?"

D. They said to him, "In order to fulfill [the requirement for] one who is not familiar (BQY) [with the details of the prayer]."

E. He said to them, "Just as he fulfills [the obligation of] one who is not familiar, so he fulfills [the obligation of] one who is familiar."

b. R.H. 34b

Comment: Here the debate occurs without the dispute which preceded it in Tos., and the two units of the debate, A-B and C-E, are in reverse order. There are differences in diction, even though the sentence structures are the same: "bring him down"/"go down", "does not know"/"is not familiar", "prepare himself"/ "arrange his prayer". All of this points to the independence of the dispute and the two elements of the debate from each other. They have been redacted slightly differently in M., Tos. and b.

We note that none of the three versions makes explicit mention of Rosh Hashanah. It is the redaction which has applied this dispute to the context of Rosh Hashanah. Perhaps the unacceptability of the augmented role of the leader, and the diminished role of the congregation, led to this restriction of Gamaliel's view to the complex New Year liturgy. This might also explain why, though all of the units in Tos. and b. reflect Gamaliel's primary position, in M. his view is secondary.

A. R. Aḥa b. ʿAvira said in the name of R. Simeon the Ḥasid, "Rabban Gamaliel used to free even the people in the fields [of their obligation to pray, through the prayer of the leader in the synagogue], and needless to say those in town."

B. . . . when Rabin came [from Palestine, he said that] R. Jacob b. Idi said, "R. Simeon the Ḥasid said, 'Rabban Gamaliel freed only the people in the fields [vicariously, of their obligation to pray]. What is the reason? Because they are forced by their work [to remain away from the synagogue]. But those in town are not [freed of their obligation by the leader].'"

b. R.H. 35a

Comment: Babylonian Amoraim, in the middle of the fourth century, attempt to determine the extent of the ability of the leader to fulfill the requirement of prayer for the community. They rely upon early fourth century tradents quoting Simeon the Ḥasid (late third century). There is a gap of about a century between Simeon and Gamaliel.

A explains that Gamaliel's lemma (M.R.H. 4.9) applies not only to persons within the synagogue, but even to those outside of the town. The lemma is understood not as applying only to the Rosh Hashanah prayer, as does Tos. (or else, what are the people doing working in the fields?) but to the regular daily prayer.

In B, Jacob b. Idi's revision of the explanation attempts to harmonize Gamaliel, as much as possible, with the sages' ruling, by restricting the power of the leader's prayer to fulfill the responsibility only of those living outside the town. Here too, the lemma is explained as applying to the daily prayer.

In both A and B, Gamaliel is not quoted directly, nor is a story told about his behavior (the two main forms of Gamaliel legal traditions). While this is not conclusive evidence of authenticity, it would still seem that Gamaliel's fairly terse lemma became detached from its context of the Rosh Hashanah prayer, and was used once more as a general statement about the prayer of the leader. This gave rise to explanations like A, and later, B.

xi. Ta'anit, Mo'ed Qatan, Ḥagigah

A. On the third [day] of Marḥeshvan, they ask for rain.

B. Rabban Gamaliel says, "On the seventh, fifteen days after the Festival [of Sukkot], so that the last of the Israelites can reach the Euphrates river."

M. Ta. 1.3 (b. Ta. 4b, 6a;
b. B.M. 28a)

Comment: Gamaliel (B) wants the prayer for rain delayed, so that rains will not interfere with the return of visitors to Jerusalem to their homes.

If this statement is indeed from our Gamaliel, and not his grandfather, he may be quoting a source from Temple times, possibly from his father, Simeon b. Gamaliel I.

A. They do not decree a public fast on the first day of the month, or on Ḥanukkah or Purim.

B. "But if they had begun, they do not interrupt [the fast]," the words of Rabban Gamaliel.

C. R. Meir said, "Although Rabban Gamaliel has said, 'They do not interrupt,' he admitted that they do not complete [the whole day]."

D. And the same with the Ninth of Av, if it fell on the eve of [P omits: eve of] a Sabbath.

M. Ta. 2.10 (b. 'Eruv. 41a)

Comment: The New Moon is considered a minor festival; a fast day would conflict with its celebratory mood. The same is true for the minor festivals of Ḥanukkah and Purim.

Gamaliel (B) disputes this anonymous rule, by restricting it to a before-the-fact prohibition. If the day has been proclaimed, he permits it to continue. Meir, in turn, uses the same method to harmonize Gamaliel with A, explaining that Gamaliel agreed with A in part. The fast is not to be continued throughout the day.

Meir's words provide an Ushan attestation for A-B. D adds that when the Ninth of Av occurs on a Friday, it also is terminated early, before nightfall; it must be subsequent to Meir.

A. (M'SH W) They decreed a fast during Ḥanukkah, in Lud. They told R. Liezer: he cut his hair; they told R. Joshua: he bathed. R. Joshua said to them, "Get out of here, and fast in addition to what you already fasted!"

B. All the time Rabban Gamaliel was alive, the halakah followed his words. After Rabban Gamaliel's death, R. Joshua sought to cancel his words.

R. Yoḥanan b. Nuri stood up and said, "*I see that the body follows the head!* All the time Rabban Gamaliel was alive, the halakah would follow his words. Now that he is dead, you're cancelling his words!"

C. He said to him, "Joshua, we will not listen to you! The halakah is set according to Rabban Gamaliel."

D. And no one objected one bit.

Tos. Ta. 2.5 [Aramaic italicized] (Lieberman ed. p. 331, lines 36-43; b. 'Eruv. 41a)

Comment: A reports the agreement of Eliezer and Joshua with the anonymous law of M. Ta. 2.10, and hence their dispute with Gamaliel. For the story to place Eliezer in Lud is understandable; for him not to be decisive in determining the law in his own town is significant. Since the people of the town follow the ruling attributed to Gamaliel, this story may be counted with those pericopae which associate Gamaliel with Lud.

B-D recounts an abortive revolt against Gamaliel's halakic authority, led by Joshua after Gamaliel's death. The point of view is pro-Gamaliel, probably from a follower of Yoḥanan b. Nuri. By itself, B does not indicate that the question of fasting on a minor holiday was the point of issue. In fact, considering that in M. Ta. 2.10 the opposite view comes first, and that Meir revises Gamaliel's position, it is doubtful that the later generations were that faithful to Gamaliel's ruling on this particular point. B-D is an independent story, and gives no indication which, or how many, of Gamaliel's "words" Joshua intended to nullify. Likewise, we cannot be sure how extensive a body of law is here defended as "set", according to Gamaliel's authority.

Significantly, the story shows Joshua in keeping with the role preserved for him in his circle as an independent authority, and with the role taken for granted by M.R.H. 2.8-9 as Gamaliel's active opponent.

A. [If a man] buries his dead three days before the feast [of Sukkot], the rule of seven [days' mourning] is annulled for him. [If] eight [days before], the rule of thirty [days] is annulled for him.

B. Because they said, "The Sabbath is included [in the first seven days] and does not interrupt [them]; but festivals interrupt and are not included."

C. R. Eliezer says, "Since the destruction [of the Temple], ʿAṣeret [Shavuot] is like the Sabbath."

D. Rabban Gamaliel says, "The New Year and the Day of Atonement are like the festivals."

E. And sages say, "It is not like the words of one, nor like the words of the other; rather, Aṣeret is like a festival, and the New Year and the Day of Atonement are like the Sabbath."

M.M.Q. 3.5-6 (y. M.Q. 3.6;
b. M.Q. 19a, 24a)

Comment: A provides an example to explain the rather cryptic formula of B. Once mourning has been observed, the intervention of a festival cancels the seven days of mourning or the thirty days of mourning. The Sabbath, on the other hand, is counted as one of the seven or thirty, but does not cancel them, even though no mourning is observed on it.

The latter units of the pericope presuppose A-B for their definition. Eliezer redefines the mourning rules of Shavuot to be like the Sabbath, now that the Temple has been destroyed (C). Gamaliel's saying (D) is dependent upon A-B but is not related to C: the New Year and the Day of Atonement are like the festivals as regards mourning. E is dependent upon all the preceding units. The sages reject both C and D. The significance of Shavuot has not been changed by the destruction of the Temple; and the New Year and the Day of Atonement are not to be considered as festivals in the annulment of the seven or thirty days of mourning.

A. They sit on a bench belonging to gentiles on the Sabbath.

B. 1. At first they used to say, "They do not sit on a bench belonging to gentiles on the Sabbath" [Vienna and London mss. add: 2. until Rabbi ʿAqiva came and taught that they may sit on a bench belonging to gentiles on the Sabbath. y. Pes. 4.1 omits B entirely].

C. (MʿSH B) Rabban Gamaliel was sitting on a bench belonging to gentiles on Sabbath, in ʿAkko.

D. They said to him, "It isn't done here, to sit on a bench belonging to gentiles on the Sabbath."

E. He did not want to tell them, "You are permitted." Rather, he got up and went away.

F. (M'SH B) Judah and Hillel, sons of Rabban Gamaliel, went in to bathe, in Kabul.

G. They said to them, "It isn't done here, for two brothers to bathe at the same time."

H. They did not want to tell them, "You are permitted." Rather, they entered and bathed one after the other.

I. (ŠWB M'SH B) Again, Judah and Hillel, sons of Rabban Gamaliel, went out [wearing] gold slippers (QWRDQYYŚYN) on Sabbath.

J. They said to them, "It isn't done here to go out [wearing] gold slippers on Sabbath."

K. They did not want to tell them, "You are permitted." Rather, they sent them with their servants.

Tos. M.Q. 2.14-16 (Lieberman
ed. p. 372, lines 4-50;
A + C-K = y. Pes. 4.1)

Comment: The reasons behind the objections to the practices mentioned are as follows: the benches (A) are used for displaying wares: it would look as if the Jew were engaged in buying or selling on the Sabbath. For two brothers to bathe together (G) would provide a possibility for homosexual practices. And since the QWRDQYYŚYN (J) are loose-fitting slippers, when they fell off one might be tempted to carry them in the street on the Sabbath, which is forbidden. In all these cases, however, the stories claim that these unusual severities were followed only in the specific places where the incidents take place.

A states the anonymous law. B mentions the prior, stricter practice. The mss. which include B. 2 must be correct. There can be no point in B. 1 by itself. B. 1 implies that someone came and changed the situation; but the Gamaliel-story does not show him teaching that it is permitted, or that anyone followed his example (as in, e.g., M. Ḥal. 4.7). B was probably added by an 'Aqivan source, to credit him for the law in A. But since B. 2 does contradict the substance of the story (crediting Gamaliel for the ruling) this may account for its disappearance from some of the versions.

The story C-E credits Gamaliel with the ruling permitting the use of a gentile's bench on the Sabbath, but states that he did not teach so publicly, because the popular practice was otherwise.

F-H and I-J are patterned after C-E: disputed lenient practice + objection + retreat. Both the stories concern Judah and

Hillel, the sons of a Rabban Gamaliel; but it cannot be our Gamaliel, who is the father of Ḥanina and Simeon. Since Judah and Hillel are mentioned by name again in the introduction to the second story, I-K may have had an independent history before being redacted here with F-H.

We have, then, a small collection of stories about the leniencies in the behavior of the patriarchal family. The stories are favorable, in that Gamaliel and his sons follow the correct practice. But they may be revisions of anti-patriarchal narratives, told to defend the Patriarch against stories criticizing his behavior, from the viewpoint of a more stringent piety. Certainly the Gamaliel presented here does not seem to be the authority-figure of other narratives, nor are his sons treated by the populace as the examples of proper behavior we would expect from the pericopae referring to "those of the house of Rabban Gamaliel."

A. Have we not learned (WHTNY'): Two brothers bathe at the same time, but two brothers do not bathe in Kabul.

B. (WM'SH B) Judah and Hillel, the sons of Rabban Gamaliel, bathed at the same time in Kabul, and the whole region laughed at them. They said, "In our whole lives, we have never seen [anything] like that!"

C. Hillel slipped away (WNŠMṬ), and went to the outer chamber. He did not want to tell them, "You are permitted."

D. They go out in slippers on the Sabbath, but they do not go out in slippers on Sabbath in Biri.

E. (WM'SH B) Judah and Hillel, the sons of Rabban Gamaliel, went out in slippers on Sabbath in Biri, and the whole region laughed at them. They said, "In our whole lives, we have never seen [anything] like that!"

F. They slipped them off (WŠMṬWM), and gave them to their servants. They did not want to tell them, "You are permitted."

G. They sit on the benches of gentiles on Sabbath, but they do not sit on the benches of gentiles on Sabbath of 'Akko.

H. (WM'SH B) Rabban Simeon b. Gamaliel [Printer's error; all mss. and early eds. read: Rabban Gamaliel, cf. Rabbinovicz, D.S. Pes., p. 147, n. 29] sat on the benches of gentiles on Sabbath in 'Akko, and the whole region laughed at him. They said, "In our whole lives, we have never seen anything like that!"

I. He slipped off (NŠMṬ), onto the ground. He did not want to tell them, "You are permitted."

b. Pes. 51a

Comment: The b. version of these stories, with the son-stories preceding Gamaliel, provides an introductory generalized law for each one (A, D, G). And b. adds a place name for D-F, which lacks one in Tos. In each story (C, F, I) the verb ŠMṬ (to slip) is used in different senses, to describe Gamaliel or his sons; it is a mark of the redaction of the three stories as a single pericope. The context in b. uses the stories to make the point that one does not teach that something permitted is in fact permitted, in a locale where the custom is otherwise.

A. When do they overturn the couches?

"From the time the deceased has gone out the court-yard entrance," the words of R. Liezer.

R. Joshua says, "From the time the rolling [stone covering the tomb] is closed."

B. And when Rabban Gamaliel died, after [the corpse] went out the court-yard entrance R. Liezer said to his students, "Overturn the couches."

When the rolling [stone of the tomb] had been closed, R. Joshua said to his students, "Overturn the couches."

They said to him, "They have already turned them over, upon order of the Elder."

y. M.Q. 3.5 (Sem. 11.19)

Comment: A is an Eliezer-Joshua dispute. Overturning the couches is a sign of mourning for the members of the household, who must sit on the ground. Eliezer has the house prepared immediately the funeral procession begins, Joshua somewhat later. In either case, the house is prepared to receive the mourners when they return from the burial.

B is a story illustrating the opinions of both men. Each follows his own rule, but Eliezer's action has pre-empted Joshua's. So just as Eliezer is placed first in the dispute, he is first in the story.

Gamaliel's funeral was famous in its effect upon later funerary custom. According to the story in b. B.M. 59b, Eliezer outlived Gamaliel. Given these two traditions, this pericope could have been formulated easily to show the advantage of Eliezer's ruling, possibly by the same tradents responsible for formulating the joint Eliezer-Gamaliel opinions.

A. Our rabbis taught (TNW RBNN): From what time do they overturn the couches?

"From [the time the corpse] goes out the doorway of his house," the words of R. Eliezer.

R. Joshua says, "From the time the rolling [stone covering the tomb] is closed."

B. (M'SH Š) Rabban Gamaliel the Elder died. As soon as [his corpse] went out the door of his house, R. Eliezer said to them, "Overturn your couches."

As soon as the rolling [stone of the tomb] was closed, R. Joshua said to them, "Overturn your couches."

They said to him, "We have already turned them over, by order of the Elder."

b. M.Q. 27a

Comment: There are few differences between b. and y. The court-yard entrance of y. is the doorway of the house in b. B here is labelled as a M'SH. The main difference is that b. identifies Gamaliel as "the Elder", which is anachronistic, and surely a contamination from the final word of the pericope.

And said R. Simeon b. Pazzi [that] said R. Joshua b. Levi in behalf of Bar Qappara, "Rabban Gamaliel and his court took a vote on these two [terminal] periods and abolished them."

b. M.Q. 3b

Comment: The question concerns the time when the Seventh Year prohibition against tilling fields actually takes effect. The Hillelites held that an orchard could be cultivated until the Feast of Weeks, and an open field tilled until Passover (b. M.Q. 3b). The court, in abolishing these two terminal dates, extended the cultivation period until the New Year in the Fall.

The tradents are first generation Palestinian Amoraim. There is reason to assume that the pericope refers to Rabban Gamaliel III (see comment on b. Ḥull. 5b).

A. Shall we say [our discussion is] like these Tannaim:

B. One whose dead lies before him eats [his meals] in another house [room]; [if] he has no other house, he eats in the house of his fellow; [if] he has no friend's house [available], he makes a partition for himself, ten handbreadths high; [if] he has nothing of which to make a partition, he turns his face aside and eats.

C. And he does not recline as he eats; and he does not eat meat; and he does not drink wine; and he does not bless [the grace after meals]; and he does not invite [others to join in the grace];

and they do not join him in grace; and they do not invite him [to join in grace].

D. 1. And he is exempt from reciting the Shema', and from the Tefillah and from tefillin,

2. and from all the commandments mentioned in the Torah.

E. But on Sabbath, he reclines as he eats; and he eats meat; and he drinks wine; and he blesses [the grace]; and he invites others [to join in grace]; and they join him in grace and invite him [to join them].

F. 1. And he is obligated for reciting the Shema', and for the Tefillah and for tefillin,

2. and for all the commandments mentioned in the Torah.

G. Rabban Gamaliel [b. Ber. 18a = Simeon b. Gamaliel] says, "Since he is obligated for these [commandments] he is obligated for them all."

b. M.Q. 23b (b. Ber. 18a)

Comment: The Amoraic discussion framework (A) identifies this as a as a Tannaitic pericope. The collection of mourning-laws begins with a discussion of meals in a house with a corpse (B) and then proceeds to other mealtime laws for mourners (C) and finally to exemption from prayers and all other commandments (D). E-F depends upon C-D, repeating the list of prohibitions and exemptions, but declaring them all to apply as positive obligations once again on the Sabbath.

Gamaliel's comment (Rabbinovicz, D.S., ad. loc., identifies M.Q. as the correct reading) appears to be connected most directly with F, through the use of the word "obligated" (ḤYYB, NTḤYYB). G appears to repeat the sense of the final phrase of F, since F has already stated that the mourner is liable for all the commandments. The phrase, "and for all the commandments mentioned in the Torah," (F. 2) seems to be a contamination from D. 2, above. If it were original to F, there would be no need to append G. Possibly, at a stage before the separate issues of B, C+E and D+F were brought together, there existed the following dispute:

> A mourner is exempt from Shema', Tefillah and tefillin,
> and from all the commandments mentioned in the Torah.
> But on Sabbath, he is obligated for reciting the Shema',
> and for the Tefillah.
> Rabban Gamaliel says, "Since he is obligated for these,
> he is obligated for them all.

Gamaliel's assertion of the force of all the commandments upon the Sabbath would, most notably, include the requirement of marital relations during the week of mourning. The phrase, "and tefillin", is an erroneous repetition from the preceeding line:

there is, of course, no obligation for tefillin on the Sabbath.

The extensive redaction of this pericope suggests at least two stages of development, though we cannot be sure of their order, or over how long a period they occurred: (1) G comments upon, or disputes with, D+F; and (2) D+F+G is brought together with B-C+E. The parallel passage in Sem. would strengthen this assumption.

A. But he eats at his friend's [house]; and if he has no friend, he eats at another house; and if he has no other house, he makes a partition for himself and eats. And if he cannot make a partition for himself, he turns his face away from the dead and eats.

B. And he does not recline as he eats, and he does not eat as much as he needs, and he does not eat meat; and he does not drink wine; and they do not invite him [to join in grace]; and they do not say to him, "Bless [the grace after meals]."

C. When does this apply (BMH DBRYM ʾMWRYM)? On weekdays. But on the Sabbath, he eats as much as he needs, and he eats meat, and drinks wine; and they do invite him [to join in grace].

D. Rabban Gamaliel says, "But on Sabbath it is as though he is not a mourner."

Sem. 10.3

Comment: As in b. M.Q. 23b, above, Gamaliel appears to comment on the pericope with a generalization about the laws of mourning. Though the material here is parallel to b. M.Q. 23b B-C, the former pericope does not contain Gamaliel's lemma. On the other hand, Sem. contains material which in b. M.Q. is commented upon by Gamaliel:

> A mourner, as long as his dead lies before him, is free from the obligation to recite the Shemaʿ and the Tefillah, and from all the commandments mentioned in the Torah... (Sem. 10.1)

It would appear that when the two pericopae in b. M.Q. were brought together by the editor of b., Gamaliel's first statement was dropped, and the final, more inclusive generalization, that all the commandments are in force on Sabbath, was allowed to stand. It is equally possible that these pericopae circulated within the patriarchal tradition with Gamaliel's comments appended, and independently without them. In such a case, b. M.Q. supplies pericopae with Gamaliel's comment (D-G) and without (B-C); and Sem. also includes material with (10.3) and without (10.1) Gamaliel's comment.

A. Rabban Gamaliel used to eat common food (ḤWLYN) [in a state] of purity during his entire lifetime, and his napkin (MṬPḤTW) was considered _midraś_ for those who ate sacred [food of sacrifices].

B. Onqelos the proselyte used to eat food which was pure for those who ate sacred [food of sacrifices] all of his lifetime, and his napkin was considered _midraś_ for [those who handled the water of purification for] a sin-offering.

Tos. Ḥag. 3.2b-3 (Lieberman ed. p. 387, lines 5-7)

Comment: I follow the explanation of Lieberman (_T.K._, V, pp. 1309-1311). M. Ḥag. 2.7 describes an ascending order of purity: _ʿAm-ha'areṣ_, Pharisee, priest eating Heave-offering, priest eating food of sacrifices, priest handling water of sin-offering. In all these cases, the clothing of each is considered _midraś_ (transmitting uncleanness through touch) to the one above him on the scale.

The passage goes on to say that some pious individuals maintained the state of purity beyond the normal. The napkin of Yosé b. Yoʿezer, the most pious of the priesthood, was considered _midraś_ for those eating sacred food. This was the normal state for a priest who would only maintain a state of purity enabling him to eat Heave-offering. But Yoḥanan b. Gudgada, a Levite, maintained a purity-state equal to that of eating sacred food (which as a Levite he could not eat) and his napkin was considered _midraś_ for those who handled the sin-offering water.

Tos. now supplies two more examples, from the time after the destruction of the Temple, completing the genealogical categories of the nation: an Israelite and a proselyte. Gamaliel, the Israelite, is in a purity-state fitting for a priest (A). Onqelos, the proselyte, however, maintains a purity-state equal to a priest able to eat sacrificial food (B). In point of fact, there is no practical difference between these two states. After the destruction there is no sacrificial food. The only difference is in the intention of the person who immerses himself. Thus far Lieberman.

There may be nothing invidious in the comparison between Onqelos, the proselyte, who chooses to maintain a higher level of priestly purity than Gamaliel, the Patriarch. After all, Gamaliel, as an Israelite, _is_ observing a state of purity appropriate for priests. And further in M., we have the instance of a Levite who is stricter than the most pious of the pre-70 priesthood. Gamaliel may here represent the norm of Pharisaic piety, while Onqelos goes beyond it.

However, there is at least a suspicion of such an invidious distinction. In Tos. Miqv. 6.4, Gamaliel and Onqelos appear together. There the issue is the permissibility of a gentile bath-house. Gamaliel immerses in the bath-house, while Onqelos uses the sea. We must assume that the story there is uncomplimentary to Gamaliel, since its content is immediately revised by Joshua b. Qibusai, who declares that Gamaliel followed the stricter view. In our pericope too, then, Gamaliel may be only a foil for the superior piety of Onqelos.

xii. Yevamot

A. Rabban Gamaliel says, "There is no [valid] *geṭ* [divorce document] after [another] *geṭ*, and no *ma'amar* [statement of bethrothal] after [another] *ma'amar*, and no [act of] consummation after [another act of] consummation, and no *ḥaliṣah* [dissolution of the levirate bond] after another *ḥaliṣah*."

B. And sages say, "There is a [valid] *geṭ* after [another] *geṭ*, and there is a [valid] *ma'amar* after [another] *ma'amar*; but nothing [valid can take place] after consummation or after *ḥaliṣah*."

M. Yev. 5.1 (b. Yev. 95a)

Comment: Deut. 25:5-7 explains levirate marriage, the special relationship between a man and the widow of his childless deceased brother (levir = brother-in-law). A *de facto* marriage exists between them, which must be consummated, in order to provide an heir for the deceased man.

The situation of "*geṭ* after *geṭ*" would arise if a levir sent a *get* (divorce document) first to one of the co-wives of his deceased brother, then to the other; or, where two brothers each sent a divorce to the same widow of their deceased brother. In either case, Gamaliel asserts that the second *get* has no force whatever (A), and the sender of the second *geṭ* may marry the close relatives of the recipient. (Under normal circumstances he would not be permitted to marry the sister, or other close relation, of his divorcée.) The sages rule that a *geṭ* has some power (B), even though it cannot dissolve the levirate bond. While the sender of the first *geṭ* would require receipt of *ḥaliṣah* to be free of the bond, the sender of the second get would be unable to marry the close relations of his "divorcée".

The ma'amar, or "statement of betrothal" is understood as the normal betrothal formula, spoken in conjunction with the presentation of a ring or coin -- in other words, standard qiddušin. This is insufficient to consummate levirate marriage: only intercourse can do that. The situation envisioned is where the levir betrothes two co-wives of his deceased brother, or where two brothers betrothed the same brother's widow. Again, Gamaliel asserts that the second betrothal has no force; but the sages hold that the second betrothal must be severed by a get, and the one who sent the second get is then forbidden to the close relatives of the divorcée.

In the final two instances, however, both Gamaliel and the sages agree: just as intercourse consummates the levirate marriage, the ḥaliṣah ceremony dissolves the levirate bond. A second instance of either has no validity whatever.

Gamaliel's lemma, as we have seen, expresses a great deal of legal theory in a highly compact form. But the principle it expresses is straightforward: once a valid legal act has been performed, other similar acts have no consequence. The sages' response, in the dispute (B), seems to have been formulated in answer to A. Even though B could stand independently, the correspondence is too exact for B to have been developed apart from A.

A. [If] he addresses a ma'amar to his yevamah, her rival is rendered unfit.

[If] he gives a get to his yevamah, [both] she and her rival are rendered unfit.

[If] he submits to ḥaliṣah from her, her rival is rendered unfit.

B. And sages say, "There is a get after a get, and a ma'amar after a ma'amar."

C. Rabban Gamaliel agrees with the sages that there is (1) a get after a ma'amar, and a ma'amar after a get, (2) a get after intercourse [following] a ma'amar, and a ma'amar after intercourse [following] a get.

D. How did Rabban Gamaliel say, "There is no get after a get"?

E. [If there are] two yevamot, and one levir, and he gives a get to one of them, and then gives a get to the other --

Rabban Gamaliel says, "He submits to haliṣah from the first, and he may marry the close relatives of the second."

And sages say, "He is forbidden to marry the close relatives of both of them, and he must submit to *ḥaliṣah* from [either] one of them."

F. [If] he addresses a *ma'amar* to one, and then addresses a *ma'amar* to the other --

Rabban Gamaliel says, "He gives a *geṭ* to the first one, and submits to *ḥaliṣah* from her, and he may marry the close relatives of the second."

And sages say, "He is forbidden to marry the close relatives of both of them. Two *giṭṭin* are required, and *ḥaliṣah* from one of them."

G. The same [viewpoints hold] for two levirs and one *yevamah*.

Tos. Yev. 7.2B (Lieberman ed. pp. 22-23, lines 6-15; D = b. Yev. 27b)

Comment: A explains the power of *ma'amar*, *geṭ* and *ḥaliṣah*, following the viewpoint of the sages in the M. Yev. 5.1B. Though the *ma'amar* does not consummate a levirate marriage, it has enough force to disqualify a co-wife from the need to fulfill a levirate marriage. Though the *geṭ* does not sever the levirate bond, it has enough force to prevent both co-wives from marrying the levir (since he has, in effect, shown his refusal to *build up his brother's house* (Deut. 25:9) he may not undertake the levirate marriage again again); rather he must receive *ḥaliṣah*; and the co-wife is freed of the levirate bond too.

B quotes the passage from the M. Yev. 5.1B above, as a context for Gamaliel's statement (C). Slotki (Soncino *Yev.*, p. 168, n. 12) explains the force of a *geṭ* given to one co-wife after a *ma'amar* given to the other (C. 1) and vice versa, as follows: "If the *ma'amar* was made first, the subsequent divorce forbids the marriage of the second and also that of the first, the *ma'amar* to her not being regarded as actual marriage; and if the divorce was first and the *ma'amar* afterwards, the second widow also requires a divorce, the divorce of the first not having the force of *ḥaliṣah* to invalidate the *ma'amar* addressed to the second."

Lieberman (*T.K.*, VI, p. 61) explains the situation of "*geṭ* after intercourse [following] a *ma'amar*" (C. 2) as follows: a *ma'amar* is addressed to co-wife A; intercourse follows with co-wife B; a *geṭ* is then required for co-wife A. However, Lieberman also quotes the explanation of y., to the effect that the situation concerns *three* co-wives, as follows: (y. Yev. 6.1): a *ma'amar* is addressed to wife A, followed by intercourse with wife B; a get presented to wife C still has force to disqualify her relatives to the levir.

The second formula, "ma'amar after intercourse [following] a get," is similarly identified by Lieberman: a get is presented to co-wife A, followed by intercourse with co-wife B; a ma'amar addressed to co-wife A still has legal force. Lieberman does not explain the effect of the ma'amar, but it must be to require the levir to give a second get to co-wife A, in order to dissolve its force. Here too, y. explains things in terms of three wives: a get to A, followed by intercourse with wife B, followed by a ma'amar to wife C.

All the materials of the pericope serve to explain M. Yev. 5.1, though some of them may possibly antedate it. A. explains M. Yev. 5.1B, as we have seen. It could as well follow B here, which is a quotation from M. there. But C also depends upon B; it harmonizes Gamaliel with the sages' viewpoint, in some intermediate cases which M. gives as undisputed anonymous law in M. Yev. 5.4-5.

D-G explains Gamaliel's view in M. Yev. 5.1A. The editor has joined two disputes, E and F. E deals with the problem of "get after get" in a dispute concerning one levir and two co-wives; F concerns the problem of "ma'amar after ma'amar" under the same circumstances. The editor has provided an introduction (D), showing that he is commenting on the Mishnah, and the postscript, explaining that the same rule holds true for the case of two levirs and one wife. E and F may be materials which were eventually reworked into the more comprehensive dispute of M. Yev. 5.1; or different groups may have preserved these materials in co-extant different forms.

A. [As to] two brothers married to two sisters who are minors and orphans, if the husband of one of them dies, she is exempt [from levirate marriage] by virtue of being the sister of his [the levir's] wife.

B. So too, [with] two sisters who are deaf-mutes.

C. If one is of age and the other a minor, and the husband of the minor dies, she is exempt [from levirate marriage] by virtue of being the sister of his wife.

D. [If] the husband of the one who is of age dies --

E. R. Eliezer says, "They instruct the minor to exercise the right of refusal against him."

F. Rabban Gamaliel says, "If she exercises her right of refusal, she refuses [i.e., it is valid].

G. "And if not, she waits until she is of age, and then the other goes free [of the levirate bond] as the sister of his wife."

H. R. Joshua says, "Woe to him because of his wife [who is lost to him], and woe to him because of the wife of his brother [also lost to him]! He divorces his wife with a get, and the wife of his brother with ḥaliṣah."

M. Yev. 13.7 (y. Yev. 13.7,
b. Yev. 18a, 79b, 109a)

Comment: The point in A relevant to us is that, when two brothers are married to two sisters, and one husband dies, the widow is exempt from the levirate bond. This is because of Lev. 18:18, which prohibits a man from marrying his wife's sister.

In B, again we have the case of two sisters, wed to two brothers. This time they are deaf-mutes, which means that in any case the option of ḥaliṣah is closed to them (M. Yev. 12.4: a deaf-mute may not validly participate in ḥaliṣah). In C, one sister is of age, the other a minor. If the husband of the minor dies, the case is similar to the preceding: she is exempt from the levirate bond, as the sister of the levir's wife. But in D, it is the husband of the adult sister who dies. The question now concerns the relative strength of the two different relationships. On the one hand, the marriage of the minor may be considered a "potential" marriage. Even though it requires a divorce to be dissolved, it is not consummated until she comes of age; and she may reject the marriage before that time. Further, it is a rabbinical ordinance. On the other hand, the levirate bond between the adult sister and the levir, though biblically-ordained, may also be considered a "potential" marriage, since it requires consummation. Which of these two obligations is the stronger?

In his analysis of this pericope (Eliezer, pp. 172-174) Neusner points out that D, F-G and H are all formulated as answers to the topic-sentence D. Further, Gamaliel's answer (F-G) responds to Eliezer's (E) as well as to the topic (D). Gamaliel could as well have completed the topic-sentence with the substance of G. And Joshua's opinion likewise responds to all that has gone before.

Eliezer (E) considers the levirate bond paramount. The minor sister is instructed to reject the marriage, and the elder sister consummates the levirate marriage with her brother-in-law.

Gamaliel (F) holds the marriage already contracted to be the stronger. The minor may exercise the right of refusal, in which case the elder may marry the levir; but if not, the elder sister must wait until the minor's marriage is consummated, when she will be freed of the levirate bond via Lev. 18:18.

Joshua (H) considers the two obligations exactly equal, each with the power to enforce a cancellation of the other. The levir must submit to ḥaliṣah from the elder sister, and also divorce his minor wife. W. Green's analysis (Joshua, pp. 221-229) locates the source of the view assigned to Joshua in the Houses-dispute of M. Yev. 3.5:

> 1) [Concerning] three brothers, two of whom [were] married to two sisters, and one [of whom] was unmarried,
>
> 2) [If] one of the sisters' husbands dies and the unmarried [brother] performs a ma'amar for the widow, and afterwards his second brother dies,
>
> 3) The House of Shammai say, "His [bespoken] wife [remains] with him, and the other is exempt [from levirate marriage] because [she is] the sister of the [levir's] wife."
>
> 4) And the House of Hillel say, "He sends out his wife with a geṭ and [with] ḥaliṣah, and his brother's wife with ḥaliṣah."
>
> 5) And this is [the case] of which they said, "Woe to him on account of his wife, and woe to him on account of his brother's wife [since he loses both]."

Both pericopae test the levirate bond against the strength of another, additional bond. In 3.5 the added factor is the ma'amar, while in 13.7 the added factor is the unconsummated marriage to a minor. Regarding 3.5, Green continues: "If we reverse the order of 4-5 and drop "and [with] ḥaliṣah" from the first part of 4 (it is inappropriate to 13.7), then the position of the Hillelites is identical to Joshua's. Since the ruling and the proverb occur together in Mishnah-Tosefta only in these two pericopae, it seems that the opinion has been taken from the Houses-dispute, ascribed to Joshua, and appended to 13.7. In order to ascribe the proverb and the ruling to Joshua, it was necessary to reverse their order. Joshua's tradition, then, is probably pseudepigraphic."

Whereas Eliezer (holding the levirate bond to be paramount) stands apart from the Houses-dispute, Green notes that "both Gamaliel and the Shammaites hold that the unconsummated marriage remains in force, in effect voiding the competing levirate claim . . . the Houses' opinions have been transposed to 13.7 from 3.5 and attached to appropriate names. Joshua has, almost verbatim, the Hillelite view, and Gamaliel, mutatis mutandis, the Shammaite."

Whether or not we accept the view that Joshua's lemma and proverb are imported from the Houses-dispute, Green's analysis conclusively demonstrates the following: (1) that Eliezer's lemma is primary to the pericope, (2) that Gamaliel's lemma is shaped to respond to Eliezer, and (3) that Gamaliel's opinion is congruent to -- but not transferred from -- the Shammaite ruling.

With Eliezer's lemma as central, the adaptation of the Houses' views, and their ascription to Eliezer's contemporaries follows easily. Whether Gamaliel's identification as a Shammaite here is more than mechanical, given the identification of Joshua as a Hillelite, is difficult to determine.

One other observation may be made about the postures of the three men, aside from their specific views on the relative strength of the betrothal-bond vs. the levirate bond. Eliezer requires action changing the status of both girls, so that the levir marries the elder sister. Joshua requires action changing the status of both girls, so that the levir winds up married to neither. Gamaliel requires that the levir take no action to change the situation at all, unless the minor breaks the betrothal by her refusal. These three views are parallel to the positions taken on an entirely different issue, in M. Ter. 8.8 (a jar of Heave-offering exposed to uncleanness). Eliezer requires action to protect the contents, Joshua requires their actual defilement, and Gamaliel says that nothing new should be done.

Rabban Gamaliel says, "[In a case where two brothers are married to two sisters, one of the latter being a minor, and the husband of the elder dies, if the younger] exercises her right of refusal, she refuses [i.e., it is valid and her husband performs levirate marriage with her sister]. If not, he waits until she is of age, and marries her, and the other goes free [of the levirate bond] as the sister of his wife."

Tos. Yev. 13.6 (Lieberman
ed. p. 47, lines 32-33)

Comment: This is identical with M. Yev. 13.7 E-F except for the omission of a conjunction at the beginning of F, and the addition of and marries her.

A. R. ʿAqiva said, "When I went down to Nehardea to ordain a leap-year, I met Nehemiah of Bet Deli. He said to me, 'I have heard that in the Land of Israel [the sages], except for R. Judah

b. Baba, do not allow a woman to marry [again] on the evidence of one witness.' I answered, 'Those words are correct.'

"He said to me, 'Tell them in my name: You know that the land is in turmoil because of the [marauding] troops -- I have received [a tradition] from Rabban Gamaliel the Elder that they allow a woman to marry [again] on the evidence of one witness.'

"And when I came and told the matter before Rabban Gamaliel, he rejoiced at my words and said, 'We have now found a fellow for R. Judah b. Baba.'"

B. Through these words, Rabban Gamaliel remembered that certain men were killed at Tel Arza, and Rabban Gamaliel the Elder allowed their wives to marry again on the evidence of one witness.

C. And the rule was established to allow a woman to marry [again] on the evidence of a witness [who testifies what he has heard] from [another] witness, or from a slave, or from a woman, or from a bondwoman.

D. R. Eliezer and R. Joshua say, "They do not allow a woman to marry on the evidence of one witness."

E. R. ʿAqiva says, "[They do] not [allow a woman to remarry] on the evidence of a woman, or from a slave, or from a bondwoman, or on the evidence of relatives."

F. They said to him, "Once certain Levites went to Zoar, city of palms, and one of them fell sick by the way, and they brought him to an inn. When they returned there, they asked the hostess, 'Where is our companion?' She said to them, 'He died and I buried him.' And they allowed his wife to marry again."

G. They said to him, "And should not a priest's wife be [assumed as trustworthy] as the hostess of an inn?"

H. He said to them, "Only when the mistress of an inn could be deemed trustworthy. For in this case the mistress of the inn brought out to them his staff and his bag, and the scroll of the Torah that belonged to him."

M. Yev. 16.7 (y. Yev. 16.8,
b. Yev. 122a)

Comment: This pericope is the full, narrative version of the law reported in ʿAqiva's name in M. ʿEd. 6.5: "R. ʿAqiva testified in the name of Nehemiah of Bet Deli that a woman is permitted to marry [again] on the evidence of one witness." We have other first-person reports by ʿAqiva dealing with laws involving Gamaliel (M. Suk. 3.9, M. Ker. 3.7, M. Neg. 7.4).

Units C and D have become reversed. A + B + D and C + E + F + G + H are two separate pericopae, related in subject, from

ʿAqivan tradents. The first pericope, A + B + D is itself not unitary. Neusner (Pharisees, i, pp. 348-50) shows that in A, the tradition of Gamaliel the Elder is reported in the form of a law: "They allow a woman to marry again . . ." In B, however, Gamaliel reports the same law in terms of a story about his grandfather: "Rabban Gamaliel the Elder allowed their wives to remarry . . ." Thus, two traditions about Gamaliel the Elder, one a generalized law and the other a story, preserve the same law in the same language. It is this forgotten view, reported by Nehemiah, which is represented by Judah b. Baba (A). The majority view, according to the narrative in A, is expressed by Eliezer and Joshua (D).

From Gamaliel's reported joy in A, he is sympathetic to granting such permission. But the narrator represents him as having forgotten the authority for such a ruling. He requires ʿAqiva's message to refresh his memory. Thus, though Gamaliel is not represented unsympathetically, he is shown to be dependent upon ʿAqiva for the actual decision of the law, and even for information concerning the patriarchal house itself. Further, ʿAqiva claims to have been part of the court which temporarily emigrated to Babylonia in order to determine the calendar. This was an authority carefully guarded by the patriarch (M.R.H. 1.6, 2.8; M. Ed. 7.7) -- yet ʿAqiva is represented as saying that Gamaliel remained in the land of Israel.

The latter pericope, C + E + F + G + H, is not directly connected to the earlier one. It is a dispute between ʿAqiva and the sages, followed by a debate in which ʿAqiva wins. Both pericopae display ʿAqiva more favorably than his colleagues.

A. For we have learned there (DTNYNN TMN): Ten families of unbroken lineage (YWḤŚYN) returned from Babylonia.

B. According to the view of R. Liezer b. Jacob [y. Yev. 8.2: R. Eliezer b. Jacob], eight.

C. According to the view of Rabban Gamaliel and R. Liezer [y. Qidd. 4.3: Eleazar], nine.

D. According to the view of the rabbis, ten.

y. Yev. 4.2 (y. Yev. 8.2;
y. Qidd. 4.3)

Comment: Pure family lines were of special concern to the priests, especially those who had preserved their family records from pre-exilic times. Gamaliel and Eliezer are paired on a question of marriage into the priesthood in M. Ket. 1.8, 9. As there,

Gamaliel is mentioned first. However, B-D is not a series of lemmas; it rather appears to be an Amoraic listing of the various views.

A. It was taught (DTNY'): Said Rabban Gamaliel, "Once I was travelling by ship. I saw a ship that was wrecked, and was saddened over [the loss of] a scholar who was in it."

B. And who was it? Rabbi ʿAqiva.

C. "When I landed, he came to me and sat down and discussed matters of halakah. I said to him, 'My son, who picked you up?'

D. 1. He said, 'The plank of a ship came my way,

2. "and to every single wave that came to me I bent my head.'"

E. Based on this, the sages said that if wicked persons attack a man, let him bend his head to them.

F. "At that hour I said, 'How great are the words of the sages who said [that if a man fell into] water which has [a visible] end, [his wife] is permitted [to marry again; but if into] water which has no [visible] end, she is forbidden [to remarry]."

b. Yev. 121a

[Aramaic italicized]

If a husband disappears, his wife may not remarry without evidence of his death. If he were lost in a relatively small body of water she may remarry since we assume that the husband's return would be reported. If the body of water were too extensive for its far shores to be visible, it is possible that the husband may have emerged from the water elsewhere; so the wife may not remarry.

Our pericope represents a first-person report by Gamaliel of a scholar lost at sea (A) who was saved (B) by grasping a floating plank (D. 1). Gamaliel commends the wisdom of the sages' view that a wife may not remarry, since here the man was lost at sea, yet turned up safely ashore (F).

B, the sole Aramaic element in the pericope, is a gloss identifying the name of the scholar. E too is an addition to the story, connecting it with a well-known proverb. It is possible that D. 2 may have been added simultaneously with E. In any case, the story must already have been associated with Gamaliel's name before the addition of E. The redactor may have seen a special relevance of E to Gamaliel, who was reported to have humbly accepted his deposition from leadership of the academy. That this confers the title of "wicked persons" on those who attacked the Patriarch may identify the tradent as a supporter of the Patriarch, and suggests that the pericope was close to final form before its redaction in b.

There are difficulties in the relation of F to the preceding. Its distinction of visible-end *vs*. no-visible-end is irrelevant to the story, A+C+D. Further, F is certainly anachronistic. The case of a husband lost at sea was an Ushan problem. The position of the sages here (F) is identified as that of R. Yosé in M. Yev. 16.4, in opposition to the view of R. Meir. F assumes, in Gamaliel's name, that the sages' view is already accepted as law, though it was the subject of Ushan dispute. Gamaliel could not be quoted approving a prior decision of this issue. On the other hand, to excise F would leave the story without any real point.

Weiss-Halivni, in his discussion of this pericope (*Meqorot*, pp. 126-127) suggests that the original lemma approved by Gamaliel was: "If a man fell into waters, his wife is forbidden to remarry." This exactly fits the point of the preceding story, and solves the anachronism by positing a Yavnean law which was further refined at Usha. There, Meir and Yosé introduced the distinction between visible-end and no-visible-end, as recorded in M. and the *baraitot*. Their formulation of the issue was transmitted by b.

Before discussing the relationship between Gamaliel and the story, we must compare it with the almost-identical narrative immediately following it. (The parallel version of the latter narrative, b. Yev. 121a, has also been quoted from y. Yev. 16.4.)

b. Yev. 121a	b. Yev. 121a	y. Yev. 16.4
A. It was taught: Rabban Gamaliel, "Once I was travelling by ship. I saw	A. Said R. ʿAqiva, "Once I was " "	A. Said R. ʿAqiva, " " "
a ship that was wrecked	a ship foundering at sea	a ship sunk at sea
and was saddened over [the loss of] a scholar who was on it	" " " " " "	" " " " " "
B. *And who was it?* Rabbi ʿAqiva.	" " Rabbi Meir.	- - - -
C. When I landed - - - -	" " in the province of Cappadocia	" " " " " "
he came to me and sat down	" " " "	and he began to come before me -
and discussed matters of *halakah*	" " " "	and ask me questions
I said to him, 'My son, who picked you up?'	" " " "	I asked him, 'My son how did you escape?'

b. Yev. 121a	b. Yev. 121a	y. Yev. 16.4
D.1. He said, 'The plank of a ship came my way	He said to me, 'One wave tossed me (TRDNY)	" " " " (TRPNY)
	to another and another	" "
2. and to every single wave that came to me I bent my head.'"	to another until it spewed me onto dry land.'"	" " " " " "
E. Based on this, the sages said that if wicked persons attack a man let him bend his head to them.	-	-
F. "At that hour I said, 'How great are the words	" " "	" " -
of the sages who said, etc.'"	" "	" "

The same story has been reported told by ʿAqiva about Meir as was reported told by Gamaliel about ʿAqiva. (More legendary, moralistic developments of this story with ʿAqiva as hero are found in Av. deR. Nat. I, iii and Eccl. R. 11.1) Comparing the two stories in Yev., whether in the version here or in the source-versions suggested by Halivni, we can note the following differences: The ʿAqiva story (1) adds the detail of the name of Cappadocia (C); (2) is more miraculous in the way the scholar is saved (D); (3) is more literary, in being influenced by the book of Jonah (D: "spewed me onto dry land"); and (4) omits E, which our analysis suggested was a gloss suggestive of Gamaliel's reputation. On these literary grounds, we may argue that the ʿAqiva-story is more highly developed than the Gamaliel-story. Further, we may speculate that the Gamaliel-story was revised as an ʿAqiva-story in order to support Yosé's view against Meir's. Such a story, in which Meir himself turned up alive, amounts to a strong argument against his own view, in the hands of Yosé's supporters.

Similar reasoning may be used to explain the Gamaliel-story of our pericope. The editor of M. incorporated Meir's view as the anonymous law beginning M. Yev. 16.4, together with a supporting story in Meir's name. A Gamaliel-story, praising the sages' opinion which parallels Yosé, would be an effective counter to the pro-Meir redaction of M.

However, there may be reasons internal to the traditions of Gamaliel for the story. A lenient view is recorded about him, permitting remarriage for widows of men killed in battle (M. Yev. 16.7). This pericope may have its origin in the need to explain why Gamaliel did not hold a similar leniency in the case of a man lost at sea.

(MʿSH B) The daughter of Rabban Gamaliel was married to his brother, Abba, who died without children; and Rabban Gamaliel performed levirate marriage (VYYBM) with her co-wife.

b. Yev. 15a

Comment: The House of Hillel exempt the co-wife of a daughter, widow of a man's brother, from the levirate bond (M. Yev. 1.2). However, the Shammaites permit levirate marriage between such a co-wife and the surviving brother (M. Yev. 1.4, M. Ed. 4.8). Gamaliel is reported to have followed Shammaite law in this matter.

xiii. Ketuvot

A. [One] who marries the woman and did not find in her the tokens of virginity (Deut. 22:14).

B. She says, "After you betrothed me, I was raped, and your field was laid waste,"

C. And the other says, "Not so, but before I betrothed you [it happened], and my purchase was an erroneous purchase,"

D. Rabban Gamaliel and R. Eliezer say, "She is believed."

E. R. Joshua says, "We do not rely upon her word [lit., not from her mouth do we live]; but lo, this one is in the presumption of having had intercourse (BʿWLH) before she was bethrothed, and she deceived him, unless she will bring proof for her claim (DBRYH)."

M. Ket. 1.6 (y. Ket. 1.6;
b. Ket. 12b, 13a)

A. She claims, "I am injured by [a piece of] wood," and he says, "Not so, but you have been trampled by man,"

B. Rabban Gamaliel and R. Eliezer say, "She is believed."

C. And R. Joshua says, "We do not rely upon her word; but lo, this one is in the presumption of having been trampled by a man, unless she will bring proof for her claim."

M. Ket. 1.7 (y. Ket. 1.7;
b. Ket. 11b, 13a)

A. They saw her speaking with one [man] in the market. They said to her, "What is the character of this man?"

B. "He is so-and-so, and a priest,"

C. Rabban Gamaliel and R. Eliezer [N: Eleazar] say, "She is believed."

D. And R. Joshua says, "We do not rely upon her word; but lo, such a one is in the presumption of having had intercourse with a Netin or a Mamzer, unless she will bring proof of her claim."

M. Ket. 1.8 (y. Ket. 1.8;
b. Ket. 13a)

A. She was pregnant. They said to her, "What is the nature of this embryo?"

B. "He is from so-and-so, and he is a priest."

C. Rabban Gamaliel and R. Eliezer say, "She is believed."

D. R. Joshua says, "We do not rely upon her words; but lo, such a one is in the presumption of having been made pregnant by a Netin or a Mamzer, unless she will bring proof for her claim."

M. Ket. 1.9 (y. Ket. 1.9;
b. Ket. 12b, 13a, 16a;
b. Qid. 74a)

If they saw her go in with someone into a secret place or a ruin, and they said to her, "What sort of person is he?" and she said, "He is a priest and the son of my father's brother. . . [The rest as above.]"

b. Ket. 13a-b

Comment: Neusner (Eliezer, pp. 182-3) writes: "This little collection of rulings on several examples of the same problem follows a disciplined form: (1) statement of the situation; (2) ruling of Gamaliel and Eliezer . . . (3) ruling of Joshua . . . The statement of the problem in M. Ket. 1.7, 8 and 9 depends upon 1.6A, so the collection is a unity."

In 1.6 and 1.7, the problem is whether the ketuvah is to be paid: were she unfaithful, she would forfeit this financial right. Gamaliel and Eliezer accept the woman's testimony, but Joshua requires proof of any claim. In 1.8 and 1.9, the issue is marriage into the priesthood. Were the woman to have had intercourse with a Netin or Mamzer, she would be ineligible to marry a priest. Again, Gamaliel and Eliezer, accepting the woman's testimony, permit her to marry into the priesthood. Joshua requires proof.

It is commonplace for either Gamaliel or Eliezer to dispute Joshua; but it is unusual to have a joint Gamaliel-Eliezer lemma in a pericope. The simplest form of this dispute would be: She is believed vs. She is not believed. Since Joshua's view is given in expanded form, to illustrate his principle that a claim requires proof, we may suspect that the pericopae were shaped by a Joshuan tradent, who spun out the collection, expanding Joshua's lemma and telescoping the views of his opponents. This would assume that independent lemmas of Gamaliel and Eliezer were redacted into a single, joint statement: however, we cannot be sure at which point in the process the joining took place.

A. [If] she was pregnant, [and] they said to her, "What is the nature of this embryo?"

B. "From so-and-so, and he is a priest."

C. Rabban Gamaliel and R. Liezer say, "She is believed, for this is testimony which a woman is fit [to give]."

D. R. Joshua says, "She is not believed."

E. R. Joshua said to them, "Do you not agree concerning the woman taken captive by gentiles, who has witnesses that she was taken captive, and she says, 'I am clean,' that she is not believed? [Likewise here there is adequate presumption that the woman has had intercourse.]"

F. They said to him, "No, if you [pl.] have said so concerning the woman taken captive who has witnesses [that she was taken captive], will you say so concerning this one, who has no witnesses [that she has had intercourse with someone who renders her unfit for the priesthood]?"

G. He said to them, "And what evidence is greater than this, for lo, her belly is between her teeth!"

H. They said to him, "Because gentiles are suspected (ḤŠWDYN) concerning forbidden sexual relations."

I. He said to them, "There is no guardian [guaranteed] to [prevent] forbidden sexual relations."

J. In what circumstances? In respect to testimony concerning [the woman about] herself. But as to the child, all agree he is a šetuqi [= of unknown parentage].

Tos. Ket. 1.6 (Lieberman ed.
p. 59, lines 41-48; b. Ket. 13b)

Comment: A-D is a different version of the dispute in M. Ket. 1.9. The statement of the topic-situation is identical (A-B). The ruling of Gamaliel-Eliezer (C) includes an apposite phrase, which is nevertheless not a reason. Joshua's reply (D) is not identical with the rhetoric of M., but it means the same.

A debate (E-I) follows. Joshua challenges the position of Gamaliel-Eliezer twice. They reply to both challenges, but cannot respond to his final answer. At first (E) Joshua compares the pregnant woman to the case of a woman who has witnesses to her captivity: the claim of the latter not to have been raped is not accepted. (Had there been no witnesses, her claim would be accepted. Since she need not have admitted to being captive in the first place, we accept both the admission of captivity and the claim not to have been violated.) Gamaliel-Eliezer reply that the cases are different, since the captive woman had witnesses to her captivity; but here there are no witnesses to her intercourse with someone unfit. Joshua then points out that there is evidence to her intercourse (pregnancy) comparable to the evidence of captivity. The claim of the latter to be unviolated is comparable to the claim of the father's genealogical fitness: both are unacceptable. This time, Gamaliel-Eliezer answer that the cases are not comparable, because with gentiles there is a presumption of rape, while with women there is a presumption of selecting a lover who would be socially acceptable. Joshua dismisses this (I): there are no guarantees about sexual conduct or misconduct. Here the dialogue stops.

J appears to be an editorial comment, on behalf of Gamaliel-Eliezer. The woman is believed, so far as her own status is concerned; she may marry a priest. As for the child, all agree that he is a <u>šetuqi</u>. (The latter remark occurs in y. Ket. 1.9, attributed to "R. Liezer", so that we may be sure that J represents his side in the debate.) However, we cannot be sure what it means for Gamaliel-Eliezer to declare that the child is a <u>šetuqi</u>, of unknown parentage. As discussed by the Amoraim, this can either mean "unknown", and therefore she is presumed fit to marry into the priesthood, or, "unknown" and therefore presumed to be unfit (<u>T</u>.<u>K</u>., VI, p. 197, line 48). If the latter, the editor has declared that Gamaliel-Eliezer agree part-way with Joshua; if the former, the editor has supplied an answer for them, defending their point of view, appending it to a dialogue in which Joshua has triumphed. But at least through A-I, the pericope is Joshuan in focus, strengthening the assumption of M. Ket. 1.6-9 as a collection by Joshua's circle.

A. [Concerning] the woman who inherited goods before she was betrothed, the House of Shammai and the House of Hillel agree that she sells them or gives them [away], and it is valid.

B. [If] she inherited them after she was betrothed --

The House of Shammai say, "She sells."

And the House of Hillel say, "She does not sell."

C. Both agree that if she sells them or gives them [away], it is valid.

D. Said R. Judah, "They said before Rabban Gamaliel, 'Since he [the husband] attains [possession of] the woman, does he not attain [possession of] her goods?'

"He said to them, 'We are embarrassed [to find reason for giving him rights] over the new [possessions], and would you even burden us with the old?'"

E. [If] she inherited [goods] after she was married, both agree that if she sells them or gives them [away], the husband may take them out of the hands of the buyers.

F. [If she inherited them] before she was married and [then] married --

Rabban Gamaliel says, "If she sells them or gives them [away], it is valid."

G. Said R. Ḥananiah b. ʿAqavya, "They said before Rabban Gamaliel, 'Since he attains [possession of] the woman, does he not attain [possession of] her goods?'

"He said to them, 'We are embarrassed [to find reason for giving him rights] over the new [possessions], and would you even burden us with the old?'"

M. Ket. 8.1

H. R. Simeon makes a distinction between different possessions. Possessions known to the husband she shall not sell; and if she sells or gives, [her act] is invalid. [Possessions] unknown to the husband she shall not sell; but if she sold or gave, [her act] is valid.

M. Ket. 8.2

Comment: The question here concerns the extent of control by a husband over the property of his wife. The Houses agree on two extreme cases: (1) property inherited by a woman prior to her betrothal is controlled by her, even after her marriage (A); and (2) property inherited by her after her marriage is totally controlled by her husband (E). The focus of debate concerns property she inherits during the period of time of her betrothal (normally one year), the period after she has been betrothed but before she is married.

Normally, in a Houses-dispute, the superscription and antithetical lemmas would be followed by any agreements. But since A handles the material chronologically (betrothal, then marriage), the protasis includes the Houses' agreement that the wife controls her pre-betrothal inheritance. B then presents the topic for dispute, which depends upon A for its full definition, followed by the Houses' answers.

In C, the Hillelites concede the wife's post facto right to control her inheritance. They have relinquished their position as stated in B. In Judah's report (D) the anonymous sages question this concession, in the light of the Hillelite position. Gamaliel acknowledges the weakness of that position; even the husband's rights over the wife's property inherited after marriage (something agreed on by the Houses) are not so firmly-based. They may not be extended back to cover the period of betrothal. In this half of the pericope, Judah provides the terminus ante quem for the Houses-dispute as well as for Gamaliel's dialogue.

E is the continuation of the Houses' agreement in A, and depends upon it for its context. (The nucleus of the pericope is probably A + E.) F in turn depends upon E. In view of what follows, F appears to be a truncated dispute, lacking, "And the sages say, 'It is not valid.'"

Neusner (Pharisees, ii, p. 211) points out that F is really the same issue as A-B, inheritance after betrothal, and that Gamaliel's ruling in F shows no knowledge of the Houses' agreement to the same effect. He (Neusner) concludes that the Houses' pericope would have been formulated after Gamaliel's ruling. Gamaliel's rule deals with the wife's control after her marriage; by implication, he would also agree that she controls the property prior to marriage, during the betrothal period. The latter case is presented as a Houses-agreement in C. In B-C, the phrase "after she was betrothed" is used, and there is no reference to her marriage later, as in F. The Houses' statement is more inclusive, when taken out of context. It appears to apply to any time after the betrothal. But as redacted into the pericope, the difference in formulation ("After betrothed" vs. "before married, then married") implies its restriction to the betrothal period only.

The elements of the pericope, considered chronologically, would be as follows:

Goods	Question of wife's control
A. Inherited before betrothal	during betrothal period and after marriage
B. Inherited after betrothal	during betrothal period
F. Inherited after betrothal	after marriage
E. Inherited after marriage	after marriage

G presents the same dialogue as D, but with Ḥananiah b. ʿAqavya as tradent. Seen here, however, the sages appear to oppose Gamaliel's ruling, while his answer successfully defends it: the authority for the Houses' agreement about the husband's rights after marriage (E) is weak, and cannot be extended. While Gamaliel's answer occurs in a number of parallel passages, the sages' question (D, G) occurs only here. Elsewhere, other questions elicit this reply.

The relation of Judah and Ḥananiah to the identical material must be considered below. But at this point, let us observe in advance that the Ushans and their successors possess firmly the tradition of Gamaliel's reply, but are less clear about the exact question to which it responds. Further, in H we have an Ushan, Simeon, who introduces a totally new principle: the effect of the husband's knowledge. Simeon retains the Hillelite prohibition on selling, but discards the distinctions among the single, betrothed and married states which Judah and Hananiah attest as so important to both the Houses and the Yavneans. The traditions are unclear as well as complex.

The redactor of M. often uses material favorable to Gamaliel. Here he presents a pericope (B-D) which reports a ruling of Gamaliel as something agreed upon by the Houses. In the dialogue(s) (D, E) Gamaliel is in a position of authority (ʾMRW LPNY RBN GMLYʾL) and has the last word.

A. Said R. Judah, "They said before Rabban Gamaliel, 'Since [the woman when] betrothed, is his wife, and [when] married, is his wife -- as with the latter (ZW) her sale is invalid, so with the former (ZW) [her sale should be] invalid.'

"He said to them, 'We are embarrassed [to find reason for giving him rights] over the new [possessions], and would you even burden us with the old?'"

B. Said R. Ḥananiah b. ʿAqavya, "Rabban Gamaliel did not answer them that way. Rather it was thus he said to them:

"'No! If you [pl.] say that [i.e., her sale is invalid] about a married woman whose husband has rights over what she finds or makes, or has power to void her vows, shall you say it of a betrothed woman [whose husband] does not have rights over what she finds or makes, or the power to void her vows?'

C. "They said to him, 'What about [the case of a woman who] came into possessions before she was married, and was [then] married?'

D. "He said to them, 'Even that one may not sell. Yet (Š) if she sells or gives [away], it is valid.'

E. "They said to him, 'Since the former (ZW) is his wife, and the latter (ZW) is his wife -- as with the former, her sale is invalid, so with the latter, her sale should be invalid.'

"He said to them, 'We are embarrassed [to find reason for giving him rights] over the new [possessions], and would you even burden us with the old?'

F. "And our rabbis reconsidered and voted, concerning possessions which she obtained before she was married, and was [later] married, that if she sells or gives [them away], it is valid [Vienna, and first printed edition: invalid]."

G. R. Simeon makes a distinction between different possessions. Possessions known to the husband she shall not sell; if she sells or gives, [her act] is invalid, for she was married on that condition [that he would have control over her known property]. And [property] unknown to the husband she may sell, for if she sells or gives [her act] is valid. [Vienna: she may <u>not</u> sell, <u>but</u> if she sells or gives [her act] is valid, for she accepted it on that condition].

Tos. Ket. 8.1 (Lieberman ed.
pp. 83-84, lines 1-13; A =
y. Ket. 8.1A; E = b. Ket. 78b)

<u>Comment</u>: A provides, in Judah's name, an alternate version of the question to Gamaliel about goods inherited "after she was betrothed". The force of the argument is similar (that the husband's authority should extend back to cover the betrothal period) but the language implies that we are dealing with the power of the husband during the betrothal period: since she is his wife when betrothed, and his wife when married, the same conditions should apply to both periods, i.e., that her sale should be invalid. Gamaliel's reply is that of M.

B depends upon A. It is Ḥananiah's revision of the dialogue, markedly different from M., where he repeats Judah's words verbatim. Accepting the sages' question, he gives Gamaliel an argument which contrasts the authority of the husband during the betrothal period with that of the marriage, thus directly countering the virtual identity between the two, which the sages attempt to stress. The husband, when married, has many more rights than during the betrothal period; how can the two be compared? The answer suggests an argument created to fit the position known from the lemma "We are embarrassed over the new, etc.," rather than a tradition.

C is another version of M. Ket. 8.1F, used here as a continuation of the sages' argument. If Gamaliel draws a distinction between the husband's rights during betrothal and after the marriage, what about his rights <u>after</u> the marriage over the goods inherited during the betrothal period? Gamaliel maintains that the husband's rights may not be retrojected.

D-E makes explicit what is only implicit in M. Ket. 8.1F, Gamaliel's affirmation of the Hillelite position, though with reservations. The woman may not dispose of the goods, though her sale is valid, if she does. E repeats the material used by Judah in A.

According to Lieberman (<u>T.K</u>. VI, pp. 309-310) the correct reading for F states that the sages reconsidered and decided that the sale was <u>invalid</u>, after questioning Gamaliel; in other words, they made the Hillelite position consistent. This repudiation of Gamaliel's view does not appear in M., in line with the favorable tendency toward him there.

G provides an expansion of Simeon's view in M. Ket. 8.2; this refinement of the problem does not directly concern us.

M. and Tos. are seen to have alternate versions of Gamaliel-traditions on this issue, in formulations by the Ushans Judah and Ḥananiah. Judah connects Gamaliel to the Houses' dispute on the husband's control after betrothal; Ḥananiah attaches the same dialogue to Gamaliel's lemma on the husband's control after marriage.

Basic to the material seems to be (a) the lemma, M. Ket. 8.1F and (b) the questioning of the Hillelite position, "We are embarrassed over the old, etc." The materials in Tos. appear to be constructed to provide the proper context for the latter statement, but there is no clarity about where it applies: during betrothal, or after marriage.

A. R. Judah said, "They said before Rabban Gamaliel, 'Since [the woman, when she is] betrothed is his wife, and [when she is] married is his wife -- as with the latter (ZW), her sale is invalid, so with the former (ZW), her sale should be invalid.'

"He said to them, 'We are embarrassed [to find reason for giving him rights] over the new [possessions], and would you even burden us with the old?'"

B. What are the "new"? Since her marriage.

What are the "old"? Before her marriage.

y. Pe. 6.2
(A = Tos. Ket. 8.1A)

Comment: A is identical with Tos. Ket. 8.1A. B, like A, explains M. Ket. 8.1B, understanding it as applying to the betrothal period. B is not part of Judah's pericope.

A. R. Judah said, "They said before Rabban Gamaliel, 'Since [the woman, when] betrothed, is his wife, and [when] married, is his wife -- as with the latter (ZH), her sale is invalid, so with the former (ZH) her sale should be invalid."

"He said to them, 'We are embarrassed [to find reason for giving him rights] over the new [possessions], and would you even burden us with the old?'"

B. What are the "new"? Since her marriage.

What are the "old"? Before her marriage -- and she was [later] married.

y. Ket. 8.1

Comment: Except for the difference in pronoun (ZH *vs*. ZW) A is identical with y. Ket. 6.2A. The redactional comment here, B, applies the dialogue to M. Ket. 8.1F, rather than M. Ket. 8.1B.

A. We have learned (TNYNN), "She sells or gives [away] and it is valid.

B. R. Ḥiyya learned (TNY RBY HYYʾ) "She does not sell or give [away] but (W) if she sells or gives [away] it is valid."

C. R. Ḥanina b. ʿAqavya said, "Rabban Gamaliel did not answer them that way. Rather, it was thus he answered them:

"'No! If you say that about a betrothed woman, whose [husband] does not have rights over what she finds or makes, or the power to void her vows, shall you say it of a married woman whose [husband] has rights over what she finds or makes, and has power to void her vows?'

D. "They said to him, '[A case in which she found property or made something] before she married and then married proves it: for he does [then] have rights over what she found or made, and power to void her vows. Will you agree with us that she does not sell or give [away]?'

E. "He said to them, 'I agree with you that she does not sell or give [away] but if she sells or gives [away] her sale is valid.'"

y. Ket. 8.2

Comment: The difference in text between Gamaliel's lemma in M. and in A here is small but major, since this version makes him a Shammaite. Lieberman considers this text unreliable (T.K., VI, pp. 308-309). R. Ḥiyya's version in B is identical with Tos. Ket. 8.1D, and Lieberman considers it the correct text of the Mishnah.

C is identical with Tos. Ket. 8.1B; and D here spells out the question in Tos. Ket. 8.1C, in terms of what precedes it, C.

A. It was taught (TNY'): Said R. Ḥananiah b. ʿAqavya, "Rabban Gamaliel did not answer the sages that way. Rather it was thus he answered them:

"'No! If you [pl.] say that about a married woman, whose husband has rights over what she finds or makes, or has power to void her vows, shall you say it of a betrothed woman, whose husband does not have rights over what she finds, nor over what she makes, nor the power to void her vows?'

B. "They said to him, 'Master, [we can understand your view concerning something she inherited and] sold before she was married; but if she married and then sold, what then?'

C. "He said to them, 'Even that one sells and gives [away], and it is valid.'

D. "They said to him, 'Since he attains [possession of] the woman, does he not attain [possession of] her goods?'

E. "He said to them, 'We are embarrassed [to find reason for giving him rights] over the new [possessions], and would you even burden us with the old?'"

b. Ket. 78b
(A = Tos. Ket. 8.1B)

Comment: A is identical with Tos. Ket. 8.1B. B here clarifies the question of Tos. Ket. 8.1C, spelling out the difference between the betrothal period and the marriage, as regards the husband's authority.

C perpetuates the error of y. Ket. 8.2A, stating that the wife's power to dispose of her goods is absolute.

D-E is a quotation from M.

Thus b. has taken the Tosefta (A), clarified its question (B), and synthesized it with the Mishnah (D-E).

A. [Concerning] a widow who said, "I do not wish to leave my husband's house," the heirs cannot say to her, "Go to your father's house, and we shall support you." Rather, they support her in her husband's house, and they give her a dwelling befitting her station.

B. [If] she said, "I do not wish to leave my father's house," the heirs can say to her, "If you are with us you have no support."

C. If she pleaded [to remain with her father, on the grounds] "that she is a child", and they are children, they support her, though she be in her father's house.

D. "All the time she is in her father's house, she collects her *ketuvah* at any time. All the time she is in her husband's house, she collects her *ketuvah* up to twenty-five years, since in the twenty-five years she spends there, she receives the equivalent of her *ketuvah*," the words of R. Meir, who said it in behalf [K, N, Camb.: MŠWM; P: MŠM] of Rabban Simeon b. Gamaliel [K, P, N, Camb.: Rabban Gamaliel].

E. And sages say, "All the time she is in her husband's house, she collects her *ketuvah* at any time. All the time she is in her father's house, she collects her *ketuvah* up to twenty-five years.

F. [If] she died, her heirs claim her *ketuvah* up to twenty-five years.

M. Ket. 12.3-4
(D = Tos. Ket. 12.3)

Comment: Besides the cash value of her *ketuvah* [marriage document], a widow is entitled to support from her husband's estate while continuing to reside in his household. Under certain conditions she is also supported while living with her own parents. Thus far, A-C.

According to D, Gamaliel allows the widow to collect the cash value of her *ketuvah* without any time limit, while living in her father's house, since she is not drawing upon the estate of her late husband, However, if she is being supported by her husband's estate she may only collect the value of the *ketuvah* throughout a period of twenty-five years: beyond that time, Gamaliel considers the value of the *ketuvah* to have been paid off by the support she received in the household of her husband. In other words, the husband's estate owes the widow continuous support, but a limited time for support-plus-*ketuvah*. The estate is protected against the double claim after twenty-five years.

The sages in E turn Gamaliel's ruling around. They do not consider her support, in the husband's house, as drawing upon the *ketuvah*, but as an addition to it. Therefore, she may collect it at any time. If she resides with her father, they do set a time limit on her collection of the value of the *ketuvah*. The twenty-five year period is applied as a limitation of the liability of the husband's estate: after that time one may assume that, since she is supported by her father, she has waived her right to the value of the *ketuvah*, because she does not need it. The sages do not restrict the liability for support-plus-*ketuvah*, except where it is clearly superfluous.

F completes the anonymous law of A-C. Supported either in her husband's house or her father's house (depending upon her age) the widow has had no need to claim her *ketuvah*; but her heirs may do so up to twenty-five years after her death. F is probably the source of the limitation period of twenty-five years, which the dispute of D-E attempts to apply to the distinction between father's and husband's estate. D-E is an Ushan dispute, but Meir attributes his position to Gamaliel.

To this point we have followed K, P, N and Camb. in discussing the subject of D as our Gamaliel. However, the printed editions of M., as well as the parallel passage to D (Tos. Ket. 12.3), all identify him as Rabban Simeon b. Gamaliel. Further, while Rabban Gamaliel appears in only three other pericopae in M. Ket., none of which deal directly with the subject of the *ketuvah*, Simeon b. Gamaliel appears in eleven other pericopae of the tractate, six of which deal with matters of the *ketuvah*. Epstein (*Mišnah*, p. 1201) notes the main difficulty of the identification: Simeon b. Gamaliel is Meir's junior, and it is anachronous for Meir to quote him. Epstein suggests that the Simeon may be Simeon b. Gamaliel the Elder (the father of our Gamaliel).

We do have one other example of a pericope in which Meir speaks "in behalf of" Gamaliel, the non-legal parable of Tos. B.Q. 7.2. If this passage is another, despite the contrary evidence, then it is Gamaliel's sole ruling on the *ketuvah*, limiting its effective duration in order to protect the husband's estate.

A. Admon says seven [rulings].

B. [Concerning] one who died and left sons and daughters: when the possessions are many, the sons inherit and the daughters are supported. And when possessions are few, the daughters are supported and the sons go begging.

C. Admon says, [The son can argue] "Must I lose because I am a male?"

D. Said Rabban Gamaliel, "I see [approve] the words of Admon."

M. Ket. 13.3
(M.B.B. 9.1)

A. [Concerning] one who claims [the return of] jars of oil from his fellow, while [the latter] admits to the [empty] jars,

B. Admon says, "Since he admits a part of the claim, he takes an oath [that he is not liable for the rest]."

C. And sages say, "This is not an admission of the same type as the claim."

D. Said Rabban Gamaliel, "I see the words of Admon."

M. Ket. 13.4
(M. Shav. 6.3)

A. [Concerning] one who promises money to his son-in-law, and goes bankrupt, [his daughter] sits [unmarried] until her hair grows white.

B. Admon says, "She can say, 'If I myself had promised, I would sit until my hair grows white; now that Father promised it for me, what can I do? Either marry me or set me free.'"

C. Said Rabban Gamaliel, "I see the words of Admon."

M. Ket. 13.5

Comment: Of the seven Admon-decisions in the collection, the first three are approved by "Gamaliel". One of these three, and all of the remaining four, involve disputes with "sages", pre-70 Pharisees.

On the basis of the contemporaneity of Admon with Gamaliel the Elder, Neusner (Pharisees, ii, pp. 350-351) assigns this pericope to him, rather than to our Gamaliel. The Gamaliel of this pericope fits Gamaliel the Elder also: his approval of the permission for the betrothed girl to be either married or freed is consistent with the ruling granting permission for women to remarry (cf. M. Yev. 13.7). Analysis of M. Shav. 6.3 confirms this attribution (as we shall see). Yet it also reveals what appears true for this pericope as well: the editor of the Mishnah evidently assumed that the pericopae refer to Gamaliel II. In M. Ket. 13.1-2, Yoḥanan b. Zakkai approves two decisions rendered by Admon's fellow-judge, Ḥanan b. Avishalom. In M. Ket. 13.3-5

Gamaliel approves Admon's three decisions. The implication of the editing of M. Ket. 13.1-9 seems to be: just as Yoḥanan b. Zakkai carried the chain of authority from pre-70 Jerusalem into Yavneh, Rabban Gamaliel continued that same tradition, from pre-70 Jerusalem, beyond Yavneh. Gamaliel is, then, the equal of Yoḥanan.

R. Yosé b. R. Judah said, "Admon and the sages did not differ concerning [a case] where her father promised it for her. For she could say, 'My father promised it for me; what can I do? Either marry me or set me free.' [Then] about what did they differ? Over [a case] where she herself promised it: for Admon says, 'She may say: "I had thought my father would give me [the money]. What can I do? Either marry me or set me free.'"

"Rabban Gamaliel said, 'I approve the words of Admon.'"

Tos. Ket. 13.1B (Lieberman ed. p. 98, lines 38-42)

Comment: Yosé revises the Mishnah, claiming that the sages agreed with Admon's position in M. Ket. 13.5. He applies the dispute to a more moot case. Gamaliel's words remain the same.

A. (M'SH B) Rabban Gamaliel once knocked out the tooth of Ṭabi, his slave. He came to R. Joshua.

B. He said to him, "I have found a way of freeing Ṭabi, my slave."

C. He said to him, "What [grounds] do you have (WMH BYDYK) [y. Shev.: you have nothing (LYT BYDYK)]? There is no fine except through a court and witnesses [y. Shev.: through witnesses and a court]."

y. Ket. 3.10 (y. Shev. 5.6)

Comment: The pericope presupposes the genre of stories about Ṭabi's piety and exemplary character. Gamaliel desires to free him. However, Joshua points out that the biblical law emancipating a slave under these conditions is in the nature of a fine imposed upon the master (Ex. 21:27). The law governing fines does not accept a confession as evidence; witnesses are required in order for a court to impose a fine. Therefore Ṭabi is not freed by the injury.

Joshua, not Gamaliel, is the hero of the story, since he reminds Gamaliel of a basic legal principle. However, given the background of Gamaliel-Ṭabi stories, this pericope may merely use all three names as an illustration of the law, and not reflect a tradition from Joshua's circle at all.

A. (GWP':) Said R. Huna, said Rav, "Concerning one who admits liability for a fine, and afterward witnesses come [to testify that he is liable], he is exempt."

B. R. Ḥisda raised an objection to R. Huna [based on the following]:

C. (M'SH B) Rabban Gamaliel put out the eye of Ṭabi, his slave. He was rejoicing a great rejoicing. He met R. Joshua. He said to him, "Didn't you know that Ṭabi, my slave, went free?"

He said to him, "Why?"

He said to him, "Because I put out his eye."

D. He said to him, "There is nothing to what you've said, because he doesn't have any witnesses. Now, if he has witnesses you are obligated [to set him free]."

E. But was it not taught: He said to him, "There is nothing to what you've said, because you have already confessed."

b. B. Q. 74b-75a

Comment: As observed above (y. Ket. 3.10), the emancipation of an injured slave is categorized as a fine imposed upon his master. Rav's generalization (A) states that an admission of liability for a fine, in the absence of witnesses, exempts one from later legal action. Ḥisda (B) uses the Gamaliel-Ṭabi story to contradict the generalization. According to Joshua, in D, witnesses' testimony would have emancipated Ṭabi despite Gamaliel's prior admission. However, another version of the story is quoted (E) in which Joshua's words accord with Huna/Rav's lemma: since Gamaliel confessed, he would be exempt from the fine, even though witnesses might later coroborate his testimony.

The story C-D identifies Ṭabi's injury as a lost eye, instead of a tooth, as in y. Ket. It also omits the reference to the emancipation as a fine, though that law is taken for granted. Aside from these major variations, b. appears to be an expansion of the story in y. Since b. has a late third-century attestation, in the names of Huna and Rav, the value of E is questionable. The existence of D (illustrating emancipation as a fine) and E (illustrating confession as a solvent for liability) as well as the difference in the details of tooth (y.) and eye (b.) strengthens the supposition of the paradigmatic nature of the story, which could be used for different purposes.

A. Someone came before Rabban Gamaliel. He said, "I found an 'open door' [my bride was not a virgin]."

He said to him, "Perhaps you moved aside.

B. "I will give you a parable. To what may this be likened? To a man who was walking in the deep darkness of night [and came to his house and found the door locked. If] he moved the bolt aside, he found it open; if he didn't move it aside, he found it locked."

C. Some say he said this to him: "Perhaps you moved aside intentionally, and tore away the door and the bar.

D. "I will give you a parable. To what may this be likened? To a man who was walking in the deep darkness of night [and came and found the door locked. If] he moved the bolt aside intentionally, he found it open; if he didn't move it aside intentionally, he found it locked."

b. Ket. 10a

Comment: The context is a series of stories, concerning R. Naḥman, Rabban Gamaliel, Rabban Gamaliel son of Rabbi, Rabban Gamaliel the Elder and R. Judah the Patriarch, all of whom find ways of reassuring a bridegroom that his bride was a virgin, despite appearances to the contrary.

In A, Gamaliel suggests that the groom performed intercourse without rupturing the hymen. B may be a gloss.

In C, the alternate version, Gamaliel suggests that the groom may have ruptured the hymen without noticing it. There is only one word's difference (MZYD) between B and D, suggesting a closer relationship between the glosses than between the two versions of Gamaliel's answer. It is possible, however, that C may be a glossed version of Gamaliel's reply in A.

xiv. Nedarim, Soṭah, Giṭṭin

A. If a man's wife vowed to abstain from any thing the absence of which causes her affliction of soul, whether the matter be between him and her, or between her and others, he shall revoke it.

B. Something [the absence of] which does not afflict the soul, whether between him and her or between her and others, he shall not revoke.

C. How? If she said, "Qonam [for me shall be] anything I do for the benefit of my father, for your father, for my brother, for your brother, that I will not give fodder to your cattle," he shall not revoke [her vow] because it is between her and others.

D. [If she said,] "I will not use kohl [eye-paint], I will not use rouge, I will not wear jewelry, I will deny you the privilege of my bed," this he shall revoke, because it is between them.

E. [If she said,] "I will not spread the mattress, I will not soak your feet, I will not mix the wine [cup] for you."

F. he does not have to revoke [it]: he forces her [to do so] against her will.

G. Rabban Gamaliel [Rashi, contra most mss.: R. Simeon b. Gamaliel] says, "He shall revoke it,

H. "for it is said: He shall not break his pledge (Num. 30:3)."

Tos. Ned. 7.1 (Lieberman ed.
p. 120, lines 1-7; b. Ned. 81b)

Comment: Scripture empowers a woman's husband, like her father, to revoke vows she makes, on the day he learns of them (Num. 30:13). This is the background of A-D, which does not directly concern us. E now declares that any vow a wife makes, prohibiting certain wifely duties, need not be revoked by the husband. She may be forced to do them, despite a vow.

Gamaliel (G) rules otherwise. H supplies an exegetical backing for Gamaliel's dissent. The husband is required to revoke his wife's vow, in order that she not transgress her pledged word, even under the compulsion of a greater responsibility. H may be a gloss, since exegeses are rare in M. and Tos. disputes. But the point it makes is significant enough not to rule out the possibility entirely. Without it, we would understand Gamaliel to mean only that these details of personal life are no different from the others listed in D. Revoking the vow is permitted. However, with the exegesis, the husband is required to revoke the vow, in order to avoid making his wife violate Num. 30:3.

A. [Vienna ms. and first printed ed.: During the war of Vespasian, they decreed against the custom of the crowns of bridegrooms.]

B. What are the crowns of bridegrooms? They are of salt and of sulphur.

C. But they permitted those of roses, and of myrtle.

D. [Vienna ms. and first printed ed.: During the war of Titus they decreed against the custom of the crowns of brides.]

E. What are the crowns of brides? They are of gold [Vienna ms. and first printed ed.: gold-embroidered crimson].

F. But she does go out with a royal cap.

G. [Vienna ms. and first printed ed.: They also decreed that one should not teach his son Greek.]

H. They permitted those of the house of Rabban Gamaliel to learn Greek, because they are close to the government.

Tos. Śoṭ. 15.8

Comment: This small collection of decrees presents some effects of the Roman wars of 69-70. A-F describes which wedding customs were restricted as the result of hardship and (later) mourning (A, D), and then mentions which aspects of the customs remained (C, F). The rulings are glossed with explanations of the customs (B, E) which suggests at least an Ushan terminus ante quem for the rulings. A-C and D-F are identical in form: Decrees + explanation of term + remainder of custom.

G-H reflects the xenophobic aftermath of the war, in the reaction against Hellenistic language and culture. It differs in form from the earlier two: Decree + exception + reason for exception; so it is probably independent of them. As in Tos. ʿA.Z. 3.5, the Patriarchal house is seen as political, and the sages ("they") are the religious authorities over their representative.

A. Who prohibited [the study of] Greek Wisdom? For Rav Judah said, Samuel said on behalf of R. Simeon b. Gamaliel,

B. "What does it mean, which is written, 'My eye affects my soul, because of all the daughters of my city (Lam. 3:51)'?

C. "There were a thousand children in my father's house; five hundred learned Torah, and five hundred learned Greek wisdom. And there remained of them only me and the son of my father's brother in Asya."

D. *It was different* with those of the house of Rabban Gamaliel, *for they were* close to the government.

E. For it was taught (DTNY'): To cut [the hair] *qoma* [Roman style] -- this is of the "ways of the Amorites". They permitted Avtilus b. Reuben to cut [his hair] *qoma*, because he was close to the government.

F. They permitted those of the house of Rabban Gamaliel [to learn] Greek wisdom because they are close to the government.

b. Śoṭ. 49b
[Aramaic italicized]

Comment: The Amoraic discussion (A, D) cites a story from which one might infer the absence of the famous prohibition of the study of "Greek Wisdom" (B-C). It quotes Rabban Simeon b. Gamaliel (early 2nd c.) lamenting the destruction of the great numbers of his father's students, incidentally mentioning the large number who studied Greek. The story, in the name of Samuel (early 3rd c.) has a late-3rd century attestation. Since a century separates Samuel from Simeon b. Gamaliel, this description of the great number of students may be based upon the tradition about the Greek studies of Gamaliel's house from Tos.

E-F cites a *baraita* justifying the adoption of foreign customs for diplomatic reasons. F is identical to Tos. Soṭ. 15.8H.

A. [A man] who brings a *geṭ* [divorce document] from abroad (MMDYNT HYM) must say, "It was written in my presence and it was signed in my presence."

B. Rabban Gamaliel says, "Even [one] who brings [it] from Reqem or from Ḥeger."

C. R. Eliezer says, "Even from Kefar Ludim to Lud."

D. And sages say, "He must say 'It was written in my presence and it was signed in my presence' only if he brings it from abroad, and if he takes it [abroad] (HMWLYK)."

M. Giṭ. 1.1 (y. Giṭ. 1.1, 2;
b. Giṭ. 4a)

Comment: Neusner points out (*Eliezer*, p. 205) that A was a law known to Eliezer and Gamaliel; they glossed the phrase "from abroad", Gamaliel including lands adjacent to eastern and southern Palestine, Eliezer including nearby villages within Palestine:

"The sages in D differ from B-C, repeating the rule of A and taking into account the opinions of B-C. D has not generated A, but must depend upon it.

"In M. Giṭ. 1.2, Judah refers to Reqem; therefore he knew 1.1 in its present form. But he has Ashqelon instead of Ḥeger, and adds a northern locale."

It is unusual for Gamaliel's gloss to precede Eliezer's. But perhaps the geographical sequence explains it: overseas (A), then lands adjacent (B) and finally, within Palestine (C).

A. Any document (GṬ) which has a Samaritan witness is invalid, except a document (GṬ) for [divorcing] women or for emancipating slaves.

B. (M'SH Š) They brought a woman's divorce document (GṬ) before Rabban Gamaliel at Kefar 'Otnai, and its witnesses were Samaritan; and he declared it valid (WHKŠYR).

C. All writs (ŠṬRWT) which are drawn up in registries of the gentiles are valid, even though those who signed them are gentiles, except a document for [divorcing] women or for emancipating slaves.

D. R. Simeon [Epstein, Mišnah, p. 1199, corrects to: Simeon b. Gamaliel] says, "Even those are valid; they were mentioned [as invalid] only if made by one unauthorized (BHDYWṬ)."

M. Giṭ. 1.5

Comment: A and C are symmetrically-shaped laws, which rule on the status of Samaritan and gentile legal documents. A writ of divorce or emancipation with a Samaritan as one of its two witnesses is valid; but no other documents thus witnessed are valid (A). according to C, in our texts of M., the reverse is true for documents executed by a gentile court. (Weiss-Halivni suggests -- on the basis of Tos. Giṭ. 1.3 -- that the text should read "invalid" instead, so that A and C become parallel in content. In any case, A and C are revised, by B and D respectively.) D is Simeon b. Gamaliel's Ushan revision of C: all documents of gentile courts are valid.

Gamaliel's act of validation (B) illustrates the law for a bill of divorce (A). But B does not mention emancipation and both of its witnesses (not just one) are Samaritans. B is independent of A, since it appears to disregard one aspect of A (emancipation) and go beyond it in another (two witnesses). The story, B, has been redacted to create a dispute, or at least a revision of the anonymous law: A declares that one Samaritan witness is valid;

Gamaliel accepts two (cf. b. Giṭ. 10b). The probable origin of this revision may be found in Tos. Giṭ. 1.4, which will be discussed below.

Kefar ʿOtnai, near the border of the Galilee and Samaria, would be a reasonable setting for the names of Samaritan witnesses to appear on a document. It is commonplace to describe Gamaliel as an itinerant authority, and his actions as legal precedent, as we have seen.

A. R. Judah says, "Even though both of its witnesses [of a GṬ] are Samaritans, it is valid."

B. Said R. Judah, "(MʿSH Š) They brought a woman's divorce document (GṬ) before Rabban Gamaliel, at Kefar ʿOtnai, and the signatures on it were of Samaritan witnesses. They pronounced it valid (WHKŠYRW)."

Tos. Giṭ. 1.4

Comment: Judah differs from M. Giṭ. 1.5A: a divorce document is valid even if both its witnesses are Samaritans (A). In B we have the story which appears in M., though the language is not identical. Here it is attributed to Judah, whose view it matches exactly.

Judah is a frequent tradent of Gamaliel, and often provides marked revisions of the views attributed to him. In this case there is no difference between Judah's version and that of M; he may be the source of M. There is no way to determine here whether B is his creation. Though the editor of M. did not use Judah's lemma as a dispute with M. Giṭ. 1.5A, he did accept the story for that purpose. This is in keeping with his penchant for Gamaliel-materials as precedents.

A. As it was taught (KDTNYʾ): At first [a witness] used to write: "I, peloni signed as witness." If his handwriting was found elsewhere, [the geṭ] was valid, and if not, it was invalid.

B. Said Rabban Gamaliel, "A great decree was set down, [when the rabbis required] that [the witnesses] spell out their names [in full] on giṭṭin, to prevent suffering (MPNY TYQWN HʿWLM)."

b. Giṭ. 36a

Comment: Munich ms. and Tos. Giṭ. 9.13 read: Simeon b. Gamaliel (cf. Epstein, Mišnah, pp. 1201-1202). M. Giṭ. 4.2-3 is a collection of decrees concerning divorces by Rabban Gamaliel the Elder. The decree mentioned in B occurs anonymously there. If it is to be attributed to a Gamaliel, rather than Simeon b. Gamaliel, it would be Gamaliel the Elder.

Said R. Judah that said Samuel, "Orphans do not require a *prośbul*."

So too Rami b. Hama learned (TNY), "Orphans do not require a *prośbul*, because Rabban Gamaliel and his court are the parents of orphans."

b. Giṭ. 37a (b. B.Q. 37a)

Comment: The reference to Gamaliel sounds like a popular saying about the responsibility of the Patriarchal court.

xv. *Bava Qamma*, *Bava Meṣia'*, *Sanhedrin*, *Shavu'ot*

A. Why did they say that they do not raise small animals in the Land of Israel? Since they bring small animals from outside the Land to the Land, but they do not bring large animals from outside the Land to the Land.

B. 1. Even though they said [that] they do not raise small animals in the Land of Israel, nevertheless they raise it ('WTH) thirty days before a festival, [or] thirty days before the [wedding] feast of his son,

2. provided that it does not go out to graze in the marketplace [i.e., at will] but [rather] that it is bound to the leg of the bed.

C. They asked Rabban Gamaliel, "What [is the law] about [permitting] raising small animals [in the Land of Israel]?"

D. He said to them, "They keep the last (H'GWNH) one for thirty days, and the butcher takes it and sells it,

E. "provided that the last one of the (H'ḤRWNH ŠBHM) does not remain more than thirty days."

Tos. B.Q. 8.11-12

Comment: M. B.Q. 7.7 prohibits raising small cattle in the Land of Israel. This is explained by Bertinoro and Maimonides as protection for the trees and for the crops: the small animals would otherwise graze in the newly-sown fields. Tos. (A) explains the ruling as an economic control: small cattle can be easily imported from neighboring countries, while large cattle cannot.

However, B also mentions that the small cattle which are permitted to be raised thirty days before a festival must be kept tethered, so that they do not graze freely. Both reasons probably stand behind the ruling.

Jastrow has been followed (p. 1042) in translating Hʿ GWNH (lit., the tied one) as the last one; he bases himself on the reading of b. B.Q. 80a, which is provided they do not keep Hʿ GWNH ŠBHM for thirty days, etc. He assumes that it is an error for Hʾ ḤRWNH the last one, in the last clause of the previous sentence there (79b). However, since B mentions the proviso that the animal must be tethered, we can also understand D more literally, as, "They keep the one (which has been) tied up, for thirty days, etc."

In either case, E still appears to be a gloss on Gamaliel's answer; but at least the gloss is not a redundancy, using the latter translation.

The pericope presupposes and comments upon the anonymous pericope in M. B.Q. 7.7. The Gamaliel-dialogue seems only to illustrate the Toseftan ruling in B. The question (C) pre-supposes it and the answer (D) re-affirms it. C-D seems to have been created to illustrate the easing of the prohibition by Tos. It is most likely that Gamaliel appears in the illustration because of the reference in B to permission to raise an animal "thirty days before the wedding of his son". The ʿAqivan traditions in M. Ker. 3.7 and b. Hul. 91b mention Gamaliel shopping for an animal for his son's wedding feast in the marketplace of Emmaus. Gamaliel's behavior in those stories would not contradict the ruling here.

A. Another [baraita] taught (TNY ʾYDK): They do not raise small animals in the Land of Israel; but they do raise [them] in the desert of Judea, and in the desert of the border of ʿAkko.

B. And even though they said, "They do not raise small animals", nevertheless they raise large animals, because "They do not impose a decree upon the community unless the majority of the community is able to stand it." [That is:] It is possible to bring small animals from outside the Land; it is impossible to bring large animals from outside the Land.

C.1. And even though they said, "They do not raise small animals," nevertheless he keeps [them] thirty days before a festival [or] thirty days before the [wedding] feast of his son;

2. provided that he does not keep the last one [more than] thirty days.

D. For you might think [Munich ms. omits: For you might think] that if the festival is over [lit., has gone], and from the time he bought it until now they did not count thirty days [Munich ms. omits: they did not count thirty days] [you might say, "Then let him keep it the full thirty days." No:] we do not say that thirty days are permitted for keeping it. Rather, since the festival is over he must not keep it [any longer].

E. And the butcher buys it and slaughters it, [or] buys it and keeps it [for market]; provided that he does not keep the last one (HʿGWNH ŠBHN) for [more than] thirty days.

F. His students asked Rabban Gamaliel, "What [is the law] about raising [small animals]?"

He said to them, "It is permitted."

G. (But didn't we learn, "They do not raise . . ."? Rather this is what they asked him:)

H. "What [is the law] about keeping [small animals]?"

He said to them "It is permitted, provided that it does not go out to graze with the flock, but [rather] is tied to the legs of the bed."

b. B.Q. 79b-80a

Comment: A and B supply two other exemptions, additional to Tos., for the rule of M. B.Q. 7.7 (not raising small animals). A mentions two desert areas where the animals' grazing would not damage new crops. B explicitly permits raising large animals, something implied but not stated by Tos. B.Q. 8.11A. C. 1 is practically identical with Tos B. 1; while C. 2 is the same as Tos. E. And D is obviously a gloss, both late and confused.

E in the *baraita* here is anonymous, though it is the same as Tos. D, which is attributed there to Gamaliel. On the other hand, H here is a quotation attributed to Gamaliel, while in Tos. B. 2 it is anonymous!

An indication of the difficulties that the Amoraim, too, had with the text is seen in F-G, where the Gamaliel-dialogue is first quoted and then revised, both in a way which seems neither to know the Toseftan version, nor to be known by it.

In brief, b. adds nothing which could amplify the concluding comments on Tos. B.Q. 8.11-12.

A. A man lends his tenant-farmers wheat [in return] for [repayment with] wheat, for seed but not for eating.

B. For Rabban Gamaliel would lend his tenant-farmers wheat for wheat, for seed [K, P, N, Camb. omit: for wheat, for seed].

C. [If he lent it when the price was] expensive, and it became cheap, or [if he lent it when it was] cheap, and it became expensive, he would take it [lit., he takes it, i.e., the repayment] from them at the cheaper price --

D. not because the halakah is that way, but because he wished to be more stringent with himself.

M. B.M. 5.8

Comment: Because agricultural prices may fluctuate sharply, a loan of wheat in return for wheat, to be repaid other than immediately, is prohibited (M. B.M. 5.9):

> A man does not say to his fellow, "Lend me a kor of wheat until threshing time and I will repay you." But he says, "Lend it to me until my son comes," or, "until I find the key." And Hillel forbids [even this].

In the interim the price may have risen, and the repayment would include a kind of "interest" (forbidden by Lev. 25.36).

In our pericope A exempts the tenant-farmer from this prohibition, in the case of a loan for seed grain. The issue does not appear to be a question of greater vs. lesser quantity, since an amount for seed purposes can be quite substantial. Bertinoro explains A as a special provision for the tenant-farmer, who would lose his field if he could not plant it. The loan of grain is considered to belong to the owner, as does the field. The percentage of the crop received by the tenant is viewed as payment for his labor, after the owner's share (here including the seed grain) has first been deducted. Thus the repayment to the owner, even if it has increased in value, is not considered to be "interest".

B provides an illustration for the law. Gamaliel's precedent (according to K, P, N and Camb.) may have consisted only of lending his tenants wheat. This is so ambiguous that it could stand even as a dispute with the anonymous law of M. B.M. 5.9, at the other extreme from the position attributed to Hillel there. But in B it is redacted here to support the anonymous law, which may require a prestigious precedent, since it overrules Hillel.

C is understood by the standard commentators to be a continuation of B. (The reason will become clear when we reach D.) But the transition from B to C is abrupt, and the present-tense verb NWṬL would have to be either HYH NWṬL or NṬL to continue the Gamaliel-narrative. Further, C is unusual for a story about Gamaliel. Though we have narratives describing his piety, none of them uses the language of stringency: ŠRṢH LHḤMYR 'L 'ṢMW. He recites the Shema' on his wedding night (M. Ber. 2.5) explaining, "I will not remove the kingship of Heaven even for a moment." He refuses a gift of fish (M. Beṣ. 3.2) saying, "They are permitted, but I do not wish to accept them." On the other hand, he is described as an opponent of extremes in piety (y. Ber. 2.9, y. Pe. 1.1) and in M. ʿEruv. 4.5 his opponents Joshua and Aqiva are described as wishing "to act stringently with themselves".

Rather, C appears to be apodictic in form, and a continuation of A: A man lends his tenants wheat, in return for wheat, for seed grain; if the price became cheap, he takes repayment at the cheaper price, in order to avoid the possibility of usury.

A-C thus permits a loan of wheat for a period of time (in contrast to M. B.M. 5.9) but places a ceiling on the value of the repayment to avoid usury. The tenant has no possibility of loss, and the owner's rental profit may shrink slightly if the price of wheat rises.

The gloss D now removes C's restriction on repayment in kind, assuring the owner of his loan even if the price of wheat rises (probably in order to encourage loans for seed grain). D does this by transforming C from a law into a description of saintly behavior, which exceeds the requirement of the law. D joins C to B by referring back to Gamaliel, making C refer to him as well. With B-D now a unit, Gamaliel's ambiguous precedent has been reworked into something no longer a precedent: a pious exemplum illustrating what the law is not, a story not anti-Gamaliel (since the redaction stresses his saintliness) yet in which he does not appear as a definer of the norm of <u>halakah</u>.

In view of his ancestry and position, Gamaliel would be assumed to own sufficient land for tenant-farming. The story need not be considered historical evidence.

A. A man says to his fellow, "Weed with me and I will weed with you," or, "Hoe with me and I will hoe with you." But he may not say, "Hoe with me and I will weed with you."

B. All days of the dry season are one and all days of the rainy season are one: a man may not say to another, "Plow with me in the rainy season and I will plow with you in the dry season."

C. Rabban Gamaliel says, "There is interest that is [paid] in advance and interest that is [paid] afterward."

D. How? If a man intended to borrow from another (HYMNW) and sent him [a gift] and said, "That you may lend me (ŠTLWNY) [money]" -- that is interest [paid] in advance.

If a man borrowed from another and returned his money, and then sent him [a gift] and said, "This is for your money [K has dropped: and then sent him [a gift] and said, "This is for your money . . ." by homoioteleuton] which was out of use while it was with me" -- that is interest [paid] afterward.

E. R. Simeon says, "There may be interest [paid in] words: a man may not say to him [his creditor], 'Know that such-a-man has come from such-a-place'."

M. B.M. 5.10

Comment: A-B gives examples to show that, even in the case of physical labor, if the effort used in repayment of a kindness exceeds the original effort, the excess is considered as "interest". Hence the repayment must be in the same kind of labor, and at the same season of the year.

C-D is unrelated to the foregoing, though it is also concerned with a definition of "interest", in the broader sense. Its refinement of definition suggests a development of commercial law not evidenced by the pre-70 Pharisees or Eliezer. Gamaliel's lemma is immediately followed by an explanatory gloss (D) joined to it by KYṢD, "How?". In E, Simeon adds a further refinement of the idea, and supplies an Ushan terminus ante quem for the pericope.

A. You may deduct interest from loans to foreigners, but not from loans to your countryman (Deut. 23:21a). You may deduct interest from loans to a foreigner -- [this is] a positive commandment; but not from loans to your countryman -- [this is] a negative commandment.

B. Rabban Gamaliel says, "What is taught by but not from loans to your countryman? For [Scripture] had already said, You shall not deduct interest from loans to your countryman (Deut. 23: 20a). Rather, [this is to teach that] there is interest that is [paid] in advance and interest that is [paid] afterward."

C. How? If a man set his eyes to borrow from another (MMNW), and sent him [a gift] and said, "That he may lend me (ŠYLWYNY) [money]" - that is interest [paid] in advance. If a man borrowed from another and returned his money, and then sent him a gift and said, "This is for his money which was out of use while it was with me" -- that is interest [paid] afterward.

Sifré Ki Teṣé. 263 (B = Midr. Tann. on Deut. 23:21, ed. D.S. Hoffman, vol. ii, p. 151, lines 13-14)

Comment: Except for use of the third person, in some places, C here is identical with M. B.M. 5.10D. But rather than being an independent lemma, the Sifré pericope is structured as an exegesis.

B connects the two kinds of interest with two Biblical verses. Gamaliel's words aside from the stock exegetical phrases introducing the verses, are identical with M. B.M. 5.10C; so they may have been incorporated here into an exegetical frame, though originally without it. It is less likely that this may have been the origin of Gamaliel's lemma, which entered the Mishnah shorn of its introduction.

(WTNY) We have learned: If two men were claiming ownership of a document, one saying, "It is mine and I lost it," the other saying, "It is mine, and I paid you [the debt recorded on it]" -

"The document with its signatures shall be carried out," the words of Rabbi.

Rabban Gamaliel says, "Let them divide [the sum]."

y. B.M. 1.5

<u>Comment</u>: The text here should read "Rabban Simeon b. Gamaliel", as in Tos. B.M. 1.15 and y. Git. 1.1.

A. Every Sanhedrin in which there are two [judges] who know how to speak [the seventy languages of mankind], and in which all are able to understand [them] is worthy to act [as a Sanhedrin]. A Sanhedrin with three [able to speak the seventy languages] is intermediate [in quality; one with] four [is considered] wise.

B. The [seating of the] Sanhedrin was [arranged] like half of a round threshing-floor, so that they would all see each other. The Patriarch would sit in the center, and the elders would sit to his left and right.

C. Said R. Eleazar b. R. Ṣadoq, "When Rabban Gamaliel was in session in Yavneh, my father and another (W'ḤR) [scholar sat] at his right, and the elders at his left.

D. "And why did one ('ḤD) sit to the right of the elder [R. Ṣadoq]? In order to give honor to the elder."

Tos. San. 8.1

<u>Comment</u>: Eleazar's reminiscence of his father has been added to the pericope to illustrate the seating arrangements of the Sanhedrin, described in B. It is originally independent, however, since it does not describe symmetrical seating; the Patriarch is not in the center. Ṣadoq and one other sit on one side, all the other sages on the other.

C-D does constitute a claim of Eleazar b. Ṣadoq to be directly intimate with the Patriarch and his traditions (as in Tos. Y.Ṭ.

2.12). As J. Lightstone ("Ṣadoq", p. 69) notes, the pericope places him in Yavneh at the time of Gamaliel's patriarchate. Furthermore, Eleazar's father, R. Ṣadoq, is the only one of the elders to sit to Gamaliel's right on his own merits. The other scholar is there only as an honor to R. Ṣadoq, not as an intimate of Gamaliel.

A. The Sanhedrin was like half of a circular threshing-floor. The Patriarch would sit in the middle, so that they would [both] see and hear him.

B. R. Leazar b. R. Ṣadoq said, "When Rabban Gamaliel was in session in Yavneh, Father and his brothers (ʾḤYW) were sitting to his right, and the Elders to his left, out of respect to the elder."

y. Sanh. 1.4

<u>Comment</u>: This parallel to Tos. San. 8.1 is almost identical. However, the "other one" (ʾḤR, ʾḤD) who sat beside Ṣadoq there has become Ṣadoq's "brothers" (ʾHYW) here. Since there is no other mention of the brothers of Ṣadoq (cf. Lightstone, "Ṣadoq", <u>ad. loc</u>.) I assume that the text in y. is faulty.

A. What is [the law concerning eligibility] for colleagues to enter [a session] for the intercalation of the year? We may learn from the following:

B. (MʿSH B) Rabban Gamaliel said, "Have them call seven elders to the upper chamber for me." Eight entered.

C. He said, "Who entered without permission?"

D. Samuel the Little rose and said, "I came up without permission: I needed a [decision in] <u>halakah</u>, and entered to ask about it."

E. Said Rabban Gamaliel to him, "Even though all Israel know that Eldad and Medad are [but] two, I say that you are one of them [fit to join them]."

F. Yet even so, they did not intercalate [the year] on that day. They digressed into words of Torah, and intercalated it on the following day.

y. Sanh. 1.2

<u>Comment</u>: A makes explicit use of the story it quotes as a legal precedent -- something implicit throughout the Gamaliel traditions. The setting for the story is an "upper chamber", which also appears in a story in b. Ber. 37a ("an upper chamber in Jericho"). B does not indicate the purpose of the meeting for

which the seven elders are summoned; the story turns on the fact that Gamaliel did not invite specific individuals. The key word of the story is "permission": only those invited may enter (C, D). Up to this point, we might seem to be heading toward another kind of "humiliation-story", in which the rabbi who runs afoul of the Patriarch is subjected to punishment (M.R.H. 2.7, y. Ber. 4.1). But in E Gamaliel praises Samuel and accepts him, in spite of his not being invited. The reference to Eldad and Medad is appropriate (Num. 11:24-29). When Moses assembled seventy elders to receive the Holy Spirit and prophesy, these two young men were not invited; yet the Holy Spirit rested upon them. They prophesied outside of the camp and Moses praised them. Gamaliel's remark indicates that Samuel is both worthy of being present and worthy of the Holy Spirit (cf. Tos. Soṭ. 13.3). The story appears to end here. It is another of the praises of Samuel the Little, from Samuel's circle, in which Gamaliel himself testifies to Samuel's eminence. Samuel is indeed aggressive. He enters without permission, just as he volunteered to compose the prayer against the Minim (b. Ber. 28b-29a). But this assertiveness was for a good purpose (D) and he is praised for it.

F completes the pericope with the first mention of intercalation. Only those appointed may intercalate; therefore the subject of the meeting is changed, out of deference to Samuel's presence. Though F appears to be an addition, its phrasing indicates that it takes for granted that the story refers to intercalation, rather than adapting it for that purpose. The superscription, A, must have been a part of the pericope before F's comment. The function of F is to strengthen the rule, in the face of the exception Gamaliel is reported to have made. We have seen that the authority to intercalate was carefully guarded by the Patriarch (M. ʿEd. 7.7). For the possible response of the patriarchal tradition, see Tos. Pes. 1.27-28 and comment.

Traditions about Gamaliel preserve four different stories about public confrontation between him and other scholars. In three of them, Gamaliel humiliates Joshua. In M.R.H. 2.8-9, from patriarchal tradents, Gamaliel is triumphant and magnanimous. In y. Ber. 4.1 the confrontation is over the evening prayer (b. Bek. 36a says it is over R. Ṣadoq's lamb); and it leads (in the versions of ʿAqivan tradents) to Gamaliel's deposition. Here the tradition of confrontation is used by Samuel's tradents to show the acknowledged eminence of their master. The story of confrontation, in both instances, marks Joshua and Samuel as rabbinic antagonists of Gamaliel. Yet their challenge seems to come from different quarters. Joshua, we recall, is presented as a proponent of the power of the rabbis to interpret law, without regard to heavenly voices (b. B.M. 59b). Samuel, on the other hand is described as worthy of the Holy Spirit, and as a disciple of Hillel would not be considered averse to reliance upon its successor, the BT QWL, the divine echo.

A. Our rabbis taught (TNW RBNN): They intercalate the year only with those [scholars] who have been appointed for it.

B. (M'SH B) Rabban Gamaliel said, "Have seven [men] get up early for me, to [come to] the upper chamber [to intercalate the year]." He got up early and found eight.

C. He said, "Who is it that came up [here] without permission? Let him go down."

D. Samuel the Little stood up and said, "I am he who came up without permission. But I didn't come up to intercalate the year; rather [the reason was] that I needed to learn the actual practice of a law (HLKH LM'SH) [from you]."

E. He said to him, "Sit down, my son, sit down. Any year is fit to be intercalated by you; only the sages said, 'They intercalate the year only with those who have been appointed for it.'"

F. *And it was not Samuel the Little* [who was the uninvited person], *but another man; and he did it* [to avoid] *the result of* [the other person's being put to] *shame*.

b. Sanh. 11a (Aramaic italicized)

Comment: The redactor's point in y. Sanh. 1.2 A+F, that only those appointed to the court may intercalate, is stated at the outset here as an anonymous law (A). B-D is almost identical with y., with slight additions ("get/got up early", "Let him go down," "HLKH LM'SH"). Gamaliel's words in E have been revised to fit the opening statement of the law exactly, retaining praise of Samuel. The narrator of b. seems to be sensitive to the situation as a potential humiliation-story: he adds a moral (in Aramaic) which interprets Samuel's admission as an act to avert someone else's humiliation, and which also absolves Samuel of having violated the rule of A by attending a court to which he had not been invited.

Our rabbis taught (TNW RBNN): *Justice, justice shall you follow* (Deut. 16:20). This means: follow scholars to their academies. [Follow] after R.Eliezer to Lud, after R. Yoḥanan b. Zakkai to Beror Ḥayyil, after R. Joshua to Peki'in, after Rabban Gamaliel to Yavneh, after R. 'Aqiva to B'nai Beraq, after R. Mattia to Rome, after R. Ḥanania b. Ṭeradion to Sikni, after R. Yosé to Sepphoris, after R. Judah b. Batyra to Nisibis, after R. Joshua [GRA: R. Ḥanania, nephew of R. Joshua] to the Exile, after Rabbi [Judah the Patriarch] to Bet She'arim, after sages to the Chamber of Hewn Stones.

b. Sanh. 32b

Comment: The list is not chronological. In some cases it mentions rabbis in connection with their place of residence, in others with their place of retirement. These were probably the most well-known place-names associated with the men on the list, so that Gamaliel's connection with Yavneh is significant.

A. If he claimed [the return of] wheat from him, and he admitted to him [a claim for] barley, he is exempt from taking an oath that he does not owe him wheat.

B. And Rabban Gamaliel declares him liable.

C. [Concerning] one who claims [the return of] jars of oil from his fellow, while [the latter] admits to the [empty] jars.

D. Admon says, "Since he admits a part of the claim, he takes an oath [that he is not liable for the rest]."

E. And sages say, "This is not an admission of the same type as the claim."

F. Said Rabban Gamaliel, "I approve [lit., see] the words of Admon."

M. Shav. 6.3 (Tos. Shav. 5.9: b. B.M. 5a, 100b; C-F = M. Ket. 13.4)

Comment: A man admitting to partial validity of a claim against him must take an oath that he is not liable for the rest of the claim. In A-B, Gamaliel differs from the anonymous law; he requires an oath even when the admission is to a liability of a kind different from the claim.

The second case, C-F, is part of the collection of Admon-laws in M. Ket. 13.3-9, seven dissents by Admon followed by the approval of Gamaliel. Here it is joined to A-B, to illustrate the underlying principle followed by Gamaliel: an oath is required, even when the admission is not identical with the claim.

But there is a significant difference between A-B and C-F. In the latter, Gamaliel agrees with Admon's reasoning: jars and oil are a different aspect of the same claim. All three parties, Gamaliel, Admon and the sages, share the same view that an "admission of the same type as the claim" requires an oath. They differ only on its application to the example of jars and oil. However, the Gamaliel of A-B differs in principle from both Admon and the "sages" of A and of E. They both require an oath only when the admission is of the same type as the claim. He requires an oath even when they differ (wheat and barley). Thus the Gamaliel of A-B would agree with Admon's decision, but not with his reasoning, while the Gamaliel of C-F would agree with the sages of A, and not with the Gamaliel of B.

As we have seen, (M. Ket. 13.4) Neusner considers C-F to refer to Gamaliel I, while the editor of the Mishnah assumed him to be Gamaliel II. Here the redactor assembled the two traditions without bothering to distinguish between them. Yet surely the Gamaliel of A-B is represented as our Gamaliel. His view is more extreme than the principle underlying C-F, in requiring an oath.

xvi. 'Eduyyot, Avodah Zarah

A. [There are] four things [which] Rabban Gamaliel declares [capable of becoming] unclean; and sages declare them clean:

B. (1) the metal cover of a basket belonging to houseowners, (2) the hanger of a strigil, (3) unfinished metal vessels and (4) a plate (TBL') broken in two.

C. And the sages agree with Rabban Gamaliel that if the plate was broken into two pieces, one large and one small, the large one is [capable of becoming] unclean, and the small one is clean.

M. 'Ed. 3.9 (M. Kel. 12.6)

Comment: See M. Kel. 12.6.

A. In three things Rabban Gamaliel [gives the more] stringent [ruling], according to the words of the House of Shammai,

B. "They do not cover up hot [food] on a festival day for the Sabbath; and they do not re-assemble a candelabrum on a festival; and they do not bake bread in large loaves but only as thin cakes."

C. Said Rabban Gamaliel, "Never did my father's household bake bread in large loaves, but only as thin cakes."

D. They said to him, "What shall we do with your father's household, who used to be strict with themselves, but lenient with all Israel, so that they [Israel] could bake large loaves and thick cakes!"

E. Moreover (ʾP) he said three things [which are more] lenient, "They sweep between the couches, and put spices on the fire, on a festival; and they prepare [lit., make] a kid roasted whole for Passover evening."

F. And sages prohibit.

M. ʿEd. 3.10-11 (M. Beṣ. 2.6-7; A-C = b. Shab. 39b; D = b. Pes. 36b-37a)

Comment: See M. Beṣ. 2.6-7.

A. They testified that they intercalate the year [declare it a leap-year] during all of Adar.

B. For they used to say "Until Purim".

C. They testified that they may intercalate the year conditionally.

D. (WMʿSH B) Rabban Gamaliel went to Syria to receive authority from the [Roman] governor (HGMWN) in Syria, and he was delayed in returning. So they intercalated the year on condition that Rabban Gamaliel would wish it so. When he returned, he said, "I wish it." And the year was considered as intercalated.

M. ʿEd. 7.7

Comment: "They", who testify in A, are shown from the context of M. ʿEd. 6.6 (and from Tos. Sanh. 2.13C, below) to be R. Joshua and R. Pappias. Their testimony would be part of the Yavnean work of reconstructing the legal corpus, which would suggest that B represents the practice of Temple times.

C is independent of A, though it also follows the testimony-form (HM HʿYDW Š). D is cited as both an illustration and a precedent. That is, it defines conditional intercalation as intercalation in the absence of the Patriarch and pending his approval; and it suggests that the Gamaliel-story is the precedent for the law. We shall see immediately below, however, an alternate explanation to that supplied by the redactor of M.

As in other pericopae, Gamaliel's authority regarding the calendar is emphasized.

A. They do not intercalate the year [Vienna ms., first printed ed. add: except (ʾLʾ)] in Judea; but if they do intercalate it, it is [validly] intercalated.

B. Ḥananiah, man of Ono, testified before Rabban Gamaliel that they do not intercalate the year except in Judea; but if they intercalate it in the Galilee, it is [validly] intercalated.

C. And they intercalate the year all [through the month of] Adar. For at first they used to say [that] they only intercalate [the year] until Purim, until R. Joshua and R. Pappias came and testified that all of Adar is fitting for intercalation.

D. 1. R. Simeon b. Gamaliel and R. Eleazar b. Ṣadoq say, "They do not intercalate the year,

2. "and they do not do what is for the needs of the community,

3. "except (ʾLʾ) conditionally;

4. "so that the majority of the community will accept it upon themselves."

E. They do not intercalate the year at night; and if they do intercalate it, it is not [validly] intercalated.

F. They do not sanctify the new moon at night; and if they do sanctify it, it is not [validly] sanctified.

Tos. San. 2.13, 14

Comment: A declares the validity of fixing the calendar outside of Judea. B specifically permits performing the intercalation in Galilee; Ḥananiah's testimony is given "before Rabban Gamaliel," which implies a formal session of the Patriarchal court, with Gamaliel presiding. The information from C, with the key phrases reversed, occurs in M. without the names of Joshua and Pappias.

Normally, the double-negative phrase ʾYN ʾLʾ is translated as "only". In this pericope it has been rendered as, "They do not ... except" in order to indicate the separation of the two negatives. This is of significance in D, which bears signs of glossing in 2 and in 4. (2 breaks into the lemma, and 4 supplements it.) The question is, where does the "except (L)" of 3 fit? Is it a continuation of 2, or is all of 3 a continuation of 1? If we note that both E and F are simple prohibitions ("They do not . . . They do not . . ."), D may also be, in its pre-glossed state, a simple prohibition: "They do not intercalate the year conditionally." In other words, Simeon and Eleazar have a tradition different from M. While M declares that they may intercalate conditionally, and redactionally modifies that rule to stress the subsequent agreement of the Patriarch, Simeon and Eleazar are more extreme -- they declare the necessity of the Patriarch's presence.

If, on the other hand, we assume that ʾLʾ is integral to 3, Simeon and Eleazar may themselves be the glossators and recasters of D. In that case, they would be supplying a different explanation for the tradition of conditional intercalation. While the redactor of M. explains it in terms of Patriarchal authority they understand it as: subject to ratification by a majority of the community. Though their lemma could be understood in a way not to conflict with the Mishnah -- i.e., the calendar is fixed pending the approval of the Patriarch, so that a majority of the community will accept it -- the absence in Tos. of any reference to the Patriarch seems decisive. At least for these Ushans, conditional intercalation means majority approval, not Patriarchal approval. It is doubly significant that Simeon is Patriarch himself, and Eleazar in the patriarchal circle. Their names provide an Ushan attestation for the substance of M. ʿEd. 7.7C. The content of their gloss may indicate a loss of Patriarchal authority at Usha, while the use of the Gamaliel-story by the redactor of M. may suggest a later attempt to recoup that pre-eminence. At the very least, M. has selected the tradition more favorable to the Patriarch. This does not imply, however, that Gamaliel did not exercise veto power over the calendar during his own patriarchate, as M. ʿEd. 7.7 asserts. M. R.H. 2.7 makes it plausible that he did.

A. Our rabbis taught (TNW RBNN): They do not intercalate the year unless the Patriarch (NSYʾ) wishes it.

B. (WMʿSH B) Rabban Gamaliel went to receive permission from a ruler (ŠLṬWN) in Syria, and he was delayed in returning. So they intercalated the year, with the proviso that Rabban Gamaliel would wish it so. When Rabban Gamaliel returned and said, "I wish it," the year was considered as intercalated.

b. Sanh. 11a

Comment: The b. baraita makes explicit the redactional point of M. ʿEd. 7.7: conditional intercalation means "pending the approval of the Patriarch".

A. R. Joshua testified with (W) R. Judah b. Bathyra concerning the widow of [one who belonged to] an ʿIsah [family], that she is fit to [marry into] the priesthood.

B. For [K, P, Camb.: And] [a member of] an ʿIsah [family] is fit to declare unclean and to declare clean, and to send away and to bring near.

C. Said Rabban Simeon b. Gamaliel [P, Camb.: Rabban Gamaliel], "We accept your testimony,

D. "but what shall we do since (Š) [P, Camb.: W] Rabban Yoḥanan b. Zakkai decreed that courts not be set up for this.

E. "The priests [will] listen to you [concerning] sending away, but not [concerning] bringing near."

M. ʿEd. 8.3

Comment: The term ʿIsah designates those families with whom priests would not intermarry, out of fear that they might contain persons of unfit status. Joshua and Judah testify to two things: first, that the widow of a man from one of those families may marry into the priesthood (A). Her husband's possible unfitness does not affect her own fitness. Second, they claim that a member of such a family may testify concerning the fitness of other family-members' personal status (B).

Epstein (Mišnah, p. 1202) accepts the reading of "Gamaliel" (in P and Camb.) as correct. Joshua and Judah could not have testified before the first or second Simeon b. Gamaliel. In C, Gamaliel is clearly in a position of authority. He accepts the testimony of Joshua and Judah, implying that he agrees with them. He attributes to Yoḥanan b. Zakkai the acceptance of the futility of imposing this Pharisaic leniency upon the priestly families: there is not way to force the priests to accept marriage with people they regard as unacceptable. Gamaliel's reply, like their testimony, appears composite: D appears to respond to B, while E responds to A; no court would be necessary to identify the widow (A), while a court would be required to hear the testimony of the ʿIsah (B).

W. Green (Joshua, ad. loc.) points to a number of Joshuan traditions "advocating a relaxation of the restrictions which surrounded the priesthood." Gamaliel seems to concur. However, Neusner (Life, p. 285) speculates that Gamaliel may have suppressed some of Yoḥanan's enactments concerning the priests, as the price of their co-operation with his leadership. Here he appears to employ Yoḥanan's own prestige to make Joshua and Judah accept his inaction, concerning legislation affecting the priesthood.

A. Asked Proqlos, son of Plosfos (PRWQLWŚ BN PLWŚPWŚ; Midr. Tann.: PLWŚLWŚ) of Rabban Gamaliel, in ʿAkko, when he was bathing (MRḤṢ) in the bath-house of Aphrodite (ʾMR LW), "It is written in your Torah, Let nothing that is to be destroyed (ḤRM) stick to your hand (Deut. 13:18). Why then do you bathe in the bath-house of Aphrodite?"

B. He said to him, "One does not give a reply [concerning religious law] in the bath." And when he came out,

C. 1. he said to him, "I did not come into her boundary; she came into my boundary.

2. "They do not say, 'Let us make a bath-house for beautiful Aphrodite.' Rather they say, 'Let us make a beautiful Aphrodite for the bath-house.'

D. "Another explanation (DBR ʾḤR): If they would give you much money, you would not enter for your idolatrous worship (ʿBWDH ZRH) naked, or having had an emission, or urinate in her presence. Yet this one stands before the sewer-pipe, and all the people urinate in her presence!

E. "It only says [Cut down the images of] their gods (Deut. 12:3): that which he treats as a god is forbidden; that which he does not treat as a god is permitted."

M. ʿA.Z. 3.4 (Midr. Tann. on Deut. 13:18, ed. D.S. Hoffman, vol. i, p. 68, line 30--p.69, line 1)

Comment: A number of pericopae dealing with Jewish-gentile relations place Gamaliel in the vicinity of ʿAkko (e.g., Tos. M.Q. 2.14). Here we have a debate between Gamaliel and a gentile, which incorporates both a challenge to Gamaliel's personal behavior and a question of biblical exegesis.

Proqlos was the name of the teacher of Marcus Aurelius Antoninus. Since the latter appears in many legends together with Rabbi Judah the Patriarch, his mentor's name may have found its way into the Patriarchal tradition. It may then have been added to the Gamaliel-story as a proper title for a cultured gentile. Alternatively, it is possible that the name could be a distortion of Onqelos: the last four letters are identical (QLWS) and the initial letters may be easily confused (פ, ע). Proqlos' family name may be symbolic (Plosfos = Philosophos?). In any case, he claims that Gamaliel's use of the ʿAkko bath-house violates the law of the Torah. The idol is something to be destroyed (ḤRM), so Gamaliel should have no proximity to it. The core of his challenge is the question: "Why then do you bathe . . .?" The exegetical point may be an addition, concurrent with E.

B also appears to be an addition. In other pericopae, too, Gamaliel does not answer until the environment is suitable (e.g., Tos. Pes. 1.27). C. 1 is the first reply, and probably the core of the pericope. The statue is an intrusion into the bath-house, not a central feature of it; therefore it does not transfer any idolatrous meaning to the institution as a whole. C. 2 expands the answer, with a popular saying. D provides a second answer: the statue is not treated with reverence, so that it cannot be considered as an object of worship. E repeats the point exegetically.

Standing behind the story is certainly a tale uncomplimentary to the Patriarch. As one in frequent contact with the Romans, and permitted greater familiarity with their religion and culture (Tos. Šoṭ. 15.8, Tos. 'A.Z. 3.5) he was fair game for questions about his personal piety.

The pericope would be a pro-Patriarchal answer to such stories. First, it places the challenge to Gamaliel in the mouth of a pagan, hostile to the Torah, rather than in the mouth of a pious Israelite -- thus identifying opposition to the Patriarch with the camp of idolaters. Second, it provides Gamaliel's defense: using a pagan bath-house is permitted. Gamaliel is provided with two answers, each one doubled, where one would have sufficed. This excess may suggest the seriousness in which the patriarchal tradents held the attack on their representative.

A. Another incident (ŠWB M'SH), in the heights of Bet'Anat, where there were gathered more than two thousand kor [of water], they came and asked R. Ḥananiah b. Ṭeradion, and he declared it unfit, [saying] "I say that gentiles entered during the night and emptied it and returned and filled it with a swipe."

B. (WM'SH B) Rabban Gamaliel and Onqelos the proselyte came to Ashqelon. Rabban Gamaliel immersed himself (ṬBL) in a bath-house, and Onqelos the proselyte [immersed] in the sea.

C. Said R. Joshua b. Qibusai [alt.: Qipusai, Quipunai], "I was with them, and Rabban Gamaliel immersed himself only in the sea."

Tos. Miq. 6.3

Comment: Tos. Miq. 6.1 presents a series of disputes over the status of various types of pools. Pericopae 6.2 and 6.3 then provide a number of stories illustrating the disputes.

B-C, which concerns us here, deals with a dispute between Meir and Judah, about pools belonging to gentiles within the towns of the Land of Israel. Meir declares them unfit for use by Israelites who have had an emission; Judah declares them fit, since someone who has had an emission may immerse himself in any pool of 40 se'ahs' volume. The story given in B and then revised in C is added to provide support for Meir's side of the dispute. The anonymous tradition of B has it that when Gamaliel and Onqelos the proselyte came to the gentile town of Ashqelon, Gamaliel made use of the bath-house, while Onqelos used the sea. The redactor understands the tradition to mean that both men had had emissions; and the operative word is ṬBL, rather than MRḤṢ as in M. ʿA.Z. 3.4. Gamaliel's behavior would then reflect the view later espoused by Judah, while Onqelos' behavior would support Meir. But Joshua b. Qibusai (C) revises the tradition on the basis of his personal experience, claiming that Gamaliel held the stricter view also, and did not use the gentile bath-house for his immersion. Gamaliel's example thus also supports Meir. Since Judah is closely identified with Gamaliel's traditions, this is a strong argument against him.

Clearly, Joshua (or the redactor who supplied C in his name) considered B to be uncomplimentary to Gamaliel. Though M. ʿA.Z. 3.4 reports Gamaliel's view that using a gentile bath-house is permissible, C ignores this, or is ignorant of it. B displays Gamaliel as inferior to Onqelos in the strictness of his observance; C defends him against this invidious comparison by denying the allegation.

The possibility must at least be considered that both M. ʿA.Z. 3.4 and Tos. Miq. 6.3 are reflections of a single anti-Gamaliel story: Gamaliel uses the bath-house and Onqelos uses the ocean; then Onqelos questions Gamaliel about the propriety of his act. This tradition becomes distorted into the Gamaliel-Proqlos-ʿAkko debate, and the Gamaliel-Onqelos-Ashqelon story. In both cases, the story is taken up by patriarchal tradents, incorporating defenses of Gamaliel which are contradictory in nature, but more powerful than the attacks upon him.

A. An Israelite taking a haircut from a gentile [barber] looks in the mirror.

B. [Taking a haircut] from a Samaritan, he does not look in the mirror.

C. They permitted the house of Rabban Gamaliel to look in the mirror, because they were close to the government.

Tos. ʿA.Z. 3.5

Comment: This is related to M. ʿA.Z. 2.2 (and b. ʿA.Z. 29a): "'And they [Israelites] do not have their hair cut by them [gentiles] in any place,' the words of R. Meir. And sages say, 'In public it is permitted, but not just the two of them [alone].'" The issue is personal saftety; the gentile with the sharp instrument in his hand is presumed capable of murder.

Our pericope, A-B, serves to restrict the sages' view: when taking the haircut in public, the Israelite must look in the mirror, in order to be aware of any hostile motion. But a Samaritan is presumed to be subject to the same moral laws as the Israelite, and need not be suspected of murderous intent.

C is redacted as if it were an illustration of A-B, but it is not. A and B are stated as requirements, C as a leniency which is permitted; so C contradicts A-B. It presupposes a prohibition on the use of a mirror, something which may be implied, but is not stated, by A-B. (An Amoraic comment (b. Shab. 94b) bases the prohibition on Deut. 22:5, but the origin of the ruling is obscure.) The issue of C is related to y. ʿA.Z. 2.2: "They permitted three things to the house of Rabbi: that they would look in the mirror, that they would cut their hair qoma [fringed Roman style], and they would teach their children Greek wisdom -- since they were close to the government."

Even though the meaning of C is not clear, we may note the position of the house of Gamaliel in the statement. We see the house of the Patriarch not as religious authorities, but rather as political figureheads. The law is in the hands of others, who "permit" the household of the Patriarch certain latitudes of cultural deviance for political necessity.

A. An objection was raised (MYTYBY): [As to] barrels or leather bottles of idolaters, wine of an Israelite which has been kept in them is forbidden for drinking, but permitted for [other] benefit.

B. Testified Simeon b. Gudda (GWDʾ) before Rabban Gamaliel's son, concerning Rabban Gamaliel, that the latter drank from one [of those containers] in ʿAkko.

C. But they did not accept [his testimony].

D. A contradiction (WRMYNHY): Wine which comes in leather bottles of idolaters is forbidden for drinking but permitted for [other] benefit.

E. Testified Simeon B. Gudda (GWDʿ) before Rabban Gamaliel's son, concerning Rabban Gamaliel, that the latter drank from one in ʿAkko.

F. And they accepted [his testimony].

b. ʿA.Z. 32a

Comment: M. ʿA.Z. 2.3 forbids the use, in any way, of wine belonging to gentiles, since that wine was intended for use in libations honoring foreign gods. M. ʿA.Z. 2.4 considers the problem of containers belonging to gentiles, which hold Israelite wine. Meir holds that such wine is permitted neither for drinking nor for other use, while the sages permit other benefit from the wine.

In our pericope, A presents the viewpoint of the sages in that Ushan dispute. B presents a view more lenient than the sages', drawing upon patriarchal precedent; but that view is rejected (C). D-F presents the same story with a reversed decision.

Added to the contradiction between the two versions of the story is a problem of attributions.

The parallel pericope in Tos. ʿA.Z. 4.9 reads:

> A. [As to] barrels or leather bottles of gentiles in which wine of an Israelite has been kept, [the wine] is forbidden for drinking but permitted for [other] benefit.
>
> B. Testified Simeon b. Gudda (GWDʿ) before the son of Rabban Gamaliel, saying (Šʾ MR) on behalf of Rabban Gamaliel the Elder [Vienna ms.: Testified Simeon b. Gudda (GWDʿ) before his son Gamaliel the Elder] that drinking [it] is permitted.
>
> C. But they did not accept [his testimony].

On the basis of the Vienna ms. reading, Lieberman (T.R., ii, p. 193) suggests that the correct reading should be, "Testified Simeon b. Gudda on behalf of the son of Rabban Gamaliel the Elder that drinking [it] is permitted." This would be the source of R. Ḥananel's text of b. ʿA.Z. 32a A-B, which reads, "Testified Simeon b. Gudda concerning the son of Rabban Gamaliel [i.e., the Elder], that he drank from one in ʿAkko. But they did not accept [his testimony]." In other words, Simeon reports a lemma of Simeon b. Gamaliel the Elder that such is permitted, and also reports him doing so in ʿAkko. From Lieberman's analysis, none of this refers to our Gamaliel.

The testimony-form of the pericope would support this supposition, since it would mark the pericope as more likely to be Yavnean than Ushan (as b. would have it).

The condition of that precedent-story is seen from both the confusion between b. and Tos. over whom it concerns, and between b. ʿA.Z. 32a C and F over the acceptance of the testimony.

Accepting Lieberman's reconstruction, we may observe that as the lemma in Tos. has been transformed into the chria of b., the story has been assimilated into the Gamaliel-corpus in two ways. First, we have other pericopae concerning Gamaliel's contacts with gentiles in the ʿAkko area, one of them involving the drinking of wine (Tos. Pes. 1.27). While the Toseftan pericope here does not mention ʿAkko, b. does add that detail. And second, we have other pericopae about testimony before Gamaliel concerning the deeds of his father and grandfather: this story concerns him, and the testimony is given before his son.

xvii. Zevaḥim, Ḥullin, Keritot

A. The Altar sanctifies what is designated for it.

B. R. Joshua says, "Everything designated for the fires [of the Altar] and goes up [there] does not come down.

C. "As it is said, *This is the Whole-offering on the hearth upon the Altar* (Lev. 6:9). As with the Whole-offering, designated for the fires, if it goes up it may not come down again, so everything designated for the fires, if it goes up it may not come down."

D. Rabban Gamaliel says, "Everything designated for the Altar, if it goes up it may not come down."

E. "As it is said, *This is the Whole-offering on the hearth upon the Altar*. As with the Whole-offering, designated for the Altar, if it goes up it may not come down again, so everything designated for the Altar, if it goes up it may not dome down."

F. The words of Rabban Gamaliel differ from R. Joshua only regarding the blood and the Drink-offering, [about] which Rabban Gamaliel says, "They may not come down," and R. Joshua says, "They may come down."

G. R. Simeon says, "[Whether] the sacrifice be fit and the Drink-offerings unfit, or the Drink-offerings fit and the sacrifice unfit, or even both of them unfit: the sacrifice may not come down, and the Drink-offerings come down."

M. Zev. 9.1 (A-D = b. San. 34a:
E-F = Sifra, Ṣav 1.5-6)

Comment: A is accepted Temple law: something brought to the altar as an offering may not be returned to profane use, even if it has become unfit to be offered as intended.

B-F is a Gamaliel-Joshua dispute. Joshua explains A to refer only to that which is to be burned in the fire. Gamaliel (D) explains A to refer to everything connected with a sacrifice. Joshua's view is given first, and is further favored by F (which depends upon the preceding) through its implication that Gamaliel dissents from Joshua (ʾYN BYN DBRY RBN GMLYʾL LRBY YHWŠʿ).

The basic dispute B+D has been supplied with Scriptural exegeses on behalf of each man, interpreting the same verse in accordance with each view. Joshua's position is further from the plain meaning of both A and the scriptural verse; the analogy with the Whole-offering (C) was probably felt to be necessary to support him. Gamaliel's exegesis (D) is self-explanatory, and the verse may have been supplied for balance. It may be that Gamaliel represents early Temple practice on the matter.

G is independent of the foregoing. Simeon does not mention the blood, and he introduces the term "sacrifices (ZBḤ)", which has not appeared in the pericope before. Simeon adds the point that, whichever aspect of the offering becomes unift, the Drink-offerings may be freed for profane use. Simeon's lemma agrees with Joshua, and was redacted here to support him. But the pericope may well have been complete long before this independent Ushan summary of the problem. Clearly, the pericope reflects a Joshuan viewpoint throughout, on an issue which was, despite its significance, entirely theoretical.

A. The words of Rabban Gamaliel differ from the words of R. Joshua only over the blood and the Drink-offerings.

B. According to the words of Rabban Gamaliel, he sprinkles the blood beside the Fire-offerings; [and] he puts (NWTNW) the Drink-offerings into the bowls.

Tos. Zev. 9.1

Comment: A is identical with the beginning of M. Zev. 9.1F. B must be a stray tradition, somehow redacted into the Tosefta. It is unconnected with the issue of A; and certainly Joshua would not dispute it, in cases where he holds that the blood and wine are offered.

A. Blood which was mixed into water is regarded as if it were all wine.

B. If it were mixed with wine, it is regarded as if it were water.

C. If it were mixed with the blood of a [domesticated] animal, or with the blood of a [wild] beast, it is regarded as if it were wine.

D. [If it were mixed] with water: if its appearance was [completely] changed (BṬLW) it is unfit, but if not it is fit.

E. R. Judah says on behalf of Rabban Gamaliel, "Blood does not nullify (MBṬL) [the power of] blood."

F. The only thing you have which atones is the blood of a living being, as it is said, <u>For it is the blood of a living being which atones</u> (Lev. 17:11).

G. What is <u>the blood of a living being</u>? That which spurts. And it is the "last blood" when it does not spurt.

Tos. Zev. 8.16-17

<u>Comment</u>: The text of Tos. is confusing here, and probably defective: the last word of A, and of C, should probably read "water".

D-E alone concern us; they are paralleled by M. Zev. 8.6. The issue concerns the blood to be sprinkled upon the altar. When does it lose its usefulness, having become mixed with some other liquid? D follows the Mishnah, stating that it may be used so long as it is visible, but Gamaliel holds that the blood never loses its status, and always may be used, no matter if it has been mixed into another liquid.

The important difference between D-E and M. Zev. 8.6 is that, there, E appears not as a quotation by Judah or Gamaliel, but as a lemma in Judah's own name. We have other examples of pericopae which occur in one place as Gamaliel-quotations, but elsewhere in Judah's own name (M. ʿEruv. 10.2 [Gamaliel] = Tos. ʿEruv. 11.14 [Judah]; Tos. Pes. 1.4 [Gamaliel] = M. Pes. 1.5 [Judah]). This must be discussed later, in terms of the handling, by Judah's tradents, of Gamaliel's tradition.

A. [Concerning the animal a man] slaughters, the blood on the knife and the blood on the wings require covering.

B. R. Simeon b. Gamaliel says, "Since the blood of the slaughter is covered, it is free (PṬWR) [of this requirement] of being covered."

C. R. Judah says, on behalf of Rabban Gamaliel, "Blood does not nullify [the power of] (MBṬL) blood."

Tos. Ḥul. 6.8

<u>Comment</u>: The blood of an animal slaughtered for food must be covered (Lev. 17:5, 6, 13). A extends this rule to the incidental splashings, even though the blood from the slaughtering has been covered. Simeon does not require this, agreeing with Judah's view in M. Ḥul. 6.6.

Now C adds Judah's quotation of Gamaliel. In this context, it seems to be saying that the fact that the main quantity of blood has been covered does not free the remaining splashings from the necessity to be covered. Judah/Gamaliel seem to be disputing Simeon, and his/their own view in the Mishnah as well! So Tos. here becomes markedly different from Tos. Zev. 8.17.

It may be that this tradition of Gamaliel was a free-floating lemma, with no clearly-accepted context, and that different editors or scribes added it where they felt appropriate. Some of the material connected with the mixture of blood and water appears in both Zev. and Ḥul., and so a lemma from one context could be inserted into the other context as well.

For it was taught (DTNY'): R. Judah says, on behalf of Rabban Gamaliel, "Blood does not nullify blood; saliva does not nullify saliva; and urine does not nullify urine."

b. Zev. 79a

Comment: Here Gamaliel's lemma is one of three examples sharing a rejection of the principle of nullification. The saliva and urine do not concern sacrifices. They pertain to a zav, whose bodily issue is unclean. If either of these fluids were dissolved in greater quantities of similar fluids from a person not afflicted, the mixture would still remain unclean.

This small collection points to the redaction of Gamaliel-materials, which passed through Judah's hands, in some more comprehensive way, by Judah's tradents.

A. [As to one] who slaughters [an animal] at the point of death (MŚWKNT) -

B. Rabban Simeon b. Gamaliel [K, P, N, Camb.: Rabban Gamaliel] says, "As long as it can jerk a fore-leg and a hind-leg [its slaughter is valid.]"

C. R. Eliezer says, "It is sufficient if [when it is slaughtered the blood] spurts forth."

D. Said R. Simeon, "Even if he slaughters at night, and the next morning rises and finds the walls [of the neck] filled with blood -- [the slaughtering] is valid, since it spurted; and [this is] according to the rule of R. Eliezer."

E. And sages say, "[It is valid] so long as it can jerk either a fore-leg or hind-leg, or move its tail.

F. "It is the same, whether it is a small animal or large animal."

G. [Concerning] a small animal which stretched out its fore-leg and did not pull it back, [its slaughter] is invalid, since this was merely [the sign of] its dying.

H. To what [situation] does this statement apply? [To a case in which] it was considered to be at the point of death (BḤZQT MŚWKNT). But if it was considered to be healthy (BḤZQT BRY'H) even if it shows none of these signs [of life, its slaughter] is valid.

M. Ḥul. 2.6 (b. Ḥul. 37a, 38a)

Comment: Eating meat of an animal which died without having been slaughtered is prohibited (Lev. 22:8, Deut. 14:21). The issue of the pericope concerns an animal which might have died before the completion of the process of slaughtering, thus being rendered unfit.

The pericope appears to originate with a Yavnean dispute which has been highly edited and glossed. We follow Epstein (Mišnah, p. 1202) who agrees with K, P, N and Camb., and the mss. of numerous commentators, in assigning B to Gamaliel II; the name of Simeon in B may be a contamination from D, below. The dispute would consist of the topic sentence (A), Gamaliel's ruling (B), Eliezer's ruling (C) and the sages opinion (E). Gamaliel requires substantial evidence of life, the movement of two limbs. Eliezer requires an absolute minimum life-sign, the beating of the heart at the time of slaughter. The sages modify Gamaliel's view, requiring only the movement of a single limb or the tail.

Simeon's lemma is almost identical with Tos. Ḥul. 2.11, a statement of Simeon "on behalf of (MŠWM) R. Eliezer." D here has been adapted for the pericope, to amplify Eliezer's lemma. F joins G-H to the dispute. F + G-H is a further elaboration of the sages' position, and need not concern us.

This pericope is another example of redaction which gives Gamaliel precedence over Eliezer.

R. Ḥanan said [that] R. Jacob b. Idi said [that] R. Joshua b. Levi said in behalf of Bar Qappara, "Rabban Gamaliel and his court took a vote on [the status of] the slaughtering [done] by a Samaritan (KWTY); and they prohibited it [as food].

b. Ḥull. 5b

Comment: M. Ḥul. 1.1 begins: "All may slaughter, and what they slaughter is valid, except only for a deaf-mute, an imbecile and a minor..." Since our pericope records a formal vote contradicting M., Rashi (ad loc.) assigns this pericope to Rabban Gamaliel III, son of Rabbi Judah the Patriarch. The vote would have been taken after the publication of the Mishnah.

The superscription is a chain of three contemporaries, all first generation Palestinian Amoraim. Bar Qappara was a member of the circle of Rabbi Judah the Patriarch (Hyman, Toledot, i, p. 288). Assuming the correctness of Rashi's supposition, the previous reference to "Rabban Gamaliel and his court" (b. M.Q. 3b) reported by Joshua/Bar Qappara must also refer to Gamaliel III.

With the exception of Tos. Ḥull. 6.8, which is probably a quotation from Tos. Zev. 8.16-17, our Gamaliel appears in M. Tos. Ḥull. only once (M. Ḥull. 2.6).

A. It was taught (TNY'): Rabban Gamaliel says, "[As to a bird] that seizes [its food] and eats, it is well-known that it is unclean.

B. "[If] it has an extra talon, and a craw, and its gizzard can be peeled off, it is well-known that it is clean."

C. R. Eleazar b. R. Ṣadoq says, "They stretch out a cord for it in a line [and when it perches] if it divides its feet, two [claws] on one side and two on the other, it is unclean; three on one side and one on the other, it is clean."

D. R. Simeon b. Eleazar says, "Every bird which catches [its food] in the air is unclean."

b. Ḥul. 65a

Comment: M. Ḥul. 3.6 reads:

A. The signs [of fitness] in cattle and wild animals are stated in the Torah, but the signs for a bird were not stated.

B. But the sages said, "Every bird that seizes [its food] is unclean.

C. Every one that has an extra talon, and a craw, and [whose] gizzard can be peeled off, is clean."

D. R. Eleazar b. Ṣadoq says, "Every bird which divides its feet is unclean."

The relationship between b. and M. should be clarified.

Except for some minor differences in language ("it is well-known" in b.) A-B of our pericope is the same as M. Ḥul. 3.6 B-C. But M. attributes the lemma to the sages, while b. assigns it to Gamaliel.

The point of the baraita in b. is the fuller explanation of Eleazar b. Ṣadoq's lemma about "divided feet", which b. distinguishes more carefully (2+2 vs. 3+1).

It is unusual for a Gamaliel-lemma to be incorporated into M. as a saying of "the sages". The language of A-B implies that Gamaliel is referring to an older tradition ("it is well known") and not an original ruling of his own. Eleazar b. Ṣadoq is a frequent tradent of Gamaliel's; perhaps this could be the reason for the lemma being cited in his name here, while M. relies upon the earlier formulation.

A. Our rabbis taught (TNW RBNN): It is written: And he shall pour it... and he shall cover it (Lev. 17:13). [That is,] he that poured [the blood of the sacrifice] shall cover it up.

B. [If] he slaughtered and did not cover it, and another saw it, how do we know that the latter must cover it? Since it is said, And say to the children of Israel (Lev. 17:14) - a warning to all the children of Israel.

C. It was also taught (TNY' ʿYDK): And he shall pour it... and he shall cover it. [That is,] with that which he poured it he shall cover it, so that he shall not cover it with his foot (in order that the miṣvot not be treated disrespectfully by him).

D. It was also taught (TNY' ʿYDK): And he shall pour it... and he shall cover it. [That is,] he that poured it shall cover it up.

E. (MʿSH B) Someone slaughtered, and his fellow [came] before him and covered it. And Rabban Gamaliel obliged [the friend] to pay him ten gold coins [as a compensation].

b. Ḥul 87a (E=b. B.Q. 91b)

Comment: The pericope is a small collection of exegeses of Lev. 17:13. B is identical to D, while B and E are the complementary consequences of the principle of A and D. A and D say that the one who slaughters an animal must cover its blood. B says that if he does not, everyone else is obligated to do it. E says that no one else may deprive him of doing so, if he is capable of it. E is not an illustration of this side of the principle, but is rather its expression in story form. If E were composed parallel to B, it could read: "If he intended to do so, no one may replace him." This would suggest that this is an independent tradition redacted here, rather than one created for D. E appears independent of the rest of the pericope, and as a Gamaliel-tradition it is in the form we would expect.

A. (MʿSH Š) the lower jaw [protruded] more than the upper, and Rabban Simeon b. Gamaliel sent to [M. text in b., both printed and Munich ms.: Rabban Gamaliel] [asked] the sages [a message of inquiry]. And they said, "Behold, this is a blemish."

B. [As to] the ear of a kid which was folded, said sages, "When it [grows from] a single bone, it is a blemish; and if it is not from a single bone, it is not a blemish."

C. R. Ḥananiah b. Gamaliel says, "[As to] the tail of a kid which resembles that of a pig, and which does not have three joints, behold this is a blemish."

M. Bek. 6.9

Comment: Epstein (Mišnah, p. 1202) notes that the b. text of Nachmanides and R'Š also read "Rabban Gamaliel". However, in Mevo'ot (p. 164) he appears to accept the reading of M. It would be unusual for a Gamaliel-tradition to describe Gamaliel inquiring about the law from unnamed sages, while Simeon does quote "sages" (M. Giṭ. 7.5). Only the presence of Ḥananiah (C) might link the collection to Gamaliel; but C does not attest to A, nor does Gamaliel appear elsewhere in M. Bek. His closest association with the substance of the tractate is the tale of R. Ṣadoq's firstling (b. Bek. 36a). See also Epstein Mišnah, p. 1149.

Said R. ʿAqiva, "I asked Rabban Gamaliel and R. Joshua, in the market of Emmaus, where they went to buy an animal for the [wedding] feast of the son of Rabban Gamaliel, [saying] '[Concerning a man] who has sexual relations with his sister and his father's sister and his mother's sister during one [act of] forgetting, what [happens]? Is he liable for one offering for them all or one offering for each of them?'

"They said to me, 'We have not heard [any tradition about this], but we have heard [a tradition that if a man] has sexual relations, during one [act of] forgetting, with his five wives [who are] menstruants, he is liable for each one of them; and we see that those words [apply] still more so (QL WḤMR) [in the other case].'"

[b. continues: since, in the case of the menstruants, which is one category [of violation] he is guilty concerning each individual [act], here where there are three [separate categories, would it not be the case?]

M. Ker. 3.7 (b. Mak. 14a)

Comment: This is the first of three Mishnaic pericopae, in which ʿAqiva poses a problem to Gamaliel and Joshua, and receives an answer extrapolated from some other case. Of the three, which follow in succession, this is the only one quoting ʿAqiva directly, or specifically mentioning the setting of the bazaar in Emmaus, and the occasion of purchasing meat for the wedding feast of Gamaliel's son.

The problem concerns multiple sex acts during one period of forgetting; the answer is that the single acts with different individuals, like sexual relations with different menstruants, are considered separately, and they require separate sin-offerings. This question represents the other side of the theoretical problem of "one act of forgetting" found in M. Shab. 12.6, and elsewhere. There Gamaliel is involved in a discussion of acts which, taken together, would add up to a violation of the Sabbath. Here he is concerned with acts which, each one being a violation, might all be considered as one because of the single time-frame in which they occur. Gamaliel's position is represented as consistent, in that he evaluates the act, rather than the time-period, throughout. We have noted earlier (M. Shab. 12.6) the importance of this problem to the Yavnean legal agenda.

The narrative places Gamaliel, Joshua and ʿAqiva together. Gamaliel is Patriarch, and the pericope does not reflect any conflict between him and Joshua. Joshua's presence on such an errand may be significant, in view of his reported opposition to ascetic trends, specifically the abstention from meat and wine, in mourning for the destruction of the Temple (b. B.B. 60b). A wedding celebrated by the Patriarchate would be a major national event. Yet there were undoubtedly groups which would consider it a violation of national mourning. They would be eager to use such a charge to discredit the Patriarch, vulnerable through his close dealings with the Roman authorities. Joshua's appearance in the story would demonstrate that Gamaliel's celebration was within the bounds of propriety, indeed an indication of opposition to ascetic extremes. The story thus helps support Patriarchal authority in the definition of religious norms.

This is another example of an ʿAqivan first-person pericope. But ʿAqiva is not in any way superior to his colleagues.

Moreover, R. ʿAqiva asked them, "What happens if a limb of a beast hangs loose?"

They said to him, "We have not heard [any tradition about this], but we have heard [a tradition] about a limb of a man that hangs loose, that it is clean; for this is what those in Jerusalem, who were afflicted with boils used to do: on the eve of Passover he would go to the physician and he would cut [the boil] and leave but a hair ['s breadth]; he then stuck it on a thorn and pulled himself away from it. Thus the man was able to bring his Passover-offering and the physician was able to bring his Passover-offering. And we see that those words [apply] still more so (QL WḤMR) [in the other case]."

M. Ker. 3.8

The second of the three pericopae reports ʿAqiva's question in the third person, rather than in the first person. There is no mention of the setting, nor of Gamaliel or Joshua by name. The content deals with the application of the rules of corpse-uncleanness to a partially-severed limb of an animal, which they rule to be clean, based on a human analogy. There is no question of liability for sin-offerings.

The pericope is joined to the preceding by WʿWD, "moreover". It is possible that it was assigned to this collection because of its similar structure, but there is no reason to doubt Gamaliel's agreement with the content of the pericope.

A. Moreover, R. ʿAqiva asked them, "If a man slaughtered five animal-offerings outside [the Temple Court] during one [act of] forgetting, what happens? Is he liable for one offering for them all, or one for each of them?"

R. Joshua said, "I have heard [a tradition] about one who, during one [act of] forgetfulness, ate of one animal-offering out of five dishes, that he was liable on each count under the law of Sacrilege; and I see that those words [apply] still more so (QL WḤMR) [in the other case]."

B. R. Simeon said, "R. ʿAqiva did not ask about such a case, but [concerning one] who ate Remnant from five animal-offerings during one [act of] forgetting. What happens? Is he liable for one Sin-offering for them all, or one for each of them?"

"They said to him, 'We have heard no tradition about this.'

"R. Joshua said, 'I have heard [a tradition] about one who, during one [act of] forgetting, ate of one animal-offering out of five dishes, that he was liable for each of them under the law of Sacrilege; and I see that those words [apply] still more so [in the other case].'

C. "R. ʿAqiva said, 'If it is <u>halakah</u> we must accept it, but if it is only an inference, there is an answer.'

"He said to him, 'Answer it.'

"He said to him, 'If you say [that] of Sacrilege, where he who gives another to eat [is as guilty] as he who eats, or he who gives for another's use [is equally guilty] as he who uses it, even if what is needed to make up the forbidden quantity is consumed only after long time -- would you say it of [a case of] Remnant, which has none of these [characteristics]?"

M. Ker. 3.9

Comment: The subject-matter of the pericope returns to the question of single or multiple sin-offerings. As above, ʿAqiva is quoted in the third person, and "they" are not specified. Joshua alone is named as the one who replies. Further, in B an alternate version of the question is reported in the name of R. Simeon; in the conclusion of that version (C) ʿAqiva provides a rebuttal of Joshua's a fortiori reasoning.

All this suggests the unreliability of this pericope insofar as it relates to Gamaliel and the Emmaus setting. As part of the ʿAqivan tradition, and because of its similarity in form, it was redacted together with the other materials. We may note the pericope immediately following, M. Ker. 3.10, which also concerns single and multiple sin-offerings. The tradent is again ʿAqiva; he reports in the first person. But there his interlocutor is Eliezer, whom he rebuts twice.

xviii. Kelim

A. An oven which was heated from outside [lit., from behind], or without [the owner's] knowledge, or which was heated up in the craftsman's house, is [capable of becoming] unclean.

B. (MʿSH Š) A fire broke out among the ovens at Kefar Signah. And [when] the case came to Yavneh, (W) Rabban Gamaliel declared them [capable of becoming] unclean.

M. Kel. 5.4

Comment: Once the work is completed on an oven, by firing it, it becomes susceptible to uncleanness. The fire mentioned in B heated the ovens without the owner's knowledge; but it was also from the outside [we cannot assume fire starting inside a number of ovens simultaneously], and most probably in the factory. So the example given in B combines all three circumstances mentioned in the law.

Neusner writes (Kelim, i, p. 130) that the late 16th century commentary Melekhet Shelomo and Sens "point out that ms. evidence known to them - as in M. - gives clean for A, which would mean [that] Gamaliel holds a contrary opinion." In that case, the redactor has used the Gamaliel-story to create a dispute.

A. An oven which was heated in order to roast [something] in it is [capable of becoming] unclean; [if it were heated] to store away bundles of flax [for the purpose of drying them] it is clean, since it does not do work directly (BGWPW).

B. An oven which was heated before the work of making it was finished is [capable of becoming] unclean.

C. R. Judah says, "Clean."

D. Said R. Judah, "This was the incident (MʿSH) of the oven[s] of Kefar Sugna, and Rabban Gamaliel would [declare them capable of becoming] unclean, and sages would [declare them] clean."

Tos. Kel. B.Q. 4.4

Comment: In previous pericopae, heating was considered as the final stage of manufacture, which rendered the oven susceptible to uncleanness. The issue of B is an oven which was heated before the completion of its manufacture. Judah cites Gamaliel's ruling in M. Kel. 5.4B, but the context there does not refer to ovens prior to the completion of their manufacture. D may be independent of B-C. By adding it the redactor has assimilated B to the situation of "the craftsman's house" in M. Kel. 5.4A. Neusner (Kelim, i, p. 132) writes, "The precedents in M. and Tos. are otherwise identical, and that must mean [that] exactly what happened is not known to either redactor; each then is able to cite the 'famous' story for his own purpose."

A. An earth-oven (BWS: alt.: KWR, crucible) which has a place for setting [a pot] is [capable of becoming] unclean; and one of glass-makers, which has some place for setting [a pot] is [capable of becoming] unclean.

B. A furnace of lime-burners, or of glass-blowers or of potters, is clean.

C. A large furnace (PRNH), if it has a rim (LZBZ), is [capable of becoming] unclean.

D. R. Judah says, "If it has a [perforated] roof."

E. Rabban Gamaliel says, "If it has borders."

M. Kel. 8.9

Comment: A furnace made for baking or cooking (A) is unclean, while one not made for that purpose (B) is clean. C-E present a separate rule about a "large furnace", i.e., a baking oven. The issue is whether the furnace is built to be attached to the ground -- or to be moved about. In the latter case it is unclean. Slotki (Kelim, p. 43) alternately explains the "perforated roof" of D as an "outlet for smoke" or "mouldings"; but he considers them all as types of ovens which would be movable rather than fixed to the earth (following the explanation of Tos.).

Judah's view (D) differs from C, and strangely precedes Gamaliel, whose tradent he often is.

Gamaliel's view (E) does not seem to differ from C, except in language. C-E appears to be a series of examples; but below Tos. shows it to be a dispute, among Ushans, as to Gamaliel's exact words.

A. A large furnace (PWRN'), lo, this is clean, for it is made only to be used on the ground.

B. R. Meir says in the name of (MŠM) Rabban Gamaliel, "If it has a rim (LYZBZ), it is unclean."

C. R. Judah says on behalf of (MŠWM) Rabban Gamaliel, "If it has a [perforated] roof."

D. R. Yosé says in the name of (MŠM) Rabban Gamaliel, "If it has borders."

E. And all are for the same reason.

Tos. Kel. B.Q. 6.17

Comment: The characteristics of the unclean furnace of M. Kel. 8.9C-E are given again here, in identical language, together with a reason: only an immovable furnace is clean; one made to be moved receives uncleanness. However, each detail is presented by a different Ushan authority, and all three are given in the name of Gamaliel. Meir assigns the rule of M. Kel. 8.9C (there anonymous) to him; M. Kel. 8.9D is there in Judah's own name, but here assigned to Gamaliel; and D here presents Yosé giving in Gamaliel's name what M. attributed to Gamaliel directly.

B and D seem to be saying the same thing, so that Meir and Yosé appear to have different formulations of the same tradition. But B and C are completely different: Meir and Judah have a real dispute about the kind of furnace Gamaliel considers unclean. This is another instance in which Judah markedly revises a Gamaliel-tradition.

Now we may be in a better position to understand M. Kel. 8, 9C-D. It is the result of the Meir/Yosé vs. Judah dispute recorded in Tos. Epstein (Mevo'ot, p. 99) assigns the Mishnaic pericope to Meir. This is plausible, since it presents his dispute with Judah, giving Meir's version of Gamaliel as anonymous law, and Judah's revision as an opinion in Judah's own name. Thus far Meir's redaction.

To account for M. Kel. 8.9E we may posit another stage of redaction: the editor of the Mishnah, with his interest in Gamaliel-materials, adds Yosé's version of Gamaliel in Gamaliel's own name. But this does not explain the absence of all the Toseftan Gamaliel-traditions in M.

A. [Concerning] the metal cover of a basket belonging to house-owners,

Rabban Gamaliel declares it [capable of becoming] unclean,

And sages declare it clean.

B. The [metal] door of a tower [-shaped] cupboard belonging to house-owners is clean, but that of physicians is [capable of becoming] unclean.

C. Smelters' tongs are [capable of becoming] unclean, but fire-bars are clean.

The scorpion [-shaped hook] in an olive-press is [capable of becoming] unclean, but the hook in a wall is clean.

M. Kel. 12.3

Comment: A metal object which is part of a utensil is not susceptible to uncleanness; an object which is separate can become unclean. Gamaliel considers the metal basket cover an independent utensil.

A is in dispute-form, with Gamaliel's opinion first. The rest of the pericope lists other objects, superficially similar, which differ according to whether or not they are independent utensils, alternating the clean and unclean. B-C is independent of A.

A is probably the source of M. ʿEd. 3.9, above.

A. Said R. Judah, "Why [is the hook] of a peddler [which is carried] before him [capable of becoming] unclean? Because he hangs [something] from it. [And why is the hook protruding] from behind him clean? Because it is made for protection (LŠMYRH)."

B. [Concerning] the metal cover of a basket and belonging to house-owners -

Rabban Gamaliel declares it [capable of becoming] unclean.

And sages declare it clean.

C. And a wooden one is clean.

D. If it were inserted down halfway, or even to one third, it is [capable of becoming] unclean, because it is like the cover of a box.

Less than that it is clean, because it is like the cover of a chest.

E. And why is the [metal] door of a tower [-shaped cupboard] belonging to physicians [capable of becoming] unclean? Because he places compresses on it, and hangs scissors from it.

F. R. Yosé [in the name] of R. Judah says, "Because he manipulates an infant ['s limbs] upon it."

G. They said to him, "If so, let it [be capable of becoming] <u>midraś</u>-unclean."

Tos. Kel. B.M. 2.9

<u>Comment</u>: Tos. repeats the dispute of M. Kel. 12.3A, with the following additions: C adds that a wooden basket-cover is clean (which would be a concession by Gamaliel to the sages); D declares that the position of the cover, inserted one-third or more into the basket, can make it susceptible to uncleanness. D thus moves back toward Gamaliel's view, that the cover is an independent utensil.

The dispute in B stands apart from the rest of the pericope. All the other materials, A, D, E, F, provide reasons for declaring the object clean or unclean, while B does not. This would suggest C-D as a later elaboration of B.

A. [There are] four things [which] Rabban Gamaliel declares [capable of becoming] unclean, and sages declare clean:

B. (1) the metal cover of a basket belonging to house-owners, (2) the hanger of a strigil, (3) unfinished metal vessels and (4) a plate (ṬBLH) broken in two.

C. And the sages agree with Rabban Gamaliel that if the plate was broken into two pieces, one large and one small, the large one is [capable of becoming] unclean, and the small one is clean.

M. Kel. 12.6 (M. ʿEd 3.9,
b. Ḥul. 25a)

<u>Comment</u>: A fragment of a utensil, or a utensil before its manufacture is complete, is not susceptible to uncleanness. Three

of the objects listed (1, 2, 4) are considered by Gamaliel to be objects in their own right, while the sages disagree.

As for the objects in 3, Gamaliel considers the unfinished metal utensils to be fully manufactured nevertheless, while the sages do not. Neusner (Kelim, ii, pp. 13-15) points out that this principle [unfinished metal utensils are susceptible] occurs only here and in a gloss by ʿAqiva in M. Kel. 14.1. But exactly what an "unfinished metal utensil" is, is subject to dispute, so far as ʿAqiva is concerned (see Neusner, Kelim, on M. Kel. 14.1 and Tos. Kel. B.M. 4.1). For Gamaliel, Tos. Kel. B.M. 2.10 says it is one unpolished (Š̌WP).

In C, the sages agree that the larger half of a plate (we assume from the context of B that it is metal also, but Maimonides considers it to be clay) is to be considered useful in its own right, and therefore susceptible to uncleanness. Neusner points out that the sages are here affirming the anonymous rule of M. Kel. 5.7E.

A. Said R. Nathan, "Rabban Gamaliel and the sages did not differ concerning the hook of the scrapers (MGRRWT) of the bath-houses, that it is clean, for it is made only for use in connection with the ground.

"Concerning what did they differ?

B. "Concerning the metal scraper (ḤPWT) of house-owners, which is made like a ball.

"For Rabban Gamaliel declares it unclean, because slaves scrape with it.

"And sages declare it clean."

C. Said R. Judah, "Rabban Gamaliel and the sages did not differ concerning a plate which was divided in two [pieces] where one of them was twice as large as the other, that the large one is unclean and the small one clean.

"Concerning what did they differ?

D. "Concerning the case in which one of them is not larger than the other, for the two are equal.

"Rabban Gamaliel declares unclean.

"And sages declare clean."

Tos. Kel. B.M. 2.12, 13

Comment: Tos. supplies two explanations of M. Kel. 12.6. Nathan says Gamaliel and the sages actually agree that the hanger of bath-house scrapers is clean, since it is attached to the ground (via the wall) and is not a separate utensil. They differ over another scraper, which Gamaliel considers a utensil because slaves can make use of it. But the sages do not consider it as such, because it is not normally used that way. Nathan's comment has, in effect, decided the Yavnean dispute in favor of the sages, and narrowed down the purported dispute to a finer disagreement.

Judah (C-D) explains that Gamaliel and the sages agree about the case of an unequally-divided plate. (The words "twice as large" cannot be meant literally there.) They differ on an equally-divided plate: Gamaliel considers the halves to be still useful, hence unclean.

Judah's comment may be the source of M. Kel. 12.6C, "the sages agree with Rabban Gamaliel..." If so, the redactor has restated it without his name and omitted the imprecise detail about the larger piece being twice as large as the other. If not, his comment appears to add nothing not already implicit in M. In contrast to Nathan's comment, which is clearly an Ushan refinement of a Yavnean dispute, Judah's comment (D) appears to be the formulation of the dispute prior to its redaction into the list of "four things" in M. Kel. 12.6. This would tend to strengthen Judah's claim to transmit Gamaliel's traditions in other instances, where he appears drastically to revise them.

A. A goatskin [bottle is clean if it has holes] that something the size of warp-pegs will pass through.

B. If it does not hold warp-pegs even though it will hold woof-pegs, it is [capable of becoming] unclean.

C. A dish-holder that will not hold dishes, even though it will hold trays, is [capable of becoming] unclean.

D. A chamber-pot that will not hold liquids, even though it will hold excrement, is [capable of becoming] unclean.

E. Rabban Gamaliel declares [it] clean,

F. since [men] do not allow it to remain [that way].

M. Kel. 17.2 (b. Ḥul. 138a)

Comment: This pericope has proved difficult for its interpreters (cf. Epstein, Mevo'ot, pp. 215-216, Neusner, Kelim, ii, pp. 89-92, plus traditional commentaries mentioned by them). Since Gamaliel's participation in the dispute is confined to D-F, the textual problems of the pericope will be treated only briefly.

A is the continuation of M. Kel. 17.1. The general principle of M. Kelim is that a utensil is capable of becoming unclean so long as it is useful. In 17.1, Eliezer declares that a vessel with any kind of hole is now clean, because it is not useful for its specific purpose. Joshua supplies a specific measure; a hole larger than that size renders the vessel clean. In our pericope, A takes a position similar to Joshua's: a goatskin bottle with holes larger than a specific size (warp-pegs) is clean. Eliezer would, in any case, have declared it clean with a hole of any size.

The language of B is problematic: the phrasing of the protasis seems to imply the opposite of what is stated by the apodosis. GRA removes the contradiction by emending the apodosis: "If it does not hold warp-pegs, even though it will hold woof-pegs [which are much larger] *nevertheless it is clean*." However, the contradiction might also be solved by removing the phrase "even though" from B. The pericope is built upon this construction -- B, C and D all use ʾP ʿL PY Š -- and is difficult throughout. Neusner's solution is to disregard it, and to read B as: "If it does not hold warp-pegs, and will hold woof-pegs, it is unclean." In other words, as in C-D, usefulness for some related purpose makes the vessel capable of being unclean. A is thus disputed either by all of B-F or just by C-F.

Whichever way we understand B, C and D declare that a vessel useful for some related purpose is unclean. Gamaliel appears to agree in principle with C-D, and thus disagree with Eliezer. Use for some other purpose would render the vessel unclean. However, in the specific example of the chamber pot, he disagrees. If the chamber pot were normally used in a broken state (that is, used solely for excrement) Gamaliel would agree with D. But he claims that, once broken, the pot will be repaired if it is to be used at all. Otherwise it will be discarded. Therefore, he declares it clean (E-F).

Gamaliel's view, Neusner points out, though in disagreement with his contemporaries, is in accord with the later views of the Ushans. They too hold that so long as a utensil may be used for some purpose it remains unclean (e.g., 17.4). Thus far we have considered E-F as unitary. But F may well be a gloss, restricting Gamaliel's agreement only to the single case, and implying his agreement with D. If F is indeed a gloss, then Gamaliel agrees instead with Eliezer: any kind of hole renders the pot clean. F would have been supplied by someone who wanted to convert Gamaliel's agreement with Eliezer into a dispute, in order to support the views of the Ushans.

Epstein's solution to the problem involves extensive emendation, changing B, C and D-E to *clean*. He attributes all of B-F to Gamaliel, whose views -- agreeing with Eliezer -- were heavily revised by the redactor of M. (except for E). This solution by emendation has not been followed here. However we take the difficult ʼP ʻL PY Š, it would seem that the most reliable part of the tradition here is the apodosis.

A. "Scroll-wrappers, whether or not they are decorated [with figures], are [capable of becoming] unclean," according to the words of the House of Shammai.

And the House of Hillel say, "Decorated [with figures] -- they are clean; not decorated [with figures] -- they are [capable of becoming] unclean."

B. Rabban Gamaliel says, "Both of them are clean."

M. Kel. 28.4

Comment: The Houses agree that an ordinary cloth used as a scroll-wrapper is considered as an object of ordinary use, and is subject to uncleanness. They differ on the question of a scroll-wrapper with decorations indicating its purpose. The Hillelites consider the latter to be clean since it is a cover to decorate a utensil, rather than an object for ordinary use. The Shammaites say that people do use them, in connection with the scrolls; therefore, they are unclean.

In B, Gamaliel glosses the dispute, and extends the Hillelite position further: even an unfigured wrapper is to be considered decorative rather than useful. It is also not subject to defilement. So we have a standard Houses-dispute, glossed by Gamaliel with a ruling more lenient than the Hillelites.

R. Yosé and R. Simeon say, "The words of Rabban Gamaliel concerning scroll-wrappers are seen [to be correct] and we agree with his words (WBDRBYW ʼNW MWDYM) [HD = WKDBRWB ʼNW MWRYM]."

Tos. Kel. B.B. 6.9B

Comment: Yosé and Simeon agree with Gamaliel's ruling that scroll-wrappers are clean, providing an Ushan attestation for M. Kel. 28.4 as a Yavnean pericope.

Said R. Yosé, "(MʻSH Š) They brought, from Kefar ʻAdim [Sens: ʻRYM] before Rabban Gamaliel, more than sixty troughs, and he would measure them: a large one for a *śeʼah,-śeʼah*; and the small one, two *logs*. The measure of a *śeʼah,-śeʼah*; holds nearly nine *qavs* [HD: that is, a large trough holds a whole *seʼah* and a bit more, and this measure is equal to nearly 9 qavs]."

Tos. Kel. B.M. 11.2J

Comment: Tos. Kel. B.M. 11.1, 2 discuss the susceptibility of baking troughs of various sizes to midraś-uncleanness, and how they become purified. Three sizes are mentioned: troughs of less than two logs, troughs between two logs and nine qavs, and troughs "larger than that". Much of the law is in the name of R. Yosé b. R. Judah.

This pericope quotes R. Yosé's story about the way Gamaliel would measure baking-troughs, to determine which laws applied to them. Lieberman (T.R., III, p. 67) asserts that the measurements here have no meaning.

The ms. of Sens read Kefar ʿAdim as "Kefar ʿArim", and Gamaliel as "Simeon b. Gamaliel", (See Rengstorf, Die Tosefta, Seder Ṭaharot, Stutgart, 1967, p. 127, n. 57).

xix. Negaʿim, Parah, Ṭoharot, Niddah, Yadayim

A. [Concerning] a Bright Spot (BHRT) like [the size of] a split bean, surrounded by healthy [flesh] like [the size of] a lentil, with another Bright Spot outside the healthy [flesh],

B. the inner [Bright Spot is] to be shut up, and the outer one to be certified [unclean].

C. Said R. Yosé, "Healthy flesh is not a sign of uncleanness for the outer one since the [inner] Bright Spot is within it."

D. [If the healthy flesh] decreased and went away,

Rabban Gamaliel says, "If it disappears from the inner [side], it is a sign of spreading of the inner [one], and the outer [one] is clean. And if [it disappeared] from outside, the outer [Bright Spot] is clean, and the inner [one] is shut up."

E. R. ʿAqiva says, "In either case they are clean."

M. Neg. 6.5

Comment: Lev. 13:2-8 deals with the diagnosis of a ṣaraʿat, a skin eruption which renders the afflicted person unclean. Our pericope concerns a "Bright Spot" (white skin area which may or may not be a ṣaraʿat) and its status of cleanness/uncleanness. The symptom described is a central Bright Spot, surrounded by an area of healthy flesh, in turn surrounded by another Bright Spot area (A). Since a Bright Spot with inner healthy flesh is unclean (Lev. 13:10, 14) the outer one is certified as unclean immediately; the inner one requires quarantine and later examination (B). Yosé disagrees with the anonymous law declaring the outer spot unclean; he holds that because there is another spot within the healthy flesh, the latter does not fall under the category of healthy flesh which would make a Bright Spot unclean (C).

Gamaliel (D) adds another complication. If the central spot spreads, covering the previously-healthy area, the inner area is declared unclean (since it has spread, Lev. 13:8); the outer area is clean (because the healthy flesh within it has disappeared). If the outer area spreads inward, covering the previously-healthy area, the outer area is clean, for the same reason; the inner area requires the person to be quarantined, so that a decision can be made about it. 'Aqiva (F) declares the inner area to be clean in both cases. He does not consider the spreading in this case to be the "spreading" referred to in Lev. 13:8, since it takes place within the larger Bright Spot.

D depends upon A for its definition. D-E contains two contrasting opinions, but they are not balanced. D-E is a dispute in the form of an 'Aqivan comment upon a Gamaliel-pericope. We have two other cases of this 'Aqivan use of Gamaliel materials (M. Ber. 4.3, 6.8). Yosé's Ushan comment in C provides a terminus ante quem for the pericope as a whole. It is outside the framework of A-B and D-E.

A. [Concerning] a Bright Spot like [the size of] a split bean, surrounded by healthy [flesh] like [the size of] a lentil, with another Bright Spot outside the healthy [flesh] -

B. if this healthy [flesh] decreased and became a Bright Spot -

C. Rabban Gamaliel says, "If it decreases from the inner side, the inner one is to be certified [unclean] and the outer one is to be shut up. [If it decreases] from the outside, the inner one is to be shut up, and the outer one is clean."

D. R. 'Aqiva says, "In either case, the inner one is to be shut up and the outer one is clean.

E. "If it is because of the spreading [of the inner Bright Spot], we are not concerned about the inner one since a plague does not spread into another plague [-infected area]. If it is because of the spreading [of the outer Bright Spot] we are not concerned about the outer one, since the [inner] Bright Spot is inside it."

Tos. Neg. 2.9

Comment: The Toseftan parallel to M. Neg. 6.5 mostly differs from the Mishnah version. Units A of both pericopae are identical, but after that both language and ruling diverge. Tos. deals only with Gamaliel and ʿAqiva. For Gamaliel, the differences are as follows:

M.	Tos.
Disappears from inner side:	Decreases from inner side:
inner = unclean	inner = unclean
outer = clean	outer = shut up
From outer side:	From outer side:
outer = clean	outer = clean
inner = shut up	inner = shut up

Thus for Tos., the difference is that if the healthy flesh disappears from the inside, the outer Bright Spot must be shut up for the seven-day quarantine.

ʿAqiva's rulings differ more markedly. In M. he considers the inner spot clean in all cases, while in Tos. it is to be shut up. Tos. is in standard dispute-form, with A-B setting forth the topic followed by opposing rulings in C-D.

ʿAqiva's ruling (D) is provided with an explanation (E) which is probably a gloss.

The differences between M. and Tos. are small enough to suggest variations on the same tradition of Gamaliel, rather than two separate traditions. The editor of M. has used the more lenient of the variants, of both Gamaliel and ʿAqiva.

A. [If a man] pulls out the signs of uncleanness or cauterizes healthy flesh, he transgresses a negative command.

B. And concerning his cleanness, [if he removed the signs] before he came to the priest, he is clean; but if after he had been certified unclean, he is still unclean.

C. Said R. ʿAqiva: "I asked Rabban Gamaliel and R. Joshua when they were on the way to Narwad, 'What would happen [if he removed the signs of uncleanness] while he was shut up?'

D. "They said to me, 'We have heard no tradition about this, but we have heard that if he did so before he came to the priest, he is clean; but if after he had been certified unclean, he is still unclean.'

E. "I began to bring them proofs.

F. "It is all one whether he stands before the priest or whether he is shut up; he is clean, unless the priest has certified him to be unclean."

M. Neg. 7.4

Comment: A-B indicates that a man is considered clean until pronounced otherwise by the priest. Even if he removed the signs of uncleanness, he still is clean. C-F is a first-person report by ʿAqiva, testifying to the views of Gamaliel and Joshua about a similar problem.

The structure of C-F here follows that of other similar, pericopae (M. Ker. 3.7-9, b. Mak. 14a): ʿAqiva reports his question to Gamaliel and Joshua; they respond that they have not heard any tradition concerning it, but report another applicable tradition.

There are some differences from the pattern: the setting here is on the way to Narwad; they do not conclude their reply with an a fortiori, though it is implied; ʿAqiva does not dispute their view, but cites a law covering the case he raised together with the case they mentioned.

A. If cattle or wild animals drink from it [the water of purification] it is unfit.

B. All birds render it unfit, except the dove, since it sucks [the water].

All creeping things do not render it unfit, except the weasel, since it laps [the water].

C. Rabban Gamaliel says, "Even (ʾP) the serpent, since it vomits."

D. R. Eliezer says, "Even (ʾP) the mouse."

M. Par. 9.3 (y. Ter. 8.3;
b. Ḥul. 96)

Comment: The context deals with the water of purification prepared from the ashes of the Red Heifer (Num. 19). The water is made unfit by foreign matter, in this case the spittle of various animals drinking from it. Though the structures of the three sentences in A-B are not identical, they are a unit. A sets the topic, mentioning animals; then B includes birds and insects. Considering that A-B is subjected to quite minor Yavnean glosses, this part of the pericope could represent quite early law, perhaps from Temple times.

In C-D, Gamaliel and Eliezer gloss the general statement with two specific additions. It is unusual for Eliezer to gloss a pericope which includes Gamaliel; usually when they appear together Eliezer's view comes first. Since, as Neusner notes (Eliezer, i. p. 309) Eliezer is omitted from the general discussion of this topic in M. Par. 11.1 (which includes a reference to Gamaliel) his gloss must have been added sometime later to this Gamaliel-pericope.

A. [Concerning] a flask that [someone] left uncovered, and came and found covered, [the purification-water in it is] invalid.

B. [If] he left it covered and came and found it uncovered, and a weasel could have drunk from it or, according to the words of Rabban Gamaliel, a serpent, or if dew fell into it in the night, [the water of purification is] invalid.

C. Sin-offering [water] is not saved [from uncleanness] by an airtight lid (ṢMYD PTYL); but water which is not sanctified [by mixture with the ashes] is saved [from uncleanness] by an airtight lid.

M. Par. 11.1

Comment: In a further elaboration of possibilities of contamination of the water from the ashes of the Red Heifer, the Mishnah refers to Gamaliel's gloss on the list of contaminating creatures, above (M. Par 9.3).

R. Yosé and R. Simeon say, "The words of Rabban Gamaliel are seen [to be correct] concerning a serpent, and we teach according to his words (WKDBRYW ʾNW MWRYM)."

Tos. Par. 9.6C

Comment: Yosé and Simeon provide an Ushan attestation for M. Par. 9.3 and 11.1.

A. From what time do olives receive uncleanness?

"After they exude the moisture that comes out of them when they are in the vat (Zʿ T MʿTN) but not the moisture that comes out of them when they are yet in the store-basket (ZʿT HQPH)," according to the words of the House of Shammai.

B. R. Simeon says, "The time for the moisture [before it renders the olives capable of becoming unclean] is three days."

C. The House of Hillel say, "After there is moisture enough for three olives to stick together (MŠYTḤBRW ŠLŠH ZH LZH)."

D. Rabban Gamaliel says, "After the preparation is finished."

E. And sages say according to his words.

M. Ṭoh. 9.1

Comment: The Houses dispute the time olive-moisture renders the olives subject to uncleanness. The Shammaites say (A) it is when the olives are in the vat, rather than in the harvest-basket. R. Simeon (B) either explains or revises the Shammaite position: the moisture of olives in the vat must be three days old. The Hillelites say: even later, when at least three olives stick together. Gamaliel decides that it is even later: when work is done, and the olives are ready to be pressed (D). The Houses' opinions, in their simplest form, are two balanced five-syllable words: MŠYZY'W us. MŠYTḤBRW. Gamaliel's opinion is also balanced: MŠTGMR.

The decision by Gamaliel identifies the pericope with the Yavnean consolidation of the Houses' positions. The comment of R. Simeon on the Shammaite position helps provide a terminus ante quem. Sometimes Simeon will introduce a totally different principle into the pericope (e.g., M. Ket. 8.2, M. Git. 5.1). He does that here too, adding a three-day time limit. However, if the sages' agreement with Gamaliel (E) were Yavnean, it would be difficult to imagine Simeon revising the Shammaite position in the face of such Yavnean unanimity (unless B is only a theoretical explanation of the Shammaite position, rather than a revision of it). Therefore, E must be at least contemporary with Simeon, if not after him: the terminus ante quem is Ushan, but possibly post-Ushan.

Once again, Gamaliel comments upon a Houses' dispute, expressing a position more extreme than the Hillelites.

A. [Both] son and daughter, even though they said, "We do not know on whose behalf (LŠM MY) we vowed, or on whose behalf we dedicated [something to the Temple]," their vows are vows, [and] their dedications are sanctified.

B. (M'SH B) The father of R. Ḥananiah b. Ḥananiah vowed him to be a Nazirite. His father brought him before Rabban Gamaliel, and Rabban Gamaliel was inspecting him to see whether he had come to [display] any signs [of physical maturity].

C. R. Yosé b. R. Judah said, "Whether he had reached the stage of [making his own] vows."

D. He said to him, "Why are you troubled? If I am in Father's jurisdiction, Father's jurisdiction is upon me and I am a Nazirite. And if I am under my own jurisdiction, behold, I am a Nazirite as of now."

He rose and kissed him (NŠQW) [HD: NS'W, carried him] on his head [and] said, "I am certain about this one, that he will not leave the world without teaching with authority in Israel."

E. And he did not leave the world without teaching with authority in Israel.

F. Said R. Eliezer b. R. Ṣadoq, "I saw that he was teaching with authority in Israel."

Tos. Nid. 5.15

Comment: The context discusses the age at which a young person is no longer bound by the vows made by his father, and when his own vows become binding. A points out that, before that age, even if the child understands the meaning of the vow, it is not binding, while after that age it is binding even if the child did not understand the vow.

In the story which follows, B-E, Gamaliel appears only incidentally. The story is focused on Ḥananiah b. Ḥananiah and is a kind of narrative commonly told about the youthful precocity of holy men. Gamaliel's role is that of the religious authority who recognizes the acumen of the young hero.

Though the official status of Nazirite terminated with the destruction of the Temple, many traditions attest to the continuation of Nazirite-like vows of self-restriction, even into the early Middle Ages. So the presence of Gamaliel and Eliezer in such a pericope is not anachronistic.

A. (MʿSH BY) Rabban Ḥanina b. Ḥanina's father vowed him [while a child to be a Nazirite] and Rabban Simeon b. Gamaliel inspected him to see whether he had grown two [pubic] hairs.

B. He said to him, "Why are you inspecting me? If my father's Nazirite [vow] is upon me, I am a Nazirite; and if not, I am a Nazirite [by my own vow]."

C. Rabban Gamaliel rose, kissed him on his head, and said, "I am certain that you will not leave old age without teaching with authority in Israel."

D. R. Eleazar b. Ṣadoq said, "I saw him sitting and expounding in Yavneh."

y. Naz. 4.6

Comment: The y. version of the story about Ḥananiah's intelligence is not identical in language to Tos.; it is either independent or loosely retold. The authority-figure is described as Simeon b. Gamaliel in A and as Gamaliel in C.

Whereas Eleazar's words in Tos. Nid. 5.15 merely repeat the last line of the story, his words in D here are more vivid; they may point to a later development of the tradition.

A. (DTNY') For it taught: (M'SH B) R. Ḥanina's father vowed him to be a Nazirite, and brought him before Rabban Gamaliel. Rabban Gamaliel was inspecting him, to know whether or not he had grown two [pubic] hairs.

B. R. Yosé says, "Whether or not he reached the stage of [making his own] vows."

C. He said to him, "Master, do not trouble to inspect me. If I am a minor, I shall be [a Nazirite] because of Father; if I am an adult, I shall be [a Nazirite] because of myself."

D. Rabban Gamaliel rose and kissed him on his head. He said, "I am certain about this one, that he will teach halakah in Israel."

E. They said it was only a short time before he taught with authority in Israel.

b. Naz. 29b

Comment: b. seems to be aware of some of the details of both Tos. and y. versions, but retells the story much more briefly.

A. At first, the poor would bring [food] to the house of a mourner in colored glass [utensils, and] the rich in white glass. They reversed [themselves] and would bring out [the food] in either colored or white glass, out of respect to the poor.

B. At first, for anyone to whom a death occurred, bringing [the deceased] out [for burial] was harder than his death. Everyone began to set down their dead and flee. Rabban Gamaliel acted casually toward himself. Everyone acted as did Rabban Gamaliel.

Tos. Nid. 9.17

Comment: Tos. Nid. 9.16-18 is a small collection of materials stating At first they would do x, then they decreed y. Five of the practices mentioned concern funerals, the sixth ritual purity. A-B deals with the problem of the expense of funerals for the poor; and in B, Gamaliel is credited with setting the precedent for modest funerals by his own instruction. The reference here is quite brief, and obviously to a well-known story. Gamaliel is portrayed as a popular public figure, whose aura of respect, as well as wealth, could make him a model in this regard.

At first, bringing out the dead [for burial] was harder for his relatives than his death, so that his relatives would set him down and flee. Then Rabban Gamaliel came and acted casually toward himself, and went out [to be buried] in linen garments. And the people followed his custom, to go out [to be buried] in linen garments.

b. M.Q. 27b (b. Ket. 8b)

<u>Comment</u>: The before/after collection supplied by b. consists of eight items, all concerned with mourning. Five are the same as Tos. Nid. 9. 16-18; the final item there, not pertaining to mourning, does not appear, and three others are added. As is usual in b., the text is smoother and more detailed. The item about Gamaliel adds the detail of "linen garments" to explain the nature of Gamaliel's simplification of the mourning rites. This is probably the substance of the tradition alluded to in Tos., attributing the change in custom to Gamaliel.

A. (M'SH B) Ṭabita, Rabban Gamaliel's maidservant, used to carry wine for pouring,

B. and she used to check [herself] with every single jar.

C. She said to him, "Master, I saw a red stain."

D. Rabban Gamaliel was upset.

E. She said to him, "I checked]myself after] every single jar, and I had not become unclean, except after this one."

y. Nid. 2.1

<u>Comment</u>: According to the view of the sages (M. Nid. 1.1) a menstruant conveys uncleanness retroactively, either for the twenty-four hours prior to the time of discovering her flow, or from the time of the previous self-examination, whichever is the shorter interval.

In B, Ṭabita knows this, and so she checks herself at brief intervals, in order not to render the wine jars unclean.

The emphasis of the story, as in others of this genre, is on the wisdom of the servant, whose behavior demonstrates the law. In this narrative Gamaliel is passive and Ṭabita is the central character. Her name, the female form of Ṭabi, may be constructed for the purpose of the story. No references to her occur in the earlier strata.

A. (T'ŠM': M'SH B) Rabban Gamaliel's maidservant was baking ('PH) loaves of [bread which were] <u>terumah</u>.

B. And after each one she would rinse her hand[s] with water and inspect [herself, to see if she were menstruant].

C. With the last one, she inspected and found herself unclean. She want and asked Rabban Gamaliel [about the status of the loaves.

D. He said to her, "They are all unclean."

E. She said to him, "[But] Master, didn't I have an inspection after every one?"

F. He said to her, "If so, that one is unclean and all [the rest] are clean."

b. Nid. 6b

A. (T'ŠM': ŠWB M'SH) Again, Rabban Gamaliel's maidservant was corking (GPH) wine jugs.

B. And after each one she would rinse her hands with water and inspect [herself].

C. And with the last one, she inspected and found herself unclean. She went and asked Rabban Gamaliel [about the status of the wine].

D. He said to her, "They are all unclean."

E. She said to him, "[But] didn't I have an inspection after every one?"

F. He said to her, "If so, that one is unclean and all [the rest] are clean."

b. Nid. 6b

Comment: In both of these stories parts B-F are identical (with the exception of adding a conjunction and dropping "Master" in the second story. Gamaliel first rules that all the jugs his maid touched while working were unclean, since they were touched within the same 24-hour period. Then she reminds him of her examinations, and he agrees that only the object touched since the last examination is considered unclean.

The difference between units A of the stories, describing the situation, might be accounted for by scribal error. The key verbs are similar in form: 'PH (baking) vs. GPH (corking). The phrases following the verbs may be glosses to explain the verbs: baking loaves of terumah vs. corking jars of wine.

In any case, the same story has been adapted to two situations. The wine jug story illustrates the issue of retrospective uncleanness. On the other hand, the baking story introduces an additional problem, by specifying terumah. On b. Nid. 6a, R. Huna is quoted as ruling that a menstruant conveys uncleanness to hallowed things only, not to terumah. The story is one of the materials used in opposition to his view.

As for the substance of the stories, apart from their differing superscriptions, these are further examples of the genre describing the intelligent and pious servant of the Patriarch, whose behavior reflects proper observance of the law. (cf., Ṭabi-stories, M. Ber. 2.7 et. al.).

A. Ṭabita, maidservant of Rabban Gamaliel, was inspecting jars [of wine]. When she felt [the start of menstruation] she paused.

B. He said to her, "Have they gone stale?"
She said, "No."

C. When he understood, he said, "Woe, that wine has gone!"

D. She said to him, "I was checking with every single jar, and I did not feel anything until this one."

E. He said to her, "May your life be given to you as you have given me my life."

Lev. R. 19.4

Comment: This elaboration provides additional suspense and new dialogue.

A. (M'SH B) The servant girl of Rabban Gamaliel was cleaning out of every room all its cups and jars, and she would inspect herself with every single jar.

B. At the last one she inspected herself and was found to be unclean.

C. Rabban Gamaliel was afraid, saying, "Perhaps all the clean [jars] became unclean. He said to her, "Weren't you inspecting yourself?"

D. She said, "By your life, my Lord, I was inspecting myself after every single jar, and with the last one I inspected myself and was found to be unclean."

E. Said Rabban Gamaliel, "If this woman had been lazy, all the clean [jars] would have been unclean."

Tanḥ. Yitro, 10 (Pes. de R.K. Baḥodeš 15 [Mandelbaum ed., p. 215, lines 8-14])

Comment: E adapts the story to its context, and exegesis praising women who take extra effort to check themselves.

A. [Concerning] an abortion with the form of a serpent, Ḥanina, the son of R. Joshua's brother ruled (HWRH), "Its mother is unclean [by reason of having given] birth."

B. R. Joshua went and told [these] words before Rabban Gamaliel.

C. He sent [a message] to him: "R. Joshua, lead your nephew and come [to me]!"

D. When they were [starting] on their way, Ḥanina's daughter-in-law came out to meet [Rashi: R. Joshua]. She said to him, "Master, what [is the law concerning] an abortion like a serpent?"

He said to her, "Its mother is clean."

E. She said to him, "But wasn't it in your name my mother-in-law told me, 'Its mother is unclean'?"

F. And he said to her, "For what reason?"

"Since its eyeball is round like a man's."

G. From her words, R. Joshua remembered. He sent [a message] to Rabban Gamaliel: "Ḥanina ruled on [the basis of] what I said (MPY)."

H. Said Abbayé, "*Let the students of the rabbis learn from this, that when he says a word* [of law] *he should also give its reason, so that he will remember it from its wording.*"

B. Nid. 24b (Aramaic italicized)

Comment: The point of the law here (cf., M. Nid. 3.2) is that a foetus must be human in form in order to render the mother unclean; if the foetus appears non-human, she is clean. Ḥanina's ruling appears to contradict this principle.

This story shares some of the characteristics of the Gamaliel-Joshua conflict-stories. As in b. Ber. 27b, an unknown student brings a story to Gamaliel which gets Joshua into trouble. As in M.R.H. 2.7, the ruling is by a third party, but Gamaliel addresses himself to Joshua and summons him to appear before him. As in b. Ber. 27b. and b. Bek. 36a, Joshua is asked the disputed point of law (D) - though not by Gamaliel - and responds with the majority opinion. He is asked "But wasn't it said in your name...?" (E).

However, the focus of the story does not seem to be conflict between Joshua and Gamaliel. When Joshua remembers the reason for his ruling, he merely informs Gamaliel that he had so ruled, without explaining further. As we have the story, with Abbayé's early fourth-century Aramaic comment, its purpose is to show how Joshua's nephew's daughter-in-law reminded Joshua of his own ruling, by remembering the reason (F: the serpent-shaped foetus still has one humanoid resemblance).

If this was originally another conflict-story, it is not possible now to recover its pristine form. The pericope is here an Amoraic tale, and Ḥanina's unnamed daughter-in-law has become a major figure. Her presence, though it leads to a justification for Joshua's original ruling, need not be seen in terms of a specifically-Joshuan pericope. After all, he has forgotten his own teaching, and must be reminded of it. At this late stage of the pericope, we are far from the Gamaliel-Joshua conflict, and from the tradents of either man.

A. "Foods and vessels which have been made unclean by liquids make the hands unclean in the second degree," the words of R. Joshua.

B. And sages say, "[Something] made unclean by a Father of Uncleanness makes the hands unclean; if it were made unclean by an Offspring of Uncleanness, it does not make the hands unclean."

C. Said Rabban Simeon b. Gamaliel [K, P, Camb. and Munich ms. of b.: Rabban Gamaliel], "(M'SH B) A woman came before [my] father. She said to him, 'My hands entered the air [-space] of an earthenware vessel.'

"He said to her, 'My daughter, what was its [degree of] uncleanness?'

"And I did not hear what she said to him."

D. Said sages, "The matter is clear: [something] made unclean by a Father of Uncleanness makes the hands unclean; [if it were made unclean] by an Offspring of Uncleanness, it does not make the hands unclean."

M. Yad. 3.1

Comment: Foods and vessels are made unclean in the second degree through contact with unclean liquids. According to Joshua (A) such objects make the hands also unclean in the second degree. The sages state a general rule (B): only something unclean in the first degree makes the hands unclean, while something unclean in the second degree does not.

We follow Epstein (*Mišnah*, p. 1151) in accepting the ms. readings of "Rabban Gamaliel." The point of the story lies in the question of Simeon b. Gamaliel the Elder. He implies that it makes a difference whether the vessel were unclean in the first or second degree. The sages take this as confirmation of their rule. From Joshua's viewpoint it would make no difference whether the vessel were unclean in the first or second degree.

On formal grounds, A-B appears to be an artificially created dispute. In normal dispute-form, a proper response to Joshua's lemma would have been simply, "They do not render unclean." The general rule of the sages has been added to oppose Joshua.

Likewise, Gamaliel's story has been cited to provide an even earlier precedent for such opposition, from the time of Simeon b. Gamaliel; it gives the opportunity for claiming an early-Yavnean source for the substance of the rule articulated by the sages.

As in M. ʿEruv. 6.2, Gamaliel recounts a story about his father. But the preservation of such materials is seen here to have reached an extreme. Only a fragment of an incident has been transmitted, yet it is used as a valuable legal source.

A. On that day (BW BYWM) Judah (YHWDH; Midr. Tann. = HWDH) An Ammonite proselyte, came and stood before them in the house of study. He said to them, "May I enter into the congregation?"

Said Rabban Gamaliel to him, "You are forbidden."

Said R. Joshua to him, "You are permitted."

B. Said Rabban Gamaliel to him, "Scripture says, An Ammonite or a Moabite shall not enter into the assembly of the Lord, even to the tenth generation (Deut. 23:4)."

C. Said R. Joshua to him, "And are the Ammonites and the Moabites in their [same] places? Sennacherib, king of Assyria, long ago came up and put all the nations into confusion, as it is written, I have removed the bounds of the peoples and have robbed their treasures, and I have brought down as a valiant man them that sit [on thrones] (Is. 10:13)."

D. Said Rabban Gamaliel to him, "Scripture says, But afterwards I will restore the former condition of the children of Ammon (Jer. 49.6): so they have already returned."

E. Said R. Joshua to him, "Scripture says, And I will restore the former condition of my people Israel and Judah, says the Lord (Jer. 30:3); but they have not yet returned."

F. They permitted him to enter into the congregation.

M. Yad. 4.4 (A-F = Midr. Tann. on Deut. 23:7, ed. D.S. Hoffman p. 146, lines 14-20)

Comment: A is a Gamaliel-Joshua dispute, connected to a story about the status of an Ammonite proselyte. Gamaliel forbids the proselyte to marry a Jewish girl ("enter the congregation") while Joshua permits it. F reports a decision of the rabbis in favor of Joshua.

The "Tanna" quoted on b. Ber. 28a, in his attempt to synthesize traditions, connects all references to "that day" with the day Eleazar b. ʿAzariah was made head of the Academy. Epstein (Mevoʾot, pp. 423-425) argues that "on that day" refers rather to the particular context of any passage, the law or laws immediately prior to whatever is being discussed. In the case of this pericope, M. Yad. 4.2 contains a reference by Simeon b. ʿAzzai to a tradition about the day Eleazar was appointed. This implies that "on that day" here means the day Simeon b. ʿAzzai spoke, which was long after that appointment, and long after Gamaliel's restoration.

B-E presents an exegetical debate, with two exchanges. Joshua has the last word, and the better argument, in both of them. In B, Gamaliel applies the prohibition of Deut. 23:4 to Judah the Ammonite; Joshua quotes the verse from Isaiah to show that we cannot identify who is really a descendant of the proscribed nations nowadays (C). Gamaliel's answer is subtle: he notes (D) that mention of the restoration of the Ammonites in Jer. 49:6 omits reference to the "end of days" cited in connection with both Moab (Jer. 48:47) and Elam (Jer. 49:39). This would imply that the restoration of the Ammonites to their territory has taken place, and that someone called an Ammonite is really a member of the proscribed nation. Joshua replies with a quotation mentioning the return of Israel and Judah from exile (Jer. 30:3) which also has no reference to the "end of days", and points out that nevertheless no restoration has taken place. Joshua's decisive argument is followed by the precedent-setting decision, F.

The entire pericope has been carefully shaped; it is difficult to consider the dispute apart from the debate, especially since the scriptural issue of the debate does stand behind the dispute. Though Gamaliel speaks first in the dispute, as befits the Patriarch, Joshua is the preeminent speaker; clearly, his circle is responsible for the pericope.

A. On that day (BW BYWM) Judah, an Ammonite proselyte, stood before them in the house of study. He said to them, "May I enter into the congregation?"

Said Rabban Gamaliel to him, "You are forbidden."

Said R. Joshua to him, "You are permitted."

B. Said Rabban Gamaliel to him, "Behold, it is written, *An Ammonite or a Moabite shall not enter into the assembly of the Lord* (Deut. 23:4).

C. "And are [the peoples of] Ammon and Moab standing in their [same] places? Sennacherib long ago came up and mixed all of the peoples, as it is said, *I have removed the boundaries of the peoples and have robbed their treasures* (Is. 10:13)."

D. Said Rabban Gamaliel to him, "Scripture says, *But afterwards I will restore the former condition of the children of*

Ammon, as in the beginning says the Lord (Jer. 40:6)." He said, "By now have they not returned?"

E. Said R. Joshua, "Scripture says, And I will restore the former condition of My people Israel (Jer. 30:3). In the same way [that] the latter have not returned, so the former have not returned."

F. Said Judah, an Ammonite proselyte, to them, "What shall I do?"

They said to him, "I have already heard from the mouth of the elder that you are permitted to enter into the congregation."

[Midr. Tann.: A student of sages spoke up and said to me, "What did you say to him, Master?"

He said, "I said to him, 'You have already heard that the elder said, "Permitted."'"]

G. Said Rabban Gamaliel to them, "Then even an Egyptian [should be treated] similarly."

H. They said to him, "Scripture gives an Egyptian a conclusion [to the time of exile] as it is said, In forty years I will gather Egypt from the nations among which they were scattered, and they will return to their land (Ez. 29:13)."

Tos. Yad. 2.17-18 (F = Midr. Tannaim on Deut. 23:8, ed. D.S. Hoffman p. 146, lines 20-21)

Comment: A-E are almost identical with M. Yad. 4.4 A-E; the few variations are minor. Instead of the flat statement of permission of M., Tos. has another exchange of dialogue; this is parallel to M. in content. Only in G-H does Tos. add something new. Gamaliel offers another challenge, pushing Joshua's argument to the extreme: If an Ammonite is admissible, an Egyptian should be too. H replies in the name of the rabbis, rather than Joshua: the Egyptian exile concluded after forty years, so that the biblical proscriptions against Egyptians apply to contemporary Egyptians. G-H has thus spun out another implication of the exegetical line.

xx. Mekilta, Mekilta RŠY, Sifra, Sifré, Sifré Zuta

A. Rabban Gamaliel says, "...but the owner of the ox is not to be punished [lit., clean] (Ex. 21:28). [This means:] free of paying the price of the slave.

B. "For the following argument might have been advanced: The mu'ad is subject to death by stoning, and the tam is subject to death by stoning. Now since you have learned that in the case of the mu'ad the owner must pay the price of the slave, also here [in the case of a tam] he also should have to pay the price of the slave. But [adding these words] it teaches us [that] the owner of the ox is not to be punished."

Mek. Nez. 10 (Laut. ed., iii, p. 81, line 93 - p. 82, line 97)

Comment: Ex. 21:29-32 discusses the liability of the negligent owner of an ox known to be dangerous (mu'ad), toward the victims of the animal. While the ox is to be stoned, the master must pay damages. In contrast, a single verse discusses the ox with no previous record of danger (tam). It is likewise stoned, but its owner "is not to be punished (Ex. 21:22)."

Mek. Nez. 10 presents a series of exegeses on the latter verse, in the names of the Yavneans Judah b. Batyra, Simeon b. 'Azzai, Gamaliel and 'Aqiva. They explain the owner's freedom from punishment, respectively, as: freedom from divine punishment, payment of half-damages, payment of the full price of the slave, payment of damages for causing a miscarriage.

The logical method is the same throughout. The mu'ad is contrasted with the tam; then a specific liability connected with the mu'ad, which might have been thought applicable to the case of the tam, is declared inapplicable because of the verse. The language used in the Judah and Gamaliel-pericopae is almost identical. In effect, this is an editorially-created exegetical dispute.

Gamaliel's exegesis (A) states that the essential difference between the two oxen is that the owner of the tam need not pay the fine indemnifying the owner for the loss of his slave. This is the single ruling on torts attributed to Gamaliel among all the traditions in his name.

A. Abba Yudan, a man of Sidon (alt.: Saidan), says on behalf of (MŠWM) Rabban Gamaliel, "From whence [do we know] that a man should not say, 'I am not worthy to pray for the Temple and for the Land of Israel'?

B. "Because it is taught, I shall surely hear him cry. (Ex. 22:22). Now which aspect (MDH) [of God] predominates, the aspect of goodness or the aspect of punishment? I would say that the aspect of goodness predominates.

C. "So since [in a case involving] the lesser aspect of punishment, an individual prays and the Ever-present (HMQWM) hears his prayer, [in a case involving] the predominant aspect of goodness it logically follows (DYN HWʾ) that an individual prays and the Ever-present hears his prayer."

Mek. RŠY, Mišpaṭim 24.23
(Epstein-Melamed ed. p. 211,
lines 3-8)

Comment: The pericope constitutes an exegetical *a fortiori*, concerning Divine response to prayer (B-C). Ex. 22:22 promises God's quick response to punish mistreatment of the poor. Since God's propensity to reward is greater than His desire to punish it follows that God will respond to prayer asking for His mercy. However, the question (A) and its answer to (B-C) do not directly correspond. The question is related to specific topics of prayer, "the Temple and the Land of Israel"; the answer is general, "goodness predominates... an individual prays and the Ever-present hears..." and mentions neither the Temple nor the Land. If we read B-C without A, it seems to answer the question, "How do we know that God rewards the prayers of the righteous?" -- or something similar -- with the reply, "Since the Torah indicates I will surely hear his cry, in a matter of punishment, *a fortiori* this will be true of reward." The focus of the argument of B-C considered alone, is on the phrase, "and the Ever-present hears his prayer."

This exegesis appears to have been adapted, by its introduction (A), to answer a different question: may a member of a sinful people pray for God's goodness? This question shifts the emphasis of B-C. It now appears to answer, "A man should pray, (since God is even readier to respond with reward)." The focus is the phrase "an individual prays", which is understood prescriptively, rather than descriptively.

The issue of the revised pericope is support for prayers on behalf of the restoration of the Temple, and for the Land of Israel. This would appear to refer to the second and third blessings of the Grace after meals, though it may also intend to include three of the Eighteen Blessings (#9, for the land and crops; #14, for rebuilding Jerusalem; and #17, for restoring the Temple service). In either case, the attribution to Gamaliel is appropriate, since he was credited with requiring the reciting of the Grace (M. Ber. 6.8) and the Eighteen Blessings (M. Ber. 4.3).

Abba Yudan of Sidon (or possible Bet Saida, BYT ṢYYD', near Tiberias) is identified by Hyman (Toledot, ii, p. 617) as a Tanna, also tradent of a single Eliezer-pericope. The ascription "on behalf of (MŠWM)" may be intended literally, an argument presented to support Gamaliel. The earlier exegesis on the response to prayer may have been revised to support the Yavnean liturgical program at almost any time after the promulgation of its official texts.

Yet the pericope does appear to address itself to the mood of despair following the Destruction. The school of Joshua preserved stories about Yoḥanan b. Zakkai and Joshua dealing with the problem of that despair. The answer associated with the figure of Yoḥanan was that deeds of lovingkindness atoned for sin in the absence of the Temple (ARNA 4); the response of Joshua was that mourning was proper in measure, but not in excess (b. B.B. 60b). (Cf. Neusner, Life, pp. 217-218, Development, pp. 125-126.) The strategy of response to the Destruction implied by this exegetical pericope is a complementary one: liturgy substitutes for the Temple, and will help effect its restoration. It declares: "Despite feelings of guilt and despair, a man still prays for God's goodness; and he is heard." So the exegesis may have been created close to Gamaliel's own time by his circle of tradents, revising the earlier exegesis to support his liturgical program.

A. He shall be put to death (Lev. 20:2): [This means] by [agency of] the court. From whence [do we know that] if the court does not have the power [to execute], the people of the land assist it? Since it is taught, the people of the land shall pelt him with stone[s] (Lev. 20:2b).

B. Another explanation (DBR'ḤR) for the people of the land: The people of the land [refers to the people] for whose sake the land was created.

C. Rabban Gamaliel says, "The people who are destined to inherit the land, by means of these matters."

D. Shall pelt him: but not cover him [with stones].

E. With stone [lit., with a stone]: This teaches that if he dies by a single stone, the obligation has been fulfilled.

Sifra, Qedošim, 10.4

Comment: This is a small collection of comments on Lev. 20:2. A declares that, in the case of an impotent court, the populace has the authority to execute. B provides a second interpretation of the phrase, "people of the land", unrelated to the topic of capital punishment. Gamaliel's comment (C) offers a parallel exegesis of the phrase, but one which re-orients it toward the original question. The final phrase, "by means of these matters," may be a gloss adapting B and C to the purposes of the pericope; they may have been a unit by themselves before entering here. D and E return to explaining the verse in terms of capital punishment, rather than in praise of the "people of the land."

This pericope is the sole Gamaliel-tradition associated with capital punishment; and as we noted, it may be a simple exegesis unrelated to that legal issue.

A. [And if any of those falls] into it [a clay vessel] (Lev. 11:33). [This means that] something which has an inside is unclean and that which has no inside is clean, as for example: a bed, chair, bench, table, boat or candelabrum of clay.

B. This is the testimony [that] Hezekiah, father of ʿIqeš testified before [b. Bek. 38a: Rabban Gamaliel in Yavneh, in behalf of (MŠWM)] Rabban Gamaliel the Elder,

C. "Any clay vessel which has no inside [is considered as] having no outside."

Sifra, Šemini, 7.5

Comment: Maimonides on M. Kel. 1.8 explains the principle involved: a hollow utensil is susceptible to uncleanness via its air space, while a solid one is not (but cf. J. Neusner, The Mishnaic Law of Purities, Mishnah Kelim, on M. Kel 2.3).

As for Gamaliel's relation to B.: Hezekiah b. ʿIqeš appears only in this pericope (A. Hyman, Toledot, ii, p. 420). If the text of b. Bek. 38a is correct, the pericope would provide another instance of a tradition about Rabban Gamaliel the Elder which our Gamaliel did not know, similar to M. Yev. 16.7 (pp. 132-134, above). If the text of b. is incorrect, the pericope would not concern our Gamaliel at all.

A. Another explanation of Lover, indeed, of the people (Deut. 33:3): This teaches that the Holy One did not apportion love to the peoples of the world in the same way he apportioned it to Israel. You may know that it is so, for they said, "The robbery of a gentile [by an Israelite] is permitted, while the robbery of an Israelite [by a gentile] is forbidden."

B. And once the government sent two officers (ŚRDYṬ'WT) and said to them, "Go, make yourselves proselytes, and see what is the nature of the Torah of Israel."

C. They went to Rabban Gamaliel at Usha, and read the Scriptures, and studied the Mishnah and _midrash_, _halakot_ and _aggadot_.

D. At the time they were leaving, they said to them, "All of your Torah is lovely and praiseworthy, except for one thing, [that] the robbery of a gentile is permitted, and the robbery of an Israelite is forbidden. And this thing we shall not make known to the government."

Sifré Deut. 344

Comment: According to a _baraita_ on b. B.M. 111b, the reasoning behind the view permitting "robbery of a gentile" is as follows: Lev. 19:13 prohibits the coercion or robbery of "your brother". The latter is defined as an Israelite. Here A quotes the _baraita_ to illustrate the exegesis of a special love for Israel. B-C adds a story of the Roman officers who adopt the guise of proselytes. In contrast with A, which seems to see no problem in the robbery of gentiles, B-C considers it to reflect poorly upon the Torah as a whole. Impressed by the rest of the Torah, the officers volunteer to suppress information about this one embarrassment.

Gamaliel is located at Usha (C) in this pericope, which makes the story unique.

A. [M'SH Š] The government (MLKWT) sent two officers ('YSṬRṬYWṬWT) to learn Torah from Rabban Gamaliel. They learned from him Scripture, Mishnah, Talmud, _halakhot_ and _aggadot_.

B. In the end, they said to him, "All of your Torah is lovely and praiseworthy, except for these two things: that you say, 'An Israelite woman may not be midwife to a gentile woman, but a gentile woman may be midwife to an Israelite; an Israelite woman may not suckle the child of a gentile woman, but the latter may suckle the child of an Israelite woman within her domain (M.'A.Z. 21);'

C. and [that you say that] robbery of an Israelite [by a gentile] is forbidden, while that of a gentile [by an Israelite] is permitted."

D. At that time Rabban Gamaliel decreed, concerning the

robbery of a gentile, that it was to be forbidden, because of the desecration of the Name [of God].

E. "'The ox of an Israelite which gored the ox of a gentile is free, etc. [from liability while the ox of a gentile is liable for damages] (M.B.Q. 4.3).' Concerning this matter, we shall not make it known."

F. Nevertheless, they did not travel [so far as] to the Ladder of Tyre before they had forgotten all these things.

y. B.Q. 4.3

Comment: The story of the Roman officers is much longer in y. than in Sifré. In B the officers mention "two things", not one. But the listing which follows includes four different laws: midwife to a gentile, nurse for a gentile, robbery of a gentile, and ox of a gentile. Even if we assume that the first two laws, found in a single *mishnah*, (M. ʿA.Z. 2.1) count as a single topic, there are still three items; so it is obvious that at least E, if not C, too, is an addition to the story. Further, C and E are both followed by comments, while B has no comment or response.

In C the officers raise the issue of "robbery of a gentile". D comments that in response Gamaliel decreed such actions to be blasphemy: the most intense expression of religious and social disapproval for something not actionable in a court. With E the officers raise another legal inequity, but declare that they will suppress the information. F appears to comment on the pericope in its entirety. Whether or not C-D and E were added separately or together, F refers to more than C-D+E (KWLN, "all of them"). The final redactor does not know of the association of Gamaliel with Usha, as in the Sifré. He has in mind the background of stories about contacts between Gamaliel and gentiles in the ʿAkko area (e.g. Tos. M.Q. 2.14). The Roman officers appear to be headed from there north (Tos. Pes. 1.27) towards Syria, which is identified by M. ʿEd. 7.7 as the seat of the government of the region.

Most significant for the pericope is the attribution to Gamaliel of the decree categorizing robbery of a gentile as blasphemy. The reason for this action (on a question of exegeses then entirely theoretical) is attributed to the needs of diplomatic relations rather than the inner dynamic of legal discussion. Such concerns were entirely appropriate to Gamaliel's position.

A. Another explanation of *Lover, indeed of the people* (Deut. 33:3): This teaches that the Holy One apportioned glory to Israel, more than to all the peoples of the world:

B. as we have learned there (DTNYNN TMN): "The ox of an Israelite which gored the ox of a gentile is free [from liability] while the ox of a gentile which gored the ox of an Israelite is liable [for damages] (M.B.Q. 4.3):

C. "An Israelite woman may not be midwife to a gentile woman, but a gentile woman may be midwife to an Israelite; an Israelite woman may not suckle the child of a gentile woman, but the latter may suckle the child of an Israelite woman within her domain (M. ʿA.Z. 2.1):

D. "The robbery of an Israelite [by a gentile] is forbidden, while that of a gentile [by an Israelite] is permitted. [The possession of] the lost property of an Israelite [by a gentile] is forbidden, while [the possession of] the lost property of a gentile [by an Israelite] is permitted."

E. They said: (MʿSH Š) The government sent two astrologers (ʾSṬRWGWLYN), saying to them, "Go and learn the Torah of the Jews, and come back and make known to us what is written in it."

F. They went off to Rabban Gamaliel in Usha, and learned from him _midrash_, _halakot_ and _aggadot_. When the time came to leave, they said to him, "Master (RBYNW) all your Torah is lovely and praiseworthy, exept for this matter, that you say,

G. "The ox of an Israelite which gored the ox of a gentile is free from liability while the ox of a gentile which gored the ox of an Israelite is liable [for damages] (M.B.Q. 4.3):

H. "An Israelite woman may not be midwife to a gentile woman, but a gentile woman may be midwife to an Israelite; an Israelite woman may not suckle the child of a gentile woman, but the latter may suckle the child or an Israelite woman within her domain (M. ʿA.Z. 2.1).

I. "The robbery of an Israelite is forbidden, while the lost property of a gentile is permitted.

J. "But this thing we shall not make known to the government."

K. At that hour, Rabban Gamaliel arose and prayed concerning them. They looked for something, of the things in their possession, and they did not find it.

Midr. Tann. Deut. 33:3, ed.
D. S. Hoffman, p. 212, lines 1-12

Comment: Midr. Tann. appears to expand the story, using all available sources. In A, the term "love" used by Sifré has been replaced by "glory". Further, the idea of Sifré that divine love for Israel is different from that for the nations is here converted to an invidious distinction: Israel's glory is more than that of the nations.

B and C are quotations from the Mishnah, as noted.

D quotes Sifré.

In E, dependent upon Sifré, the change to "astrologers" from "officers" must be scribal error.

In F-J, the story is expanded by repeating quotations from M.

K appears to depend upon the conclusion to the story added by y., though it has lost the point: the well-disposed officers forget all they have learned. But it has added the detail about Gamaliel's power of prayer which obviously supplies the reason for their forgetting in y. This ascription of theurgic power to Gamaliel is unique.

Thus, though not well-transmitted, the pericope in Midr. Tann. has combined Sifré and y., and filled them out through quotations from the legal materials of M. The exegetical intent of Sifré has fallen away.

A. (TNW RBNN) Long ago the Roman government sent two officers (ŚRDYWṬWT) to sages of Israel [saying], "Teach us your Torah."

B. They read and reviewed and [studied a] third [time]. At the time they were leaving, they said to them, "We carefully examined your Torah, and it is true, except for this one thing: that you say, 'An ox of an Israelite which gored the ox of a Canaanite is free [of liability]; that of a Canaanite which gored an ox of an Israelite, whether tam or muʿad, [the owner] pays full damages (M.B.Q. 4.3).'

C. "How can you say this? For if [the law of damages applies only to those described as] literally brother (Lev. 19:13) even the [ox of a] Canaanite that gored an [ox of an] Israelite should be exempt [from liability]; and if [the law applies to someone] not literally brother, then even that of an Israelite which gored that of a Canaanite should be liable.

D. "But [as to] this matter, we shall not make it known to the government."

b. B.Q. 38a

Comment: The story of the visit by Roman officers here occurs between them and the "sages of Israel," who are not named (A). The topic of B is shared with y., ox-goring and liability for the damages. But C supplies the officers with an analysis of the law to support their objection. There is no counter-argument offered in the pericope. D is common to all the versions.

Of the four versions of this tradition, three use the same word for the Roman officers (ŚRDYṬ'WT, 'YSṬRṬYWṬWT); Midr. Tann. has the more familiar word, "astrologers". In all of them the officers praise the Torah, take exception to something, and declare that they will not publicize the embarrassing law. The Sifré version deals with robbery of a gentile, b. with ox-goring. Midr. Tann. starts with ox-goring, then midwife/nurse and robbery/lost property. Midr. Tann. makes the only reference to lost proprerty. Only in y. do we have Gamaliel's decree against robbery of a gentile, and the miraculous amnesia of the officers after they leave the academy. It is apparent that y. has made use of traditions available to Sifré and to b., though not in the exact texts found there (e.g., the detail locating Gamaliel at Usha, in the Sifré, indicates lateness compared to y., while the absence of Gamaliel's decree suggests an earlier development). Midr. Tann. shares the detail of Usha, but its conclusion indicates a garbling of the tradition of miraculous amnesia mentioned in y.

Thus, while Gamaliel is associated with this story as a theoretical problem in Sifré, the decree is first attributed to him in y.

A. Whence do you say [that] a man is permitted to give his consecrated [gifts] to a single priest? [Since] it said, [The sacred donations] that the Israelites shall offer shall be the priest's [sing.] (Num. 5:9).

B. Rabban Gamaliel presented [lit., said] an *a fortiori* (QL WḤWMR) [argument] before R. 'Aqiva [as follows], "In the case of something in which I have no share, if they give it to me it is mine; [then concerning] something in which I have a share, if they give it to me should it not be mine?"

C. Said to him R. 'Aqiva, "No! If you say of something in which you have no share, if I give it to you it will be yours, [that is] because no one else shares it with you. Would you say [the same] in the case of something in which you have a share, [that] if I give it to you it is yours, (ŠKN) since someone else does share [it] with you?"

D. Said Rabban Gamaliel, "What of a woman, whom I do not share: if I betrothe her she is mine [and] I have the power to void her vows, and no one can prevent me [Horowitz adds: then in the case of a woman whom I share, if I betrothe her, will she not be mine, with [my] power to void her vows and [with] no one preventing me?]"

E. Said R. ʿAqiva to him, "No! If you say about a woman, whom you do not share, that if you [lit., I] betrothe her she is yours [and] you have the power to void her vows, and no one can prevent you, that is because no one shares with you. [Horowitz adds: Shall you say, about a woman, in whom you share, that if you [lit., I] betrothe her, that she is yours and you have the power to void her vows with no one preventing you, that someone actually shares her with you?] [So therefore,] shall you say [concerning] something in which you have a share, that if I give it to you it is yours, since someone else does share with you?"

F. He said, "_Each priest shall keep what is given to him_ (Num. 5:10b)."

Sifré Zuṭa, Naso 5.9
(Horowitz ed., p. 231, line 12-
p. 232, line 3)

Comment: A presents an exegesis, to the effect that one may give his priestly gifts to a single priest even though in theory all priests may equally claim a share in the consecrated objects.

In B, Gamaliel advances an _a fortiori_ argument to prove the same ruling, independent of the exegesis. He is refuted in C, by ʿAqiva. The introduction to the debate ("Rabban Gamaliel presented an _a fortiori_ before R. ʿAqiva") is unusual. Even in those Gamaliel-pericopae, preserved by ʿAqivans, in which ʿAqiva bests Gamaliel, it is Gamaliel, rather than ʿAqiva, who rests in the most prestigious position. It would be more normal for ʿAqiva to speak "before" (LPNY) Gamaliel.

B-C is an adaptation, to the issue of priestly gifts, of the argument D-E which concerns a husband's rights over his betrothed. That argument appears to come from Tos. Ned. 6.5 (b. Ned. 74b). There it is connected to an Eliezer-ʿAqiva dispute. Eliezer claims that any of a number of levirs may void the vows of a _yevama_ prior to the consummation of the levirate bond; the same _a fortiori_ is advanced here by Gamaliel and refuted by ʿAqiva. Evidently the structure of the debate was preserved in ʿAqivan circles, and applied to several contexts, with several antagonists.

Rabban Gamaliel says, "_She shall be unharmed and able to retain seed_ (Num. 5:25b): this is to exclude one who has already retained seed. That is to say, a pregnant woman does not drink [the bitter waters]."

Sifré Zuṭa, Naso 5.28 (Horowitz
ed. p. 237, lines 17-18)

Comment: Horowitz notes that this exegesis appears only in the Yalqut Simeoni text of its larger midrash-passage, and not in other texts. M. Śoṭ. 5.3 quotes Meir to the effect that a woman pregnant by a former husband does not drink the waters of the jealousy-ordeal; the anonymous law of Tos. Śoṭ. 5.3 states that a woman pregnant by her own husband does drink, an issue that M. does not raise. So if, despite its shaky textual warrant, the pericope here were to be early, it would have to precede the distinction between pregnancies established by the Ushans.

Gamaliel is associated with only one other lemma on the subject of the suspected woman, the non-legal comment of M. Śoṭ. 2.1.

A. This is the question which R. Yosé b. Taddai, [lit., man] of Tiberias, asked of Rabban Gamaliel [Yalq. Šim.: Simeon b. Gamaliel]: "If [in the case of] my wife, with whom I am permitted [to have sexual intercourse] I am prohibited [from marrying] her daughter, then the wife of [another] man, concerning whom I am prohibited [from having sexual intercourse], does it not logically follow (ʾYNW DYN) that I should be prohibited [from marrying] her daughter?"

B. He said to him, "Go out and provide me [a wife] for the High Priest, about whom it is written, A virgin of his own people shall he take to wife (Lev. 21:14), and I will provide you [with wives] for all Israel.

C. "Another argument (DBR ʾḤR) [Yalq. Šim. omits DBR ʾḤR]: We do not use an a fortiori argument to uproot something from Scripture."

D. And Rabban Gamaliel put him under the ban (WNDHW) [Yalq. Šim. omits D].

D.E.R. 1.6 (Yalq. Šim., Emor)

Comment: Yosé's a fortiori argument is a non-practical exercise in logic. It would, on the grounds of the ban on incest, forbid any man to marry anyone except the daughter of someone not the wife of another man, or of his own wife, hence only the daughter of a widow or divorcée. Gamaliel's reply shows that the reasoning is faulty: it would render inoperative the scriptural command for the High Priest to marry, since that verse implies freedom of choice (any unmarried virgin). C states the principle in succinct form; since it is really the point of B, the reading of the version in Yalq. Šimeoni makes sense, omitting DBR ʾḤR. That version also omits D entirely; indeed, there is no reason for Yosé to have been placed under the ban for such a question, though D is in keeping with the reputation for high-handed behavior established in b. Ber 27b, and elsewhere.

All in all, the emergence of this issue in such late texts, together with the relative superiority of the Yalqut, makes it doubtful that this pericope refers to Gamaliel.

PART TWO: THE FORMS OF THE LEGAL TRADITION

i. Listing of the Forms

The 169 pericopae of Gamaliel's legal traditions appear in no less than ten distinct forms. However, on closer examination they are seen to be variations of four basic forms. Forms (A), (B), (C), (D) and (E), discussed below, are all variations of one basic form, the dispute. (F) contains the few exegeses, (G) the lemmas, or simple sayings. And (H), (I) and (J) are all types of narratives. (I have bracketted those pericopae which analysis in Part I showed not to concern our Gamaliel, or which are identical with other listed pericopae. These will be omitted from later discussion of the proportions of different forms or subjects.)

A.

Many Gamaliel-pericopae are cast in the standard dispute-form used for the disputes of the Houses of Shammai and Hillel (as identified by Neusner, Pharisees, ii, pp. 1-4). The legal problem is stated in a superscription, followed by the balanced answers of named authorities in direct or (less often) indirect discourse: Legal Problem + X Says... Y Says...

1. Ate figs, grapes, etc., 3 blessings, Gamaliel, sages ʿAqiva	M. Ber. 6.8
2. After eating of 7 species, Gamaliel, sages + MʿSH	Tos. Ber. 4.15
3. Seven species not grain, Gamaliel, sages	Tos. Ber. 4.15
4. Neither 7 species nor grain, Gamaliel, sages	Tos. Ber. 4.15
5. Two sheaves, 2 seʾahs between them, Gamaliel, sages + debate	M. Pe. 6.6
6. Pickles 3 vegetables in one jar, Eliezer, Joshua, Gamaliel, halaka: Gam.	M. Shev. 9.5
[Same + introductory verse]	[Sifra, Behar 3.4-5]
7. Jar of Heave-offering suspected unclean, Eliezer, Joshua, Gamaliel	M. Ter. 8.8

8.	Israelite tenant-farmers in Syria, Eliezer, Gamaliel	M. Ḥal. 4.7
9.	Writes 2 letters, 2 times on Sabbath, Gamaliel, sages	M. Shab. 12.6
10.	Writes 2 letters on 2 Sabbaths Gamaliel, sages	b. Ker. 16b
11.	Binds a thread upon red, Gamaliel, Eleazar b. Ṣadoq	Tos. Shab. 7.11
12.	Gentiles brought man to other town on Sabbath, Gamaliel/ Eliezer, Joshua/ᶜAqiva + MᶜSH	M. ᶜEruv. 4.1
13.	Picks out pulse on festival, Houses, Gamaliel	M. Beṣ. 1.8
14.	Two *yevamot*, one levir, he sends *geṭ* to both, Gamaliel, sages	Tos. Yev. 7.2B
15.	Two sisters, deaf-mutes, one of age, one minor, Eliezer, Gamaliel, Joshua	M. Yev. 13.7
16.	Married a woman, did not find her a virgin, Gamaliel/Eliezer, Joshua	M. Ket. 1.6
17.	She claims injury, Gamaliel/ Eliezer, Joshua	M. Ket. 1.7
18.	They saw her speaking in the market, Gamaliel/Eliezer, Joshua	M. Ket. 1.8
19.	She was pregnant, Gamaliel/ Eliezer, Joshua	M. Ket. 1.9
20.	They saw her go into a secret place, Gamaliel/ Eliezer, Joshua	b. Ket. 13a-b
	[She was pregnant: same as M. Ket. 1.9 + debate]	[Tos. Ket. 1.6]
21.	Woman inherited foods before she was betrothed, Houses + they said before Gamaliel	M. Ket. 8.1
22.	If she inherited before, then married, Gamaliel, sages missing + They said before Gamaliel	M. Ket. 8.1
23.	Slaughters animal at point of death, Gamaliel, Eliezer, Simeon	M. Ḥul. 2.6

24. Metal basket-cover, Gamaliel, sages	M. Kel. 12.3
25. Healthy flesh within Bright Spot, Gamaliel, ʿAqiva	M. Neg. 6.5
26. Evening prayer Gamaliel, Joshua	b. Ber. 27b
27. Oil and myrtle Houses, Gamaliel	b. Ber. 43b
28. Sukkah on ship, Gamaliel, ʿAqiva + MʿSH	b. Sukk. 23a

B.

Similar to A, the legal problem here is phrased in the form of a question, rather than as a situation: Question + X Says... Y Says...

1. From what time do they recite Shemaʿ? Eliezer, Sages, Gamaliel + MʿSH	M. Ber. 1.1
2. What is Rikpa onion? Anonymous + Gamaliel	y. Ma. 5.3
3. When do olives receive uncleanness? Houses + Gamaliel, Simeon, sages	M. Toh. 9.1
4. Evening prayer law? Gamaliel, Joshua	y. Ber. 4.1

C.

Closely related to the above is the juxtaposition of differing opinions. In one case (2), the statements do not deal with the same topic. But the others are true disputes; the opening statement includes a statement of the problems which would have been a separate element in A. The form followed is: X Says... Y Says...

1. Gamaliel: Every day man prays 18 + Joshua, ʿAqiva, Eliezer	M. Ber. 4.3, 4A
2. Gamaliel: Stalks of fenugreek tithed + Eliezer, ʿAqiva	M. Ma. 4.6

3.	Gamaliel: 2 Dough-offerings in Syria + Eliezer [people follow Gamaliel]	M. Ḥal. 4.7
4.	Buy from professional baker in Syria, Gamaliel, sages	Tos. Ḥal. 2.6
5.	Gamaliel: <u>Etrog</u> like tree in 3 ways + Eliezer	M. Bik. 2.6
6.	Gamaliel: 3 women knead dough + sages, ʿAqiva	M. Pes. 3.4
7.	Gamaliel: 3 things more lenient, sages prohibit	M. Beṣ. 2.7
8.	Gamaliel: agent of congregation fulfills Rosh Hashanah prayer + sages + debate	Tos. R.H. 2.18
9.	Gamaliel: No <u>geṭ</u> after <u>geṭ</u> + sages	M. Yev. 5.1
10.	Sages: get after <u>maʾamar</u> + Gamaliel agrees	Tos. Yev. 7.2B
11.	Widow who did not want to leave husband's house, Meir in name of Gamaliel + sages	M. Ket. 12.3-4
12.	Four things Gamaliel declares clean, sages unclean	M. Kel. 12.6
13.	Gamaliel and sages did not differ over unequally-divided plate (Judah)	Tos. Kel. B.M. 2.13
14.	Houses-dispute on scroll-wrappers + Gamaliel	M. Kel. B.M. 2.13

D.

Here the differing opinions follow the anonymous statement of a (possibly earlier) law and comment upon it: <u>Anonymous Law + X Says... Y Says...</u>

1.	Poor make 3 searches + Gamaliel, ʿAqiva	M. Pe. 4.5
2.	<u>Sukkot</u> annuls 7 days' mourning + Eliezer, Gamaliel, sages	M. M.Q. 3.5-6

3. One bringing get from abroad + Gamaliel, Eliezer sages	M. Giṭ. 1.1
4. Altar sanctifies + Gamaliel, Joshua + their words differ only	M. Zev. 9.1
[Large furnace with rim unclean + Judah, Gamaliel = Tos. Kel. B. Q. 6.17]	[M. Kel. 8.9]
5. Large furnace is clean + Meir, Judah, Yosé [all in name of Gamaliel]	Tos. Kel. B.Q. 6.17
6. Only weasel renders water unfit + Gamaliel, Eliezer	M. Par. 9.3
7. 10 families + Eliezer b. Jacob, Gamaliel, Eliezer	y. Yev. 4.2
8. Passover dough with wine, honey + Gamaliel, sages, ʿAqiva	b. Pes. 36a

E.

In a smaller number of pericopae, Gamaliel's lemma follows, and depends for its definition upon, an anonymous statement of law. While Gamaliel's words seem to be commentary, the content shows the pericope to be a dispute, in which the law defines the problem and presents its ruling: Anonymous Law + X Says (=Gloss or differing Opinion).

1. Sicilian beans square + Gamaliel	Tos. Ma. 3.15
2. Egyptian lentils + Gamaliel	Tos. Ma. 3.15
3. Finds tefillin in field + Gamaliel	M. ʿEruv. 10.1
4. Each individual required to say Rosh Hashanah prayer + Gamaliel	M. R.H. 4.9
5. On 3rd of Marheshvan they ask for rain + Gamaliel	M. Ta. 1.3
6. They do not decree fast day + Gamaliel	M. Ta. 2.10

7. Husband revokes vow not to spread mattress + Gamaliel	Tos. Ned. 7.1
8. Man says to fellow, weed with me + Gamaliel	M. B.M. 5.10
9. Claimed wheat, admitted barley: exempt + Gamaliel	M. Shav. 6.3
10. Blood mixed with water + Judah on behalf of Gamaliel	Tos. Zev. 8.17
11. Chamber pot is unclean + Gamaliel	M. Kel. 17.2
12. Mourner says Shemaʿ on Sabbath + Gamaliel	b. M.Q. 23b
13. Mourner eats on Sabbath + Gamaliel	Sem. 10.3

F.

Exegesis: Verse + X Says...

1. You may deduct interest (Deut. 23:21a) + Gamaliel	Sifré Ki Teṣé 263
[2. Follow the scholars (Deut. 16:20) mentions Gamaliel-Yavneh	b. Sanh. 32b]
3. Owner of ox is free (Ex. 21:28)	Mek. Nez. 10
4. A man prays (Ex. 22:22)	Mek. RŠY, Mišpatim 24.23
5. People of the land (Lev. 20:2)	Sifré Qedošim 10.4
[6. Pregnant woman does not drink (Num. 5:25)	Sifré Zuta Naso 5.28]

G.

Only a minority of Gamaliel's sayings occur without being incorporated into a dispute-form. The simple saying of a named authority in the present tense, the standard legal form, appears also for Gamaliel as : X Says + Lemma (Direct or Indirect Discourse).

1. Forbids tenant-farming in Syria (Eleazar)	Tos. Ḥal. 2.5

2.	Only 1 Dough-offering in Syria (Eleazar)	Tos. Ḥal. 2.5
3.	Three lands for Dough-offering	M. Ḥal. 4.8
4.	Even if he writes 2 letters the same (Judah)	b. Shab. 103b
5.	Common food eaten through 4th hour	M. Pes. 1.5
6.	Two loaves of Thanks-offering on portico (Judah)	Tos. Pes. 1.4
7.	Must say 3 things on Passover	M. Pes. 10.5
8.	Words of House of Hillel apply to case where food more than refuse	b. Beṣ. 14b
9.	Three things more stringent ruling + debate	M. Beṣ. 2.6
10.	It was received by me... times moon travels long way	b. R.H. 25a
11.	According to words of Gamaliel he sprinkles	Tos. Zev. 9.1
12.	Blood, Saliva, urine (Judah on behalf of Gamaliel)	b. Zev. 79a
13.	Signs of clean/unclean birds	b. Ḥul 65a
14.	Shemaʿ twice in one night	ARNA 2.8

H.

In some instances, the report of an opinion is phrased in the first person, with anindication of the setting in which the opinion was given: X Says, I Asked... + Reply

1.	ʿAqiva: I asked what kind of woman, oven	b. Pes. 48b
2.	ʿAqiva: I asked Gamaliel/Joshua, sexual relations with sister, etc.	M. Ker. 3.7
3.	ʿAqiva: I asked Gamaliel/Joshua, man removed signs of uncleanness	M. Neg. 7.4

I.

A substantial number of Gamaliel's traditions appear as stories about his behavior. Often they follow an anonymous law, sometimes as precedent, sometimes as illustration. But often, too, the story itself is used as if it were a legal ruling, to dispute the cited law. The form is: Statement of Law + Story (With or Without Superscription MʿSH).

1.	Bridegroom exempt from reciting Shemaʿ + MʿSH	M. Ber. 2.5
2.	Scribes stop for Shemaʿ, not Tefillah Rabbi, Ḥananya, Eleazar b. Ṣadoq + story	Tos. Ber. 2.6
3.	Carob trees in sight of each other require Peʾah + Gamaliel: Father's house	M. Pe. 2.4
[4.	Feed Demai to the poor + story = no. 5	M. Dem. 3.1]
5.	Ḥaver must announce Demai + story	Tos. Dem. 3.15
6.	Three decrees concerning Demai + MʿSH + story	Tos. Dem. 5.24
7.	Houses-dispute: changing silver for gold + ʿAqiva: I changed for Gamaliel and Joshua	M. M.S. 2.7
8.	Fourth year fruit in Syria + MʿSH	Tos. Ter. 2.13
9.	Fruit far, must designate tithes + MʿSH	M. M.S. 5.9
10.	Gentile sets gangplank, may disembark + MʿSH	M. Shab 16.8
11.	Saying "He heals" is way of Amorites + Eleazar + House of Gamaliel	Tos. Shab. 7.5
12.	Scriptures in Aramaic stored away + MʿSH	Tos. Shab. 13.2
13.	Disembark only within Sabbath limit + MʿSH	Tos. Shab. 13.11A

14. Meir-Eliezer b. Jacob dispute: gentile or Sadducee in same court-yard + MʿSH + Judah revision	M. ʿEruv. 6.1-2
15. Eliezer-Yosé dispute: bolt with knob on Sabbath + MʿSH	M. ʿEruv. 10.10
16. Channel outside window, lower bucket on Sabbath + story	Tos. ʿEruv. 9.25
17. Passover offering not roasted on spit + MʿSH	M. Pes. 7.2
18. Finds leavened bread on road + MʿSH + stories	Tos. Pes. 1.27
19. Eleazar b. Ṣadoq: Heave-offering burned before Sabbath + story: we burned *hameṣ*	Tos. Pes. 2.9-11
20. After Passover meal man studies law + MʿSH	Tos. Pes. 10.11-12
21. Sleep under bed in *sukkah* + MʿSH	M. Suk. 2.1
22. Houses disput on shaking *lulav* + ʿAqiva: I watched Gamaliel and Joshua	M. Suk. 3.9
23. On Sukkot need own *lulav* or gift + MʿSH	Tos. Suk. 2.11
24. Traps for animal set before festival + MʿSH	M. Beṣ. 3.2
25. Profane Sabbath for 2 new moons + MʿSH	M. R.H. 1.4-6
26. So not stop multitude from *miṣvah* + Judah: officer of Geder prevented	y. R.H. 1.5
27. Sit on gentile's bench on Sabbath + MʿSH	Tos. M.Q. 2.14-16
28. Decreed not to teach son Greek + House of Gamaliel	Tos. Soṭ. 15.8
29. Document with Samaritan witness + MʿSH	M. Giṭ. 1.5
30. Permit raising small animals before festival + They asked Gamaliel	Tos. B.Q. 8.11-12
31. Lend tenant-farmers wheat + story	M. B.M. 5.8

32.	Seating of the Sanhedrin + Eleazar b. Ṣadoq: When Gamaliel was in session	Tos. San. 8.1
33.	Intercalate the year conditionally + MʿSH	M. ʿEd. 7.7
34.	Joshua and Judah testify concerning ʿIsah + Gamaliel said: we accept, but what can we do	M. ʿEd. 8.3
35.	Israelite taking haircut looks in mirror + Permitted House of Gamaliel	Tos. ʿA.Z. 3.5
36.	Oven heated from outside or without owner's knowledge + MʿSH	M. Kel. 5.4
37.	Joshua, sages dispute: food and vessels make hands unclean + Gamaliel says: MʿSH a woman came before father	M. Yad. 3.1
38.	Syrian decorated cakes on Passover + House of Gamaliel	b. Pes. 37a
39.	Reasons for leaving sukkah + Gamaliel, Liezer	y. Sukk. 2.10
40.	He that pours blood of sacrifice + MʿSH	b. Ḥul. 87a
[41.	Ḥanina rules on foetus + MʿSH	b. Nid. 24b]
42.	Robbery of a gentile + 2 officers to go study	Sifré Deut. 344

J.

In an almost-equal number of instances, stories about Gamaliel occur without being appended to a law. However, their purpose is not biographical, nor is it the expression of moral- or wisdom-sayings. They too serve as the equivalent of legal sayings: Story (With or Without Superscription MʿSH).

1.	Bathed himself first night wife died	M. Ber. 2.6
2.	Accepted condolences for Ṭabi	M. Ber. 2.7

3. Simeon HaPaquli arranged 18 blessings	b. Ber. 28b-29a
4. Gamaliel: blessings for Minim	b. Ber. 28b-29a
5. Gamaliel and court decreed 4 cubits	Tos. Kil. 4.1
6. ʿAqiva picked etrog (MʿSH)	Tos. Shev. 4.21
7. Household would bring garments to laundry (E. b. Ṣadoq)	Tos. Shab. 1.22
8. Gentile set up gangplank	Tos. Shab. 13.11B
9. House of R. Gamaliel did not fold garments	Tos. Shab. 12.16
10. Joshua decided halakah follows Gamaliel for a ship	b. ʿEruv. 43a
11. Didn't enter harbor until dark	M. ʿEruv. 4.2
12. Absolved vow at ladder of Tyre	Tos. Pes. 1.28
13. Prompted old man to release vow	b. Ned. 22a
14. House of Gamaliel used to fill pail with lentils (E. b. Ṣadoq)	Tos. Y.Ṭ. 1.22
15. In Gamaliel's house didn't reassemble candelabrum on festival + MʿSH	Tos. Y.Ṭ. 2.12
16. E. b. Ṣadoq: We ate at Gamaliel's, they never swept between couches, never brought incense	Tos. Y.Ṭ. 2.13-14
17. Gamaliel's household used to grind pepper on festival (E. b. Ṣadoq)	Tos. Y.Ṭ. 2.16
18. Gamaliel had pictures of moon + MʿSH	M. R.H. 2.8-9
19. Heavens clouded, Gamaliel did not sanctify new moon	b. R.H. 25a
20. Gamaliel freed people in field of requirement for prayer (R. Simeon)	b. R.H. 35a
21. They decreed a fast + After Gamaliel's death (MʿSH) + story	Tos. Ta. 2.5

22. Gamaliel ate common food in purity + Onqelos	Tos. Ḥag. 3.2B-3
23. ʿAqiva: I went to Nehardea, woman allowed to remarry	M. Yev. 16.7
24. Ḥananiah testified before Gamaliel that they do not intercalate	Tos. San. 2.13
25. Proqlos son of Plosfos asked when bathing	M. ʿA.Z. 3.4
26. Gamaliel and Onqelos immerse at Ashqelon	Tos. Miq. 6.3
27. They brought 60 troughs before Gamaliel (Yosé) (MʿSH)	Tos. Kel. B.M. 11.2J
28. Ḥananiah b. Ḥananiah's father vowed him a Nazirite (MʿSH)	Tos. Nid. 5.15
29. At first, burial harder than death	Tos. Nid. 9.17
30. Judah the Ammonite proselyte came, Gamaliel, Joshua + debate	M. Yad. 4.4
31. Evening prayer (MʿSH)	y. Ber. 4.1
[32.R. Yeshovav's possessions (MʿSH)	y. Pe. 1.1]
33. Gamaliel knocked out Ṭabi's tooth (MʿSH)	y. Ket. 3.10
34. Ṭabita poured wine (MʿSH)	y. Nid. 2.1
35. Gamaliel's maidservant baked/corked (MʿSH)	b. Nid. 6.b
36. Presence at intercalation-session	y. Sanh. 1.2
37. Gamaliel: I saw shipwreck	b. Yev. 121a
38. Gamaliel performed levirate marriage	b. Yev. 15a
39. Reassures husband about virginity	b. Ket. 10a
40. Roman officers study, Gamaliel decrees blasphemy (MʿSH)	y. B.Q. 4.3
[41.R. Yosé b. Taddai asked marrying daughter of widow	D.E.R. 1.6]

ii. The Disputes

(A), (B), (C) and (D) are all variations of the dispute-form, first used for the preservation of the views of the Houses of Shammai and Hillel. Form (A) is identical with the Houses' dispute-structure: the problem is stated, then the differing opinions. Form (B) is similar to (A), except that the legal case is phrased in the form of a question, rather than as a problem. Form (C) juxtaposes differing opinions. Most are true disputes: there the first opinion defines the topic, which would have been a separate element in (A). But in one case the lemmas do not deal with the same topic. Unrelated statements have been incorporated into a dispute-form. In (D), the differing opinions follow an anonymous statement of a (possibly earlier) law and comment upon it.

None of these closely-related forms appear to be connected with specific named masters, as may be seen from the comparison below (the Ushan Simeon and "anonymous" who each appear once in form (B) have been excluded):

(A) + (B) Problem/Question + X Says...Y Says
Appearing in a total of 32 pericopae:
Gamaliel-sages - 12
Gamaliel-Joshua - 10
Gamaliel-Eliezer - 12

(C) X Says...Y Says...
Appearing in a total of 14 pericopae:
Gamaliel-sages - 8
Gamaliel-Joshua - 1
Gamaliel-Eliezer - 4

(D) Law + X Says...Y Says...
Appearing in a total of 8 pericopae:
Gamaliel-sages - 3
Gamaliel-Eliezer - 4
Gamaliel-ʿAqiva - 2

So while forms (A) and (B), the original Houses' forms, predominate, all Yavnean circles felt free to use all the developing forms of the dispute for their formulations of law.

In other ways too, the dispute-form has become looser. Though (A) and (B) perpetuate the Houses-disputes in structure, they provide few examples suggesting any arrangement for mnemonic considerations. Reviewing the pericopae from that perspective, we may note the following balanced apodoses:

A. 5 -- M. Pe. 6.6
A. 9 -- M. Shab. 12.6 (= A. 10 -- b. Ker. 16b)
A. 25 -- M. Kel. 12.3
A. 26 -- b. Ber. 27b (=B.4 -- y. Ber. 4.1)
A. 28 -- b. Suk. 23a
B. 1 -- M. Ber. 1.1
B. 3 -- M. Ṭoh. 9.1
C. 1 -- M. Pe. 4.5
C. 3 -- M. Giṭ. 1.1
D. 7 -- y. Yev. 4.2

Out of all 67 items in sections (A) through (E), only 10 pericopae, or 14.9%, are possibly balanced for memorization. And these are in fact doubtful: the answers are brief: to the owner vs. to the poor, lest they increase vs. lest they decrease, etc. It seems more likely that the brevity of the answers, together with the balance inherent in the form itself accounts for this, rather than the presence of any mnemonic interest. The only clear exception would be B.3, where Gamaliel's comment on the original Houses-dispute has been fitten to it exactly, in a one-word, five-syllable answer. Yet on the other hand, in A. 27 (b. Ber. 43b) Gamaliel's comment on a Houses-dispute is not balanced at all.

Form (E) has been termed "commentary form" by Neusner (Eliezer, ii, pp. 59-73). His analysis of similar pericopae in the Eliezer corpus revealed that none there were true glosses of earlier law; all were really a variation of the dispute. Here too, only 1 and 2 appear to be glosses, but they too are probably disputes. So none of these pericopae actually glosses earlier law.

In most of the disputes in which Gamaliel appears, his opinion is quoted first. Neusner has noted (Politics, p. 102) the implications of b. ʿEruv 13b and y. Suk. 2.8, to the effect that primary placement in a pericope indicates favored treatment. It should be noted, therefore, that of the 55 pericopae in (A), (B), (C) and (D) -- excluding 5 in which Gamaliel comments on Houses-disputes, 1 Gamaliel-comment on a saying of Admon, and 1 pericope in which all three opinions are given by masters on Gamaliel's behalf -- 39 pericopae (=81.3%) place Gamaliel's opinion first.

Of the 9 in which he follows other opinions, in 6 Eliezer is first, with 1 each for Eliezer b. Jacob, sages and an anonymous law.

Further, we observed that, in the case of M. Ket. 13.3-5 and M. Shav. 6.3, the redactor of the Mishnah did not appear to distinguish between Rabban Gamaliel the Elder and Gamaliel II. The implication of the former pericopae seemed to equate Gamaliel's position in later Yavneh with that of Yoḥanan in earlier Yavneh. This would certainly fit in with the favorable treatment accorded Gamaliel by the Mishnah in the disputes and, as we shall see, in the narratives.

In sum: We have seen thus far that no variation of the dispute-form which includes Gamaliel is associated solely with any particular master. As with the Eliezer-materials, the dispute-form is looser than that used for the Houses of Shammai and Hillel; there is no evidence for any consistent attempt to impose a mnemonic form upon the apodoses of the disputes; nor does Gamaliel gloss earlier laws. And in most of the disputes, Gamaliel's opinion is presented first.

iii. Exegeses, Lemmas, First-person Reports

The examples in Form (F) are not the only exegeses. Sifra Behar 3.4,5, M. ʿA.Z. 3.4, M. Zev. 9.1, Sifra Emor 16.2 and M. Yad. 4.4, though classified under other headings, also contain exegeses. Slightly more than half of the exegeses are in the M.-Tos. stratum of the pericopae.

Relatively few lemmas occur in Form (G), unredacted into a dispute-form.

As for Form (H), the first-person reports, these may be supplemented by a number of other first-person accounts. The latter occur as stories, though the dividing line here may be hard to draw:

I. 7 ʿAqiva: I changed silver for gold dinars

I. 19 Eleazar: We burned the ḥameṣ on Sabbath

I. 22 ʿAqiva: I watched Gamaliel and Joshua wave the lulav

J. 16 Eleazar: We ate at Gamaliel's

J. 23 ʿAqiva: I went to Nehardea

J. 26 Joshua b. Qibusai: Gamaliel did not immerse

Of the 9 pericopae, 6 are attributed to ʿAqiva, 2 to Eleazar b. Ṣadoq, and 1 to Joshua b. Qibusai. So it appears that the first-person report of an opinion, or of behavior, is associated with the ʿAqivan circle. (See, in addition to M. Ker. 3.7, also M. Ker. 3.8, 9 and 10.)

This fact leads us to speculate about the redactional history of three pericopae which are first-person accounts, told by Gamaliel himself about his father, Simeon b. Gamaliel the Elder. In M. ʿEruv. 6.1-2 (I. 14), we have a story of a Sadducee who shared an alley-way with Simeon's family home. The story appears to be a revision of a third-person story about Gamaliel himself, as told by Meir (b. ʿEruv. 68b); but Judah presents a different version of the story. In M. Pe. 2.4 (I. 3), a first-person account told by Gamaliel supports an anonymous law about tithing carob trees; but Eleazar b. Ṣadoq presents a more lenient version in Gamaliel's own name. The third case, M. Yad. 3.1 (I. 37), is only the fragment of a story.

It may be that, in the first two instances at least, ʿAqivan tradents at Usha made use of the first-person narrative form to revise a story about Gamaliel into a narrative about his father, Simeon b. Gamaliel. Perhaps this would render the opinions presented there more acceptable during the patriarchate of Simeon b. Gamaliel II. The formal evidence is not conclusive, but it is suggestive, especially in the light of J. 37. The latter (b. Yev. 121a), it will be recalled, is a first-person report narrated by Gamaliel about a scholar lost at sea, in which the hero turns out to be ʿAqiva. (The identical story there is told by ʿAqiva about Meir.) So clearly, the ʿAqivans were able to revise first-person narratives, perhaps with greater freedom than other forms, as an enterprise characteristic of their circle.

iv. The Narratives

The significance of narratives within the corpus of Gamaliel's legal traditions may be seen from the following comparison. Among the traditions about Eliezer, legal narratives represent 14 pericopae out of a total of 228, or 6.1%. Of all the legal pericopae concerning the pre-70 Pharisees, legal narratives represent 54 out of 323, or 29%. To arrive at a comparable figure for Gamaliel, we take from the listing of forms, above, the total number of pericopae from (H), (I) and (J), adding to that number the four narratives included in sections (A) and (B): A. 2, A. 12,

A. 28 and B. 1. These stories were too closely connected to the disputes of which they are a part to be listed separately. The total number of this form from the legal corpus, thus arrived at, is 81 narratives, or 47.9% of the 169 pericopae.

We have seen overwhelmingly, in our analysis, that the stories do not appear to have been created as illustrations for the laws they often accompany. Almost always do they show signs of independent origin (exceptions may be Tos. Shab. 12.6, M. B.M. 5.8, and M. ʿEd. 7.7). This does not assert the historicity of these narratives; some of them (for example, M. M.S. 5.9) were probably created to illustrate legal principles. But in only two instances can we find cases of a teaching, in the form of a lemma, which has been _also_ expressed as (probably developed into) a story: Tos. Beṣ. 1.22 and b. Suk. 23a. For the rest, the stories are used within their respective contexts as if they are legal lemmas. _Rabban Gamaliel did x_ is treated the same as if it were _Rabban Gamaliel says x_. Since the personal biographical interest in Tannaitic traditions is so low as to be almost nonexistent, we must assume that the legal narratives expressed paradigmatic actions for those who formulated and circulated them. They are the equivalent of other forms of legal statement.

The Gamaliel narratives share this narrative form with the pre-70 Pharisaic masters (aside from the Houses). Lightstone (_Ṣadoq_, p. 137) has observed that tradition has assigned to those masters the titles of _nasi_ (=patriarch) or _av bet din_ (= subordinate to the patriarch). He concludes that the narrative form of legal statement is probably connected to the patriarchal circle. Is it possible to be more specific about the significance of narrative form, beyond labelling it as "patriarchal"? Gamaliel does not merely continue the use of narrative form of the pre-70 _nasi_ traditions: he far exceeds them in the proportion of such materials. Let us now compare Gamaliel's traditions to the traditions of his son. Rabban Simeon ben Gamaliel held the office of patriarch during the Ushan reconstruction following the Bar Kokhba defeat, in the mid-second century. Since the bulk of reliable traditions are found in the M.-Tos. stratum, we may compare them as an indicative sample, as follows:

	Narrative	Non-Narrative	Total	%
Gamaliel	61	64	125	48.5
Simeon b. Gamaliel	15	331	346	4.3

Clearly, then, whatever emphasis within the patriarchal circle was placed upon paradigmatic action, through use of the narrative (as derived from the pre-70 nasis) is especially important only to Gamaliel. His predecessors' traditions bulked less than 1/3; his own also 1/2; and his son and successor's legal narratives less than 1/20.

The only other group in 2nd-century Palestine, whose record we possess, engaged in formulating narratives about a master was that of the Christians. Their comparison might be instructive. For them, stories about Jesus were both theological and political in purpose: the narratives revealed the nature of divinity, and provided the basis for the authority of the Church and its faith. For the patriarchal group, such theological purpose for the Gamaliel traditions is, of course, lacking. But its political purpose may be analogous. The patriarchate was a new institution, linked with a religious movement, the emergent rabbinical group, itself relatively new. The legal narrative form looks back towards the pre-70 Pharisees, who represent the Jewish validation of the patriarch as nasi. Its marked increase in frequency, to 47.9% within the Gamaliel traditions, records establishing the legitimacy of the new figure of authority. Since the patriarch's power derived from the Romans, his claim to Jewish legitimacy was centrally important.

A parallel significance may be seen in that 52.1% of the traditions which were redacted into the dispute-form. From within the rabbinic movement, the rabbinic credentials of the patriarch were crucial. This is the meaning to be perceived in the use of the dispute-form, which in effect records the "rabbinization" of the patriarch. Though usually appearing first, the Gamaliel of the disputes is one rabbi among others. By late Yavnean or early Ushan times, both kinds of forms served Gamaliel's tradents equally well, and his traditions were considered important enough by the ʿAqivan tradents to be given pride of place in the disputes they formulated. Morton smith has observed that the Sitz im Leben for the precendent-story (MʿSH) would be the court, while that of the dispute-form would be the school. If this observation is correct, Gamaliel's traditions were important enough to be preserved through both forms, in both the patriarchal court and the ʿAqivan-dominated schools.

While the narratives do not fall into forms so clearly defined as the dispute and the debate, one formal superscription (MʿSH) is frequent, and a number of recurrent types or patterns may be seen.

When the pericopae, some of them built up of more than one narrative unit, have been separated into their narrative parts, 36 of them have the superscription MʿSH, as compared to 47 which do not. Most of the MʿSH superscriptions are located in section I, (Law + story). Section I has 23 MʿSYWT and 18 stories, while J has only 11 MʿSYWT and 28 stories. This may be explained simply by the function of MʿSYWT as precedent cited to support the preceding law. But as may be seen from J, this is not always rigidly followed; a MʿSH superscription may introduce a story which does not follow the citation of a law.

The types of stories in sections I and J may be described as follows:

1. Simple narrative declaration: Gamaliel + action. I. 4, I. 9, I. 10, I. 17, I. 18, I. 20, I. 31, I. 39, I. 33, J. 19, J. 20, J. 22, J. 29.

2. More-developed narrative declaration: Situation + Gamaliel + action. I. 23, I. 25, I. 26, I. 40, J. 13, J. 32, J. 38.

3. Precedent associated with a place: MʿSH + problem + place + Gamaliel-decision. I. 15, I. 16 (omits MʿSH), I. 29, I. 36, J. 27.

4. Example or consensus: Gamaliel's household/Rabban Gamaliel and court + action. I. 2, I. 3, I. 11, I. 28, I. 35, I. 41, J. 5, J. 7, J. 9, J. 14, J. 16, J. 17, J. 34, J. 35.

5. Narrative with dialogue: (a) Situation + question to Gamaliel + Gamaliel's reply or action. I. 13, I. 27, I. 30, J. 8, J. 11, J. 12, J. 18, J. 25, J. 30, J. 40. Also, perhaps, I. 12 (b. Shab. 115a supplies a response for Gamaliel).

(b) Gamaliel's action + question to Gamaliel + Gamaliel's reply. I. 1, J. 1, J. 2.

(c) Other's action + Gamaliel's question + reply. I. 6, J. 15, J. 36.

6. Record of ruling: Situation + brought before Gamaliel + said/decreed. I. 24, I. 34, J. 28, J. 31. Also, perhaps, J. 3, J. 24 and J. 39 which contain the phrase, "before Rabban Gamaliel".

7. First-person narratives, by Gamaliel or others: I. 7, I. 14, I. 19, I. 22, I. 37, I. 38, J. 16, J. 23, J. 26, J. 37.

8. Narratives about others, incidentally mentioning Gamaliel: I. 32, I. 42, J. 4, J. 6, J. 10, J. 21, J. 33.

9. Laws derived from preceding story: Story + from this we learned. I. 18, I. 21, J. 12 = above, #5 (a).

The patterns of narrative serve to emphasize the following aspects of the legal tradition: As we have observed, the simplest stories carry the premise that Gamaliel's behavior itself is prescriptive, demonstrative of a legal opinion, not merely of saintly or pious deeds. And not only Gamaliel himself (1, 9) or the action of his court (4) but even the behavior of his servant and members of his household teaches law (4). A seeming exception (M. B.M. 5.8 = I. 31) is the story of Gamaliel lending his tenants wheat, and accepting payment only at the cheapest rate. Analysis showed this pericope to have revised a story of prescriptive behavior to one of special, extreme piety.

The stories emphasize Gamaliel's role as authority. The most carefully-developed single narrative in M.-Tos. (M. R.H. 2.8-9) describes Gamaliel's defense of his prerogatives in fixing the calendar. The later elaborate deposition narrative (b. Ber. 27b) describes Gamaliel's liturgical authority. Both assertions of patriarchal primacy are associated with the public humiliation of Joshua. Later traditions (y. Sahn. 1.2, b. Sanh. 11a) suggest that there may have been a number of humiliation-stories, in which a rabbi suffers from infringing upon Gamaliel's authority. When Gamaliel travels with other sages, he is the leader: he provides them with a <u>lulav</u> for Sukkot, and advises when it is proper to disembark from a ship on Sabbath. The single most popular type of narrative emphasizes this authoritative role: a case is brought before him, or question asked of him, and he replies or takes action about it (5, 6). Sometimes the question to him is critical of his own behavior; his answer provides a justification of his position. Yet, even where a story is critical of him, he is described befitting his office.

Of special interest are the precedents associated with a particular place (3). Though these may have originally formed a small collection, the Ushan tradents seem to have had no firm tradition about the details of some of them, beyond that of problem and location. Allon takes these references as an evidence for regular, official trips of Gamaliel's court to various parts of Palestine, as a means of establishing its rule as well as administering local problems (Toledot, i. p. 146). He is probably correct in reading Tos. Ter. 2.13 as a reference to such a circuit: "Segavyon ... came to ask Gamaliel, who was traveling from place to place."

The great majority of narratives take for granted Gamaliel's position to enforce the laws. Even a tradition like Tos. Dem. 5. 24 (I.5) in which ʿAqiva is credited with establishing the rule about the status of Samaritan produce, the ʿAqivan tradents assumed that Gamaliel was the one who put the decree into effect. Therefore, the few stories to the contrary draw our attention. The latter assert cases in which Gamaliel's rulings are not acceptable to the people, so that he does not teach them publicly (Tos. Ter. 2.13, the Fourth-year vineyard in Syria, and Tos. M. Q. 2.14, the permission to use a gentile's bench on Sabbath). Similarly, the two rulings on learning Greek (Tos. Soṭ. 15.8) and adopting a Greek-style haircut (Tos. ʿA.Z. 3.5) both appear to assume that the patriarchal household is "permitted" to do so by the rabbis, rather than being a source of authority in itself.

If the latter pericopae be taken as evidence of restiveness, by the rabbis, in the face of patriarchal power, such evidence is rather sparse. Looming large, though, is the great disposition narrative of y. Ber. 4.1, with its assertion of Gamaliel's arrogance and high-handedness. Especially important there, analysis has shown, is the charge of Gamaliel's misuse of his powers against the rabbis as a group, rather than against a single individual. The theme appears only in this pericope, and is not found in the M.-Tos. stratum. Yet we have noticed that in the later materials, the proportion of unfavorable stories drops, in comparison to the M.-Tos. materials. Indeed, the deposition narrative is the only openly unfavorable narrative in the later group. So it is striking, not only in its length and complexity, but in terms of its content and location. Despite its singularity its indication of patriarchal-rabbinic conflict is convincing.

v. Collections, Composites

1. M. Ber. 2.5, 6, 7 -- 3 stories: Shemaʿ, bathed, Ṭabi
2. Tos. Ber. 4.15 -- 3 rulings on blessings
[3. Tos. Dem. 5.24 -- Three things concerning Demai]
4. Tos. Ma. 3.1 -- 2 definitions: beans, lentils
5. M. Ḥal. 4.7 -- Tenant-farmers in Syria

[6. M. Ḥal. 4.8 -- Three lands for Dough-offering]
7. Tos. Pes. 1.27 -- Finds bread: We learned three things
8. Tos. Pes. 1.28 -- Absolved vow: we learned four things
[9. M. Pes. 10.5 -- Say three things on Passover]
10. M. Beṣ. 2.6 -- Gamaliel says three things more stringent
11. M. Beṣ. 2.7 -- Three things more lenient
12. M. Ket. 1.6, 7, 8, 9 -- 4 rulings on status of woman
13. M. Ket. 8.1 -- 2 rulings on woman's inheritance
14. M. Kel. 12.6 -- Declares four things unclean

In the listing of collections immediately above, Arabic numerals describe the elements of the collections (e.g., 3 rulings, 4 things); while the use of the word itself (three, four) indicates that the numeral is actually mentioned within the pericope itself (e.g., "There are three things that Gamaliel etc.").

Of the kinds of collections in pericopae of the Houses and Eliezer (discussed by Neusner, Eliezer, ii, pp. 56-59), Gamaliel's collections do not share the mnemonic formulations characteristic of many of the Houses' materials. His collections are more similar to those of Eliezer: some contain rulings or disagreements which share both a common theme and a common legal principle (5, 12, 14) while others are collections sharing only a common theme or problem (2, 4, 10, 11, 13).

Unique to Gamaliel, however, are 6 and 7, lists which cannot really be termed composites. They are rulings which derive from the analysis of a story ("We learned three things . . . we learned four things . . . "). They would appear to be a natural development of the tendency to use stories about Gamaliel as legal precedents. Here, more complex narratives are subjected to analysis, in order to bring out their fullest legal significance.

Three items in the listing resemble collections superficially, but have been bracketted for the following reasons. Nos. 6 and 9 are not individual rulings which have been developed into a more complex pericope. The three lands regarding the Dough-offering and the three things recited on Passover are each individual units. It is improbable that they were redacted out of separate lemmas even though they include a number of details. Concerning no. 3, as discussed in the analysis of the pericope, Simeon's mention of the three things concerning Demia may derive from an analysis of the story though it is more likely the cause of the story which follows. But in either case it is not a real collection, despite its superscription.

Of all those listed, only 10, 11 and 14 are true composites, fully integrated units sharing the same theme and principle and redaction.

Significant in this listing are nos. 7, 8, 10, 11 and 14. All are numbered collections, the superscriptions indicating that they were redacted with that fact in mind: "There are three things '. . . We learned three things . . ." Such numbered collections do not occur, for example, in the materials of Eliezer. But numbered collections do occur as a redactional formula for the pre-70 masters (Neusner, Pharisees, iii, p, 118) as well as in the tractates Avot and ʿEduyyot (the single numbered collection in the ʿAqiva materials is ʿEd. 2.7, 8, 10). So the numbered collection, like the predilection for narrative, may also be associated with the patriarchal redactional circle.

PART THREE: THE CONTENT OF THE LEGAL TRADITION

i. Over-view of the Laws

The complete picture of the shape of Gamaliel's tradition must include its non-legal materials: historical, exegetical, biographical and legendary. Here, however, it is possible to make some generalizations about the content of the legal tradition as a whole, on the basis of the materials we have surveyed.

In the list below, pericopae discussed in Part I which turned out not to be our Gamaliel have been omitted. Likewise omitted are parallel passages, unless a passage introduces a version different either in form or content.

		Mishnah	Tosefta	Other
1.	When to recite *Shema'*	Ber. 1.1		
2.	Recited on wedding night	Ber. 2.5		
3.	Bathed night wife died	Ber. 2.6		
4.	Accepted condolences for slave	Ber. 2.7		
5.	Pray the 18 Blessings	Ber. 4.3, 4A		
6.	Simeon Hapaquli arranged 18 Blessings			b. Ber. 28b
7.	Ate figs, etc., says 3 blessings	Ber. 6.8	Ber. 4.15	y. Ber. 6.1 b. Ber. 37a
8.	Didn't stop for *Shema'*		Ber. 2.6	
9.	Evening prayer law			y. Ber. 4.1 b. Ber. 27b
10.	*Shema'* twice in one night			ARNA 2.8
11.	Oil and myrtle			b. Ber. 43b
12.	Tithing olive, carob	Pe. 2.4		
13.	Poor make 3 searches	Pe. 4.5		
14.	Two sheaves, 2 *se'ahs*	Pe. 6.6		
15.	Feed *Demai* to poor	Dem. 3.1		
16.	Must announce *Demai*		Dem. 3.15	
17.	Three decrees on *Demai*		Dem. 5.24	
18.	Decreed 4 cubits		Kil. 4.1	
19.	Pickles 3 vegetables	Shev. 9.5		Sifra, Behar 3.4-5
20.	Jar of Heave-offering	Ter. 8.8		
21.	Fourth-year vineyard in Syria		Ter. 2.13	

		Mishnah	Tosefta	Other
22.	Fenugreek stalks tithed	Ma. 4.6		
23.	Sicilian beans defined		Ma. 3.15	
24.	Change silver for gold	M.S. 2.7		
25.	Designating tithes	M.S. 5.9		
26.	Tenant-farmers in Syria	Ḥal. 4.7	Ḥal. 2.5	
27.	Three lands for Dough-offering	Ḥal. 4.8		
28.	Professional baker in Syria		Ḥal. 2.6	
29.	Etrog like a tree	Bik. 2.6		
30.	ʿAqiva picked etrog		Shev. 4.21	
31.	Brought garments to laundry	Shab. 1.9	Shab. 1.22	b. Shab. 19a
32.	Writes two letters	Shab. 12.6		
33.	Even 2 letters of same kind			b. Shab. 103b b. Ker. 16b
34.	Sets up gangplank	Shab. 16.8	Shab. 13.11B	
35.	Says, "He heals!"		Shab. 7.5	
36.	Binds a thread		Shab. 7.11	
37.	Did not fold garments		Shab. 12.16	
38.	Scriptures in Aramaic		Shab. 13.2	b. Shab. 115a
39.	Brought to other town	ʿEruv. 4.1		
40.	Joshua decided law			b. ʿEruv. 43a
41.	Didn't enter until dark	ʿEruv. 4.2	Shab. 13.11A	
42.	Gentile, Sadducee in courtyard	ʿEruv. 6.1-2		b. ʿEruv. 68b

		Mishnah	Tosefta	Other
43.	Finds tefillin	ʿEruv. 10.1-2		
44.	Bolt with knob	ʿEruv. 10.10		
45.	Channel of Tripolis		ʿEruv. 9.25	
46.	Two loaves on portico	Pes. 1.4-5	Pes. 1.4	
47.	Three women bake	Pes. 3.4		b. Pes. 48b
48.	Passover-offering	Pes. 7.2		
49.	Say 3 things	Pes. 10.5		
50.	Finds bread on road		Pes. 1.27-28	y. ʿA.Z. 1.9 b. ʿEruv. 64b b. Ned. 22a
51.	Burn ḥameṣ on Sabbath		Pes. 2.9-11	b. Pes. 49a
52.	Study Passover laws		Pes. 10.11-12	
53.	Passover dough with wine, honey			b. Pes. 36a y. Pes. 2.4
54.	Syrian decorated cakes			b. Pes. 37a
55.	Sleep under bed	Suk. 2.1		
56.	Ṭabi put on tefillin			Mek., Pisḥa 17
57.	When to shake lulav	Suk. 3.9		
58.	Lulav as gift		Suk. 2.11	b. Suk. 41b
59.	Reasons for leaving sukkah			y. Sukk. 2.10
60.	Sukkah on ship			b. Sukk. 23a
61.	Picks pulse on festival	Beṣ. 1.8	Y.Ṭ. 1.22	b. Beṣ. 14b

		Mishnah	Tosefta	Other
62.	Three stringent rulings, 3 lenient	Beṣ. 2.6-7/ ʿEd. 3.10-11	Y.Ṭ. 2.12-14	
63.	Grind pepper on festival		Y.Ṭ. 2.16	
64.	Animals trapped on festival	Beṣ. 3.2		
65.	Profane Sabbath for 2 new moons	R.H. 1.4-6		y. R.H. 1.5 b. R.H. 22a
66.	Had pictures of moon	R.H. 2.8-9		
67.	Sometimes long way			b. R.H. 25a
68.	Did not sanctify new moon			b. R.H. 25a
69.	Agent of congregation	R.H. 4.9	R.H. 2.18	b. R.H. 43b
70.	Freed people in fields			b. R.H. 35a
71.	Ask for rain in Marḥeshvan	Ta. 1.3		
72.	No fast on new moon	Ta. 2.10		
73.	While Gamaliel lived		Ta. 2.5	
74.	Sukkot cancels mourning	M.Q. 3.5-6		
75.	Gentile's bench in ʿAkko		M.Q. 2.14-16	
76.	Mourner says Shemaʿ on Sabbath			b. M.Q. 23b
77.	Ate common food		Ḥag. 3.2B-3	
78.	No geṭ after geṭ	Yev. 5.1	Yev. 7.2B	
79.	Two brothers, 2 sisters	Yev. 13.7		
80.	Allow a woman to remarry	Yev. 16.7		
81.	10 families			y. Yev. 4.2

		Mishnah	Tosefta	Other
82.	Gamaliel saw shipwreck			b. Yev. 121a
83.	Gamaliel performed levirate marriage			b. Yev. 15a
84.	Marries non-virgin	Ket. 1.6		
85.	Claims injury	Ket. 1.7		
86.	Spoke with man	Ket. 1.8		
87.	She was pregnant	Ket. 1.9	Ket. 1.6	
88.	Entered a ruin			b. Ket. 13a-b
89.	Woman inherited goods	Ket. 8.1-2	Ket. 8.1	
90.	Widow won't leave	Ket. 12.3-4		
91.	Knocked out Ṭabi's tooth			y. Ket. 3.10
92.	Reassures husband			b. Ket. 10a
93.	Will not spread mattress		Ned. 7.1	
94.	Learn Greek wisdom		Soṭ. 15.8	b. Soṭ. 49b
95.	<u>Geṭ</u> from abroad	Giṭ. 1.1		
96.	Samaritan witness valid	Giṭ. 1.5		
97.	Raising small animals		B.Q. 8.11-12	
98.	Roman officers study			Sifré Deut. 344
				y. B.Q. 4.3
				Midr. Tann. Deut. 33:3
				b. B.Q. 38a
99.	Lend tenants wheat	B.M. 5.8		
100.	Interest in advance	B.M. 5.10		Sifré, Ki Teṣe, 263

		Mishnah	Tosefta	Other
101.	Seating of Sanhedrin		San. 8.1	
102.	Presence at intercalation session			y. San. 1.2
103.	Claimed wheat, admitted barley	Shav. 6.3		
104.	Intercalate on condition	ʿEd. 7.7		
105.	Widow of ʿIsah	ʿEd. 8.3		
106.	Bath-house of ʿAkko	ʿA.Z. 3.4		
107.	Immersion at Ashqelon		Miq. 6.3	
108.	May look in mirror		ʿA.Z. 3.5	
109.	Altar sanctifies	Zev. 9.9		
110.	Sprinkles the blood		Zev. 9.1	
111.	Blood doesn't nullify		Zev. 8.16/17 Ḥul. 6.8	b. Zev. 79a
112.	Slaughters animal	Ḥul. 2.6		
113.	Signs of clean/unclean birds			b. Ḥul. 65a
114.	Pours blood of sacrifice			b. Ḥul. 87a
115.	Sexual relations with sister, etc.	Ker. 3.7		
116.	Ovens of Kefar Signah	Kel. 5.4	Kel. B.Q. 4.4	
117.	Large furnace unclean	Kel. 8.9	Kel. B.Q. 6.17	
118.	Metal basket-cover unclean	Kel. 12.3		
119.	Four things unclean	Kel. 12.6/ ʿEd. 3.8	Kel. B.M. 1.12-13	
120.	Chamber-pot clean	Kel. 17.2		

		Mishnah	Tosefta	Other
121.	Scroll-wrappers unclean	Kel. 28.4	Kel. B.B. 6.9B	
122.	Troughs of Kefar ʿAdim		Kel. B.M. 11.2J	
123.	Bright Spot	Neg. 6.5	Neg. 2.9	
124.	Removed signs of uncleanness	Neg. 7.4		
125.	Weasel renders water unfit	Par. 9.3/ 11.1	Par. 9.60	
126.	Olives become unclean	Ṭoh. 9.1		
127.	Ḥananiah b. Ḥananiah's vow		Nid. 5.15	y. Naz. 4.6
128.	Burial harder than death		Nid. 9.17	b. M.Q. 27b
129.	Ṭabita poured wine			y. Nid. 2.1
130.	Gamaliel's maidservant baked/corked			b. Nid. 6b
131.	Woman came before father	Yad. 3.1		
132.	Judah the Ammonite proselyte	Yad. 4.4	Yad. 2.17-18	
133.	Owner of ox is free			Mek. Nez. 10
134.	A man prays			Mek. R.Š.Y., Mišpatim 24.23
135.	People of the land			Sifré Qedošim 10.4
136.	Marrying daughter of widow			D.E.R. 1.6
137.	Mourner eats on Sabbath			Sem. 10.3

Since Gamaliel succeeded Yoḥanan b. Zakkai as leader of the academy in Yavneh, it is useful to compare his legal traditions with the earliest Yavnean efforts formulating the traditions of the Houses. The 142 Houses-pericopae (non-historical pericopae listed in Neusner, Pharisees, iii, pp. 225-7, 231-3) compare in subject-matter with Gamaliel's 137 legal pericopae roughly as follows:

	Houses	Gamaliel	Difference
Sabbath, Festival Laws	22.5%	29.2%	+6.7
Uncleanness	28.1%	11.7%	-16.4
Liturgy	5.6%	13.9%	+8.3
Civil, criminal	2.1%	8.8%	+6.7
Agricultural	21.8%	13.9%	-7.9
Family, inheritance	13.4%	13.9%	+ .5
Temple, oaths, vows	5.6%	4.4%	-1.2
Gentiles	N/L	4.4%	(4.4)

The most significant changes in proportions of the laws occur in the marked drop in laws concerning uncleanness and agricultural laws, and the increase in laws about liturgy, followed by Sabbath/Festival and civil/criminal laws. Family law remains about the same, while Temple law declines to further insignificance. It should be noted that while the proportion of agricultural laws decreases substantially, this category still represents a number equal to liturgy and family law.

Before turning to the content of the tradition, we may observe that it is not uniformly distributed throughout the various collections in which it is found. There are some differences between the proportions within the M.-Tos. traditions, in which a little over 3/4 of the pericopae are found, and the remaining pericopae from the later collections. The differences are shown to be as follows:

	M.-Tos.		Later		Total	
	#	%	#	%	#	%
Sabbath/Festival	31	29.5	9	28.1	40	29.2
Uncleanness	13	12.4	3	9.4	16	11.7
Liturgy	12	11.4	7	21.9	19	13.9
Civil/Criminal	6	5.7	6	18.8	12	8.8
Agricultural	19	18.1	0	0	19	13.9
Family, Inheritance	13	12.4	6	8.8	19	13.9
Temple, Oaths, Vows	5	4.8	1	3.1	6	4.4
Gentiles	6	5.7	0	0	6	4.4
	105		32		137	

Immediately we observe that traditions on agricultural laws and relations with gentiles are confined to the M.-Tos. group (though one pericope on civil law deals with "robbery of a gentile"). The uncleanness laws drop even more in the later collections, as do family and Temple laws. Liturgy and civil/ criminal laws advance, and Sabbath/Festival laws remain about the same proportion.

With these differences in mind, let us attempt to characterize the tradition as a whole. Compared with the Houses, Gamaliel's traditions still share, in the main, the preoccupations of the pre-70 Pharisees, in terms of uncleanness, agricultural and family laws; yet the first two of these have declined in number. Sabbath and Festival laws bulk larger than they do with the Houses. And an interest in both liturgy and civil/criminal law has become important, growing in importance in the later materials.

Gamaliel's rulings may be summarized as follows:

In Sabbath laws, Gamaliel follows the pre-70 Pharisees in setting down definitions for the 'eruv for private dwellings, as well as the Sabbath limit for a town. He deals with the question of shipboard travel, and contact with gentiles, as these situations affect the Sabbath. It is asserted that he followed Shammaite practice in bringing garments to the laundryman three days before the Sabbath, and other Shammaite rules. But we also noted cases where he rules more leniently than the Hillelites. The importance of the Sabbath is emphasized, in the later stratum, by the rulings suspending various mourning restrictions on that day.

The single largest number of rulings is in the area of festival law. Passover is the single most central subject: preparation of massah (including a prohibition of added flavorings), details of burning the hames, the conflict between burning the hames and the Sabbath prohibitions. He outlines elements of the Passover seder, and is credited with the practice of studying the laws of Passover after the seder meal. He also originates the practice of a "chain gift" of a lulav, so that a number of people can fulfill the biblical commandment of the Sukkot festival. In rulings about the New Year, his liturgical interest is again apparent. He stresses the function of the Agent of the Congregation in prayer, lending it significance of an almost-priestly role. This no doubt follows the precedent of Yohanan b. Zakkai, who attempted to find new equivalents for the destroyed

Temple. Gamaliel carefully guards the prerogative to determine the calendar, as a sign of his authority.

In the area of uncleanness and purity laws, the bulk of his rulings drops (compared to the Houses) by more than half. Gamaliel rules on the uncleanness of a number of utensils and ovens, and on the fouling of the Water of Purification by a serpent (an entirely theoretical issue). He is described immersing himself, by two possibly-related pericopae, and is alleged to have maintained the status of purity of a Levite throughout his life. A later ruling defines the characteristics of unclean birds; and some stories deal with keeping check on the onset of menstruation.

A number of laws concerning liturgy appear in Gamaliel-pericopae. We have already noted the Passover seder liturgy. ʿAqiva refers to Gamaliel's behavior to establish the norm for waving of the lulav during Hallel. Whereas the Houses had disputed the physical position for reciting the Shemaʿ, the Yavneans dispute the time limits for it. Both earlier and later pericopae deal with this. Gamaliel's interest in liturgy includes both public and private prayer. We have noted the import- and function of the leader of the service, for him. Gamaliel also rules on the blessings for grace before and after various foods, and presides over the official fixing of a text for the 18 Blessings of the Tefillah. He rules that the official text of the Tefillah is obligatory for the individual, thrice daily. The obligatory nature of the evening Tefillah is considered a touchstone of his authority. (It should be noted that for the first time, within his rulings, we observe the emergence of two of the hallmarks of the piety of rabbinism: stress on the study of Torah -- emphasized as an aspect of the Passover celebration -- and the specific blessings over foods, later to be elaborated by the Babylonian Amoraim as a sign of rabbinic training, cf. Neusner, History, ii, pp. 173-174, 284.)

Gamaliel's contribution to criminal law is nil. There is nothing on corporal punishment; the single, later exegesis in a pericope on capital punishment probably does not deal with the topic at all. There is a single exegesis on torts. He adds to the definition of interest, and exempts seed-grain from that category. He requires an oath in the case where a man had admitted to some responsibility toward a creditor. That is about all in commercial law, though it shows a development in complexity beyond earlier rulings.

Gamaliel's agricultural rulings prescribe laws for tithing carob trees scattered over a wide area, and a method for designating tithes of crops owned by an absentee owner. His opinions on giving Demai to worker, and on the Forgotten Sheaf, tend to favor the land-owner, but he insists on more opportunities for collecting peʾah be available to the poor. Of greatest political significance is his relinquishing of any Jewish claims to Syria, which in any case could not be enforced.

In contrast with the sparsity and elementary character of civil law, rulings on family law and marriage tend to be complex, sophisticated, and highly theoretical. He deals with conflicts between the powers of the levirate bond versus standard betrothal, the rights of a woman over her inheritance as compared with the power of her husband over her property, and the rules of evidence for determining marital status. It is alleged that he performed a levirate marriage according to Shammaite law.

Gamaliel is connected with four pericopae concerning sacrifices, and one about Nazirite vow of a minor.

Underlying a number of pericopae, in different categories, we have also noticed certain theoretical problems. One is the question of whether individual acts or items, each of which does not fall into a category of the law, may be added together and considered under that category (nos. 14, 32, 33, 115). Another is that of the conflict between the powers inherent in certain legal categories, such as betrothal vs. levirate bond, or Sabbath vs. Passover (8, 20, 51, 74, 79).

We may also observe a number of pericopae dealing with the problems of relations with gentiles, Sadducees, Samaritans and proselytes. Gamaliel makes use of a gentile bath-house in ʿAkko (106), and uses a gentile merchant's bench there on the Sabbath (75). He treats his slave as a Jew (4, 56) but declares that an Ammonite may never be accepted as such (132). He rules on the capacity of a Sadducee to restrict an ʿeruv, but we cannot be sure whether he considers the Sadducee to be like a Jew or a gentile in this respect (42). His household is described as having special permission to be familiar with gentile styles, customs and wisdom, because of their political prominence (94, 108). And last, he is credited with decreeing "robbery of a gentile" as blasphemy (98).

ii. Attestations

A more sensitive instrument for charting the development of a tradition - moreso than the simple division of earlier and later documents employed above - is the method of seeking attestations. As developed by Neusner, and exposited by him in various recent words (Eliezer, Pharisees), the attempt to find attested pericopae for a tradition helps provide a key to the strata of the tradition. Where a named tradent, standing outside of a given pericope, comments upon it, he provides the terminus ante quem for it: its substance (though not its exact language) was known by his time. Attestations, then, arrange pericopae chronologically, in terms of generations. Where chains of authorities occur, X said in the name of Y..., even more specific information is provided on the way the pericope was transmitted. An attribution of a pericope to a named authority or authorities, X said..., would appear to be more easily fabricated than an attestation or a chain; yet it provides a terminus a quo: the content of the pericope could not be attributed to anyone earlier.

Out of the list of legal pericopae, above, the following items have been selected, and arranged according to the generation of the master who transmits or comments upon the tradition.

1. Yavneh

9. M. Pe. 2.4 - Pe'ah for olive and carob trees, Eleazar (b. Ṣadoq)
26. M. Ḥal. 4.7 - Israel tenant farmers in Syria (Eleazar, Tos. Ḥal. 2.5)
31. Tos. Shab. 1.22 - Garments to laundry, Eleazar
39. M. ʿEruv. 4.1 - Brought to other town on Sabbath (Ḥanina, nephew of Joshua, b. ʿEruv. 43a)
47. M. Pes. 3.4 - Three woman bake (ʿAqiva, b. Pes. 48b)
48. M. Pes. 7.2 - Roast Passover lamb (Ṣadoq)
54. b. Pes. 37a - Syrian cakes permitted, Eleazar
61. M. Beṣ. 1.8 - Picks out pulse (Eleazar, Tos. Y.Ṭ. 1.22)
62. M. Beṣ. 2.6-7 - Sweep between couches (Eleazar, Tos. Y.Ṭ. 2.14)
63. Tos. Y.T. 2.16 - Grind pepper on festival, Eleazar
80. M. Yev. 16.7 - Woman remarried (ʿAqiva)

115. M. Ker. 3.7 - I asked, sexual relations (ʿAqiva)
107. Tos. Miq. 6.3 - Bath-house of Ashqelon (Joshua b. Qibusai)
124. M. Neg. 7.4 - I asked, removed signs of uncleanness (ʿAqiva)
127. Tos. Nid. 5.15 - Ḥananiah b. Ḥananiah's vow, Eleazar

Gamaliel's tradition is attested by 15 Yavnean pericopae, 8 bearing the name of Eleazar b. Ṣadoq. Eleazar's attestations, almost equally-divided between Mishnah and Tosefta, stand out as greater than his proportional appearance within those documents. This would support those traditions which place him as part of the patriarchal entourage (Tos. Y.Ṭ. 2.14) and the statement attributed to him (b. Shab. 11a) as part of the group of Yavnean scholars involved with the intercalation of the year, which we have seen to be a patriarchal prerogative.

ʿAqiva's 4 attestations are all first-person reports. They are the equivalent of chains, since they could easily to re-phrased as , "R. ʿAqiva said in the name of Rabban Gamaliel." Neusner (Eliezer, ii, p. 122) considers the first-person form to be an indication that the ʿAqivan tradents handed on the pericopae as they had received them, and that this is therefore a mark of authenticity. There would appear to be no reason to fabricate this form in order to lend authenticity to these issues, despite the apparent freedom of some ʿAqivan tradents to change third-person narratives into first-person ones (cf. p. 246, above).

The earliest-attested laws, then, deal with festival laws, especially Passover, Sabbath-limit, marriage, Temple, vows and uncleanness. As we would expect, the greatest number of these attestations are associated with someone closely identified with Gamaliel's own circle. And second to him is ʿAqiva himself.

2. Usha

7. Tos. Ber. 4.15 - Says three blessings, Judah (b. Ilai)
21. Tos. Ber. 2.13 - 4th year vineyard, Judah
29. M. Bik. 2.6 - Etrog like a tree (Yosa [b. Ḥalafta?] Tos. Shev. 4.21)
32. M. Shab. 12.6 - Writes two letters on Sabbath (Judah, b. Shab. 103b)
42. M. ʿEruv. 6.1-2 - Courtyard with gentile, Judah
43. M. ʿEruv. 10.1-2 - Finds tefillin, Judah, Simeon (b. Yoḥai)
44. M. ʿEruv. 10.10 - Bolt with knob, Yosé (b. Ḥalafta)
46. M. Pes. 1.4-5 - Loaves on portico (Judah, Tos. Pes. 1.4)
54. y. Pes. 2.4 - Syrian cakes permitted, Judah

62. M. Beṣ. 2.6-7 - Don't re-assemble candelabrum (Judah, Tos. Y.Ṭ. 2.13)
65. M.R.H. 1.4-6 - Witnesses to new moon, (Judah, y.R.H. 1.5)
72. M. Ta. 2.10 - Fast on new moon and Hanukkah, Meir
89. M. Ket. 8.1 - Woman inherited goods, Judah, Ḥananiah [b. ʿAqavya]
96. M. Git. 1.5 - Get of Kefar Otnai (Judah, Tos. Giṭ. 1.4)
100. M.B.M. 5.10 - Interest before and after, Simeon
110. M. Zev. 9.1 - Altar sanctifies, Simeon
111. Tos. Zev. 8.16-17/ Tos. Ḥul. 6.8 - Blood doesn't nullify blood (Judah, "on behalf of")
112. M. Ḥul. 2.6 - Animal at point of death, Simeon
117. M. Kel. 8.9/ Tos. Kel. B.Q. 6.17 - Furnace unclean (Meir, Judah, Yosé "on behalf of")
119. M. Kel. 12.6 - Utensils unclean (Judah, Nathan, Tos. Kel. B.M. 2.12-13)
121. M. Kel 28.4 - Scroll wrappers clean (Yosé, Simeon, Tos. Kel. B.B. 6.9B)
125. M. Par. 9.3 - Serpent renders water unfit (Yosé, Simeon, Tos. Par. 9.6C)
126. M. Ṭoh. 9.1 - When olives receive uncleanness, Simeon

Those Ushan masters who, in the above 22 items, attest to pericopae are, most prominently, Judah b. Ilai (14), Simeon b. Yoḥai (7) and Yosé b. Ḥalafta (5). This prominence roughly reflects their prominence within the documents of the Mishnah and Tosefta, and does not point to any special relationship to Gamaliel. Further, Judah's preeminence would indicate his role as teacher of Rabbi Judah the Patriarch (b. Shav. 13a) as well as disciple of ʿAqiva.

We may conclude from the Ushan attestations that though a small proportion of these traditions were transmitted through Gamaliel's circle, most of them were largely in the hands of ʿAqivan scholars. And though we speak of the Mishnah as patriarchal in its editing, the content primarily reflects the work of the ʿAqivan reconstruction at Usha.

In this stratum, there are additions in the areas of civil law, and especially Sabbath and festival laws, including the determination of the New Moon.

3. Beth Shearim

38. Tos. Shab. 13.2 - Translation of Job, (Yosah [b. R Judah], Rabbi, b. Shab. 115a)

This is the single identifiable pericope from Beth Shearim, apart from the anonymous items in #4, below.

4. Mishna-Tosefta

1. M. Ber. 1.1 - What time <u>Shemaʿ</u>?
2,3,4. M. Ber. 2.5-7 - Bridegroom exempt from <u>Shemaʿ</u>
5. M. Ber. 4.3-4A - Every day pray 18 blessings
7. M. Ber. 6.8 - Ate figs, etc., 3 blessings
8. Tos. Ber. 2.6 - Didn't stop for <u>Shemaʿ</u>
13. M. Pe. 4.5 - Poor make three searches
14. M. Pe. 6.6 - Two sheaves, 2 <u>seʾahs</u> between them
15. M. Dem. 3.1 - Feed <u>Demai</u> to poor
16. Tos. Dem. 3.15 - Ḥaver must announce <u>Demai</u>
17. Tos. Dem. 5.24 - Three decrees concerning <u>Demai</u>
18. Tos. Kil. 4.1 - Gamaliel and court decreed 4 cubits
19. M. Shev. 9.5 - Pickles three vegetables
20. M. Ter. 8.8 - Jar of Heave-offering
22. M. Ma. 4.6 - Stalks of fenugreek tithed
23. Tos. Ma. 3.15 - Sicilian beans, Egyptian lentils
24. M.M.S. 2.7 - Changes silver for gold <u>dinars</u>
25. M.M.S. 5.9 - Fruit far, must designate tithes
27. M. Ḥal. 4.8 - Three lands for Dough-offering
28. Tos. Ḥal. 2.6 - Buy from professional baker in Syria
34. M. Shab. 16.8 - Gentile sets gangplank
35. Tos. Shab. 7.5 - "He heals!" is way of Amorites
36. Tos. Shab. 7.11 - Binds thread
37. Tos. Shab. 12.16 - Did not fold garments
38. Tos. Shab. 13.2 - Scriptures in Aramaic
41. M. ʿEruv. 4.2/ Tos. Shab. 13.11A - Didn't enter harbor until dark
45. Tos. ʿEruv. 9.25 - Channel of Tripolis
49. M. Pes. 10.5 - Three things on Passover
50. Tos. Pes. 1.27-28 - Finds bread on road
51. Tos. Pes. 2.9-11 - Burning <u>ḥameṣ</u> on Sabbath (Eleazar)
52. Tos. Pes. 10.11-12 - Studies laws of Passover

55. M. Sukk. 2.1 - Sleeps under bed
57. M. Sukk. 3.9 - When to shake lulav (ʿAqiva)
58. Tos. Sukk. 2.11 - Gift of lulav
64. M. Beṣ. 3.2 - Traps on festival
66. M.R.H. 2.8 - Pictures of moon
69. M.R.H. 4.9/ Tos. R.H. 2.18 - Agent of congregation
73. Tos. Ta. 2.5 - While Gamaliel lived
74. M.M.Q. 3.5-6 - Sukkot cancels mourning
75. Tos. M.Q. 2.14-16 - Gentile's bench in ʿAkko
77. Tos. Hag. 3.2B-3 - Ate common food in purity
78. M. Yev. 5.1/ Tos. Yev. 7.2B - No geṭ after geṭ
79. M. Yev. 13.7 - Two brothers marry two sisters
84, 85, 86, 87. M. Ket. 1.6, 7, 8, 9 - Marries non-virgin
90. M. Ket. 12.3-4 - Widow won't leave (Meir "on behalf of")
93. Tos. Ned. 7.1 - Will not spread mattress
94. Tos. Soṭ. 15.8 - Learn Greek wisdom
95. M. Giṭ. 1.1 - Geṭ from abroad
97. Tos. B. Q. 8.11-12 - Raising small animals
99. M.B.M. 5.8 - Lend tenants wheat
101. Tos. San. 8.1 - Seating of Sanhedrin (Eleazar)
103. M. Shav. 6.3 - Claimed wheat, admitted barley
104. M. ʿEd. 7.7 - Intercalate on condition
105. M. ʿEd. 8.3 - ʿIsah families
106. M. ʿA.Z. 3.4 - Proqlos and bath-house
108. Tos. ʿA.Z. 3.5 - Look in mirror
109. Tos. Zev. 9.1 - Blood and Drink-offerings
112. Tos. Kel. B.M. 11.2J - Troughs of Kefar ʿAdim
116. M. Kel. 5.4/ Tos. Kel. B.Q. 4.4 - Ovens of Kefar Signah
119. M. Kel. 12.6 - Metal Basket cover
120. M. Kel. 17.2 - Chamber pot clean
123. M. Neg. 6.5/ Tos. Neg. 2.9 - Bright Spot
128. Tos. Nid. 9.17 - Burial harder than death
131. M. Yad. 3.1 - Woman came to father
132. M. Yad. 4.4/ Tos. Yad. 2.17-18 - Judah the Ammonite proselyte

The 69 items in Mishnah and Tosefta, almost equally divided, represent the single largest grouping of materials. Questions of liturgy attain greater importance in this stratum, along with laws concerning relations with gentiles.

iii. Chains

The following pericopae share the same form: X said in the name of [on behalf of] Y. They are also found in the listing by generation, above, and share the character of the generational strata, i.e., ʿAqiva's predominance among Yavneans and Judah's among Ushans. The chains say little about the tradition *qua* Gamaliel-materials. Perhaps they reveal only Judah's preference for using this form as a means of emphasizing for the verbatim character of his Yavnean traditions (cf. Neusner, *Eliezer*, ii, p. 124).

1. Ṣadoq

42. Pes. 7.2 - Ṣadoq said (MʿSH B) Gamaliel said to Ṭabi, Go roast

2. Eleazar b. Ṣadoq

12. M. Pe. 2.4 - *Peʾah* for olive, carob, Eleazar says in his name

3. ʿAqiva

47. b. Pes. 48b - I asked, What kind of woman, oven
80. M. Yev. 16.7 - I went to Nehardea, woman remarry
115. M. Ker. 3.7 - I asked Gamaliel and Joshua, sexual relations
124. M. Neg. 7.4 - I asked Gamaliel and Joshua, removed signs of uncleanness

4. Abba Yudan

134. Mek. RŠY - Abba Yudan of Sidon, on behalf of Gamaliel, An individual prays

5. Judah B. Ilai

7. Tos. Ber. 4.15 - Judah in his name, says three blessings
33. b. Shab. 103b - Judah in name of Gamaliel, writes two letters

46. Tos. Pes. 1.4 - Judah in name of Gamaliel, loaves on portico
62. Tos. Y.Ṭ. 2.13 - Judah in name of Gamaliel, don't re-assemble candelabrum
89. M. Ket. 8.1 - Woman inherited goods, Judah: He said to them
111. Tos. Zev. 8.16/- Judah on behalf of Gamaliel: Blood doesn't Tos. Ḥul. 6.8 nullify
117. Tos. Kel. B.Q. 6.17 - Furnace unclean, Judah on behalf of Gamaliel
119. Tos. Kel. B.M. 2.13 - Judah redefines dispute on uncleanness of broken plate

6. Meir

72. M. Ta. 2.10 - Fast on new moon and Ḥanukkah, Meir: Gamaliel has said
117. Tos. Kel. B.Q. 6.17 - Furnace unclean, Meir in the name of Gamaliel

7. Yosé b. Ḥalafta

117. Tos. Kel. B.Q. 6.17 - Furnace unclean, Yosé in the name of Gamaliel

8. Nathan

119. Tos. Kel. B.M. 2.12 - Nathan redefines dispute on uncleanness of scrapers

9. Ḥananiah b. ʿAqavya

89. M. Ket. 8.1 - Woman inherited goods, Ḥananiah: He said to them

iv. Gamaliel's Attestations of Houses-disputes

1. M.M.S. 2.7 - The Houses-dispute over changing silver for gold coins, for the pilgrimage to Jerusalem, is followed by ʿAqiva's first-person report of changing coins for Gamaliel and Joshua, in line with the Hillelite position. But Gamaliel does not attest to the dispute, which may have been created on the basis of ʿAqiva's report.

2. M. Beṣ. 1.8 - The Shammaites permit only enough seeds to be picked out for immediate eating, the Hillelites a normal quantity prepared for a meal. Gamaliel's comment attests to the dispute, and extends the Hillelite position beyond permitting the "usual" method of preparation.

3. M. Beṣ. 2.6 - Three stringent opinions of Gamaliel are attributed to the House of Shammai. Two do not occur elsewhere in the name of the Shammaites. The third, a ruling on baking thick cakes, occurs in _baraitot_ (b. Beṣ. 22b) which may have been formulated on the basis of the tradition about Gamaliel. The phrase "according to the House of Shammai" here may be a gloss. But in any case, the pericope cannot be considered an attestation.

4. M. Beṣ. 3.2 - Gamaliel permits fish which may have been trapped on a festival to be used, a position more lenient than the Hillelites. But the story does not attest to M. Shab. 1.6.

5. M. Ket. 8.1 - The Shammaites allow a woman control over property she owned before her marriage. The Hillelites restrict it. Gamaliel expresses "embarrassment" over the Hillelite view, and resists extending it further. But the portion of the pericope reported as an agreement between the Houses appears to have been formulated on the basis of Gamaliel's own ruling. So Gamaliel's comment cannot be considered an attestation.

6. M.B.M. 5.8 - The story that Gamaliel would lend his tenant-farmers wheat is used to support the law opposing the Hillelite view in M.B.M. 5.9, which prohibits this. Gamaliel does not attest to the Houses-dispute.

7. M. Kel. 28.4 - The Shammaites consider scroll-wrappers unclean; the Hillelites rule that decorated scroll-wrappers are clean. Gamaliel attests to the dispute, with his comment that both decorated and plain wrappers are clean, a position more lenient than the Hillelites.

8. M. Ṭoh. 9.1 - The Houses dispute the time that olives become unclean. The core of Gamaliel's comment, a single five-syllable word, matches those of the Houses exactly, though he supplies a different criterion (conclusion of the preparation) for determining the time of uncleanness. This clearly attests to both form and substance of the original Houses-dispute, and expresses a position more lenient than the Hillelites.

9. b. Ber. 43b - The Houses dispute over the precedence of oil _vs_. myrtle is commented upon by Gamaliel, deciding the dispute in favor of the Shammaites. Gamaliel's comment attests to the dispute.

To sum up, Gamaliel actually attests to Houses-disputes in nos. 2, 7, 8 and 9, four out of a possible nine pericopae. This does not bulk very large, in the over-200 pericopae listed by Neusner (Pharisees, ii, pp. 342-351) or compared to the attestations of ʿAqiva, or even Eliezer. However, since the greatest number of Houses-pericopae are attested by Ushans, we cannot conclude that Gamaliel played no role in the formation of the traditions about the Houses. Gamaliel's evidence provides no firm conclusions; but we may assume with Neusner (Pharisees, ii, p. 4) on other grounds that a major part of the Houses-disputes must have been given shape in early Yavneh. More noteworthy, however, is the fact that in three of the four attesting pericopae, Gamaliel's position is more lenient than the Hillelite ruling. While Finkelstein has collected the instances in which he shows a congruence between Gamaliel's rulings and the Shammaite laws (Akiba, pp. 304-306), we must set the examples above against that too-consistent depiction. Gamaliel may be seen as either Shammaite or Hillelite, or as independent of both.

iv. Favorable and Unfavorable Stories

We have seen that the disputes show respect for Gamaliel's position by assigning him first place in most pericopae. Some of the narratives also reveal bias toward him. To examine the nature of this bias, we review the stories from that standpoint. A story is considered favorable to Gamaliel here if it presents him in a position of authority, either as a legal decisor or as leader of his colleagues, or if it shows him having the last word in dialogue or debate. A simple narrative is considered favorable if it carries the assumption that Gamaliel's behavior itself teaches law. A story is considered unfavorable if it is critical of his actions, if Gamaliel is shown to be dependent upon someone else for learning, if he is compared invidiously to someone else in piety or is bested in a debate. A neutral story (often a story reflecting consensus or really about someone else) displays no perceptible bias. In addition, we discerned in our literary analysis a number of stories which appeared to have been originally critical in their conception, which have been revised to answer the criticism, and present a defense for Gamaliel. These have been marked: unfavorable made favorable.

I. Statement of Law + Story

1. Said Shemaʿ, -- Favorable
2. Did not stop for Shemaʿ -- Favorable
3. Father's house gave peʾah -- Favorable
4. Fed Demai to workers -- Favorable
[5. Same]
6. ʿAqiva tithed Samaritan produce -- Unfavorable
7. ʿAqiva changed money -- Favorable
8. Fourth year Syrian fruit -- Favorable
9. Designated tithes on ship -- Favorable
10. Disembarked on Sabbath -- Favorable
11. House of Gamaliel -- Favorable
12. Scriptures in Aramaic -- Unfavorable
13. Disembarked on Sabbath -- Favorable
14. Sadducee lived with us -- Favorable
15. Bolt with knob -- Favorable
16. Channel of Tripolis -- Favorable
17. Roast Passover sacrifice -- Favorable
18. Found bread on road -- Favorable
19. Burned ḥameṣ on Sabbath -- Favorable
20. Study Passover laws -- Favorable
21. Ṭabi slept under bed -- Favorable
22. Waved the lulav -- Favorable
23. Gamaliel had lulav -- Favorable
24. Gentile brought fish -- Favorable
25. Witnesses to new moon -- Favorable
26. Officer of Geder -- Favorable
27. Sat on gentile bench -- Unfavorable
28. Permitted to teach Greek -- Neutral, possibly Unfavorable
29. Samarital witnesses -- Favorable
30. Raising small animals -- Favorable
31. Lend wheat for wheat -- Favorable
32. Seating of Sanhedrin -- Neutral
33. Went to Syria -- Favorable
34. Testified concerning ʿIsah -- Neutral
35. Permitted to look in mirror -- Neutral
36. Oven of Kefar Signah -- Favorable
37. Woman came to father -- Favorable
38. Syrian cakes on Passover -- Favorable
39. Leaving sukkah - Favorable

40. He that pours blood -- Favorable
41. Ḥanina rules on foetus -- Unfavorable made Favorable
42. Robbery of a gentile -- Favorable

J. Story

1. Bathed self -- Unfavorable made Favorable
2. Accepted condolences -- Unfavorable made Favorable
3. Simeon arranged 18 blessings -- Favorable
4. Blessing for minim -- Neutral
5. Decreed 4 cubit -- Neutral
6. ʿAqiva picked etrog -- Favorable
7. Brought garments to laundry -- Favorable
8. Gentile set gangplank -- Favorable
9. Did not fold garments -- Favorable
10. Joshua decided law -- Unfavorable
11. Didn't enter harbor -- Favorable
12. Absolved vow -- Favorable
13. Prompted man to absolve -- Favorable
14. Filled pail with lentils -- Favorable
15. ʿAqiva assembled candelabrum -- Unfavorable
16. Eleazar: We ate at Gamaliel's -- Unfavorable made Favorable
17. Grind pepper on festival -- Unfavorable made Favorable
18. Witnesses to new moon -- Unfavorable made Favorable
19. Did not sanctify new moon -- Favorable
20. Freed people in field -- Favorable
21. After Gamaliel's death -- Favorable
22. Ate common food in purity -- Neutral
23. ʿAqiva: I went to Nehardea -- Unfavorable
24. Ḥananiah testified -- Favorable
25. Proqlos and bath -- Unfavorable made Favorable
26. Gamaliel and Onqelos -- Favorable (?)
27. Brought troughs -- Favorable
29. Burial harder than death -- Favorable
30. Judah the Ammonite proselyte -- Unfavorable
31. Evening prayer -- Unfavorable
32. R. Yeshovav's possessions -- Favorable
33. Knocked out Ṭabi's tooth -- Neutral
34. Ṭabita poured wine -- Neutral
35. Gamaliel's maidservant baked/corked -- Neutral/Favorable
36. Presence at intercalation -- Favorable
37. Gamaliel: I saw shipwreck -- Favorable
38. Gamaliel performed levirate marriage -- Favorable

39. Reassures husband about virginity -- Favorable
40. Roman officers study, Gamaliel decrees blasphemy -- Favorable

Adding one story from section A to the list (b. Suk. 23a -- Favorable) and one from section B (M. Ber. 1.1 -- Favorable) for a total of 82 stories, the proportions are: 56 Favorable, 8 Unfavorable, 7 revised from Unfavorable to Favorable, and 10 Neutral (1 possibly Favorable and 1 possibly Unfavorable). All stories with content unfavorable toward Gamaliel total 16 out of 82, or 19.5%. Since one would assume that -- for a major religious and political figure -- traditions about him would be transmitted primarily by those who hold him in esteem, such a number of critical stories is significant.

Somewhat fewer unfavorable stories appear in the later collections than in the earlier ones. If we separate out the smaller number of stories from the later collections, and compare them with the Mishnah-Tosefta group, we note:

	Favorable		Unfavorable	
M.-Tos.	47	(78.3%)	13	(21.7%)
Later	19	(86.3%)	3	(13.6%)

So the M.-Tos. stratum of the legal tradition contains a higher proportion of unfavorable material; Gamaliel's reputation "improves" in the later collections of y., b. and the _midrashim_.

Within the 60 stories of the M.-Tos. stratum, there are differences to be noted as well. Slightly more of the unfavorable-content stories are found in M. than in Tos. They represent 6 of 26 total stories in M., or 23.1%, while in Tos. they are 7 of a total of 34 stories, or 20.6%. However, only 2 of the _openly_ unfavorable stories are found in M., (compared to 4 of those revised from Unfavorable to Favorable) while 6 of the openly unfavorable stories are in Tos. (compared with 1 Unfavorable made Favorable). Though a small number of cases, this does confirm the character of the Mishnah as a patriarchal document, selecting those materials which show -- or have been reworked to show -- Rabbi Judah the Patriarch's ancestor in a favorable light.

The openly unfavorable stories in the M.-Tos. stratum, where identifiable, originate from the circles of ʿAqiva (I. 6, I. 12, J. 15, J. 23) and Joshua (J. 10, J. 30). (I. 27 and 28 bear no names of tradents.) However, the ʿAqivan tradition is not uniformly unfavorable to Gamaliel. I.7, I. 22, J. 6, and the three first-person pericopae of Section H, above, all refer to Gamaliel respectfully as a figure of authority. It is surely significant that 5 of the 6 favorable ʿAqivan pericopae are first-person accounts, while only one of the 4 unfavorable stories is a first-person narrative, the others coming from ʿAqivan tradents. In the two openly unfavorable stories of the later collections, one is ʿAqivan (J. 31) and one Joshuan (J. 10).

It should be re-emphasized that basic to the 80.5% of the stories which we have listed as "Favorable" are the many narratives which simply described an action of Gamaliel's and which have been redacted as if they were the quotation of a named master, a lemma used in the construction of a dispute.

And we note again the remarkable assertion of Tos. Pes. 1.27-28, that Gamaliel has access to supernaturally-acquired knowledge, by means of the Holy Spirit -- something which was not claimed for Hillel or Eliezer, though they were declared worthy of it. This detail seems to share the defensive interest of those stories which revised a story at first critical of Gamaliel into something more favorable to him -- a redactional attitude we have noted to be persistent, though minor, in terms of the bulk of the traditions.

Let us consider solely those pericopae which either express or react to unfavorable materials. They confirm Gamaliel's descent from a famous grandfather, and use his lineage against him -- he was not fully knowledgeable of Gamaliel I's rulings. They also confirm Gamaliel's wide travels, both within Palestine (Tiberias, ʿAkko) and abroad. It is reasonable to connect both of these details with Gamaliel's position as patriarch: the former as one of the reasons for his selection by the Romans, the latter as a consequence his activities in post-war reconstruction.

Part of Gamaliel's approach to the problem of rebuilding Palestinian society, and extending rabbinic influence, was to continue the irenic policies associated with Yoḥanan ben Zakkai. Those policies are revealed here not through the expression of pacifistic views, but rather through the reactions to his negotiations with, and co-operation with, the non-Jewish populations of Palestine and with Rome. Speculations on the nature of those contacts aside, one consequence of that policy would be the stories critical of Gamaliel's contacts with gentiles, adoption of Greek language and dress by his household, and his unwarranted ventures onto territory tainted by pagan culture. They represent the other side of the stories which credit him with the decree declaring robbery of a gentile as blasphemy.

Much of the remaining unfavorable material centers on the problem of Gamaliel's authority and its use. In the absence of any body of criminal and cival law associated with his name, the limited powers of the early patriarchate are confirmed. We must assume that the main focus of that authority concerned matters related to the rabbinic movement itself: those echoes preserved for us here deal with tithes and holiday laws. The power to determine the calendar is an important exception; first, because it was itself the power to determine reality, both sacred and profane, and secondly, because it reached beyond the bounds of the rabbinic movement to affect the lives of all Jews, in both Palestine and the Diaspora. It is understandable that the attempt to extend power over the rabbinic movement would meet with some resentment. Hence the great deposition-story. Yet we note even there that Gamaliel is considered indispensable, and he is restored to his office. Similarly, those stories which claim he did not know laws taught by his grandfather take for granted his authority to promulgate those laws.

Extension of authority may be the concern of several stories from another genre: that which quotes Gamaliel's own teachings to him to contradict his behavior. We recall the defensive nature of the small collection, with the key phrase, "Master, didn't you teach us...?", in M. Ber. 2.5-7. Two other stories similar in theme are Tos. Ber. 4.15 and Tos. Bes. 2.12-14. These are identical to each other in structure. A dispute is cited (over grace after fruit, over re-assembling a candelabrum). ʿAqiva follows the rabbis' view in the dispute and counters Gamaliel's objection with, "But you taught us <u>to follow the majority</u> (Ex. 23.2)." (Tos. Dem. 5.24 bears some resemblance to these, but it lacks the element of Gamaliel's teaching quoted against him.) A. Hyman's references to Ex. 23.2 (Hyman, <u>T.K.M.</u>, i, p. 140) indicate that Gamaliel's is the earliest name associated with this verse, insofar as it is interpreted to mean the principle of majority rule in the determination of <u>halakah</u>. Most references understand the verse as requiring an odd number of judges for a court. The famous incident of conflict between Eliezer and the rabbis (especially Joshua) over the "oven of ʿAknai" (b. B.M. 59b) <u>assumes</u> the principle; but the verse and exegesis there are quoted only in an explanatory gloss by the second-generation Amora, R. Jeremiah. They are not part of the original <u>beraita</u>.

Our stories do not mean to allege that Gamaliel was responsible for adopting the majority-rule principle for determining law. None of our sources elsewhere describe Gamaliel following this principle. Here it is used negatively, claiming he did not follow it. Yet the Toseftan stories wish to associate the exegesis on Ex. 23.2 with Gamaliel, as a means of identifying him closely with the principle. This may be understood in several ways. We may see it as a rabbinic argument aimed at Simeon b. Gamaliel and later patriarchs which states: law is decided by the majority vote of the sages, rather than by the decree of the patriarch -- no less a personage than the autocratic Gamaliel himself taught the principle!

On the other hand, given a situation of rabbinic individualism in which each sage considers himself independent, establishing the majority-rule principle may be a technique of patriarchal control. It creates discipline within the rabbinic group. Majority rule and patriarchal control are not so opposed as might first appear. Our Toseftan stories may thus reflect Gamaliel's actual attempts to impose greated group discipline upon the rabbis, now reflected back to him as a challenge.

v. Conclusion

Though the non-legal Gamaliel traditions are yet to be studied in detail, the bulk of traditions, and the most reliable traditions, are to be found among the legal materials. Thus, even though the survey is incomplete, and though future developments in the study of rabbinic materials will, I am sure, require a rereading of many of the pericopae previously analyzed, we may venture certain conclusions.

Gamaliel emerges as a well-attested major Yavnean figure, highly respected yet not central. The source of his traditions is mostly his own circle, the patriarchal court; some of the traditions emanate from other quarters. Though the formulation of most of his traditions took place within his circle, their transmission was mainly in the hands of the ʿAqivan scholars, who treated them respectfully (as did their master) yet ambivalently -- reflecting both legal disagreement and the early tensions between sages and patriarch. Yet the ultimate redaction of those materials was to rest in the friendly hands of Gamaliel's grandson.

The legal materials do not reveal many details of biographical importance: Gamaliel was married, had sons, was widowed. They allow deductions about the outline of his life: he survived the destruction of Jerusalem, succeeded Yoḥanan in leadership, lost his position and regained it.

We may discern certain theoretical interests within the legal traditions, namely the testing of limits and the powers of certain legal categories when opposed to each other. Thus, the importance of Sabbath is posed against that of Passover; the power of levirate responsibilities is tested against that of a unconsummated ma'amar; categories of Sabbath violation are analyzed, to see whether they may "add up" to the requirement of a sin-offering. Two other instances show the theoretical concern that positive action to intervene is a situation not be taken if it is unnecessary.

By and large, the traditions do not reveal a comprehensive legislative-administrative program or legal philosophy. But some few outlines do emerge. The traditions, in some ways, tell of a program of continuity and consolidation, appropriate to Gamaliel's succession of Yoḥanan ben Zakkai. Many of Gamaliel's rulings may be seen to effect the continuation of religious life past the trauma of the destruction of the Temple, in keeping with Yoḥanan's path. Gamaliel claims the authority for defining sacred time, the only remaining aspect of Temple-holiness to survive the destruction. He furthers the replacement of the Temple by establishing a fixed, obligatory daily liturgy for each individual. He defines the task of the Reader of the prayer service in quasi-priestly terms; and he adds a blessing to the ʿAmidah preventing a min from serving in that role. The pilgrimage festivals, once a Temple-centered function, increase in proportion among his extant traditions. Clearly, this reflects a redefinition of the seasonal festivals, now without the focus of pilgrimage to Jerusalem. In a time of despair, he strengthens the celebration of Passover -- festival of liberation and redemption -- and emphasizes its explanation in the most intimate surroundings, through the seder symbolism. He assures the transition from cultic celebration to rabbinic piety by stressing the study of Torah within his Passover eve gathering.

Gamaliel's patriarchate had to negotiate among a number of competing forces. Politically, on one side, stood the Roman government, with its overriding requirement for civil order; on the other, the various mixtures of religious and nationalistic sentiments, from the remnants of Zealot sympathy to simple resentment of alien rule. Gamaliel faced the task of contributing to civil peace, and extending the influence of Pharisaic-rabbinic Torah among the Jewish population of Palestine and in the Diaspora. Simultaneously he attempted to bring inner discipline to the rabbinic movement, while attempting to exert his personal authority over it. He may have helped unite the sages by uniting them against him.

For someone whose role was fraught with potential and actual conflict, the few hints of Gamaliel's political life, are tantalizing and frustrating. We might expect that a tradition passed on by his own tradents would be replete with such detail. The contrary fact reveals the extent to which Gamaliel's tradition has been assimilated into the mainstream of rabbinism, for which such detail was unimportant.

The measure of Gamaliel's efforts may finally be described by one comparison. The impact of the defeat of 135 C.E. upon Jewish Palestine was immeasurably greater than that of the defeat of the year 70. Yet if we compare the traditions of the Pharisees which survived into Yavneh with the traditions of Yavneh which survived into Usha, we see the great increase of the latter over the former. Despite the greater destruction in 135, the Ushan reconstruction was able to preserve large quantities of Yavnean traditions in a way the earlier generation never could. The explanation for this must be sought in the growth in numbers and organization of the group preserving those traditions, and their consequent ability to survive -- and recover from -- the greater disaster. At least part of that growth was the result of Gamaliel's work. The leadership he exercised was not charismatic, though it was forceful. Rather, he developed an institution which would in time bear its own "charisma of office." The patriarchate he in great measure established and defined was to maintain its authority for no less than four centuries after his death.

APPENDIX

The Deposition of Rabban Gamaliel II: An Examination of the Sources

by Robert Goldenberg
From the JOURNAL OF JEWISH STUDIES
Volume xxii, No. 2, Autumn 1972
pages 167-190, reprinted by permission.

During the time that Rabban Gamaliel II presided at Yavneh, an insurgency among the Rabbis there unseated him, and he was temporarily replaced by the young priest R. Eleazar b. ʿAzariah. No other even briefly successful uprising of this kind is mentioned in surviving records,[1] although an abortive attempt was directed against Gamaliel's son and eventual successor Simeon.[2]

Gamaliel's deposition is reported in both Talmudim. The purpose of this paper is to evaluate the two reports as historical sources.

I
THE PALESTINIAN TALMUD

The following, p. Ber. 4:17c-d, has a parallel in p. Taʿan. 4:1 67d; variants will be indicated in the footnotes. Italics represent passages in Aramaic.

A. And[3] it once happened that a certain student came and asked R. Joshua, "How is the law about the evening prayer?" He said to him. "Optional."

[The student] came[4] and asked R. Gamaliel, "How is the law about the evening prayer?" He said to him, "Compulsory."

[The student] said to him, "But R. Joshua said 'Optional'!"[5] [R. Gamaliel] said to him, "Tomorrow, when I come into the meeting-house (BYT HWʿD) get up and ask about this law."

The next day[6] that same student got up and asked R. Gamaliel, "How is the law about the evening prayer?" He said to him, "Compulsory." He said, "But R. Joshua said[7] 'Optional.'"

R. Gamaliel said to R. Joshua, "Is it you who says 'Optional'?" He said, "No."

[R. Gamaliel] said to him, "stand on your feet, and let them bear witness against you." And R. Gamaliel sat and taught, and R. Joshua remained standing, until the whole assembly shouted and said to R. Huṣpit the Meturgeman, "Dismiss the assembly!"

B. They said to R. Zenon the Ḥazzan, "Say..." He began to speak; the whole assembly began, and they rose to their feet and said[11] to [R. Gamaliel], "For upon whom has not come your unceasing evil?"[12]

C.1. They went[13] and appointed (MYNW) R. Eleazar b. ʿAzariah to the Academy (BYŠYBH).

C.2. (He was sixteen years old, and all his hair turned gray.)

D.1. R. ʿAqiva was sitting sorrowfully and saying, "Not that he is more learned (BN TWRH) than I,[14] but he is of more illustrious parentage (BN GDWLYM) than I. Happy is the man whose fathers have gained him merit! Happy is the man who has a peg on which[15] to hang!"[16]

D.2. (And what was R. Eleazar b. ʿAzariah's peg? He was the tenth generation[6] in descent from Ezra.)

E. (And[6] how many benches were there? R. Jacob b. Sisi said, "There were 80 benches there of students,[17] besides those standing behind the fence." R. Yosi b. R. Abun[18] said, "There were 300, besides those standing behind the fence.")

H.[19] [This is the reference of] *what we learn elsewhere:* "On the day they seated (HWŠYBW) R. Eleazar b. ʿAzariah in the Academy."[20]

I. (*We learn elsewhere:* "This is a *midrash* which R. Eleazar b. ʿAzariah expounded before the Sages at the Vineyard in Yavneh."[21] But was there a vineyard there?! Rather, those are the students who were arranged in rows, as in a vineyard.)

J.1. R. Gamaliel immediately went to the home of each person to appease him.

J.2. *He went*[22] *to R. Joshua; he found him sitting making needles. He said to him, "Is this how you make a living?"*[23] *He said, "And are you just now trying to find out?"* Woe to the generation of which you are the steward (PRNŚ)."

K. [R. Gamaliel] said to him, "I submit to you."

L.1. *And*[6] *they sent a certain laundry-worker* (Q̣SR) *to R. Eleazar b. ʿAzariah.*

L.2. *(but some say it was R. ʿAqiva).*

O.[24] [The messenger] said to him, "The sprinkler, son of a sprinkler,[25] should sprinkle; shall he who is neither a sprinkler nor the son of a sprinkler say to the sprinkler, son of a sprinkler, "Your water comes from a cave, and your ashes from roasting'?"[26]

P. [R. Eleazar b. ʿAzariah] said to them, "Are you satisfied? You and I shall wait at R. Gamaliel's door."

Q. Nonetheless they did not depose [R. Eleazar b. ʿAzariah] from his high dignity, but rather appointed him *Av Bet Din*.

* * * * *

The text as we now have it is clearly composite. I would break it down as follows:

Main story - A, B, C.1, J, K, L, O, P, Q
Elaborations of the main story - C.2, D, J.2, L.2(?)
Interpolations - E, H, I

If later accretions are disregarded, the story can be summarised as follows: An anonymous student became aware of a disagreement between Joshua and Gamaliel. He made the dispute known to the latter, who took the opportunity to humiliate Joshua before the assembled Rabbis. Outraged, they broke up the meeting, and R. Eleazar b. ʿAzariah was brought into the Academy. It is not stated, but we infer that Eleazar became its new head. R. Gamaliel thereupon made amends to each of the offended Rabbis, and had a message sent to Eleazar, expressing his claim to an inherited right to the presidency. Eleazar voluntarily resigned, and was rewarded with the second place in the hierarchy.

The relationship between the Eleazar-story and the Joshua-story presents a problem. There is no section in the narrative in which both men play a role. Their two stories can be told without reference to each other, although admittedly each would then be somewhat episodic. Since the references to ʿAqiva (sections D.1, L.2) are both insertions, dating from a later stage in the development of the narrative, the question arises whether there was also a still earlier stage in which the Joshua-scenes and the Eleazar-scenes constituted separate traditions.[27] The present text have obviously been pieced together.[28] The narrative progression is not always smooth;[29] such flaws often indicate the interweaving of two different traditions. On the other hand, the Palestinian narrators were evidently rather unconcerned with such esthetic considerations; we should not, therefore, be too ready to see different "sources" wherever the narrative structure fails to meet our literary standards.[30] All we can say with assurance is that the Eleazar-Joshua story is the backbone of the present narrative. At a later date, references to ʿAqiva were inserted, the most important being in section D. Still later, a number of miscellaneous interpolations were added as well (sections E, H, I).

The text of section B is unclear, and apparently corrupt. The two extant versions differ concerning the speakers identity; it is not explained what anyone actually says and at one point there is a lacuna. We have here, it seems, an alternative description of the disruption of the Academy.[31] It was presumably added to a story drawn primarily from other traditions because it offered a clearer statement of the Rabbis' motivation.[32] But even if this passage was part of the "original" story, it has by now become so obscure that there is little hope of determining its meaning, or even of restoring its text.

Section E is a very late addition designed to emphasise the large number of men who collaborated in the overthrow.[33]

In three places in the Mishnah,[34] Simeon b. ʿAzzai cites a tradition which he heard "from seventy-two elders on the day they seated R. Eleazar b. ʿAzariah in the Academy." The phrase was apparently used to date certain traditions. Its insertion into our story (section H) seems to have two purposes; to explain the phrase itself, which by Amoraic times was apparently no longer understood, and also to indicate why that day was important enough to become a point of reference.

The fanciful interpretation of "Vineyard in Yavneh," found in section I, recurs in Song of Songs R. 8:11. In that place it has no connection with R. Eleazar b. ʿAzariah, nor is this exegesis there or anywhere else associated with mKet. 4:6. The reason for its insertion into our story and the identity of the interpolator are unknown. The name of R. Eleazar b. ʿAzariah provides the only possible link. It is not even hinted, however, that Eleazar expounded the *midrash* in question on the occasion of his installation.

Section D, the most important elaboration, takes careful note of ʿAqiva's own availability to succeed Gamaliel, and purports to explain why he was in fact bypassed. At a later time, ʿAqiva was so universally admired that any hearer of the story would have wondered why he had not been chosen.

The central interest of the account is political. It revolves around the presidency over the Rabbinic gathering and the question of who might legitimately exercise it. There is no tendency to turn the original incident into a pretext for moral instruction, concerning the manner in which persons in authority ought to treat their subjects. Nor is the story used as a legal precedent; the halakhic dispute between Gamaliel and Joshua appears in both Talmudim as a separate datum prior to the narrative. From the time of R. Judah the Patriarch, the hold of the Hillelite dynasty on the Patriarchate was secure. Political interest would thereafter have naturally shifted to other issues. The main story therefore seems to antedate the ascendancy of Judah the Patriarch, *ca.*185 C.E. Once formed, the composite continued to grow until fairly late in the Amoraic period. The reference to R. Yosi b. R. Abun points to the second half of the fourth century.

The story is told in Hebrew. Only the following passages are in Aramaic:

1. The introductory formulae in sections H and I. Since these sections were added by some Amoraic redactor, it need not surprise us that standard redactional language was used.

2. The indicated portions of J, and all of L. This presents a problem. In J in particular the transition from Aramaic back to Hebrew occurs in the middle of R. Joshua's retort. I doubt that a single narrator would have composed such a short statement in two languages. The final sentence ("Woe...") appears verbatim in the BT, and may have been associated with this story from an early date, but these Aramaic passages suggest some later revision. We shall return to this question below, in part III.

II
THE BABYLONIAN TALMUD

The following is from bBer. 27b-28a. Section A has a parallel in bBekh. 36a; this parallel will be introduced in an additional note to part II. As before, all Aramaic portions will be in italics.

A. *Our Rabbis taught:* It once happened that a certain student came before R. Joshua. He said to him, "Is the evening prayer optional or compulsory?" He said to him, "Optional."

[The student] came before R. Gamaliel. He said to him, "Is the evening prayer optional or compulsory?" He said to him, "Compulsory."

[The student] said to him, "But did not R. Joshua say 'Optional'?!" [R. Gamaliel] said to him, "Wait until the Shield-Bearers enter the study-house (BYT HMDRŠ)."

When the Shield-Bearers entered, the inquirer rose and asked, "Is the evening prayer optional or compulsory?" R. Gamaliel said to him, "Compulsory."

R. Gamaliel said to the Sages, "Is there anyone who disagrees in this matter?" R. Joshua said to him, "No."

[R. Gamaliel] said to him, "But did they not tell me 'Optional' in your name?!" He said to him, "Joshua, stand on your feet, and let them bear witness against you."

R. Joshua rose to his feet and said, "If I were alive and [the witness] dead - the living can contradict the dead. But now that I am alive and he is alive - how can the living contradict the living?"

And R. Gamaliel sat and taught, and R. Joshua remained standing, until the whole assembly shouted and said to Ḥuṣpit the Turgeman, "Stop!" So he stopped.

C.1.[35] *They said, "How long will he go on insulting him? Last year he insulted him* (in Rosh Hashanah),[36] *he insulted him in the incident of R. Ṣadoq* (in Bekhorot),[36] *and now he has insulted him again. Let us remove him! Whom shall we appoint* (NWQYM)? *Shall we appoint R. Joshua?* He is a party to the dispute.[37] *Shall we appoint R. ʿAqiva? He might be punished, since he has no* ancestral merit. *Let us rather appoint R. Eleazar b. ʿAzariah, since* he is wise, and he is rich, and he is tenth in descent from Ezra."

C.2. (He is wise, [that is], *if questioned, he can answer;* he is rich, [that is], *if* [R. Gamaliel] *has to go pay honor to Caesar,* [R. Eleazar b. ʿAzariah] too *can go pay honor;* he is tenth in descent from Ezra, [that is], *he has* ancestral merit, *and he cannot be punished.*)

C.3. *They came and said to him, "Would the Master consent to become head of the Academy?"*

C.4. *He said to them, "Let me go consult my household." He went and consulted his wife.*

She said to him, "They may remove you." He answered, "Let a man use a valuable cup one day, and let it be broken the next."

She said to him, "You have no white hair." That day he was eighteen years old; a miracle occurred to him, and eighteen rows of his hair turned white.

C.5. (*That is* [why] *R. Eleazar b. ʿAzariah said,* "Behold I am about seventy years old," *and not* "seventy years old.")[38]

E.1.[39] It was tuaght: That day (ʾWTW HYWM) they removed the doorkeeper, and the students were given permission to enter. For R. Gamaliel had used to proclaim: "Any student whose outside is not like his inside shall not enter the study-house."

E.2. (*On that day* (HHW YWMʾ) *a number of benches were added. R. Yoḥanan said, "The matter is disputed by Abba Joseph b. Dostai and the Rabbis; one* [view] *holds 400 benches were added, and one, 700."*)

E.3. *R. Gamaliel was greatly disturbed, and said,* "Perhaps, God forbid, I have withheld Torah from Israel." *In a dream, he was shown white casks filled with ashes.*[40] But that was not [the case]; *he was shown that just to calm his mind.*

F.1. *It was taught:* ʿEduyot was under review (NŠNYT) on that day (BW BYWM).

F.2. *(And wherever it says* "on that day" *the reference is to that day).*

F.3. and there was no law which had been left pending in the study-house which was not decided.

G. And even R. Gamaliel did not absent himself from the study-house for as much as one hour, *as we learn:* On that day (BW BYWM) Judah, an Ammonite proselyte, came before them in the study-house. He said to them, "Am I permitted to enter the congregation?" R. Gamaliel said to him, "You are forbidden to enter the congregation." R. Joshua said to him, "You are permitted to enter the congregation."

R. Gamaliel said to [R. Joshua], "But has it not already been said, 'An Ammonite or a Moabite shall not enter the congregation of the Lord'?"[41]

R. Joshua said to him, "Them do Ammon and Moab dwell in their own places? Sennacherib, King of Assyria, has already come up and mixed together all the nations, as it is said, "And I have removed the boundaries of peoples, and have plundered their treasures; like a bull I have brought down those who sat on thrones'[42] - *and anything which comes out* [of a composite mass is assumed to have] *come from its largest element.*"[43,44]

R. Gamaliel said to him, "But has it not already been said, 'And afterwards I shall bring back the captivity of the children of Ammon, says the Lord'[45] - so they have returned?"

R. Joshua said to him, "But has it not already been said, 'And I shall return the captivity of my people Israel'?[46] And they have not yet returned!"

They immediately permitted [Judah] to enter the congregation.[47]

J.1.[48] *R. Gamaliel said, "Such being the case,*[49] *I shall go and appease R. Joshua."*

J.2. *When he got to his house, he saw that its walls were black.* He said to him, "From the walls of your house, one can tell that you are a charcoal-maker."[50] He said to him, "Woe to the generation of which you are the steward (PRNŚ). You do not know of the troubles of the scholars and of how they support and sustain themselves."

K. [R. Gamaliel] said to him, "I submit to you; forgive me." [R. Joshua] *paid him no attention.*

[R. Gamaliel said further,] "Do it out of respect for my father." [R. Joshua] *was appeased.*

L. *They said, "Who will go and inform the Rabbis?" A certain washerman* (KWBŚ) *said, "I shall go."*

M. *So R. Joshua sent* [a message] *to the study-house: "Let him who wears the garment wear the garment; should he who does not wear the garment say to him who wears it, 'Take off your garment and let me wear it'?"*

N. *R. ʿAqiva said to the Rabbis, "Shut the doors, so that R. Gamaliel's servants not come and disturb the Rabbis." R. Joshua said, "I had better go to them myself."*

O. *He came and knocked on the door, and said to them,* "The sprinkler, son of a sprinkler, should sprinkle; shall he who is neither a sprinkler nor the son of a sprinkler say to the sprinkler, son of a sprinkler, 'Your water comes from a cave and your ashes from roasting'?"[51]

P. R. ʿAqiva said to him, "R. Joshua, have you been appeased? We have done nothing except for your honor. Tomorrow you and I shall wait at [R. Gamaliel's] door."

Q. *They said, "How shall we act? Shall we remove* [R. Eleazar b. ʿAzariah]*? Tradition holds that* one may increase the sanctity of an object, but not decrease it.[52] *Should each Master expound one Sabbath* [at a time]? *That will lead to jealousy. Rather let R. Gamaliel expound three Sabbaths*[53] *and R. Eleazar b. ʿAzariah one Sabbath.*

R. (*That is what the Master meant when he said,* "Whose Sabbath was it? R. Eleazar b. ʿAzariah's.")

S. (And that student [who started the whole episode] was R. Simeon b. Yoḥai.)

* * * * *

If we being with the tripartite division which we used in part I, the results are as follows:

Main story - A, C.1.3, J.1, K, L, O, P, Q
Elaborations - E.1.3, J.2, M, N[54]
Interpolations - C.2.4.5, E.2, F, G, R, S

The central narrative is broadly similar to the Palestinian version. There is, however, one major difference. Here, the Rabbis are described as acting exclusively in Joshua's interest. They cite no offenses against other members of the group. Gamaliel need offer only one apology, to Joshua himself. ʿAqiva even says (section P) that Joshua's honor was their sole motivation for removing Gamaliel.[55] This change reduces the political aspect of the narrative, and turns it into a story about a personal dispute.

The elements concerning Eleazar and Joshua have been somewhat more closely integrated. The question, "Who will go and inform the Rabbis," referring to the reconciliation between Joshua and Gamaliel, means "Who will inform Eleazar and his supporters." In section P, ʿAqiva, addressing Joshua, alludes to the deposition of Gamaliel and (presumably) Eleazar's promotion. This tightening-up of the narrative is not surprising, since we shall see (in part III) there is abundant evidence that the Babylonian story is a later development of the Palestinian.

Most of the later interpolations come at the same point in this story as in the PT, but the two sets have almost nothing in common.[56] The only shared item is the dispute about the benches,[57] and even it plays strikingly different roles in the two stories. In the PT, the reference indicates the wide backing for Gamaliel's removal. Here, it demonstrates the result of reversing one of his specific policies, the policy of limiting access to the Academy.

In general, the additions to the Babylonian story concern what might be called the Rabbinic life-style. Two of them (sections C and Q) take what was originally a political problem and use it for a display of Rabbinic dialectics. Section E, as noted, concerns the question of who was worthy to study Torah at all. In keeping with this same theme, section F provides a bit of literary history.[58] Section G, which returns to R. Gamaliel's concern for Torah, was included because it is the only Mishnah[59] beginning "on that day" which actually mentions R. Gamaliel.

These additions change the tone of the whole narrative. Political interest, as mentioned above, has faded from view. The story, considerably "improved," has been made more interesting and more edifying for later audiences. This Babylonian version cannot be dated. It mentions no names which might be useful, except for that of R. Yoḥanan, a Palestinian who died *ca.* 279. The story certainly continued to develop in Babylonia after his time. The reference to R. Simeon b. Yoḥai is clearly late, added by someone with no knowledge of Tannaitic chronology.

The Babylonian version contains much more Aramaic than the Palestinian. Apparently, the narrative "improvements" were made in the vernacular, often displacing older Hebrew material. Section E, in particular, shows a curious shifting back and forth between

Hebrew and Aramaic. The first part, here called a *baraita*, centres around R. Gamaliel's proclamation; this may well have been a proverbial expression in certain Babylonian circles - the same expression, again in Hebrew, is attributed to Rava on b. Yoma 72b. Perhaps the same explanation could be applied to R. Gamaliel's exclamation in section E.3.

ADDITIONAL NOTE

The following appears on b. Bekh. 36a. Italics denote Aramaic, as before.

> *R. Ṣadoq had a firstling. He fed it with barley* in wicker baskets of peeled willow-branches.[60] *As it was eating, its lip became split.*
>
> *He came before R. Joshua. He said to him,* "Do we distinguish at all between a *ḥaver* and an *ʿam haʾ areṣ*?"[61] R. Joshua said, "Yes."
>
> *He came before R. Gamaliel. He said to him,* "Do we distinguish between a *ḥaver* and an *ʿam haʾ areṣ*?" R. Gamaliel said, "No."
>
> *He said to him,* "But (WHʾ) R. Joshua said, 'Yes'!" He said to him, "Wait until the Shield-Bearers come up to the study-house."
>
> When they entered the study-house, the inquirer rose and asked, "Do we at all distinguish between a *ḥaver* and an *ʿam haʾ areṣ*?" R. Joshua said, "No."
>
> R. Gamaliel said to him, "But did they not (WHLʾ) say 'Yes' in your name?! Joshua, stand on your feet and let them bear witness against you."
>
> R. Joshua rose to his feet and said, "How can I act? If I were alive and he dead - the living can contradict the dead. Now that I am alive and he is alive, how can the living contradict the living?"
>
> And R. Gamaliel stood[62] and taught, while R. Joshua remained on his feet, until the whole assembly shouted and said to Ḥuṣpit the Meturgeman, "Stop!" So he stopped.

* * * * *

It is impossible that two stories should develop independently, and become so similar to one another as this one and the story in Ber. One has obviously become assimilated to the other. Since the Bekh. version begins in Aramaic and then abruptly shifts to Hebrew, it seems likely that Ber. has the earlier setting for the present narrative.[63] A number of traditions recounting disputes between Gamaliel and Joshua were in circulation; another has survived in M. R.H. 2:8-9. One of these, concerning R. Ṣadoq's firstling, eventually became an echo of the story about the evening prayer. This may have occurred because the story about the evening prayer culminated in Gamaliel's removal and thus became better known. In the end the story about the firstling was forgotten, and there remained only a tradition that *something* concerning a firstling had happened. The present narrative was supplied.[64]

The story in Bekh. has no sequel. If the narrator had known more of the story in Ber., he would have had no reason to omit it.[65] It seems safe to infer that he knew only this part; we thus have an indication that parts of the whole story at some point circulated separately.

III
SYNOPSES

Where a section appears in both Talmudim, the two versions are set side by side for detailed comparison. When a phrase used in one version is found unchanged in the other; I show this with """. If a phrase is entirely absent, I use -----. Aramaic passages appear in italics, as before. Synopses either quote or paraphrase the text, as circumstances require.

A. *The Disgrace of R. Joshua*

pBer. 4:1	*bBer. 27b*	*bBekh. 36a*
1. And it once happened that	1. *Our Rabbis taught:* It once happened that	1. *R. Ṣadoq had a firstling...Its lip became split.*
2. a certain student came and asked R. Joshua,	2. a certain student came before R. Joshua. He said to him,	2. *He came before R. Joshua. He said to him,*
3. "How is the law about the evening prayer?"	3. "Is the evening prayer optional or compulsory?"	3. "Do we at all distinguish between a *haver* and an *ʿam haʾ areṣ?"*
4. He said, "Optional."	4. """	4. R. Joshua said, "Yes."
5. He came and asked R. Gamaliel,	5. He came before R. Gamaliel. He said to him,	5. *He came before R. Gamaliel. He said to him,*

6. [=3 above]	6. [=3 above]	6. [=3 above, omitting "at all"]
7. He said, "Compulsory."	7. """	7. R. Gamaliel said, "No."
8. He said to him, "But (WHʾ) R. Joshua said 'Optional.'"	8. He said to him, "But did not (WHLʾ) R. Joshua say 'Optional'?"	8. He said to him, "But (WHʾ) R. Joshua said 'Yes.'"
9. He said to him, "Tomorrow, when I come into the meeting-house, get up and ask about this law."	9. He said to him, "Wait until the Shield-Bearers enter the study-house."	9. He said to him, "Wait until the Shield-Bearers come up to the study-house."
10. The next day that same student got up and asked R. Gamaliel,	10. When the Shield-Bearers entered, the inquirer got up and asked,	10. When they entered the study-house, the inquirer got up and asked,
11. "How is the law about the evening prayer?" He said, "Compulsory."	11. "Is the evening prayer optional or compulsory?" R. Gamaliel told him, "Compulsory."	11. "Do we at all distinguish between a *haver* and an *ʿam haʾ areṣ?"* R. Joshua said, "No."
12a. He said, "But (WHʾ) R. Joshua said 'Optional.'"	12a. -----[see 12d]	12a. -----[see 12d]
12b. R. Gamaliel said to R. Joshua, "Is it you who say 'Optional'?"	12b. R. Gamaliel said to the Sages, "Is there anyone who disagrees in this matter?"	12b. -----
12c. He said, "No."	12c. R. Joshua said to him, "No."	12c. -----
12d. -----[see 12a]	12d. He said to him, "But did they not (WHLʾ) say 'Optional' in your name?"	12d. R. Gamaliel said to him, "But did they not (WHLʾ) say 'Yes' in your name?"
13. He said to him, "Stand on your feet, and let them bear witness against you."	13. He said to him, "Joshua, stand on your feet..."	13. Joshua, stand on your feet..."
14. -----	14. R. Joshua rose to his feet and said, "If I were alive and he dead-the living can contradict the dead. But now that I am alive and he is alive-how can the living contradict the living?"	14. """ [adds "How shall I act?"; deletes "But"]

pBer. 4:1	*bBer. 27b*	*bBekh. 36a*
15.And R. Gamaliel sat and taught, and R. Joshua remained standing, until the whole assembly shouted,	15. """	15.""" [printed text has "R. Gamaliel stood ..."]
16.and they said to R. Ḥuṣpit the Meturgeman.	16."""[Ḥuṣpit the Turgeman]	16."""[Ḥuṣpit the Meturgeman]
17."Dismiss the assembly!"	17."Stop!"	17."Stop!"
18. -----	18.So he stopped	18."""

These tables leave no doubt as to how the three stories are related. In only one case (#10) is it even remotely possible that the PT is an expansion of the BT. In that case, the name of R. Gamaliel may have been added, but the different narrative schemes in #11-12 make this evidence very weak. On the other hand, the BT expands the PT in a number of cases: #1,2=5,3=6=11 (11 twice), and 13.[66] In #3=6=11, the question has been elaborated in an obviously secondary way. The word "before" in #2=5 is also a later addition. In #11, the name of the respondent is supplied, as is R. Joshua's name in #13. In all these cases, the direct literary dependence of the BT on the PT is beyond question.

The close relationship of the two Babylonian stories, and the dependence of Bekh. on Ber., are also demonstrable. In every case where pBer. and bBer. differ, bBekh. agrees with the latter, with the single trivial exception of #8. Bekh., furthermore, has expanded Ber. in #4, 7, 10 and 14. Finally, in #2=5, Bekh. has translated Ber. into Aramaic, presumably under the influence of the Aramaic narrative (#1) which introduces its story. The three narratives differ in sequence only once, in #12. In pBer., Joshua's disagreement with Gamaliel is revealed before he is forced to lie publicly, while in bBer. the revelation follows the confrontation.[67] Since #12b-c has no intrinsic connection with #12a=12d (Bekh. omits #12b-c entirely), the reversal is not important.

The language of the Babylonian version has been adapted to its surroundings. The term for "evening prayer" is consistently and characteristically TPYLT ʿRBYT. The version in *pBer.* uses the Palestinian TPYLT HʿRB, as does the Mishnah itself.[68] Similarly, the distinctively Palestinian BYT HWʾD (meeting-house) has been changes in *bBer.* to the more common BYT HMDRŠ.[69]

It has been suggested that the "Shield-Bearers" were actually armed guards at R. Gamaliel's disposal.[70] Although *bBer.* does refer (section N) to "R. Gamaliel's servants," we have no idea who these were; for all we know, the reference is altogether anachronistic. To draw any inference from the Gothic soldiers whom the Patriarch over a century later could command[71] would be most unwise. The more common, and preferable, interpretation is that the "Shield-Bearers" were the Rabbis themselves, the epithet being metaphorical.

The story in *Bekh.* ends abruptly with the order to Ḥuṣpit the Meturgeman. Ginzberg thought there was an "original *baraita*" which carried the story through to its conclusion,[72] but it is difficult, as I have said, to imagine why the narrator would have omitted the rest, had he known it.

C. The Appointment of R. Eleazar B. ʿAzariah

PT	*BT*
1. -----	1. *They said, "How long will he go on...Let us remove him!"*
2. -----	2. *Whom shall we appoint* (NWQYM)*? R. Joshua?...R. ʿAqiva?...*
3. They went and appointed (MYNW) Eleazar b. ʿAzariah into the Academy.	*Let us rather appoint R. Eleazar b. ʿAzariah, since...*
4. -----	4. (He is wise, that is...)
5. -----	5. *They came and said to him, "Would the Master consent...?"*
6. -----	6. *He said to them, "Let me go consult..." He went and consulted his wife.*
7. -----	7. *She said, "They may remove you." He said, "Let a man..."*
8. (He was sixteen years old, and all his hair turned gray.)	8. *She said to him, "You have no white hair." That day he was eighteen years old; a miracle occurred to him and eighteen rows of his hair turned white.*
9. -----	9. *(That is* [why] *R. Eleazar b. ʿAzariah said, "Behold,...")*

Two simple declarative sentences, one probably added later than the other, constitute the entire Palestinian report of

Eleazar's entrance into the Academy. The elaborate story in the BT can hardly be considered merely an expansion of the Palestinian version. It is an original creation. It may, to be sure, have roots in older narratives, but these can no longer be traced. Much of the story in any case derives from the Babylonian story-teller.

The two versions have three items in common. One of these is the report of Eleazar's prematurely gray (or white) hair. This was probably an independent tradition, attached only at a later time to Eleazar's statement in mBer. 1:5. If the story had been invented to explain that statement (as the BT might lead us to suppose), we could not account for the PT's failure to cite it. The two Talmudim disagree concerning how old Eleazar was "on that day." Variant readings in the PT report still other figures.[73] These presumably reflect different guesses at Eleazar's previously unspecified age.[74]

The second shared element is the account of Eleazar's introduction to the Academy. The accounts differ. According to PT, Eleazar was appointed to the Academy, while BT asserts that he was openly invited to become its leader. Since most of BT is obviously fictional we cannot automatically assume that is here reflects an older and more authoritative source. PT, however, may well mean the same thing. Unless Eleazar had become not merely a member, but the Academy's new president, it would be hard to account for Gamaliel's great concern or his emphasis on hereditary legitimacy. PT further implies that Eleazar's eventual appointment as *Av Bet Din* represented a demotion, since that office was the second in the standard rabbinic hierarchy.[75] It seems reasonable, therefore, to accept BT's report on this matter. Because of PT's obscurity on this important point, it was subsequently thought necessary to specify[77] that the day of Eleazar's installation was indeed the day of the events here recounted.

The final common element in the two stories is Eleazar's alleged descent from Ezra (see section D). Since section D.2 may well be a later insertion, the presence of this claim in the BT possibly offers evidence that some Babylonian additions reflect older, independent traditions.[78] The reference to Eleazar's descent also appears in p. Yev. 1:6 3a. Apparently it was a commonly accepted belief. At a time when Davidic ancestry was claimed by any politically ambitious person, descent from Ezra was an appropriate priestly counterclaim.

E. The Benches

PT	*BT*
1. -----	1. *It was taught:*
2. -----	2. That day ('WTW HYWM) they removed the doorkeeper...
3. -----	3. For R. Gamaliel had used to proclaim...
4. And how many benches were there?	4. *On that day* (HHW' YWM') *a number of benches was added.*
5. -----	5. *R. Yoḥanan said, "The matter is disputed by Abba Joseph b. Dostai and the Rabbis;*
6. R. Jacob b. Sisi said, "There were 80 benches of students there, besides those standing behind the fence."	6. *one* [view] *holds 400 benches were added,*
7. R. Yosi b. R. Abun said, "There were 300, besides those standing behind the fense."	7. *and one, 700."*
8. -----	8. *R. Gamaliel was greatly disturbed...*
9. -----	9. *In a dream, he was shown...*
10. -----	10. But that was not the case...

The PT reports that the dispute concerns the number of benches (of men) *present*; the BT, the number of benches *added*. Since the two reports contain neither the same numbers nor the same names, it is possible that they are unrelated, despite their apparent connection. If the two were found in isolation, there would be no way to determine their relationship. The rest of the material in the BT permits at least a guess.

The BT offers #1-3 as a *baraita*. This is the only portion of the episode in Hebrew. The story of the doorkeeper may have been in independent circulation - perhaps, like the story of R. Eleazar's hair, always told in connection with R. Gamaliel's ouster. When it was combined with the dispute about the benches, the change in the latter was a natural consequence. This hypothesis is strengthened by the fact that #4 is in Aramaic. In our story, this generally seems a sign of later reworking. The *baraita* itself is possibly Babylonian; we have already seen that Rava shared R. Gamaliel's concern that a student's motivation and behaviour correspond.

This episode replaces the earlier hostility towards R. Gamaliel with patronising condescension. True, Gamaliel was harsh, and true, he was wrong to be so, but still he meant well, and after all no permanent harm was done. This shift probably indicates that the episode was constructed of elements which had already taken shape before their inclusion. Whoever inserted it was unable to achieve complete consistency in the story's characterization.

F. "On that Day"[79]

Epstein's demonstration relative to the sense of "on that day" has already been referred to.[80] Tradition took the claim at face value; we can no longer trace how this understanding developed.

Epstein also rejected the tradition about ʿEduyot, but he apparently interpreted it as referring to the Mishnaic tractate. The beginning of Tosefta ʿEduyot records that the men of Yavneh set themselves the task of collecting and arranging older traditions. At the time of the uprising against Gamaliel, they may well have been at work on that project. It is in fact possible that the word ʿEDYWT here refers simply to the mass of "testimonies" which the Yavneans were trying to organize, not to the particular literary unit which later received that name. The suggested translation of the verb NŠNYT ("was under review") is designed to preserve that possibility, while the alternative reading TQNWM, cited by Epstein,[81] lends it still greater credence. The report that no pending dispute was left unresolved is fully consistent with the kind of activity we have just postulated but there is no way to determine if it is historical.

J. R. Gamaliel Makes Amends

PT	*BT*
1. R. Gamaliel immediately went to each person, to appease him in his home.	1. -----
2. -----	2. *R. Gamaliel said, "Such being the case, I shall go and appease R. Joshua."*
3. *He went to R. Joshua;*	3. *When he came to his house,*
4. *he found him sitting making needles.*	4. -----

PT	*BT*
5. -----	5. *he saw that its walls were black.*
6. *He said to him, "Is this how you make a living?"*	6. -----
7. -----	7. He said to him, "From the walls of your house, one can tell that you are a charcoal-maker."
8. *He said to him, "And are you just now trying to find out?"*	8. -----
9. Woe to the generation of which you are the steward."	9. He said to him, """
10. -----	10. "You do not know of the troubles of scholars and how they support and sustain themselves."

The relationship between the Talmudim is more complicated in this section than elsewhere. Each version has four items which are missing from the other (#1, 4, 6, 8 in PT, #2, 5, 7, 10 in BT). Each has an Aramaic portion using its own characteristic Aramaic dialect,[82] and the contents of the two in no way coincide (cf. #2-5 in BT). Finally, each also has Hebrew passages missing from the other (#1 in PT, #7, 10 in BT). Only once, in #9 do the two versions significantly agree, and then - aside from BT's introduction - they are identical.

These are the first Aramaic passages which we have encountered in PT. Earlier narratives probably contained no exchange between Gamaliel and Joshua. A palestinian narrator must have felt the need for some discussion between them, and inserted the present one. A similar situation produced the Babylonian version of the conversation; BT, however, has already shown a number of similar cases.

The cause of this parallel development is the strong rebuke to R. Gamaliel which both Talmudim have preserved (#9). Its presence in both versions makes it likely that this remark early attained the status of a proverb, or a stock rejoinder. So striking an expression attracted the attention of those who heard and repeated the story. It is not surprising that even the Palestinian narrators were tempted to supply the setting in which it appeared.

Although part of a later expansion, #7 is in Hebrew. Presumably, #10 is an expansion of #9, of the kind which has already become familiar. It is in Hebrew because #9 is in Hebrew. #7, however, is an anomaly; the narrator apparently used Hebrew for dialogue, here and in the sequel.

L. The Messenger

PT	*BT*
1. -----[see #3]	1. *They said, "Who will go and inform the Rabbis?"*
2. *So they sent a certain laundry-worker* (QṢR)	2. *A certain washerman* (KWBŚ) *said, "I will go."*
3. *to R. Eleazar b. ʿAzariah.*	3. -----[see #1]
4. *but some say it was R. ʿAqiva.*	4. -----

In both the story of the excommunication of R. Eliezer b. Hyrcanus[83] and the other recorded public dispute between Gamaliel and Joshua,[84] ʿAqiva plays the messenger. There must have been circles which considered this his characteristic role in Rabbinic politics during his youth. The reference here, however, contradicts other statements in the story, which describe ʿAqiva either as himself a candidate for the presidency (above, sections C and D), or as a ringleader of the rebellious Rabbis (below in BT, sections N and P). It has already been suggested[85] that at least part of the latter is an artificial construction, of negligible historical value, but the former presents a real problem.

G. Alon has observed that Joshua, in his dealings with the Patriarch Gamaliel, can be seen as the heir to Yoḥanan b. Zakkai.[86] When R. Meir, in the next generation, joined a conspiracy against Gamaliel's son,[87] he may well have carried a similar heritage from his own teacher ʿAqiva. In any event, ʿAqiva was no doubt deeply involved in political activity; it need not, therefore, surprise us that various groups, in ʿAqiva's and the following generation, represented him in a manner corresponding to their own political tendencies.[88] If in the eyes of his own supporters ʿAqiva appeared as a disappointed candidate, frustrated by factors beyond his control, Gamaliel's party could well picture him as a disgruntled ringleader trying to hinder reconciliation. How these different perspectives all came into one story is difficult to explain. We must note, however, that all the references to ʿAqiva the peacemaker or to ʿAqiva the recalcitrant (that is, *not* to ʿAqiva the candidate) are in Aramaic; in these texts, this has generally suggested a later, secondary addition to the story.

Both versions of this section are in Aramaic. Probably they are later inventions, designed to integrate better the metaphors of the garment and of the sprinkler into the story as a whole. What the washerman represents, or how he got into both versions, seems a matter for conjecture.[89]

The two versions of the central narrative have differed most significantly in their portrayal of the mass of the Rabbis (see above, pp. 294-5). We find striking evidence of this in the present section. In the PT R. Gamaliel had to win over all the Rabbis. We therefore now read that "they" (referring back to section J.1) sent the messenger specifically to R. Eleazar b. ʿAzariah, the others having already rejoined Gamaliel. In the BT, however, only Joshua had to be appeased, and only "they" (the two men, Gamaliel and Joshua; cf. section K) sent the messenger; the latter had merely to "inform the Rabbis." Further elaborations of this change appear below, in section P.

M. The Garment

The metaphor of the garment is in Aramaic. It was probably added simply as an artistic "improvement" on an older version of the story. Unlike the image of the sprinkler, this one lays no stress on Gamaliel's parentage. It merely implies that the job was originally Gamaliel's, and that the others had no right to take it away.

N. "Shut the Doors"

This section is inconsistent with the rest of the story. ʿAqiva appears here for the first time as a leader of the other Rabbis. More importantly, this is the only place in the BT where the Rabbis exhibit distrust of Gamaliel beyond that which their zeal for Joshua would seem to demand. Their suspicion that his "servants" may come to enforce his will hints at tyrannical behaviour extending beyond the three disputes with Joshua reported in section C. This section was evidently added to justify the presence of two messages in defence of R. Gamaliel's legitimacy when either of the two would apparently have been sufficient. The easiest way to accomplish this task was to explain why the first had not succeeded. In section M, Joshua sends a message to the study-house. Section N reports its failure, so in section O Joshua personally delivers a second. Section N thus turns redundancy into progression.

O. *The Sprinkler*

PT	*BT*
1. -----	1. *R. Joshua said, "I had better go to them myself."*
2. -----	2. *He came and knocked on the door;*
3. He said to them, "The sprinkler,..."	3. """

The text of message is precisely the same in both versions. The BT has merely added an Aramaic introduction to complete the transition from the first message, while the second is itself retained in Hebrew. This confirms the analysis offered above.

P. *"Have You Been Appeased?"*

1. He said to them, "Are you satisfied?	1. R. ʿAqiva said to him, "R. Joshua, have you been appeased?
2. -----	2. We have done nothing except for your honor.
3. You and I shall wait at R. Gamaliel's door."	3. Tomorrow you and I shall wait at his door."

In addition to the familiar expansions, we see here final evidence for the systematic Babylonian change of structure. In #1, the speaker in PT is Eleazar b. ʿAzariah. He asks the Rabbis, in the *plural*, if they have been satisfied. In the BT, ʿAqiva, acting as spokesman, asks Joshua, in the *singular*, if he has been appeased.

Q. *The Settlement*

The PT here tells us Eleazar's new title, while the BT instead supplies one detail of the new working arrangement. Either of these details, or both, might be authentic. This text alone, however, permits no firm conclusion. For further discussion, see below, part IV.

J.N. Epstein[90] took the reference to "Sabbaths" in the BT as referring to weeks, not Sabbaths. He claims that the question "Whose Sabbath was it?" means "Which student was on duty that week to serve the Rabbis?" He cites in support b. Pes. 36a, where R. ʿAqiva, alluding to such an arrangement, recalls, "It was my Sabbath."[91] Since the whole exchange in the BT is in any case artificial, it was probably inspired by the question repeated in section R.

R. "Whose Sabbath was It?"

The citation in our text is from the following story in B. Ḥag. 3a:

> Our Rabbis taught: It once happened that R. Yoḥanan b. Beroqa and R. Eleazar Ḥisma went to call on R. Joshua at Peqiʾin. He said to them, "What novelty did you learn at the study-house today?" They said to him, "We are your disciples, and we drink your water." He said to them, "Just the same, one cannot have a study-house without some novelty. Whose Sabbath was it?"[92]--"It was R. Eleazar b. ʿAzariah's."

This story, with only irrelevant changes, also appears in Tos. Soṭah 7:9 (ed. Zuckermandel, p. 307), and ARN 18:2 (ed. Schechter, p. 67). On the other hand, in three other locations (Mekhilta Pisḥa 16, ed. Horowitz-Rabin, pp. 58-9; p. Ḥag. 1:1 75d; Yalquṭ Jer. #295), we find the following variant:

> Once the disciples spent the Sabbath at Yavneh, while R. Joshua did not. When his disciples came to him, he said to them, "What did you do at Yavneh?" They said to him, "After you, Rabbi."[93] He said to them, "And who spent the Sabbath there?"[94] They said to him, "R. Eleazar b. ʿAzariah." He said to them, "Is it possible that R. Eleazar b. ʿAzariah spent the Sabbath there, and he taught you nothing new?"

Again, the three versions are not identical,[95] but they all agree on the crucial deatil that the root ŠBT appears in a verbal, not a nominal form. Now unlike its use as a noun, the *verbal* use of ŠBT is limited in its reference to the Sabbath day.[96] It does not mean "to spend a week." The more common interpretation of these passages seems preferable.[97]

IV. *Conclusions*

In reporting the deposition of R. Gamaliel, neither Talmud offers a simple coherent narrative. Both versions are composite; they expand what may be presumed were earlier versions, and insert, at undetermined moments, entirely extraneous interpolations. Yet the two versions are not independent of one another. The Babylonian recension is clearly based on the Palestinian; cf. especially Joshua's humiliation. Gamaliel's apology, and the materials surrounding the metaphor of the sprinkler.

In parts I and II, we discussed the development of each narrative. It was then observed that the Babylonian and the Palestinian interpolations break in at the same point. The basic story can be divided into a "rising" action (dispute-humiliation-deposition) and a "falling" action (apologies-appeal to heredity-reinstatement). The interpolations separate these two. If we now examine the two parts separately we see that the earlier is harsher to R. Gamaliel than the latter. To a great extent, of course, this distinction is inherent in the logic of the narrative as a whole, but we also recall that the initial episode of the story was told separately from the rest. This raises the possibility that circles favourable to R. Gamaliel took over an already circulating story of his deposition, and gave it a conclusion putting the whole incident into the best possible light. If several versions of the deposition-story existed, these same circles may have decided which particular version would thus be taken as the basis for the "complete" story. This hypothesis explains the striking triviality of the dispute over the evening prayer which reportedly led to Gamaliel's removal. It would have been in the interests of Gamaliel's followers to divert attention from whatever more serious matters were involved (see below). Apparently, however, they would not or could not wilfully alter traditions which had already received fixed form, so they chose the least damaging version, and gave it a relatively favourable conclusion.

* * * * *

These narratives show a long history of development. They were not comtemporary archival records. They may well have begun from some historical "event," but as we have them now they are full of anachronism (the "Academy," R. Gamaliel's "servants"), legend (R. Eleazar b. ʿAzariah's hair), and inconsistency. Just what role did R. ʿAqiva play? Precisely whom had R. Gamaliel offended?

Earlier scholars, while acknowledging the fragmentary nature of surviving documents, did not question their essential reliability. Their method therefore consisted of gathering as many details as they could, and then synthesising the data thus collected. L. Ginzberg, for example, thought it useful for determining the duration of the episode to cite the opinion of medical experts stating that a man's hair cannot turn gray in less than several months.[98] In the *Jewish Encyclopedia*, Wilhelm Bacher described the events as follows:[99]

> But Gamaliel manifested the excellence of his character most plainly upon the day on which he harshly attacked Joshua b. Ḥananiah, in consequence of a new dispute between them, and thereby so aroused the displeasure of the assembly that he was deprived of his position. Instead of retiring in anger, he continued to take part, as a member of the assmebly, in the deliberations conducted by the new president, Eleazar b. ʿAzariah. He was soon reinstated in office, however, after asking pardon of Joshua, who himself brought about Gamaliel's restoration in the form of a joint presidency, in which Gamaliel and Eleazar shared the honors (Ber. 27b-28a; yBer. 7c,d).

Bacher names the PT, but pays it no attention. The PT does not refer to a "joint presidency" at all. The apology to Joshua is there only one of many. Joshua has no particular part in Gamaliel's reinstatement. All Bacher offers here is a summary of *bBer.*, accepted as historically reliable on every point (except, apparently, Eleazar's hair). The problem of the passage in *bBekh.* is not even mentioned.

Taking the whole evidence into consideration, we may conclude that some serious disturbance interrupted the period of Gamaliel's leadership. This conclusion is supported by the fact that the three central characters--the Hillelite Gamaliel, the priest Eleazar, and Yoḥanan b. Zakkai's disciple Joshua--represent three of the major political factions of the early post-Destruction period. It is highly plausible that an intense power-struggle should have revolved around these three men.[100]

It is impossible to identify from these stories the range of issues separating these groups, or specific developments in their relations. Several observations, however, are germane. The Patriarchal regime was just beginning to consolidate its power. The Rabbinic conclave in general must have resented this. At least two rival groups, the priests and Yoḥanan's circle, are likely to have had aspirations of their own. The stakes in the struggle--control over the remnant of Jewish autonomy in Palestine--were large. Gamaliel's ouster must have involved more basic concerns than the trivial events which surviving records report. The men who created the Talmud forgot as much of their own past as they remembered. In consequence, beyond the basic data thus outlined, their stories may not be relied on as historical records.

Nevertheless, the sources do reveal a great deal though not necessarily that which they purport to convey. Much can be learned from them about the men who formed and transmitted them--especially in places such as this where their conscious attention was diverted from themselves--and about the way in which Talmudic narratives developed. The constant appearance of Rabbinic dialectics and folk-wisdom (e.g. the exchange between Eleazar and his wife) no doubt reflects a living ideal of the narrator and his circle. This is how the ideal Rabbi was expected to make a decision. R. Gamaliel's refusal to be deterred from Torah study, and his worry that he might have deterred others, are also certainly offered as examples. There is even an insertion-within-an-insertion, lest Gamaliel's repudiation of hypocrisy seem discredited. Finally, the triad of wealth, wisdom, and ancestry is noteworthy. In a world where a learned *mamzer* could take precedence even over a high priest, should the latter be an ignoramus, a rich Rabbi was still better than a poor one.

NOTES

APPENDIX

[1]There has been some debate over whether Gamaliel's predecessor, R. Yoḥanan b. Zakkai, died in office, retired, or was forced to resign. Cf. J. Neusner, *A Life of R. Yoḥanan b. Zakkai* (2nd ed., Leiden, 1970), p. 225, and the literature cited there, n. 1, chiefly G. Alon, *Meḥqarim beToledot Yisra'el* [Studies in Jewish History] (Tel Aviv, 1967), I, 253-73, esp. p. 271.

[2]b. Hor. 13b; cf. J. Neusner, *History of the Jews in Babylonia*, I (2nd ed., Leiden, 1969), pp. 79-85.

[3]Lacking in Ta'an. The connection is with an earlier mention of the halakhic dispute between Gamaliel and Joshua.

[4]Ta'an.--And he came.

[5]Ta'an.--But did not (WHL') R. Joshua say.

[6]Lacking in Ta'an.

[7]Ta'an.--says.

[8]Ta'an.--shouted at him.

[9]Ta'an.--Turgeman.

[10]Text apparently defective.

[11]Ta'an.--"Say. . ." They began to speak, and the whole assembly began to rise to their feet. They said. . .

Alternatively: "Say 'Begin'!" But they said "Begin," and the whole assembly rose to their feel. They said. . .

The latter alternative makes less sense, but the former, as well as the translation in the text, requires rendering the expression HTḤYL W- as "began to. . ."

[12]Nahum 3:19.

[13]Ta'an.--They immediately went.

[14]Ta'an.--than he. Used twice, the phrase is probably a euphemism for "than I."

[15]Lit., on whom.

[16]Ta'an.--a peg to hang from them.

[17]Ta'an.--benches of students there.

[18]Ta'an.--R. Yosi b. R. Bun.

[19]Sections F and G lacking in the PT.

[20]M. Zev. 1:3; M. Yad. 3:5, 4:2.

[21]M. Ket. 4:6.

[22]Ta'an.--came.

[23]Ta'an.--Do you make your living from these?

[24]Sections M and N lacking in the PT.

[25]Phrase lacking in Ta'an.

[26]The imagery refers to the ritual of the red heifer, ordained in Numbers 19.

[27]This possibility was first suggested to me by Professor Jacob Neusner in whose graduate seminar this paper was originall read.

[28]We shall see below (part II--additional note) that the first scene (section A) apparently circulated independently.

[29]The choice of R. Eleazar b. ʿAzariah is nowhere explained; he just appears. In section J, the Rabbis have not yet come back together, while in section P Eleazar can address them collectively. The PT never explicitly reports that R. Joshua "was appeased," as does the BT.

[30]It is of course possible that crucial links were lost in the process of putting things together. But if the redactors were so insensitive as to let them fall out, it may also just not have occurred to a narrator to put them in.

[31]I owe this suggestion to Professor Neusner.

[32]L. Ginzberg hypothesised that there were two steps in adjourning any meeting. After the Meturgeman ended the session, he suggested, the Ḥazzan would pronounce some formula of benediction. See his *Commentary on the Palestinian Talmud*, III (New York, 1941), pp. 176-7. This interpretation does explain the presence of both fragments in our text, but there is no evidence to support it. It also assumes the non-existent reading, "He (i.e. Ḥuspit) said to R. Zenon. . ."

[33]Cf. Ginzberg, ibid., p. 188.

[34]See above, n. 20.

[35]Section B lacking in the BT.

[36]The citation of the tractate is a later gloss.

[37]These Hebrew phrases had been absorbed into the Aramaic vernacular.

[38]Cf. mBer. 1:5.

[39]Section D Lacking in the BT.

[40]I.e., to indicate that he had acted correctly.

[41]Deut, 23:4.

[42]Isa. 10:13, RSV translation. In the Bible these words are attributed to an unnamed King of Assyria.

[43]Thus Judah is presumably a descendant of one of the other sixty-eight gentile nations.

[44]This Aramaic insertion is a common legal principle in the BT. It is not found in the parallel in M. Yad.

[45]Jer. 49:6.

[46]*Amos*. 9:14.

[47]Cf. mYad. 4:4.

[48]Sections H and I lacking in the BT.

[49]Referring to his deposition.

[50]Or "smith." Cf. PT--he was making needles.

[51]See n. 26 above.

[52]The Hebrew phrase is a common legal dictum.

[53]MS, Munich reads "two" Sabbaths, which makes more sense in the present context, but could be a learned connection.

[54]See synopsis below, part III.

[55]ʿAqiva's other reported comment, in section N, is not consistent with this new point of view. Since the change is otherwise carried through, it is likely that section N is a later addition, part of an attempt to explain the presence of two different metaphors--in sections M and O--where either would be sufficient. See synopsis below, part III.

[56]See part IV.

[57]One edition of the PT contined the reference to ʿEduyot (section F.1). Cf. B. Ratner, *Ahawath Zion We-Jeruscholaim*, I (Vilna, 1901), p. 104 bottom.

[58]J.N. Epstein has already shown that the interpretation given the expression "on that day" cannot possibly be taken at face value. Cf. his *Prolegomena ad Litteras Tannaiticas* (Jerusalem, 1957), pp. 424-5.

[59]Yad. 4:4.

[60]The Hebrew phrase is a gloss inserted to explain a corrupt Aramaic reading. I have followed the reading suggested in *Shiṭṭah Mequebbeṣet*, as indicated in the margin of the standard Vilna edition (n. 5).

[61]I.e., do we assume that a *ḥaver* would not intentionally cause such an injury, and may now therefore use the animal for his own purposes? The two expressions are italicized because they are technical Hebrew terms; they are not Aramaic.

[62]The translation follows the standard text. It is corrected in the margin to "sat."

[63]This will be corroborated by the synopsis in part III.

[64]It is possible that these were once separate versions of the story of Gamaliel's deposition and that R. Judah the Patriarch adapted for his Mishnah a version stressing Joshua's eventual reconciliation, rather than his earlier defiance. This suggestion, however, requires that we suppose that all such traditions,

although mutually contradictory, emerged very soon after the events they purported to recount. Such a hypothesis, furthermore, receives less support from the sources than does our first, and has no greater intrinsic historical probability.

[65]The context in Bekh. concerns a litigant who is forced to tell the truth because independent witnesses would reveal his lie. This is precisely R. Joshua's predicament. If, however, someone had inserted, on the basis of this connection, what he knew to be an excerpt from a longer narrative, he would have included less. The disruption of the Academy is irrelevant to such an interpolator's point.

[66]Of these, #1 represents the standard Babylonian formula TNW RBNN, while #8, reflects merely a textual variant which could accidentally have crept in.

[67]Bekh. has only the revelation, but, as we would expect, its version agrees in all relevant details with b. Ber. as against the PT.

[68]Cf. Ginzberg, *Commentary*, III, p. 175. This change occurs even in passages found in both texts. Ours is one such; cf. as well the *aggadah* that the three Patriarchs instituted the three statutory prayers--bBer. 26b, pBer. 7a-b.

[69]Ginzberg, ibid.

[70]The idea is found in the *ʿArukh*. It was adopted by R. Samuel Edels; cf. his commentary, in the standard editions, *ad* Bekh., *ad loc*. In modern times, the interpretation was accepted by N.I. Weinstein, *Zur Genesis der Agada* (Gottingen, 1901), pp. 168-70, and rejected by W. Bacher in his review of Weinstein in *Revue des Etudes Juives* 43 (1901), p. 152.

[71]Cf. p. Hor. 3:1 47a.

[72]*Commentary* III, p. 176.

[73]Cf. Ratner, *Ahawath*, I, pp. 104-5.

[74]Ginzberg observed (*Commentary*, III, p. 180) that all the numbers have the same initial letters in Hebrew. He therefore suggested that they reflect different interpretations of the same acronym. But this presupposes that the story received written form very early, and also fails to explain why all the variant readings are in the PT tradition. The interpretation suggested here seems much simpler.

[75]Cf. b. Hor. 13b.

[76]J.N. Epstein held that Eleazar's elevation took place after his entrance into the Academy (*Prolegomena*, pp. 424-5). His argument seems based primarily on technical distinctions between the terms MNH and HWŠYB, but such distinctions may well be anachronistic; Ginzberg (*Commentary* III, pp. 190-5) thought there was no difference at all between the two terms.

[77]Section H.

[78]That is, the Babylonian insertion may have been made independently of the Palestinian text, and not merely adapted from it.

79 In the interests of brevity I have omitted texts whenever no synopsis was possible. The reader may find them above, in parts I and II.

80 Section F.2, n. 58 above.

81 *Prolegomena*, p. 422, n. 7. Cf. especially the plural suffix -WM. After ʿDYWT was taken to refer to the tractate, the feminine singular NŠNYT was a natural development. We must otherwise take the form TQNWM simply as an inexplicable anomaly.

82 Cf. the use of ḤZY in the BT (the PT would more likely have ḤMY), and KDWN and ʿYLYN in the PT, both characteristic Palestinian expressions.

83 p. M.Q. 3:1 81c-d; b. B.M. 58b-59a.

84 M. R.H. 2:8-9.

85 Above, n. 55.

86 Cf. Alon, *Meḥqarim*, I, pp. 271-2.

87 See above, n. 2.

88 It is worth noting incidentally that a fuller knowledge of these different factions would provide a powerful tool for the *literary* analysis of Talmudic sources.

89 Note the equally puzzling mention of a laundry-worker in connection with the funeral of R. Judah the Patriarch. Each Talmud uses there the same word which appears here. Cf. p. Kil. 9:4 43b; b. Ket. 103b.

90 *Prolegomena*, p. 427.

91 Cf. ibid., n. 62, where Epstein cites as well tNeg. 8:2 and its parallels.

92 ŠBT ŠL MY HYTH.

93 Either, "we do not discuss Torah unless you begin," or, "we are your disciples," as in b. Ḥag.

94 WMY ŠBT ŠM.

95 The translation follows the Mekhilta.

96 Cf. the dictionaries of Levy and Jastrow, s.v. ŠBT. Levy inexplicably makes no reference even to the noun ŠBT = week.

97 Epstein refers to the version in Mekhilta, but writes as if the noun and verb ŠBT have the same ranges of meaning. He also says that p. Ḥag. "used" the Tosefta; on at least this point, however, that was apparently not the case.

Further, Mekhilta reads KBR ŠBTW TLMYDYM BYBNH WLʾ ŠBT ŠM R. YHWŠʿ. But if the weekly shifts were specifically the *disciples'* duty, as Epstein holds, the reference to R. Joshua is altogether inappropriate.

98 *Commentary* III, p. 181, n. 200.

[99]S.v. Gamaliel II, in vol. 5, p. 560.

[100]Alon already recognized the importance for our story of the fact that Eleazar was a priest. Cf. *Toledot ha Yehudim be'Ereṣ Yisra'el biTequfat haMishnah vehaTalmud* [The History of the Jews in Palestine in the Period of the Mishnah and the Talmud], I (1967), p. 200.

BIBLIOGRAPHY

Abraham ben Elijah, of Vilna. *Commentary on the Mishnah.* Jerusalem, 1948.

Albeck, Ḥanan. *Commentary to the Mishnah.* Jerusalem-Tel Aviv, 1953.

Allon, Gedaliahu. *A History of the Jews in Palestine During the Period of the Mishnah and the Talmud (Toledot HaYehudim B'Ereṣ Yisrael, Bitequfat Ha-Mišnah VeHatalmud)* Tel Aviv, 1970.

Asher ben Yeḥiel. *Commentary on the Talmud.* Jerusalem, 1948.

Beer, Georg. *Faksimile-Ausgabe des Mischnacodex Kaufmann A50, mit Genehmigung der Ungarischen Akademie der Wissenchaften in Budapest, besorgt von Georg Beer (HaMishnah al pi Ketav Yad Kaufmann).* Jerusalem, 1967.

Cohen, Martin A. "The First Century as Jewish History." J.P. Hyatt, ed., *The Bible in Modern Scholarship.*

Danby, Herbert, [translator]. *The Mishnah.* London, 1933.

Epstein, J.N. *Introduction to the Text of the Mishnah (Mavo LeNusaḥ HaMišnah).* Jerusalem, 1964.

_______. Introductions to Tannaitic Literature *(Mevo'ot leSifrut HaTanna'im).* Jerusalem, 1957.

Finkelstein, Louis. *Akiba, Scholar, Saint and Martyr.* New York, 1936.

Frankel, Zacharias. *Darké HaMišnah, ha-tosefta, mekhilta, safra ve-sifré.* Tel Aviv, 1959.

Freedman, H. [translator]. *Shabbath.* London, 1938.

Goldschmidt, E.H. *The Passover Haggadah: Its Sources and History.* Jerusalem, 1960.

Green, William S. *Joshua ben Ḥananiah.* Unpublished PhD. thesis. Brown University, 1974.

_______. "What's in a Name?--the Problematic of Rabbinic Biography". *Approaches to Ancient Judaism.* W.S. Green, ed. Missoula, 1978, pp. 77-96.

Halivni, David Weiss. *Meqorot uMesorot.* Tel Aviv, 1968.

Haberman, A.M. *Mishna in perush ha-Ram'Bam, defus rishon,* Napoli, 252 1492 *divré mavo me'et A.M. Habermann.* Jerusalem, 1970.

Hyman, Aaron. *Biographies of the Tannaim and Amoriam. (Toledot Tannaim VeAmoraim).* Jerusalem, 1964.

Hyman, Aaron. *Biblical References in Rabbinic Literature. (Torah haKetuvah veha-Mesorah).* Tel Aviv, 1936.

Jastrow, Marus. *A Dictionary of the Targumim, the Talmud Babli and Yerushalmi, and the Midrashic Literature.* New York, 1943.

Lieberman, Saul. *A Comprehensive Commentary on the Tosefta (Tosefta ki-Fshutah).* New York, 1955-1967.

_______. *Commentary on the Tosefta. (Tosefet Rišonim).* Jerusalem, 1948-1949.

Lightstone, Jack. "Ṣadoq the Yavnean," *Persons and Institutions in Early Rabbinic Judaism.* W.S. Green, ed. Missoula, 1977, pp. 49-147.

Loewe, Herbert. *The Mishnah of the Palestinian Talmud. (HaMišnah al pi Ketav-Yad Cambridge).* Jerusalem, 1967.

Maimonides, Moses. *Commentary to the Mishnah.* Jerusalem, 1948.

Mishnah. *(Shisha Sidré Mishnah, Ketav Yad Parma. . .)* Jerusalem, 1970.

Neusner, Jacob. *A History of the Jews in Babylonia,* vols. i - v. Leiden, 1965-1970.

_______. *A History of the Mishnaic Law of Purities.* Leiden, 1974---.

_______. A Life of Yoḥanan ben Zakkai. Second edition, Leiden, 1970.

_______. *Development of a Legend.* Leiden, 1970.

_______. Eliezer ben Hyrcanus. Leiden, 1974.

_______. *From Politics to Piety.* Englewood Cliffs, 1973.

_______. *The Rabbinic Traditions about the Pharisees before 70.* Vols. i-iii. Leiden, 1971.

Pardo, David. *Sefer Hasdé David.* Jerusalem, 1970-71.

Rabinowitz, R.N. *Variae lectiones in Mischnam et in Talmud Babylonicum (Sefer Diqduqé Soferim).* New York, 1960.

Rengstorf, K.H. *Die Tosefta, Seder Taharot,* Stutgart, 1967.

Samson of Sens. *Commentary on M. Kelim.* Jerusalem, 1948.

Slotki, I. [translator]. *Kelim.* London, 1948.

Slotki, J. [translator]. *Yebamoth.* London, 1936.

INDEX TO BIBLICAL AND TALMUDIC REFERENCES

BIBLE

MISHNAH

GENERAL INDEX

effects of, 75-79; women - bitter waters, 225-26, 236; property rights, 141-49, 232, 262, 272, 276-77; year, intercalation, 105-12, 172-74, 237, 239-42, 247, 250, 261, 263, 272, 274, 297
Gamaliel the Elder, marriage, remarriage on evidence of one witness, 133-34
Garments, folding of, 54, 241, 259, 273
Gentiles - 220-24, 242, 262; Jewish relations, 175-77, 242, 263, 274; robbery of, 219-20, 240, 262; superstitions, 52-53, 232, 238, 259, 273; wine of, 179-81
Geṭ: see Divorce
Ginsberg, L., 309; eighteen blessings, 8
Goldenberg, Robert, deposition of Rabban Gamaliel II, 287-311; evening prayer, 19
Grace after meals, 11-13, 231, 251, 258, 271, 275, 283
Greek wisdom, 156-57, 239, 251, 262, 274
Green, W. S., levirate marriage, 131; lulav, shaking, 89; marriage, 131; New Year, intercalation, 108-10; priesthood, marriage into, 175

Haircuts, 178-79, 240, 251, 263, 274
Halafta, scriptures, storage of, 54-56
Ḥanan b. Avishalom, remarriage, 151
Ḥananiah, year, intercalation, 173, 242
Ḥananiah b. Aqavya, women, property rights, 142, 144-48, 272, 276
Ḥananiah b. Gamaliel, slaughter, blemished animal, 188
Ḥananiah b. Ḥananiah, vows, youth, age for release from, 205-07, 242, 264, 271
Ḥananiah b. Ṭeradion, pools, types of, 177
Ḥananya b. Aqavya, Shema and Tefillah, 16, 238
Ḥanina, abortion, 240; Sabbath, limits of movement, 58-59, 270
Ḥanina b. Ṭeradion, scholars, confrontations, 170
Heave-offering, unclean jar, 33-34, 132, 231, 258, 273
Hezekiah b. ʿIqeš, utensils, uncleanness, 219
Hillel, House of, candelabrum, assembling on festival, 98-99, 101; eighteen blessings, 9-10; festivals - foods on, 94-95, 97-99, 237, 277; laws of, 104, 277; levirate marriage, 131-32; loans, repayment in kind, 163, 277; lulav, shaking, 89; marriage, 131-32, 138; oil and myrtle, blessing of, 24-25; olives, uncleanness, 204-05, 277; Orlah and tithes, 46-47; Passover, leavened bread, 75; Sabbath, bathing and benches for gentiles, 119-20; scroll-wrappers, uncleanness, 199, 277; tithes-Orlah, 46-47; second tithe money, 38; women, property rights, 141-43, 146, 277
Ḥisda, Sabbath, letter writing, 50; slave, freeing of, 153
Ḥiyya, evening prayer, 17; travel, dispelling effects of wine, 75; women, property rights, 147-48
Horowitz, bitter waters, 226
Ḥuna, slave, freeing of, 153
Ḥispit the Meturgeman, 288, 292, 299-300; evening prayer, 18, 21
Hyman, A., Demai and the poor, 28; prayer, divine response, 218

ʿIlai, Passover, leavened bread, 72-75; travel dispelling effects of wine, 76-79
Incest, 226-27, 242, 264

Jacob b. Idi, ʿAmidah prayer, 115; slaughtering, 185
Jacob b. Sisi, 288, 302; evening prayer, 18
Jastrow, M., animals, size to be raised, 161
Jonathan b. Harsha, produce, perferations in, 37-38
Joshua, abortion, 211-12; deposition of Gamaliel II, 287-311; eighteen blessings, 7-9, 233; evening prayer, 17-21, 23-24, 233, 297-98; fasting, minor holidays, 116-17; field crops, 33; food Passover, 85; uncleanness, 212-13; grace after meals, 11; Heave-offering, unclean jar, 33-34, 231; levirate marriage, 130-32, 232; loans, repayment in kind, 164; lulav - gift of, 91-92; shaking, 89-91, 239; man,